The Handbook of Multimedia Information Management

Edited by:

William I. Grosky, *Wayne State University*
Ramesh Jain, *University of California at San Diego*
Rajiv Mehrotra, *Eastman-Kodak Company*

To join a Prentice Hall PTR Internet mailing list, point to:
http://www.prenhall.com/mail_lists/

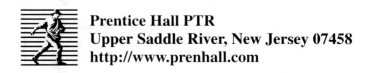

Prentice Hall PTR
Upper Saddle River, New Jersey 07458
http://www.prenhall.com

Library of Congress Cataloging-in-Publication Data

The Handbook of multimedia information management / edited by William
   I. Grosky, Ramesh Jain, Rajiv Mehrotra
      p.   cm.
   Includes bibliographical references and index.
   ISBN 0-13-207325-0
   1. Multimedia systems.   2. Database management. 3. Grosky,
   William I. II. Jain, Ramesh. III. Mehrotra, Rajiv.
   QA76.575.H36   1997
   025.04—dc21   96–47549
                                             CIP

Editorial/Production Supervision: Craig Little
Acquisitions Editor: Mark Taub
Marketing Manager: Dan Rush
Manufacturing Manager: Alexis R. Heydt
Cover Design: Anthony Gemmellaro
Cover Design Supervision: Jerry Votta

© 1997 Prentice Hall PTR
Prentice-Hall, Inc.
A Simon & Schuster Company
Upper Saddle River, NJ 07458

Prentice Hall books are widely used by corporations and government agencies for training,
marketing, and resale.

The publisher offers discounts on this book when ordered in bulk quantities.
For more information, contact:

Corporate Sales Department,
Phone: 800-382-3419; FAX: 201-236-7141; E-mail: corpsales@prenhall.com
Or write: Prentice Hall PTR, Corp. Sales Dept., One Lake Street, Upper Saddle River, NJ 07458.

Printed in the United States of America
10 9 8 7 6 5 4 3 2 1

ISBN 0-13-207325-0

Prentice-Hall International (UK) Limited, *London*
Prentice-Hall of Australia Pty. Limited, *Sydney*
Prentice-Hall of Canada, Inc., *Toronto*
Prentice-Hall Hispanoamericana S.A., *Mexico*
Prentice-Hall of India Private Limited, *New Delhi*
Prentice-Hall of Japan, Inc., *Tokyo*
Simon & Schuster Asia Pte. Ltd., *Singapore*
Editora Prentice-Hall do Brasil, Ltda., *Rio de Janeiro*

Contents

Information Retrieval Techniques

Multimedia Interfaces

Multimedia Presentation

Memory Management

Multimedia Communications

Prototype Systems

Preface

One of the major limitations of computers was that alphanumeric information used to be the primary currency, while other information modalities were, and to some extent even now are, second class citizens and were hesitatingly tolerated. On the other hand, images play such a key role in human life that all information, even alphanumeric information, is represented in pictorial form. In our daily activities, we use visual information for communicating and acquiring information much more than any other mechanism. Clearly, to make computers more natural to people, images and sound should be used at least at the same level as alphanumeric information; computers should treat them also as first class citizens. Other modes of communication used by humans should also be accorded similar status in interacting with computers.

The most amazing development in the field of computing and communications has been the development of the World Wide Web (WWW). Known only to a small group of people even in 1994, in 1996 it has become such a popular communication mechanism that you often see it on people's business cards, in TV and magazine advertisements, and even on billboards on the side of freeways. In a true sense, WWW represents a large document that contains text, audio, images, video, and even several active sensors. It is being used to provide and retrieve information by groups of people as diverse as elementary school children and CEOs of major corporations.

It is difficult to predict exactly what the nature of documents will be in the near future. It is clear, however, that these documents will be nonlinear, multimedia, and will definitely require tools for content-based access of information. Without proper tools for organization and access of large multimedia-documents, these documents will be only of limited use.

Like most fields in their early infancy, information related to multimedia information systems is distributed at several different places. Researchers are usually not aware of important research in closely related aspects of information organization and access even in closely related areas due to traditional scientific classifications. We embarked on a project to pull researchers working on disparate aspects of multimedia information systems and requested them to write tutorial chapters in their areas of expertise so that readers could get information at

1

the correct depth as well as get pointers to the literature in the field. We were pleased by the response because most people accepted our invitation and were kind enough to devote energy and time to this project. The result of this is in your hands. We believe that this collection of chapters written by experts in different aspects of multimedia information systems will provide a ready reference to the literature of the field and tutorial articles in related fields. People new to this area of study will find this volume extremely useful by presenting different aspects of multimedia information in one place.

A project of this type depends first of all on the authors of the various chapters. We are very thankful to all these authors who produced these articles and tolerated our editing suggestions and deadline reminders. We are also thankful to our families who tolerated the extra work a project of this magnitude requires.

William Grosky
Ramesh Jain
Rajiv Mehrotra

Introduction

Multimedia data has always been ubiquitous in the modern world. For many decades, organizations and individuals have acquired images in the form of photographs, magazine and book pages, and artwork. Some organizations, such as those in the entertainment industry, have accumulated movies and videos over the last 90 years. With the advent of the portable video cassette recorder, individuals have also found themselves the recipients of video data.

Until the 1990s, however, managing such data has been quite difficult. It has only been through the convergence of portions of the fields of database management, image understanding, voice recognition, and hypertext, with the support of advances in the enabling technologies of networking and communications, that we are developing a good understanding of the issues involved in managing such data. Consider the following scenarios.

A scientist has the responsibility of tracking plant growth in the Southern Hemisphere. He has many satellite images to examine. Since each image has been previously digitized and inserted into a multimedia information system, he first issues a query to gather together all the images of the Southern Hemisphere. He then applies an operation on this set of images to prioritize them, where the highest priority is assigned to the image showing the maximum change from a previous image of the same geographic area. The scientist then examines the highest priority image in more detail. Noticing new growth and unsure of the plant type, he applies a similarity operator that matches the unknown growth with the growth of known plants. He then navigates to information about this now known growth, absorbs this information, and creates a voice annotation to the new growth region of the original satellite image, also creating a snippet of it—a copy of a rectangular region that includes the new growth region of interest. Finally, this snippet, including the voice annotation, becomes the last logical frame of a video showing the selected area's changes over time.

A student examines the contents of a multimedia information system on the history of Greece. This system contains alphanumeric information, images, videos, and audios of various buildings and people of historical interest. She applies a filtering operation based on her interest in information pertaining to Aristotle. This removes any entities that have no direct or indirect reference to the entity Aristotle. She then browses the resulting subset of information. For example, one browsing path might take her from an image of Aristotle in front of a particular building to an image showing the architectural details of that building to a video about the main architect of that building. After browsing, the student has a better idea of the information she really wants. She then issues another filtering operation. This results in a still smaller subset, which she again explores by browsing.

These two scenarios illustrate that a mature multimedia information system will have to combine the properties of the three common types of present-day information systems: database management systems, text-retrieval systems, and hypertext systems. Database management systems typically allow the user to ask exact questions concerning the properties and relationships of various entities of interest, such as "Give me the social security numbers of all employees whose supervisor drives a red sports car." They have been designed and optimized for such exact queries. These queries are related to the filtering operations mentioned above. Such systems are implemented by naming the properties and relationships of interest and having their values come from predetermined domains. The queries use these names and values in a completely unambiguous fashion.

Text-retrieval systems allow for similarity retrieval. A typical query to such a system would be "Give me the citations of all articles published after 1980 in a United States journal or magazine which pertain to the wind generation of electricity." Some parts of this query are exact (the year 1980 and the publication in a United States journal or magazine), while other parts are not (the article should pertain to the wind generation of electricity). Given the same article, some people would differ as to how relevant it was to the topic of wind generation of electricity. Thus, whether a given article should be retrieved can be arguable. Typically, these systems also rank the retrieved articles as to their supposed relevance to the query, with articles below a certain relevance factor not retrieved at all. These systems are implemented by representing entities of interest in terms of properties over which similarities must be computed and then devising a distance function (preferably a metric), which evaluates how similar one entity is to another. How to represent an article in an efficient manner so as to be able to capture its contents is not an easy task and has been a matter of research for many years.

Hypertext systems support exploratory or intelligent associate retrieval. Such systems allow non-linear trajectories through alphanumeric material. For example, when one sees the phrase Julius Caesar in a text, one may directly navigate to some text which tells about his life. In a multimedia information system, one may view an image of a city, recognize the Empire State Building, and be able to directly navigate to a video concerning the life of its architect. This generalization of hypertext to multimedia data is called hypermedia.

Multimedia data are hierarchically structured encodings of information, whose corresponding decoding procedures we might know only partially. For example, the fields of image interpretation and automatic speech recognition seek to develop relevant algorithms for images and audios, respectively. Due to this structured nature of multimedia data, the semantics of a multimedia object is a function of the semantics of its parts. These semantics can be inserted into a multimedia information system manually, by having a person do the decoding, or can be semi-automated using the above algorithmic decoding procedures.

Each component of a multimedia object has attributes and can participate in relationships. Some attributes and relationships use the appropriate decoding procedures and some do not. Those attributes and relationships, the detection of whose presence depends on the application of a decoding procedure, are called content-based, while those that do not are called content-independent. Content-based attributes and relationships can be either information-bearing or non-information bearing. The former property holds if the information conveyed is not explicitly encoded in the multimedia object itself. In other words, the presence of this type of attribute or relationship adds new information regarding a particular multimedia object, information that cannot be derived from its binary encoding. For example, the name of a building shown in a particular video would usually be content-based information-bearing. However, if the video showed a person speaking outside the building identifying its name, then the building's name would be content-based non-information bearing.

The boundary between information-bearing and non-information bearing is somewhat fuzzy, as opinions could differ about whether the information appears in the binary representation of the given multimedia object or not. For example, consider the problem of identifying the composer of a never-before-heard symphony appearing in a multimedia presentation. Since each composer has an individual style, a particularly ingenious computer scientist/composer might have developed an algorithm to decide this question for a certain set of composers, based on their melodic lines. To this person, the name of the composer would be content-based non-information bearing, whereas to the average person—who does not know about this algorithm—it would be content-based information bearing.

This definition may be made more precise by characterizing content-based information as information-bearing or non-information-bearing with respect to a particular state of knowledge. Be that as it may, we believe that this concept is useful and that most people would agree on what was information-bearing versus non-information-bearing content-based information. Also, given a particular multimedia information system, there would be no problem classifying content-based information as to whether it bears information or not.

Using content-based attributes and relationships significantly expands the types of browsing and filtering operations a user can invoke. For example, you might initially issue a filtering operation to view all videos concerning universities in New York City. While watching a particular video, you might see a particular university building, stop the video at a particular frame showing the building, then browse through a sequence of icons, each representing a department having an office in that building. Choosing a particular department, you can then browse through another sequence of icons, each representing an professor of that department, and ultimately choose a particular professor. Finally, you could issue a filtering operation to find the soundtracks of all lecture presentations recorded by this professor.

This entire sequence of operations is then nothing more than a transformation from a set of videos to a set of audios. This illustrates that, in a multimedia information system, alphanumeric information, images, videos, and audios are treated equally from the standpoint of query processing. Each may participate in a query, and each may be part of a query's output.

In general, there are five types of information which a multimedia information system must represent:

> Uninterpreted multimedia information.
>
> Multimedia-related, content-independent information.
>
> Alphanumeric information.
>
> Relationships between real-world application entities and multimedia objects.
>
> Methods of constructing and representing multimedia-world relationships.

Uninterpreted multimedia information is typically represented by a blob, a binary large object. Content-independent multimedia information ranges from video synchronization information between image frames and audio to the sort of information which would have been found in image header files of image databases ten years ago. These header files specified such information as the digitization and coding methods used when these operations took place and who performed them. Normal alphanumeric information resides in a conventional database and concerns the properties and relationships pertaining to real-world application entities. The relationships between these real-world application entities and multimedia objects are all content-based information-bearing. Methods of constructing and representing multimedia-world relationships concern features extracted from the various multimedia objects and the use of these features for extracting semantics and similarity matching. As an example, an image feature can be based on texture, color, intensity, or geometry (based on points, lines, and regions). This type of information is content-based non-information-bearing.

A generic logical architecture for multimedia information is shown in Fig. Intro–1. There are three repositories of information: a standard alphanumeric

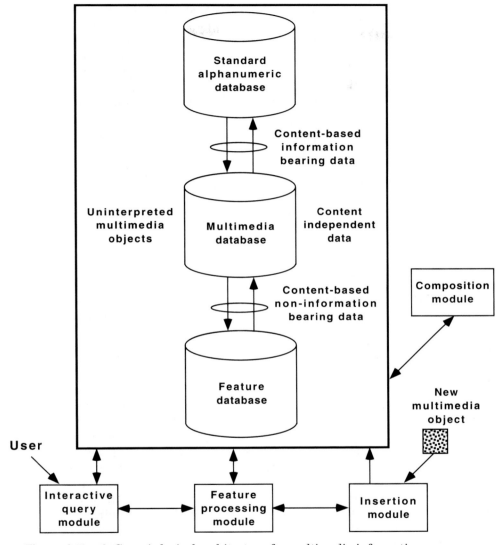

Figure Intro–1 Generic logical architecture for multimedia information.

database, a multimedia object database, and a feature database. These repositories are logically independent of one another, but any implementation may, of course, place them in a single database. The alphanumeric database holds information concerning real-world application entities. The multimedia object database contains the uninterpreted multimedia objects as well as content-independent multimedia information. The feature database contains features extracted by the feature processing module which are used for content-based matching. The composition module allows for the combination of component multimedia objects into a new multimedia object. Insertion of new multimedia objects is done using the insertion module. Note that multimedia information systems are generally insertion and query intensive, not update intensive.

Multimedia information systems can be usefully characterized based on what sorts of content-based retrieval they support, if any. Historically, multimedia has been and continues to be dominated by images and video. Few researchers have discussed managing audio information in the literature, though speech recognition is a mature field. The audio component of video data is just beginning to be used for content-based retrieval in conjunction with the video image data. This is an example of the increasing use of cross-media information relationships.

The first example of multimedia information systems were image databases. The original impetus for these systems came from the image interpretation community. Unfortunately, most of the proposals from this community were narrowly conceived. Hence, after a brief flurry of activity in the late 1970s and early 1980s, interest waned. This community conceived of an image database management system as just a way to manage images for image algorithm development testbeds. Images were retrieved based on information in header files, which contained exclusively alphanumeric information. These systems were implemented using the relational architecture. Thus, image interpretation tasks were either nonexistent or hardwired into the system. If under user control, they were extremely rudimentary. There was no notion of users composing new feature detectors during runtime.

In the last half of the 1980s, the database community expressed an interest in the development of multimedia databases as part of their development push for various sorts of non-standard database management systems. This interest grew out of the development of the object-oriented paradigm, as well as various data-driven approaches to image indexing. During this time period, the interest of the image interpretation community waned. The next generation of multimedia information systems were characterized by a more object-oriented design or by a semantically rich extension of the relational model. The image interpretation routines were, more or less, the methods of the system, and were packaged along with their respective objects. There still was no notion, however, of composing new feature detectors during runtime.

Only in the decade of the 1990s have the image interpretation and database communities begun to converge on a common conception of what a multimedia information system should be. This arose from acceptance of the belief that multimedia and alphanumeric information should be treated equally. Multimedia information should be retrievable by content and should also be integral components of the querying process. Thus, various forms of signal interpretation should be an important component of any query processing strategy.

The third generation of these systems is well on its way. These systems will allow users to manage video data, interact with the image (and audio) interpretation module, and compose new feature detectors during runtime. For the latter task, the user will have a toolbox of elementary features and their associated detectors (methods), as well as connectors that will allow the building of complex features and detectors from more elementary ones through an iconic user interface.

A good multimedia information system will ensure smooth navigation between real-world application entities and multimedia objects; it will mediate between attributes and relationships that are content-independent, information-bearing content-based, and non-information-bearing content-based. An important aspect of designing such a system is to appropriately decompose a multimedia object in terms of features, which can be either of the simple variety, treated as atomic entities, or complex, which can be further decomposed. An example of a complex image-based feature which is used quite often is a color histogram. Features of a multimedia object are analogous to attributes of real-world application entities in a standard alphanumeric database with one exception: an attribute of a real-world application entity is information-bearing, while a feature of a multimedia object, being based on its content, is non-information-bearing.

One of the key properties of a multimedia information system is how it handles semantics. Most current systems don't do this very well. One must relate the semantics of real-world application entities to the semantics of features. Since features are structured, the semantics of a complex feature should also be related to the semantics of its components. The most ubiquitous example is that of similarity. We say that two multimedia objects are similar to each other if their respective sets of content-based keys are similar, where a content-based key is a collection of features which can serve to identify a multimedia object to a high-degree of certainty. This is analogous to the concept of a key in standard alphanumeric databases. The latter notion of similarity is usually defined using some multidimensional distance function, where a point in multidimensional space represents each set of content-based keys.

Consider the following example of complex semantics which should be supported, but generally is not. Suppose one issued a query to find all videos in which Sue and Tom are dancing. One simple-minded approach would be to relate the appropriate videos to Sue and Tom through the relationships dances, which would be information-bearing content-based relationships established by a user. The weakness of this approach is that it doesn't generalize to other cases not specified by a user. The more robust, though difficult, approach would be to define dancing in the domain object set in terms of a certain sequence of events in the feature set. If this concept were not predefined in the system, the user could have a set of tools available to define dancing on the fly. Perhaps the notions of synchronous movement and synchronous leg movement were previously defined. The user should then be able to combine these definitions, add some other information, and devise a valid definition of dancing.

This introduction has tried to convince you that multimedia information systems are quite different from standard alphanumeric database management systems. In this handbook, we provide a glimpse at the state-of-the-art in their design and implementation. This handbook is divided into 7 sections: data modeling, information retrieval techniques, multimedia interfaces, multimedia presentation, memory management, multimedia communications, and prototype systems.

Section 1, Data Modeling discusses issues in the logical representation of multimedia information. The chapter by Gibbs and Tsichritzis covers the important topic of modeling time-based media and is followed by the contribution of Hardman and Bulterman, which concerns the formalization of hypermedia.

In **Section 2, Information Retrieval Techniques**, we have three contributions. The chapter by Jagadish concerns the representation of image data for efficient retrieval, while the next two chapters concern video data. The chapter by Dimitrova and Golshani discusses semantic representation techniques for content-based retrieval of image and video information, while the chapter by Patel and Sethi covers video data management from a more structural perspective.

Section 3, Multimedia Interfaces, discusses various issues in next generation information system interfaces. The chapter by Chang and Costabile develops formalisms for multiple ways of interacting with a multimedia database, while the chapter by Tonomura concentrates on approaches to content indication for video data.

The paper by Hamakawa and Atarashi makes up **Section 4, Multimedia Presentation**. This paper concerns itself with the construction of new, composite, multimedia objects from simpler multimedia components. The techniques presented in this paper will be necessary in building multimedia presentations which, themselves, are answers to queries posed by a user of a multimedia information system.

Section 5, Memory Management, discusses some of the enabling technologies which are necessary to the success of next generation multimedia information systems. The chapter by Vasudev discusses the topic of data compression in a multimedia environment, while the chapter by Buddhikot, Kumar, Parulkar, and Rangan covers the area of storage architectures for multimedia data.

In **Section 6, Multimedia Communications**, we have the paper by Baqai, Khan, and Ghafoor, which discusses issues in the synchronization of multimedia information originating from several independent channels.

Finally, **Section 7, Prototype Systems**, discusses various state-of-the-art prototype multimedia information systems. The chapter by Goble concerns itself with image database systems, while video database systems are discussed in the chapter by Oomoto and Tanaka. Finally, hypermedia systems are covered in the chapter by Buford and Rutledge.

Data Modeling

C H A P T E R 1

Modeling Time-Based Media[1]

Simon Gibbs, Christian Breiteneder, and Dennis Tsichritzis

GMD
53574 Sankt Augustin
Germany
{Simon.Gibbs, Christian.Breiteneder, dt}@gmd.de

1.1 Modeling Issues

*T*here is a qualitative difference between time-based media and the forms of data traditionally stored in database systems. Time-based media, including digital audio and digital video, music, and animation, involve notions of data flow, timing, temporal composition, and synchronization. These notions are foreign to conventional data models and, as a result, conventional data models are not well suited to multimedia database systems in general. Multimedia requires a broad perspective, one accounting for both time-

---

[1] An earlier version of this chapter appeared as "Data Modeling of Time-Based Media, *Proc. SIGMOD '94*, Minneapolis, MN, May 1994, pp. 91–102, © 1994 Association for Computing Machinery, Inc. Reprinted by permission.

encompasses many forms of time-based media found in practice and identifies three general structuring mechanisms for time-based media.

Recent proposals for multimedia database systems have introduced a *BLOB* (binary large object) data type intended for images and other very large values (e.g., [4][9][18]). While the storage of very large values is necessary for multimedia databases, it is not sufficient. The database system should also have some understanding about the internal structure of BLOBs—it must be able to "interpret" the data. There are many reasons for this. First, if the database does not maintain this structural information then the task is left to applications. In other words, information about data structure is separated from the data itself— a situation database systems were explicitly designed to avoid. Second, the structural information needed to interpret time-based media is complex, if it is lost it may be extremely difficult or infeasible to reconstruct and one is left with meaningless data. Preserving this information is crucial and the task should not be left to applications. Third, knowing the structure of time-based media permits sophisticated querying. For example, consider a digital movie with audio tracks in different languages. If the movie is represented structurally, rather than as a long uninterpreted byte sequence, it is possible to issue queries which select a specific sound track, or select a specific duration, or perhaps retrieve frames at a specific visual fidelity. Fourth, presenting time-based media requires timing information. Using a BLOB data type it is possible to read and write time-based media but, since no timing information is available to the database system, the more relevant operations of "play" and "record" have no meaning. Finally, structural information is needed when updating time-based media. For example, editing systems for digital audio and digital video take great care to perform *non-destructive* modifications: rather than reading and writing vast amounts of data in order to accomplish a modification, references to structures within the data are manipulated. The benefits of this approach include preserving the original material and supporting efficient modification operations.

To summarize, a key problem confronting multimedia database systems is the description of the structure of time-based media in a form appropriate for querying, updating, and presentation. In other words, a data model for time-based media is needed. This chapter argues that in designing such a data model it is necessary to go beyond the mere need to store large data values and consider the *stream-like* structure of time-based media.

The basic abstractions we propose for modeling time-based media are *timed streams* of media elements. The term "media element" includes such things as video frames, audio samples, and musical notes (more precise definitions are given in the next section). During playback and recording, elements are read and written not in isolation but as synchronized sequences—these are what we call timed streams. Informally, a timed stream is simply a temporal sequence of media elements. Recording and playback involve continuous access to timed streams and it is often necessary to sustain specific data rates (e.g., so many frames per second). Satisfying this requirement has many implications for database architecture and storage management but these topics are beyond the scope of this chapter. Here we focus on logical aspects of time-based media. Our goal is to identify the characteristics of time-based media differentiating it from other forms of data. Among the more unique and unusual characteristics of time-based media are:

Interpretation

If a database system knows that a unit of storage represents an integer, then interpretation of the data, i.e., determining which integer it represents, is considered a trivial problem. This is the case with traditional data types in general; their interpretation is not difficult and is largely ignored by data modeling. The same does not hold true with time-based media. In this case the storage units requiring interpretation represent timed streams. Factors that complicate interpretation include:

- heterogeneity—media elements within a stream can differ in many ways. For example, consider a stream containing a sequence of compressed digital images. Among the factors which may differ from image to image are image size, image width and height, image depth,[2] color model (e.g., RGB[3] or YUV[4]), and the type of compression used.

- interleaving—in order to simplify synchronization of streams during playback, their elements may be interleaved in a single storage unit.

- padding—storage units may be padded with unused data to match storage transfer rates to media data rates.

- out-of-order elements—some compression techniques, such as MPEG, exploit similarities between consecutive elements. "Key" elements are identified from which intermediate elements can be constructed by interpolation. Because key elements are needed at an early stage during decoding, they may be placed in storage units prior to the intermediate elements. For example, with a sequence of four elements where the first and last are "keys," the placement order could be 1, 4, 2, 3.

- scalability—certain representations for time-based media, in particular proposals for digital video [12], allow presentation at different levels of detail. For instance, a digital video sequence recorded at very high resolution may be presented in an environment requiring, or only capable of, much lower resolution. In such cases, bandwidth can be saved and processing reduced if the video sequence is "scaled" to a lower resolution by ignoring parts of the storage unit.

---

[2] The number of bits-per-pixel.
[3] Colors are represented by red/green/blue intensities.
[4] Colors are represented by a luminance (Y) and two chrominance (UV) values.

A data model for time-based media should provide constructs for timed streams. These constructs should abstract away information concerning the physical organization of media elements, for instance their physical ordering and placement, while permitting heterogeneity, interleaving, and padding, etc.

Quality Factors

Video compression algorithms such as JPEG, MPEG, and those used in DVI and QuickTime are *lossy*: encoding followed by decoding is not an identity transformation. Loss of information can be thought of as a reduction in image quality. The amount of information lost can be controlled by selection of various numeric parameters used during encoding. However, these parameters should not be visible at the data modeling level. For instance, when specifying a video-valued attribute it may be useful to specify a video quality for the attribute, but it should not be necessary to do so in terms of low-level compression parameters. Instead video quality (and the same applies for audio quality) should be specified via descriptive *quality factors*. For example a particular video-valued attribute might be of "broadcast quality" or "VHS quality."

Timing

We make two general observations concerning the role of time in time-based media: First, the handling (retrieval, storage, and processing) of media elements is subject to *real-time constraints*. For instance, video frames are presented at specific frame rates, audio samples at specific sample rates (the rates are determined when the elements are captured or generated). Second, *temporal correlations* can occur between media elements. It is often the case, for instance, that audio elements must be synchronized with visual elements. Satisfaction of real-time constraints, and assuring that temporal correlations are observed, is a performance and implementation issue rather than a data modeling issue. What is important in modeling time-based media is the ability to specify the real-time constraints and temporal correlations. In other words, the data model must address the *timing* of media elements.

Derivation

Media objects, such as audio and video sequences, are often defined in terms of other objects, and then generated when needed rather than stored explicitly. A simple example is a video transition such as a "wipe," used when one scene ends and its image is gradually wiped away to reveal the following scene. In this case there are three sequences: the first scene, the second scene, and the wipe transition. Note that the wipe is *derived* from the scene sequences; all that are needed to recreate the wipe are the two original sequences plus various parameters describing when and how the wipe takes place. A data model for time-based media should represent the relationships between derived and non-derived media objects. It should be possible to a) store derived media objects in an implicit form, and b) "expand" derived objects to produce actual (i.e.,

non-derived) objects. The decision of whether to store a derived object or to
expand and instead store a non-derived object often hinges upon resource availability: if expansion can be done in real time then the derived object is all that
needs be stored.

Composition

An essential feature of multimedia is the mixing of sound and imagery—television and films are two obvious examples, each containing both audible and visual
components. Looking at multimedia in general, one finds that complex multimedia structures are built up from simpler, perhaps "single-media," components.
The components are combined using various *composition* mechanisms which
establish relationships between components; these often are spatial relationships (e.g., relative positioning during presentation) or temporal relationships
(e.g., relative timing during presentation). A data model for time-based media, or
multimedia in general, must be capable of representing the variety of relationships that occur when combining media.

1.2   Examples of Time-Based Media

The capture and presentation of time-based media often require special hardware and often utilize compression techniques as a means to reduce storage and
communication costs. Consequently most data representations for time-based
media originate with two groups: manufacturers of platforms for multimedia
applications and the developers of data compression standards. The following
lists some of the more widely used representations that have recently emerged
from these groups. Space does not permit detailed descriptions; for more information the reader can consult the indicated references.

   Digital Video Interactive or *DVI* [19] refers to a hardware/software environment now licensed by Intel and intended mainly for PCs. DVI is based on two
digital video formats: *Production-Level Video* (PLV) and *Real-Time Video* (RTV).
PLV uses a proprietary compression algorithm allowing VHS quality video to be
produced from a data rate of about 1 Mbit/sec. The RTV format results in data
rates similar to those of PLV, however the video quality is poorer and the frame
rate may be reduced. Applications can playback both the RTV and PLV formats,
and record in the RTV format.

   The *Moving Pictures Experts Group* (MPEG), an ISO working group, has
developed two video compression standards. The first, MPEG-1, like PLV,
achieves data rates of about 1 Mbit/sec for VHS quality video [11]. The more
recent MPEG-2 provides improved compression and is suitable for the production and distribution of broadcast quality video. The MPEG standards have
strong industrial participation and many products based on MPEG-1 and
MPEG-2 are available.

The *Joint Photographic Experts Group* (JPEG), another ISO working group, has developed an image compression standard intended for continuous-tone color and grayscale images [23]. JPEG is also used with digital video by treating each frame as an image to be compressed independently (so-called *motion JPEG*, or MJPEG). Hardware implementations of JPEG are the basis of several computer-based digital video editing systems. For a given frame rate and resolution, JPEG-compressed video has a higher data rate than techniques such as MPEG and DVI's PLV which exploit similarities between frames; but, since frames are compressed independently, it is easier to rearrange the order of the frames and to play back in reverse or at variable rates.

Compact-Disc Interactive (CD-i) is a self-contained multimedia system developed by Philips and Sony [17]. CD-i specifies a data format allowing digital audio of various qualities, digital images of various resolutions, and arbitrary application data, to be stored on a CD. Support for MPEG-1 video has recently been introduced.

QuickTime [8] is an addition to the Macintosh operating system allowing real-time synchronized playback of digital audio and digital video from secondary storage. QuickTime is extensible; it allows new data representations and compression schemes to be supported through the addition of software "components." The initial release includes several components intended for both synthetic (computer-generated) images and natural (continuous tone) images. Multiple tracks of digital audio and video data are combined in a *movie* file, which can then be played by QuickTime on the various Macintosh platforms (QuickTime players are also available for PCs).

Video for Windows (VfW) is similar in functionality to QuickTime but runs on PCs under Microsoft's Windows 3.1. The file format used by VfW is called *AVI*, or Audio Video Interleaved. Like QuickTime, VfW supports several compression methods; among these is *Indeo*, a software version of DVI.

MacroMind *Director* [14] is a multimedia authoring application for the Macintosh. Director is based on a multi-track data structure (also called a movie) where individual tracks may contain graphic objects, audio and MIDI[5] events, timing information, and interactive scripts. The main tool provided by Director is the "score editor." It is used to specify track contents, how multiple graphics tracks are to be combined and overlaid, and the timing constraints between tracks. A second tool, a "movie player" is used to play back and interact with Director movies. Versions of the player tool run on the Macintosh and on the PC and soon will be incorporated in Web browsers [16].

---

[5] MIDI, or *Musical Instrument Digital Interface*, is a standard for communicating with musical devices.

1.3   Review of Related Work

There has been considerable prior work on modeling multimedia data (e.g., [3][5][10][15][25][26]) and a number of these proposals have been implemented in the context of multimedia document systems [3][5] or as multimedia extensions to existing database systems [25][26].

Much of this earlier work has focused on text and images, while time-based media have received less attention—perhaps because of their tremendous processing and storage demands (for example, one *second* of high-quality digital video can occupy tens of Mbytes). Now, however, advances in compression technology and the continually decreasing costs of memory and processing cycles are making the use of time-based media viable. As a result there is a need for multimedia databases coming from two new directions. First, new multimedia applications such as video-on-demand services and virtual environments stand to benefit from access to large databases of time-based material. Second, the vast "clip media" or "digital asset" repositories now being assembled are often loosely organized collections of files and lack the power and flexibility of databases.

The areas that have influenced the data model described in this chapter include digital video and digital audio processing systems (e.g., editors, composition tools) and developments in multimedia platforms. QuickTime in particular has served as a concrete example of the mechanics of media interpretation and timing. QuickTime defines three structures, called media, tracks, and movies—these correspond to what we have called non-derived media objects, derived media objects and multimedia objects. The main difference is that derivation is more general than QuickTime's media-to-track mapping. In QuickTime a track is created by rearranging the timing of media elements. Derivations, however, encompass changes in content and type in addition to changes in timing.

The notion of timed streams bears some resemblance to work in temporal databases. For example, Segev and Shoshani make use of *time sequences* for modeling temporal information [21]. Some of the categories of time sequences, such as continuous and discrete, are similar to the categories of timed streams. However the semantics of the two constructs differ. Time sequences identify how attributes of an object, e.g., a bank account balance, change over the object's life span. Timed streams identify what is essentially scheduling information. For instance, the start time of a video frame is not the time when the frame was captured or created, but when it should be displayed relative to other frames in the stream.

Related work on modeling time-based media has mainly been performed in the area of video authoring tools. The general notions used in most of these systems are media objects being aggregations of smaller units (that are called media elements in the context of this chapter) and in turn are temporally and spatially composed to build multimedia objects. In many of the authoring systems the timeline metaphor is used that can be found in commercially available tools as Adobe Premiere [1] and MacroMind Director.

The *algebraic video* model [24] is based on the notion of a presentation, that is a multiwindow spatial, temporal and content composition of video segments. How these segments are composed is described by *video expressions* that themselves are constructed from video algebra operations. Video expressions may contain composition information, descriptions of the information content and playback behavior. Video expressions in terms of basic operations can be played back, searched and browsed and in terms of abstractions (*algebraic video node*) can be named, stored and manipulated. An algebraic node may refer to a video segment directly or to algebraic children nodes.

The authoring system proposed by Hamakawa and Rekimoto [7] is based on a hierarchical and compositional model of multimedia objects. Objects can be composed using a *glue operator* that allows for the positioning of objects in time and space. A composite data hierarchy is employed to propagate changes of a multimedia object to all participating media objects, if necessary. Data defining a composition are kept as relative data, such as allowing changes in location and timing of one object to be easily reflected in others and in the multimedia object as well.

It was only very recently that prototypes of multimedia database systems also involved the modeling, playback, and capture of time-based media: The layered multimedia data model (LMDM) [22] for example, employs an event calculus to define complex events from simple ones, allowing the building of temporal structures and control of synchronization.

Another related area is that of real-time databases. Time-based media impose real-time constraints—the database must consume and produce (record and playback) media elements at specific rates. Note, however, the deadlines are not *hard*. Divergences from element production and consumption deadlines are certainly undesirable but can be tolerated, for example playback "jitter" can be removed by the application just prior to presentation. Support for the real-time playback of time-based media is now found in audio/video servers (e.g., [2][20]). These systems are likely precursors of more general audio/video databases.

1.4   Basic Concepts

The previous sections introduced and motivated what we believe to be the important issues in modeling time-based media. We now present a data model that incorporates many of the notions we have just introduced. First we give a series of definitions that make more precise the notion of timed streams.

Media, Artifacts, and Media Objects

The term *media* has a rich set of connotations. Often, it is related to how information is conveyed and distributed; for instance we have print and broadcast media. The term is also used to describe the materials and forms of artistic expression. This last meaning occurs when we speak of *digital media*, not in the sense of digital storage media, but in the sense of digital counterparts to *natural media*. The distinction between natural and digital media may not always be clear-cut but the idea is that natural media rely on physical elements—paper, stone, inks, and paints—while digital media rely on the computer. Suppose we call *artifacts* the objects produced in a particular medium. Prints, paintings, musical performances and recordings, films, and video clips are all artifacts. We use the term *media object* to refer to machine-readable representations of artifacts. For instance, media objects corresponding to the artifacts just mentioned consist of digital images, digital audio recordings, and digital video recordings.

Media objects represent artifacts from both natural and digital media. As an example, digital images produced by scanning photographic prints or hand drawings are representations of natural artifacts, while digital images produced by a computer paint program are representations of digital artifacts.

The Structure of Media Objects

Media objects are generally highly structured aggregates of simpler objects, often called *media elements*. Graphics objects are good examples. Complex 3D scenes contain hierarchies of graphics elements representing geometric information, shading, and lighting.

The important question from a data modeling perspective is not so much what is the structure of media objects, since this is determined by applications and standards, but what part of this structure should be captured by a database schema. The minimum a database system should know about media objects includes their type (e.g., image, audio) and encoding attributes that vary from type to type. We call such information a *media descriptor*. For example, an image descriptor includes the image width and height while an audio descriptor includes the sample size and rate.

Looking at the data representations for media objects of various types, one very general observation can be made: audio, video, and (many, but not all, representations of) animation and music use a similar manner of combining media elements. In each case elements are arranged in temporal sequences. Video is a temporal sequence of frames, audio of samples, music of notes, and animation of scenes or events. Since temporal sequences of media elements are a media-independent construct, we propose such temporal sequences, what we call timed streams, as the central abstraction for modeling time-based media.

Media Types, Discrete Time Systems, and Timed Streams

To more precisely define timed streams, we first introduce two other notions: media types and discrete time systems.

Definition 1   A *media type* is a specification of the attributes found in media descriptors and their possible values. For time-based media, a media type also specifies the form of *element descriptors* (these refer to individual elements rather than media objects as a whole).

As an example, the media type for CD audio would specify a sampling rate of 44.1 kHz, a sample size of 16 bits, and the number of channels as 2. These attributes, together with a duration, would be included in the media descriptor. In this case element descriptors are not necessary since all elements have the same form (16-bit PCM[6] samples). Now consider ADPCM[7]-encoded audio. Some versions of this compression technique involve a set of encoding parameters that vary over an audio sequence. These parameters would be part of element descriptors.

Definition 2   A *discrete time system*, D_f, is a mapping from integers to real numbers. Members of the domain of D_f are called *discrete time values*, members of the range are called *continuous time values* and measure time in seconds (or some other unit). The mapping is of the form $D_f: i \rightarrow (1/f)i$, where f is called the *frequency* of the time system.

Some examples are $D_{29.97}$, suitable for North American video (i.e., where video frames occur at a rate of 29.97 times per second), D_{25} for European video, D_{24} for film, and D_{44100} for CD audio.

Definition 3   A *timed stream* is a finite sequence of tuples of the form: $<e_i, s_i, d_i>$, $i=1, ...n$. Each timed stream is based on a media type T and a discrete time system D. In particular, the e_i are media elements of T, and the s_i and d_i are discrete time values measured in system D. The value s_i is called the start time of e_i and d_i is its duration. Start times and durations satisfy: $s_{i+1} \geq s_i$ and $d_i \geq 0$.

Generally a media type imposes restrictions on the form of timed streams based on that type. For example the CD audio type specifies a sampling rate of 44.1 kHz. Given a timed stream based on this type and D_{44100} then we must have $s_{i+1} = s_i + d_i$ and $d_i = 1$ for all i. Constraints of this form are common for time-based media and give rise to several categories of timed streams (such as depicted in Fig. 1–1):

- *homogeneous* streams: element descriptors are constant
  An example is CD audio, where all elements have the same form.
- *heterogeneous* streams: element descriptors vary
  Examples include compressed formats where encoding parameters may vary over the course of a recording.
- *continuous* streams: $s_{i+1} = s_i + d_i$, for $i = 1, ... n\text{-}1$
  In this case there is a unique element for every time value within the span

---

[6] Pulse Code Modulation (PCM), a simple encoding scheme for sample data.
[7] Adaptive Differential Pulse Code Modulation (ADPCM), a form of audio compression used in CD-i and other multimedia environments.

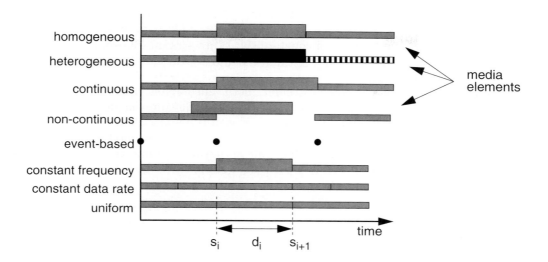

Figure 1-1 Examples of timed streams for different forms of time-based media. Media elements are represented by rectangles (or dots in the case of event-based streams). Four pieces of information are shown for each element: its start time and duration, size (area of rectangle), and descriptor (shading of rectangle).

of the stream (i.e., for all times t: $s_1 \le t \le s_n + d_n$). Digital audio and digital video are common examples of continuous media.

- *non-continuous* streams: $s_{i+1} \ne s_i + d_i$, for some i
  In this case there are "gaps" and/or "overlaps" among elements. Music and animation are examples. For instance, consider animation represented by sequences of elements specifying movement. At times when the animated object is at rest there are no associated media elements. Another example is a representation for music where media elements correspond to notes being produced. A chord would then require overlapping elements.

- *event-based* streams: $d_i = 0$, for $i = 1, \dots n$
  A special case of non-continuous streams occurs when media elements are duration-less "events." An example is MIDI where elements are musical events of the form "Start Note X" and "Stop Note Y."

- *constant frequency* streams: continuous and element duration is constant
  In this common case the durations of media elements are constant, examples include fixed-frame-rate digital video and many digital audio representations.

- *constant data rate* streams: continuous and the ratio of element size to duration is constant
  Some timed streams have a constant data rate (the data rate is the ratio of size to duration of media elements).

- *uniform* streams: continuous and both element size and duration are constant

  This is a common subcase of constant data rate streams. Examples include many "raw" (uncompressed) digital audio and digital video representations.

The above categories of timed streams both encompass, and differentiate between, a wide range of representations for audio, video, music, and animation. In this sense they also provide useful categories of time-based media. For example, one can say that audio and video are continuous media since representations for audio and video are generally continuous streams. Other categories than those shown in Fig. 1–1 are certainly possible, but appear to be less common and so less useful.

1.5   Structuring Mechanisms

Suppose we can construct multimedia objects using attributes that take media objects as their values. For instance, a VideoClip object could possess, in addition to character-valued attributes such as the title and name of the director, a video-valued attribute containing the actual content of a video clip. Clearly VideoClip objects can be related in many ways. Two may have the same director, or concern the same topic, or one may be the sequel of, or a shorter version of, the other. These relationships are domain-specific. Other relationships are generic, they represent basic ways for structuring media objects. These relationships include *interpretation*, *derivation,* and *composition*.

Interpretation

Depending upon the operation being performed, time-based media, and multimedia data in general, can be viewed at two levels. First, with low-level operations, for instance copying and deleting, there is no need to be aware of internal organization and the data can be viewed as an unstructured BLOB. However for high-level media-specific operations, such as presentation and editing, the structure of the data is important and must be visible. In this case the data is viewed as an intricately structured aggregate of media elements. Interpretation is the link between these two views. First suppose we define BLOBs as follows:

> **Definition 4** A *BLOB* is an attribute value that appears to applications as a sequence of bytes. The database system provides an interface by which applications can read and append data to BLOBs. (The database system may also support insertion and deletion of byte spans, however for time-based media these operations are not essential since non-destructive editing techniques are often used.)

Generally BLOBs can be very large in size (i.e., many Mbytes) and require special support by database systems. A BLOB may correspond to a region of contiguous storage or it may be fragmented, the layout of BLOBs is a performance issue and not directly relevant to data modeling. What is relevant to data modeling is the relationship between media streams and BLOBs:

> **Definition 5**   An *interpretation*, I, of a BLOB B, is a mapping from B to a set of media objects. For each object, I specifies the object's descriptor and its placement in B. If the object is a media sequence then for each media element I specifies the elements's order within the sequence, its start time, duration and element descriptor.

Example of Interpretation

As a specific example of interpretation, suppose a 10-minute PAL[8] video signal and an accompanying stereo audio signal are digitized and stored in a BLOB. PAL video frames occur 25 times per second. Assume frames are sampled at a resolution of 640×480 pixels, each sample providing 24 bits of RGB data. The RGB values are then converted to YUV, Y is given 8 bits per pixel, U and V are subsampled (averaged over neighboring pixels) and each is given 2 bits per pixel. There are now 12 bits per pixel. The YUV frames are then JPEG compressed using a quality factor resulting in about 0.5 bits per pixel (this will give VHS quality). Thus the original video data rate has been reduced from about 22 Mbyte/sec to roughly 0.5 Mbyte/sec. The audio data is sampled at a 44,100 Hz with a sample size of 16 bits. Since there are two channels the audio data rate is 172 kbyte/sec. The audio and video data are interleaved in a single BLOB with audio samples following the associated video frame. Suppose we call the two media objects video$_1$ and audio$_1$; their interpretation is depicted in Fig. 1–2.

The interpretation specifies the media descriptors for video$_1$ and audio$_1$, these would resemble:

video$_1$ descriptor = {
    category = homogeneous,
        constant frequency
    quality factor= "VHS quality"
    duration = 10 minutes
    frame rate = 25
    frame width = 640
    frame height = 480
    frame depth = 24
    color model = RGB
    encoding = YUV 8:2:2, JPEG }

audio$_1$ descriptor = {
    category = homogeneous,
        uniform
    quality factor = "CD quality"
    duration = 10 minutes
    sample rate = 44100
    sample size =16
    number of channels = 2
    encoding = PCM }

---

[8] Phase Alternation Line (PAL) – a European video signal standard.

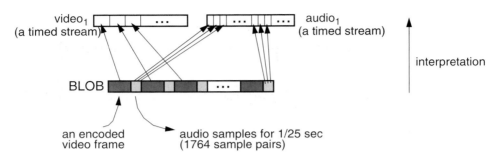

Figure 1-2   An interpretation of a BLOB.

The descriptors should also contain information that helps allocate resources for playback; this could include the average data rate for each stream, a measure of data rate variation (for non-uniform streams), and any parameters needed for decompression.

In addition to the media descriptors, the interpretation must identify element placement, timing, and element descriptors. Both $video_1$ and $audio_1$ are homogeneous streams—elements are of the same form and element descriptor attributes are subsumed by the media descriptors. However the encoded video frames are variable sized. This means that for $video_1$ the mapping from element number to BLOB placement is not a simple multiplication; the same holds for $audio_1$ because of interleaving. As a result an explicit mapping is needed, as represented by the following tables:

$video_1$(elementNumber, elementSize, blobPlacement)
$audio_1$(elementNumber, blobPlacement)

These tables have one entry for each element, i.e., for each frame of $video_1$ and each sample of $audio_1$. The tables are a logical view of the interpretation mapping—existing storage systems for time-based media use multiple index structures, allowing rapid lookup of the element occurring at a specific time and the clustering of elements for performance reasons.

The indexes used to implement interpretation should not be visible to applications, what needs to be visible are the results of interpretation—the media elements and their descriptors. In other words, interpretation supports the timed stream abstraction by encapsulating information about the low-level encoding and BLOB placement of media elements.

The information needed for interpretation depends on the category of the stream, whether it is heterogeneous, homogeneous, continuous, etc. For instance, if $video_1$ were a heterogeneous and non-continuous video object, it would require a table of the form:

$video_1$(elementNumber, startTime, duration, elementDescriptor,
        elementSize, blobPlacement)

Definition 5 does not preclude a BLOB from having more than one interpretation. For instance, from the $video_1$ table, a second interpretation can be formed simply by removing table entries or changing their element number. The effect resembles video editing which involves cutting and reordering video sequences. Similarly if an interpretation identifies many media objects within a BLOB, an alternative interpretation can be constructed by removing references to one of the objects from the original interpretation. The result is much like an alternative view of the BLOB (e.g., only the audio sequence is visible).

Generally modification of an interpretation is questionable (unless the underlying BLOB is also modified). The risk is that the original interpretation is destroyed in which case media elements within the BLOB may be effectively lost. It is probably a better practice if a BLOB has a single, complete, interpretation which is built up as the BLOB is captured or created and then permanently associated with the BLOB. Editing operations, and alternative views of the BLOB, can be achieved using derivation and composition, which we now discuss.

Derivation

In data modeling, derivation refers to how the value of a specific item (an attribute, a set of attributes, an entity type, etc.) can be computed from the values of other items. In general, the structure of the derived item is not the same as that of the items participating in the derivation. So, derivation in these cases can be considered as a simple viewing mechanism.

In the context of multimedia modeling, derivations play a prominent role and represent a very general and frequently used technique. Derivations reflect the various steps and decisions made by media designers on the way from data capture to a form of the media object ready for presentation. Information about the various production steps and their ordering are especially useful if earlier steps need to be repeated or undone. In general, it is not necessary to store the results of derivations, the *derived objects*, but the specification of each derivation step. This notion of derivation has several advantages beyond data modeling: First, derivation reduces storage utilization by allowing alternative views to be constructed without the need for replication. Second, modification operations can be performed more efficiently. For example, to delete a video sub-sequence one could copy and reassemble the frame data, but it would be much more efficient to simply create a derivation representing the edit. Third, derivation provides physical data independence by separating derived objects from the underlying stored data.

We define derivation as a mapping from a set of media objects, and a set of parameters that govern the derivation, to a new media object.

Definition 6   The *derivation* (D) of a media object o_1 from a set of media objects O is a mapping of the form $D(O, P_D) \rightarrow o_1$, where P_D is the set of parameters specific to D. o_1 is called the *derived object*. The information needed to compute a derived object, references to the media objects and parameter values used, is called a *derivation descriptor*.

The essential idea of this notion of derivation is the representation of media objects whose underlying media elements are calculated when needed. Typically, the media elements need only be stored if the calculation cannot be performed in real time (as when the time to calculate elements in a constant frequency stream is greater than their period).

The types of media objects participating in derivations are usually constrained. For example, an audio sequence cannot be concatenated to a video sequence. But there are also exceptions to this observation. As there exist many different forms of derivation, we group them into categories according to such general observations. Specific examples are given at the end of the subsection.

Derivations can be differentiated with respect to whether they change the content of a media object, its placement in time, whether they are elementary or compound, change the media type or not, allow elements of different types to participate in the derivation, or are generic and apply to all or most media types or to one or a few types only. These groups of derivations are not exclusive and a derivation can appear in more than one group.

Derivations Changing the Content

In general derivations in this group are specific to certain media types. Examples are digital filters for images, transposition of a music object to a different key, or changing the font or the font size of text. An example, in which two objects participate in the derivation is chroma-keying of one video sequence over another. In this case, the content of the first video sequence is partially replaced with that of the second. Derivations that change content often require special hardware if they are to be performed in real time. Consider video fades and wipes. In video postproduction, these derivations (known as "digital video effects") are calculated in real time by hardware that applies a function to "input" sequences and derives a new "output" sequence.

Derivations Changing Timing

Derivations involving changes in timing are generic in the sense that they apply to all time-based media. For instance, temporally translating a sequence (i.e., uniformly incrementing element start times) can be performed on video sequences, audio sequences or any other time-based value. Another example is scaling (i.e., uniformly scaling element durations).

Derivations Changing the Media Type

Synthesis is an important example of a derivation that changes the media type. Consider, for example, the synthesis of an audio object from a MIDI object, or the

Derivation	Argument Type(s)	Result Type	Category
color separation	image	image	change of content
color correction	image	image	change of content
filtering (blurring etc.)	image	image	change of content
audio edit	audio	audio	change of timing
audio normalization	audio	audio	change of content
pitch shifting	audio	audio	change of content
gap suppression	audio	audio	change of content
video edit	video	video	change of timing
video keying	video	video	change of content
video transition	video	video	change of content
tempo shift	music	music	change of timing
MIDI synthesis	music	audio	change of type
speech synthesis	text	audio	change of type
optical char recognition	image	text	change of type
text rendering	text	image	change of type

Table 1–1   Common derivations.

synthesis of a video object via rendering an animation sequence. Here the type changes from music to audio or animation to video. Other derivations result in a less radical change of type. Examples here include changing from one image encoding to another, or changing compression parameters.

Examples of Derivations

Up to now we have been discussing derivation very generally. This is due to the fact that derivations can be applied to various media types and have a rich variety of forms—a realistic enumeration of which would cover considerable space. In order to be more specific, Table 1–1 illustrates some commonly used derivations. Argument and result types in the table refer to media types only (i.e., the table does not include information about the parameters of the derivations). Each derivation is also assigned to one of the categories identified above. Several of the above forms of derivation are now discussed in more detail and some specific examples will be given.

Color separation

Printing a color image often requires a change in the color model as when images are converted from an RGB format to a CMYK[9] format (Fig. 1–3). Since the

---

[9] Colors are separated by cyan (C), magenta (M), yellow (Y), and black (K) intensities.

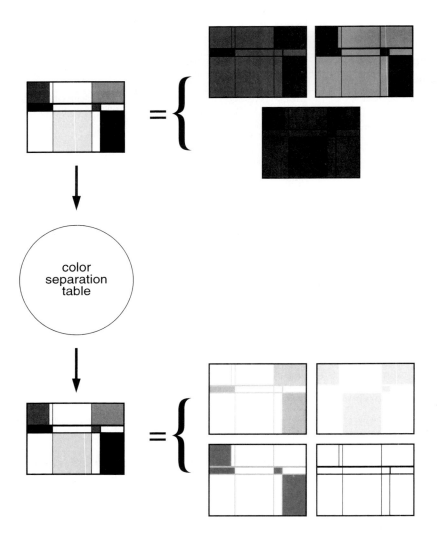

Figure 1-3 Example of a derived image object: The original image is in RGB
space, the derived image in CMYK. The large circle indicates the information
needed to perform the derivation.

mapping from RGB into the CMYK color model is not unique, additional information must be provided as parameters. In general this information is defined in
separation tables in which ink and paper qualities and levels of brightness are
accounted for to give best printing results.

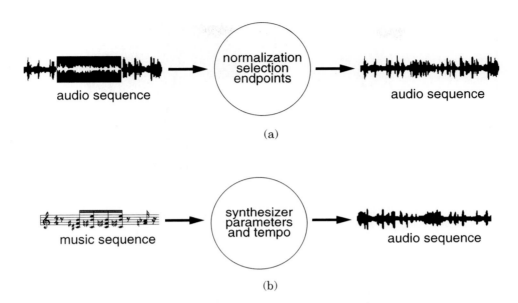

Figure 1–4   Examples of derived audio objects: (a) a normalized audio sequence, (b) a synthesized audio sequence. In each case the derived audio object is on the right and the antecedent media objects on the left. The large circles indicate the information needed to perform the derivations.

Audio Normalization

The enhancement of sound files with too little amplitude or uneven volume is done by a scaling operation called "normalization" (see Fig. 1–4(a)). The parameters needed are the start and end points of the audio sequence to be normalized. If no parameters are specified, normalization is performed for the whole audio object.

Video Keying

Chroma-keying is commonly used in video production to visually combine one video sequence with another (Fig. 1–5). Often one sequence is a "bluescreen shot" containing foreground objects, and the second sequence is the desired background. The parameters involved in the derivation of the "mixed" sequence include keying color and thresholds.

Video Editing

Editing video involves the selection and ordering of sequences that are combined to produce a new video object. The list of start and stop times of these selections is called an edit list. Edit lists are derivation descriptors, while edited video sequences are derived objects.

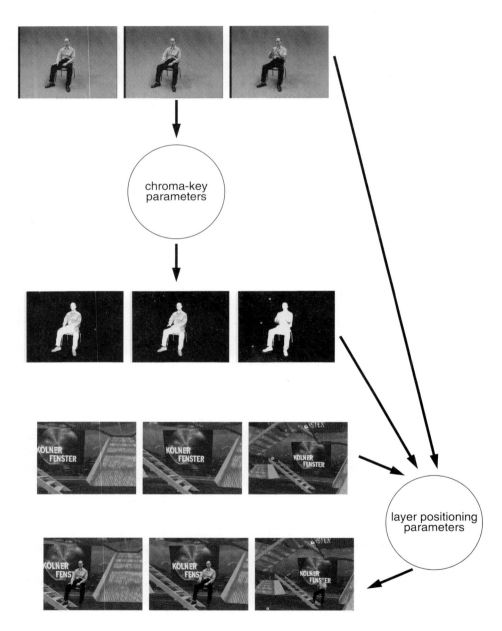

Figure 1-5 Example of a derived video object: A blue screen sequence and a synthetic background sequence are chroma-keyed together. The large circle indicates the information needed to perform the derivation.

Video Transition

In video editing, instead of directly concatenating two video objects often an intermediate video effect is used, as for example, a fade or wipe. These transitions produce video frames that consist of data stemming from both video objects (one is faded out the other is faded in). The parameters for this kind of derivation specify the type of transition, its duration, and the start time in both video objects.

MIDI Synthesis

The synthesis of an audio object from a MIDI object is an example of derivation for which argument and result types differ (see Fig. 1–4(b)). Parameters are tempo, MIDI channel mappings, and instrument parameters. These essentially identify, for example, whether a given note is played on a piano, a violin, or some other instrument.

The use of derived media objects has many advantages. First storage is saved since derived media objects and their associated derivation descriptors are relatively small (for example, a video edit list is likely many orders of magnitude smaller than a video object). Furthermore by storing derivation descriptors it is possible to keep track of, and query, manipulations to media objects. Finally, sequences of derivations can be changed and reused, this is useful in multimedia authoring environments.

Composition

The *partOf* relationship is often used to model complex assemblies of simpler components. Since the essence of "multimedia" lies in assembling different media, it appears that some form of aggregation is fundamental to multimedia modeling. Looking to music and the arts, the term "composition" describes the combining and assembling of various elements. This suggests that composition is the overall organizing principle for multimedia data—it should then be modeled explicitly. In the context of data modeling we define composition as follows:

Definition 7 *Composition* is the specification of temporal and/or spatial relationships between a group of media objects. The result of composition is called a *multimedia object*, the original objects are called its *components*.

Depending upon the nature of the media objects, a variety of forms of composition can be identified. They can be grouped into two general categories: spatial composition and temporal composition (e.g., [13]). The first deals with positioning objects in a 2D or 3D space. An example would be placing an image within a page of text or placing graphical objects in a scene. Temporal composition determines the relative timing and synchronization of time-based media. For instance, narrating a video sequence by combining it with an audio sequence is an example of temporal composition.

1.6   An Example: From BLOBs to Movies

As a more extensive example we will show how a multimedia object, in this case a multi-track movie, can be composed from several simpler objects; this example will also involve interpretation and derivation. Suppose we start with two audio sequences, $audio_1$ and $audio_2$, and two video sequences, $video_1$ and $video_2$. The two audio sequences contain music and narration. Certain sub-sequences will be presented simultaneously. For this reason the two audio sequences are interleaved in a single BLOB. Suppose the two video sequences result from a single capture operation (e.g., digitization of a single video tape) and so also reside in a single BLOB. These four sequences are the building blocks from which a multimedia sequence is to be constructed.

   The first step is to construct a derived video sequence which performs a slow (10-second) fade from $video_1$ to $video_2$ (which we can assume represent different shots from the original tape). After deriving the fade sequence, $video_F$, we concatenate it with "cut" versions of the original sequences to produce $video_3$. Finally a multimedia object is created and the three sequences—$audio_1$, $audio_2$ and $video_3$—are added to it using temporal composition.

   Fig. 1–6 shows the relationships between the various sequences and the underlying BLOBs. Also shown are the intermediate objects, such as the four derivation descriptors (cut_1, cut_2, fade, and concat), used to represent these relationships. The timeline diagram indicates the relative timing of the three components of the final multimedia object.

   In reality, producing multimedia objects will involve many more derivations and many more components. But the procedure will be similar to that followed above: raw material is created and added to the database, and then successively refined (derived) and composed.

   To summarize, interpretation, derivation, and composition give us a way of moving from simple, uninterpreted data, to complex multimedia aggregates (see Fig. 1–7). It is the higher-level abstractions, media objects and elements and multimedia objects, that are seen by applications.

1.7   Conclusion

We have presented a data model that addresses the representation of time-based media. The model includes the notions of media objects, media elements, and timed streams. Three general structuring mechanisms are used: interpretation, derivation, and composition. Many of these ideas have evolved from existing systems. Our goal has been to unify these ideas, provide a more formal foundation, and express them in a way suitable for data modeling.

   Most of the examples in this chapter deal with audio and video; we have given less attention to other media types such as graphics, music, and anima-

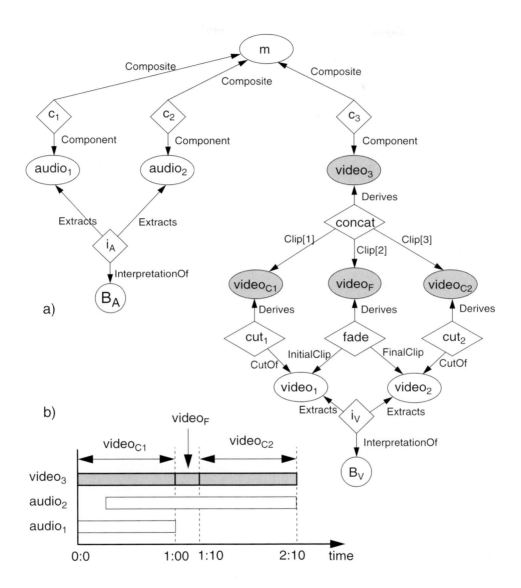

Figure 1-6 An instance diagram for a multimedia object is shown in (a). The object, m, has three components—two audio objects and one video object. These are related to m via three temporal composition relationships, c_1, c_2, and c_3. (Instances of relationships are indicated by diamond shapes, multimedia and media objects by ellipses and BLOBs by circles. Derived objects are shaded.) The second diagram (b) shows the relative timing of the three components of m.

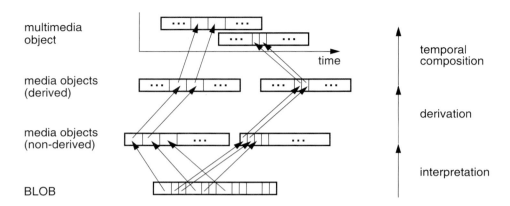

Figure 1-7　Successive interpretation, derivation, and composition.

tion. However, the data model does encompass these types. The key is derivation: animation and music deal with symbolic representations from which audio or video sequences are derived. For example, music representations allow the specification of note sequences. A synthesizer then takes these sequences and derives audio sequences. Similarly video sequences are derived (via rendering) from representations of animation.

Implementation of database systems capable of supporting time-based media presents many new problems in such areas as scheduling, synchronization, resource allocation, and storage management. Authorization and electronic copyright need to be addressed. Support for time-based media requires basic changes in database architecture and the form of the database/application interface. The notion of timed streams introduced in this chapter leads to a perspective where database operations are viewed as extended activities that produce, consume and transform flows of data. A database architecture based on activities and their interconnection is explored in [6].

References

[1] *Adobe Premiere User Guide*, 1st edition. Mountain View, CA: Adobe Systems Incorporated, 1991.

[2] Anderson, D.P., and Homsy, G. "A continuous media I/O server and its synchronization mechanism," *IEEE Computer*, Vol. 24, No. 10, Oct 1991, pp. 51-57.

[3] Bertino, E., Rabitti, F., and Gibbs, S. "Query processing in a multimedia document system," *ACM TOIS,* Vol. 6, No. 1, Jan 1988, pp. 1-41.

[4] Carey, M.J., DeWitt, D.J., Richardson, J.E., and Shekita, E.J. "Storage managements for objects in EXODUS," in *Object-Oriented Concepts, Databases, and Applications* Kim, W. and Lochovsky, F.H., Eds. Addison Wesley, 1989, pp. 341-369.

[5] Christodoulakis, S. *et al.* "Multimedia document presentation, information extraction, and document formation in MINOS: A model and a system,"*ACM TOIS*, Vol. 4, No. 4, Oct 1986, pp. 345-383.

[6] Gibbs, S., Breiteneder, C., and Tsichritzis, D. "Audio/video databases: An object-oriented approach," in *Proc. 9th International Conference on Data Engineering*, 1993, pp. 381-390.

[7] Hamakawa, R. and Rekimoto, J. "Object composition and playback models for handling multimedia data," in *Proc. First ACM International Conference on Multimedia*, Anaheim, CA, Aug 1993, pp. 273-281.

[8] Hoffert, E., *et al.* "QuickTime: An extensible standard for digital multimedia," in *Proc. of the IEEE Computer Conf.* (CompCon'92), Feb 1992.

[9] Lehman, T.J., and Lindsay, B.G. "The Starburst long field manager," in *Proc. International Conference on Very Large Databases (VLDB)*, Aug 1989.

[10] Klas, W., Neuhold, E.J., and Schrefl, M. "Using an object-oriented approach to model multimedia data," *Computer Communications*, Vol. 13, No. 4, 1990, pp. 204-216.

[11] Le Gall, D. "MPEG: A video compression standard for multimedia applications," *Commun. of the ACM*, Vol. 34, No. 4, Apr 1991, pp. 46-58.

[12] Lippman, A. "Feature sets for interactive images,"*Commun. of the ACM*, Vol. 34, No. 4, Apr 1991, pp. 92-102.

[13] Little, T.D.C. and Ghafoor, A. "Spatio-temporal composition of distributed multimedia objects for value-added networks,"*IEEE Computer*, Vol. 24, No. 10, Oct 1991, pp. 42-50.

[14] MacroMind Inc. *Director Studio Manual*, Version 3.0, 1991.

[15] Masunaga, Y. "Multimedia databases: A formal framework," in*Proc. IEEE CS Office Automation Symposium*, Gaithersburg, MD, Apr 1987. Washington, DC: IEEE CS Press, pp. 36-45.

[16] Microsoft Corp. *Microsoft Windows Multimedia Programmer's Workbook*, 1991.

[17] Preston, J.M. (Ed.) *Compact-Disc Interactive: A Designer's Overview*, Kluwer, Deventer NL, 1987.

[18] Rengarajan, T.K. "Rdb/VMS support for multi-media databases," in*Proc. of the ACM SIGMOD 1992 Conf. on Management of Data*, p. 287.

[19] Ripley, G.D. "DVI— A digital multimedia technology,"*Commun. of the ACM*, Vol. 32, No. 7, July 1989, pp. 811-822.

[20] Rowe, A. and Smith, B. A. "Continuous media player," in *Proc. 3rd International Workshop on Network and Operating System Support for Digital Audio and Video*, San Diego, 1992, pp. 334-344.

[21] Segev, A. and Shoshani, A. "Logical modeling of temporal data," in *Proc. of the ACM SIGMOD 1987 Conf. on Management of Data*, pp. 454-466.

[22] Schloss, G.A and Wynblatt M.J. "Providing definition and temporal structure for multimedia data," *Multimedia Systems*, Vol.3, No. 5/6, 1995, pp. 264-277.

[23] Wallace, G.K. "The JPEG still picture compression standard,"*Commun. of the ACM*, Vol. 34, No. 4, Apr 1991, pp. 30-44.

[24] Weiss, R., Duda, A., and Gifford, D.K. "Content-based access to algebraic video," in *Proc. International Conference on Multimedia Computing and Systems*, Boston, 1994, pp. 140-151.

[25] Woelk, D., Kim, W., and Luther, W. "An object-oriented approach to multimedia data-
      bases," in *Proc. of the ACM-SIGMOD 1986 Conference on Management of Data*,
      pp. 311-325.
[26] Woelk, D. and Kim, W. "Multimedia information management in an object-oriented
      database system," in *Proc. International Conference on Very Large Databases
      (VLDB)*, 1987, pp. 319-329.

Document Model Issues for Hypermedia

Lynda Hardman and Dick C.A. Bulterman

Interoperable Multimedia Systems Group
CWI
P.O. Box 94079, 1090 GB Amsterdam, The Netherlands
email: {Lynda.Hardman, Dick.Bulterman}@cwi.nl

A number of different systems exist for creating multimedia or hypermedia applications—each with its own internal document model. This leads to problems in comparing documents created by these systems, and in describing the information captured by a document for long-term (system independent) storage and future playback.

We discuss the components which should be considered for a hypermedia document model. These include the hierarchical and linking structure of a document and the spatial and temporal relations among components of the document. Other aspects, such as transportability of documents and information retrieval, are also addressed briefly.

We present the Amsterdam Hypermedia Model which, while expressing only a subset of all possible structures, has been used as a basis for a comprehensive authoring environment.

2.1 Introduction

Although hypermedia is often thought of as something innovative, it has been developed to make explicit already existing, but implicit, relations among pieces of information. A hypermedia model can be used to describe interactive aspects of familiar communication media. A television news program, for example, can be described in terms of a hypermedia presentation—initially there is an introduction by a newscaster; this leads into a film clip, normally accompanied by some commentary, on a particular news story; then we see the newscaster again. In this case the user is not making any choice, but the action of "jumping" to a new scene is present. By extending this example only slightly, a hypermedia presentation can be made by playing the same introduction, then giving the user the choice of which film clips to see, then returning to the newscaster for a further selection. A more static example of interaction is a book, or paper, where a reader can take notes. Sections of the text can be marked as relevant, and notes can be written in the margin either agreeing or disagreeing with the author. A future reader is able to see which notes are attached to which pieces of text.

Both examples show relations among media items (atomic pieces of multimedia data) which we would like to be able to preserve in on-line, interactive presentations. In order to be able to express these, and to enable information to be captured for later use, an information model is required in order to formally define the structure of the information, to efficiently map the structure to storage, and to support information and retrieval [7]. A model can also be used to compare the expressive power of hypermedia authoring systems, and for transporting presentations from one platform to another.

A requirement for a useful hypermedia model is that it can describe sufficient complexity so that the essence of a presentation can be preserved from one platform to another. This includes specifications of the media items used, the temporal relations among the items, layout of the items and interaction possibilities with the presentation. On the other hand, when a model becomes more complex there is a danger that it becomes too difficult to specify for any particular presentation, with consequences that an authoring system becomes very complex to use. In the extreme case a hypermedia presentation can be programmed directly in a non-specialist programming language, giving flexibility but minimal reuse. A simple model, supported by easy-to-use tools, is in turn too restrictive to allow the creation of anything more than, say, the sequential presentation of a slide show. The creation of a useful model is to find a pragmatic trade-off between these two extremes.

We present the different aspects of hypermedia modelling in this chapter through the use of an intuitive three-dimensional representation of a multimedia presentation, for example see Fig. 2–3. This consists of the notion that media items are displayed on a screen for some duration with timing and layout relations specified among them. A solely time-based model such as this is insufficient, since at some, normally unpredictable, time the user may interact with choice points and jump to another part of the presentation. On the other hand, a model based only on the hypertext notion of interaction [15] is also insufficient since it lacks the timing constraints among the media items. Often the term hypermedia is used to describe linked, multiple media, where time is only relevant when playing a particular media item and not for the presentation as a whole. We take a more multimedia-based approach, that time needs to be integrated into the document model.

As well as a model satisfying the direct issues of recreating a presentation in a different environment, a hypermedia model also has to take into account other issues, for example information storage and retrieval. While the main purpose of a hypermedia model is not to satisfy these sorts of requirements, it should remain compatible with them.

In this chapter we do not address authoring issues of hypermedia, these are discussed at length in [18]. Nor do we address issues of different data types or storage models for data, nor playback issues of a presentation, such as synchronization of remote sources (see the Baqai, Khan, and Ghafoor chapter in this volume). We do discuss briefly a number of languages for expressing a hypermedia model (see the subsection Transportability on page 57) but this is not a main theme of the work.

We begin our discussion on hypermedia documents models with an example of a hypermedia presentation to give a base on which to discuss the abstractions in the model. We then discuss a number of issues that need to be addressed in a hypermedia model, with reference to other systems and models.

2.2   An Example Hypermedia Presentation

As a starting point for our discussion on models, we consider the characteristics of a "typical" hypermedia presentation. Hypermedia presentations vary widely in terms of their interactivity. For example, an entertainment application such as watching a video is comparatively passive for the user. A video game, in contrast, is a highly interactive activity for the user. An activity falling between these two extremes might be the reading of a (hypermedia) newspaper, where the user can choose which news items to watch, and sit passively while an item (perhaps video, perhaps text) is presented. Both the more passive and the more interactive ends of this interaction spectrum demand the transmission of data and the synchronization of the constituent media items. Often the term multimedia is used to describe more passive presentations, where interaction is deemed of lesser importance than the (pre-specified) interactions among the media items.

An example of a "medium interactivity" presentation is shown in Fig. 2–1, which illustrates three fragments from a tour of the city of Amsterdam. In the top fragment, which is analogous to a table of contents, a user is given a description of the tour and a number of choices that can be selected within the presentation. One of these choices is illustrated—containing a description of walks through the city, highlighting several features found on the tour, which is itself sub-divided across a number of other fragments. From a media perspective, each fragment consists of a number of media items displayed for some duration on screen or played through loudspeakers. This structure is shown from a time perspective in Fig. 2–2. Here, a number of items are presented simultaneously, then

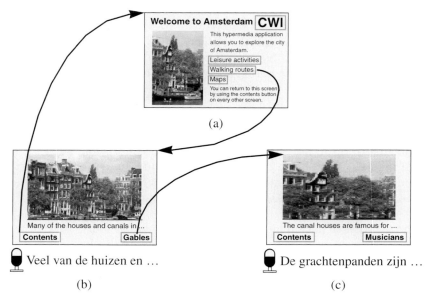

Figure 2-1   An example interactive multimedia presentation.
(a) Contents screen of the Amsterdam tour. Four media items (3 text, 1video)
are displayed. There are three interaction choices from the long text item
and one choice from the CWI item. Selecting the *Walking routes* option takes
the user to (b).
(b) The first scene in the walking route. Three text items and one image are
displayed; a fifth item is a Dutch spoken commentary. Selecting *Contents*
takes the reader to the contents screen in (a); *Gables* takes the reader to the
scene in (c).
(c) The gables scene in the walking route, similar in composition to (b).

when the user makes a choice to jump to the walking route, the currently running presentation is left and a new presentation is started. Here a number of
items are again started simultaneously, but after a few seconds the subtitle
changes to keep in time with the spoken commentary. These time relations are
an example of the types of information that need to be captured by a hypermedia
document model.

2.3   Model Issues

The issues that need to be addressed in a hypermedia model can be broadly categorized into document specification, document transportation and information
representation. Document specification is of the main importance in this work,
where we are interested in specifying sufficient information for recreating the
hypermedia presentation on a number of heterogeneous platforms, and for

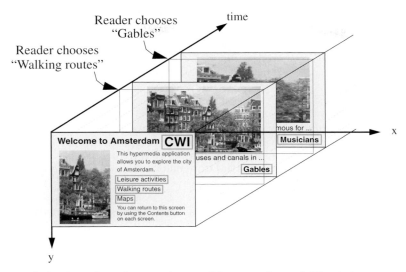

Figure 2-2 Time-based view of a possible route through Fig. 2–1.

ensuring that future systems will also be able to interpret the information. We address these issues in the four sections: the section Media Items on page 44, the section Structure on page 45, the section Presentation on page 51 (including timing and layout relations), and the section Interaction on page 56. Structural relationships define logical connections among items, including the grouping of items to be displayed together and the specification of links among these groupings. Layout specifications state where screen-based media are to be sized and placed, either in relation to each other or to the presentation as a whole. Timing relations specify the temporal dependencies among media items, possibly stored at different sites. Interactions, including navigation, give the end user the choice of jumping to related information.

Document transportation, although not within the scope of the model, influences the translation of the model to some language expressing the model. This is discussed briefly and then followed by some observations on the storage and retrieval of information and their implications for requirements of a document model.

While we prefer to use the term hypermedia to refer to collections of multimedia presentations through which the user can navigate, we will sometimes return to the term multimedia. We use the term *multimedia presentation* to indicate a collection of media items related temporally and/or spatially, or, in other words whose presentation is defined in terms of the same space and time coordinates. We show in the subsections on Composition (page 45) and Links (page 48) that a hypermedia presentation can be composed of not only a single multimedia

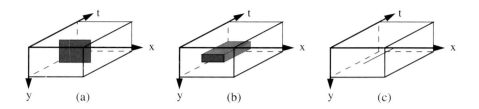

Figure 2-3 Spatio-temporal dimensions of media types.
(a) Text or graphics—spatial but no intrinsic temporal dimension.
(b) Video or animation—spatial and temporal dimensions.
(c) Sound—temporal but no spatial dimension.

presentation, but of multiple independent multimedia presentations playing simultaneously.

Media Items

It is useful to discuss the properties of the media items making up a presentation before going into the more complex aspects of document modelling. A media item may consist of a single monomedium, such as text or sound, or a composite medium such as interleaved video and sound. In either case, we use the term *media item* to refer to a data object used as part of a presentation.

Media items have data-type dependent properties, the most important of which for multimedia is their relation to space and time. Fig. 2–3 shows representations of these in a three-dimensional space. Text, an ordering of letters, requires two dimensions for display. The aspect ratio of the display area is relatively unimportant, since words can be wrapped without losing the meaning of the sentences. A time dimension can also be applied to text; for example the time it takes for a user to read the text. This timing, however, is not part of the data structure of the object. Images also require two space dimensions for display, but aspect ratio is important, since real-world representations of objects can be distorted, not to mention aesthetic considerations. (We treat image items such as pixel-based images and vector graphic images as being fundamentally the same in this spatial view of the data. The editor CMIFed [32], for example, treats a number of different image data types as the same type of object.) For both text and image media items a duration can be assigned by an author. Video requires all three dimensions of space and time to be displayed, and can be regarded as a sequence of images, each image being displayed at a particular time. As is the case for an image the aspect ratio is important, and the rate of display of frames should also remain constant for faithful reproduction. We regard animations (normally vector-based graphics) as having properties similar to video. The final media type, sound, has one time dimension and no spatial dimensions.

A media item does not necessarily have to be a complete file or object. It might be a reference to part of a physically stored object. The media item is then a combination of a reference to the stored data item and a (media-dependent) specification of the part of the item to be played. In the case of text the object may be a complete book, where only a section is required. For an image, a portion of the image is cropped. In sound, for example, a selection from a music item may last a number of seconds, but may also be only one track for the length of the complete item. A video segment might be a combination of temporal and spatial cropping operations, where a number of frames are selected from the complete sequence (cropping in time) and only a part of the image is shown (cropping in space).

Other media item types that may be included in a presentation are outputs from external processes—for example a video camera pointing at a scene outside, or the reading from a monitoring device in a chemical plant or power station. We can still treat it as an object of similar space dimensions (video in the first example, a text string or image in the second), but then with an unknown or indefinite time dimension. Alternatively, it may be a media item of known type and duration, but generated on-the-fly from an external program. For example, financial results are generated from a market simulation program and displayed as an image in the presentation, [20].

Structure

Composition

A hypermedia presentation can be regarded as a hierarchical structure with media items at the leaf nodes, [21]. This allows groups of items to be treated as one object. The MET^{++} system [1], for example, allows an author to group media items into a composite object and then manipulate the composite by, e.g., increasing the time duration of the composite and distributing the changes among the constituent children. This is analogous to a graphics editor which allows grouping of diagram elements and stretching/shrinking of the group as a whole.

Although a number of multimedia authoring systems allow parallel and serial composition ([1], [16], [23]) and treat these as fundamental divisions, they are in fact two extremes of one form of composition—*time-dependent composition*. This is where two, or more, items (or groups of items) are grouped together in one composite and a time relation is specified among them. In the serial case, Fig. 2–4(a), the time relation is that one starts when the other finishes; in the parallel case, Fig. 2–4(b), that the items start together. An intermediate case is that one item starts and at some time later, but before the other finishes, the second one starts. (We continue the discussion of timing relations in the subsection Temporal Layout on page 52.) Normally items are displayed on the screen without any thought of spatial relations, although mostly they are implicit, for example subtitles appear at the bottom of the video they apply to. The determining

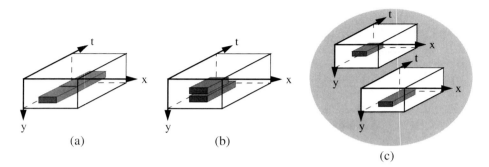

Figure 2-4 Composition.
(a) Time-dependent composition, serial.
(b) Time-dependent composition, parallel.
(c) Time-independent composition.

factor is that the items are being grouped in the same space/timeline. Fig. 2–4 is perhaps misleading, since it implies that serial composition requires that the two objects occupy the same screen position. The only condition that may apply is that two items in parallel cannot occupy the same position (unless the author explicitly specifies overlap).

The other form of composition is *time-independent composition*. This allows the grouping of items that have no time or spatial relations with each other, see Fig. 2–4(c). They *may* be played at the same time, but there is *no pre-defined* relation between them. The utility of this is perhaps not at first clear, but it enables a number of situations to be modeled. For example, two or more presentations may be played at the same time: in Fig. 2–1 if the reader selects the CWI logo, then a spoken commentary is given about the institute. The timing of the spoken commentary is not bound to the other media items already on the screen, but is conditional on the reader selecting the logo. This "unpredictable" behavior can be modeled by explicitly separating the time bases of the two presentations. Another example is where a presentation is built up of several subscenes. A number of items remain playing on the screen (e.g. a heading, background music, a link back to a contents screen) while the reader selects the different subscenes (e.g., a picture with spoken commentary)—again, there is no timing relation between the items that remain on the screen and those playing in the subscenes. In each of these examples, the timelines of the two presentations that are playing are independent. The spatial relations between the two presentations are also independent (there is no explicit constraint), but when playing the presentations they should not, normally, occupy the same screen position. A practical way of ensuring this is to use separate windows for each of the presentations in the

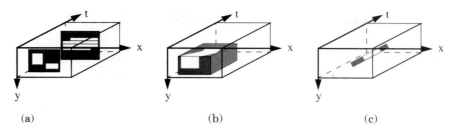

Figure 2-5   Anchor values.
(a) A text anchor is likely to be a text string, a graphics anchor, or an area.
(b) A video anchor is ideally an area changing with time.
(c) A sound anchor is a temporal extent, e.g. in music a temporal extent within an instrument.

first example, or to restrict playing of a subscene to a specific subwindow in the second example.

When the time-dependent compositions, serial and parallel, are supported in an authoring system, these can be used to calculate timing constraints for the presentation, as is the case in Mbuild [16] and CMIFed [23].

Anchors

Anchors were introduced in the Dexter model [15] as a means of referring to part of an item in a presentation in a media-independent way: they are an abstraction which allows data dependencies to be kept hidden. An anchor value specifies a part of a media item (there are other aspects to an anchor object which we will discuss as part of the model in the section Structural Information on page 59). The main use for anchors is to provide a source or destination object for linking within and among presentations, when they are used in conjunction with links (see the subsection Links on page 48). Another use is to provide a base on which to attach temporal relations so that parts of media items can be synchronized with one another (see the subsection Temporal Layout on page 52), or even as a base for spatial relations (see the subsection Spatial Layout on page 51).

In Fig. 2–5 a graphical interpretation is given for text, image, video, and sound anchor values. A text anchor normally specifies a sequence of characters within a text item. An image anchor specifies an area in a pixel-based image, where most systems implement the area as rectangular, although there need be no restriction on the shape of the area and any contour[1] could be defined to specify the extent of the area. In a vector graphic image an anchor may refer to any

---

[1] It need not even be a connected contour.

object (single or grouped) in the image—the point is that the internal specification of the anchor value is data format dependent.

Within a video item an anchor may be chosen as a sequence of frames, as is used in a number of systems [12], [24]. This allows the user to select at most one link to follow to another presentation at any frame in the video. A more desirable approach is to specify the area on the screen for the extent of the frame sequence [35]. This allows several choices for each frame, but the choices do not vary during the sequence. A complete description is given when each area is specified per frame in the sequence, see reference [10]. This allows moving or changing objects in the video to be followed, so that clicking on an object becomes a more natural option. This last description is illustrated in Fig. 2–5(b).

For sound items it is intuitive to describe the sound anchor, e.g. it is a stretch of sound (illustrated in Fig. 2–5(c)), or it might be a stretch of sound in one sound channel, for example a number of bars of violin solo. The problem starts when the reader tries to interact with the sound item, since with the normal mode of interaction with hypermedia presentations (clicking an object on the screen) there is nothing tangible with which to interact—although links *to* sound items remain possible. An example of interacting with "hyperspeech" is given in [3].

Anchors are not restricted to identifying parts of single media items, but can also be used to specify parts of groups of items. For example, in Fig. 2–1(b) the word "houses" might be a text anchor, one of the houses in the picture an image anchor, and the Dutch word "huizen" part of a sound anchor. All three anchors may be combined to form a composite "house" anchor which can be referred to from other parts of the presentation.

As well as defining the extent of part of a media item via the anchor value, an anchor can also have attributes associated with it. These can be used for labeling the parts of the media item they refer to, see [10]. This labeling of anchors becomes a route into attaching information to media items which can be used for retrieval of items—we discuss this further in the section Retrieval of Information on page 57.

Links

Links are defined as part of the Dexter hypertext model [15] for explicitly representing relations among objects. They specify a logical connection between two (or more) end points, specified via anchors. Most hypertext systems allow a user to follow a link as the basic form of interaction with the document structure. The use of links in hypermedia similarly allows the user to make choices as to which presentations to view and captures this in the document structure. The problem with links in multimedia is that a presentation normally consists of a number of media items playing simultaneously, and any one of these may have its own duration. In other words, links are not from static text or image items, as is generally the case in hypertext, but from a complete multimedia presentation. This leads to the question of where links fit into this more dynamic and complex document structure.

In the Dexter model a link has source items and destination items. Systems supporting the model do not often use composition of items, so that the structure is often fairly flat—one media item is displayed, a link is followed, and a new item is displayed. In the multimedia case, where the presentation is invariably composed of a number of media items the question is how many of the items are associated with each end of the link. For example, in Fig. 2–1, following the link from *Walking routes* in (a) to the screen in (b) results in the complete window being cleared and the new presentation being displayed. In the case of following the link from *Gables* in (b) to the scene in (c) all the items except the *Contents* text are cleared. In this case, the scope of the information associated with the link is only a part of the original presentation. We call this scope specification a *context* [22].

A consequence of associating a context with sources and destinations of links, is that the same anchor can be used in different links with different contexts. An example is when following a link from an anchor, say *Gables* in Fig. 2–1(b), not all of the presentation is cleared (in this case everything except the *Contents* item). Following a link to the same anchor with the whole scene as destination context, however, would result in playing *all* the items in (b).

Presentation specifications can also be associated with a link. These become more varied in hypermedia. When following a link in hypertext, systems generally display the destination items of the link, and either remove or leave the source items. The problem is that it is not specified in the model what the action should be, but is left to the particular system to interpret the action in its own way. The required action on following a link can be specified in a model by recording what happens to the link's source and destination contexts on following the link. For example, in Fig. 2–6(a) a presentation is playing and when the user follows the link the new presentation is played, while the original presentation continues playing. In Fig. 2–6(b) the situation is similar, but in this case the original presentation pauses while the new presentation plays. The only difference between these two cases is brought about by the fact that the original presentation can pause or continue playing. The third case, in Fig. 2–6(c), is where the original presentation is removed and the new presentation is played on its own.

Other presentation specifications can be associated with a link. For example it might specify that the anchor in the destination context blink to make it more visible. A further presentation feature, normally found in multimedia systems, is the transition [34]. Here, for example, when an image is replaced by a new image there is a choice of a number of actions such as fading the original image out and fading the new image in; similarly videos can dissolve into one another. Transitions can also be specified as a presentation attribute of the link when the destination context of a link is played in the same screen area as the source context. The transition might even be a sequence in its own right. For example, if a user chooses to zoom in to Amsterdam from a map of the earth,

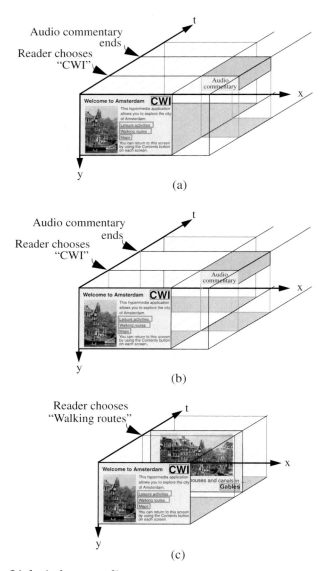

Figure 2-6   Links in hypermedia.
(a) New presentation plays in addition to original presentation.
(b) Original presentation pauses while new presentation plays.
(c) New presentation replaces original presentation.

actioning the link doesn't make the presentation jump to a presentation about Amsterdam, but increases the scale of the earth gradually then dissolves into the new presentation.

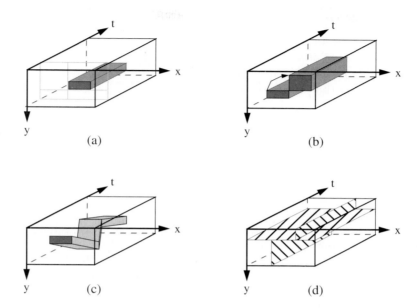

Figure 2-7 Spatial layout.
(a) Position defined relative to window.
(b) Position defined relative to another item.
(c) Object moves as a function of time.
(d) Channels predefine screen or window areas.

Links specify relations among objects, and, when labelled with semantically relevant attributes, can be used for building up information structures. We discuss this further in the section Retrieval of Information on page 57.

Presentation

Spatial Layout

Spatial layout specifications of items can be given in a number of ways. The most common method is to define an item's position per item and relative to the window (or screen) in which it will be displayed. Examples of authoring systems using this approach, illustrated in Fig. 2–7(a), are Eventor [14], Mbuild [16], Authorware, and Director [36]. Just as valid a method of specification, but to our knowledge not used in multimedia authoring systems, is to define the coordinates of a media item relative to some other media item, illustrated in Fig. 2–7(b), or relative to an anchor within an item. This would be useful for displaying, for example, subtitles next to the video they belong to, since if the position of the video is changed, the subtitles will remain in the same neighbor-hood relative to the video. (We, and others, make similar arguments for relative timing constraints, see the subsection Temporal Layout on page 52.) While it is not (yet) common to specify position relative to other items, some systems do allow the movement of objects with time, for example the MET++ [1] and Eventor [14] systems. This is illustrated in Fig. 2–7(c).

While defining the position of each item explicitly is relatively common, for large presentations it can become difficult to maintain an overview of the different layouts used. An approach to solving this is implemented in CMIFed [23], where layout objects (called channels) are defined which predefine areas of the window into which media items can be played. This is illustrated in Fig. 2–7(d). This allows an author to make changes to a channel which then apply to all the items played in the channel. While the current implementation plays an item in the middle of a channel, there is no reason why the position of a media item should not be specified relative to a channel.

A combination of the methods mentioned could be made, where a channel can move in time, another channel can be defined relative to the first, and an item's position within a channel can change with time. While this does not per-haps seem immediately useful, it should be included in an encompassing hyper-media model.

Channels, as used in CMIFed, are also used for defining high-level presen-tation specifications. These may be media-independent, for example background colour, or media dependent, for example font style and size. This is again useful for making global presentation changes to the presentation. This high-level pre-sentation specification is used as a default and can be overridden by specific lay-out specifications from individual media items.

The channels define areas relative to the window, so that in an environment where the window size can be changed, the channels also change in proportion. This means that a presentation is not defined for a fixed window size. The aspect ratio of the window may also change. In the current implementation images are scaled to fit into the available area—preserving the image's aspect ratio. (Crop-ping, as described in the section Media Items on page 44, could also be used.) A font scaling algorithm would also be useful for preserving the "look and feel" of the overall presentation.

While layout is, in theory, independent of the logical structure of a presen-tation, it is clear that presentations created from different levels of structure need to have coordination of layout among the different items. This resolution is not specified in the model, but is left to the system authoring the presentation. For example, CMIFed restricts the playing of media items in a channel to only one at a time.

Temporal Layout

Temporal layout is the determining characteristic of multimedia, in the same way that links form the basis of hypertext. In this sense, temporal properties

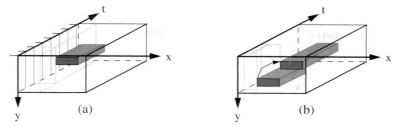

Figure 2-8   Temporal layout.
(a) Time specified with respect to a timeline.
(b) Time specified with respect to another media item.

take on a much greater importance than a small section of a hypermedia model. Our intention, however, is to make explicit where these temporal relations fit in with other relations in such a model, and give an overview of the types of temporal information that can be specified. We do not discuss, for example, how these relations can be encoded, nor how a system can strive to execute the specified relations. The issues discussed in this section are derived from the work described in [6] and [13].

Timelines   When specifying when a media item should be played in a presentation there are two different ways of providing this information. The first is to specify when the media item should start in relation to a timeline, Fig. 2–8(a), the second by specifying the relation with respect to another object in the presentation, e.g. another media item Fig. 2–8(b) or a group of objects. Both cases are supported by a number of systems: the former approach, for example, by Director [36] and the Integrator [34]; the latter, for example, by Firefly [5] and Eventor [14]. Each approach has advantages and disadvantages. The use of a timeline makes it possible to make changes to the timing of one object without affecting other objects in the presentation. This, however, requires the re-specification of all items if, e.g., one item is removed and the others have to be brought forward to fill in the gap. Specifying relations among objects, in contrast, provides more flexibility when editing the presentation later, but requires that all the relations be specified.

When defining temporal relations among the objects themselves, there remains an implicit timeline, if only the "real-time" timeline that is moved along when the presentation is being played to the user. In both cases (implicit and explicit timelines) the rate of traversal along the timeline can be varied, in a similar way that music can change its tempo when being performed. A number of systems use the timing relations specified among objects to generate a timeline, [14], [16], [23].

Durations, points in time, and intervals   The duration of a media item may be explicit or implicit, that is derived from relations with other objects. For example, a video has an explicit time associated with its data (the number of

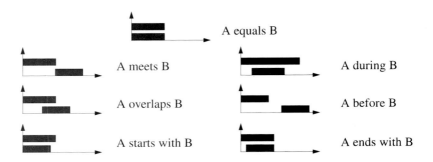

Figure 2-9 The "13" time relations. Apart from the first *equals* relation, each relation has an inverse.

frames in the clip divided by the frame rate), or an image is given an explicit display duration. An example of a derived relation is where a subtitle starts when a spoken commentary begins and remains on display until the commentary has finished. In order to achieve this type of derived duration, media items need to have the property that they can be scaled. (We consider the properties of scaling in the subsection Scaling on page 55.)

A part of a media item may be a point in time (e.g. a frame number in a video, or "5 seconds after the start" of a sound item, or "the beginning of the word *gables* in a spoken commentary), or an interval (e.g. a number of frames in a video, "between 3 and 5 seconds" in a sound item, or the duration of the word *gables* in a spoken commentary). An interval may be specified by a combination of points or intervals (e.g. "from the beginning of the word *distinctive* to the end of *gables* in a spoken commentary").

Temporal relations   Temporal relations among objects can be defined in terms of whole media items, parts of media items, or groupings of items. Examples are: (a) a video starts simultaneously with its audio track; (b) each word in a subtitle is highlighted when it is spoken in an audio commentary (synchronization between parts of media items); (c) background music is required to start with the beginning of a sequence of slides and finish at the end of the sequence.

A commonly cited ([4], [6], [13]) categorization of temporal constraints, put forward in [2], is given in Fig. 2–9. These allow all possible combinations of temporal relations between two items to be expressed. More complex relations can be built up out of this set. Using the three examples above we can illustrate a number of cases. (a) the video *starts with* the audio; (b) the highlighting of the word in the subtitle *equals* the duration of the spoken word; (c) the music *equals* the sequence of slides *meeting* each other.

Tolerance and Precision

The above temporal layout issues—such as duration of media items, synchronization constraints, interaction constraints—provide a specification of how a multimedia presentation should be played given sufficient computing resources. This is unlikely to be the case, so that variations in tolerance need to be given so trade-offs can be made. These trade-offs can be given in the form "desired timing relation, maximum allowed deviation from relation." For example, no information content is lost if a subtitle for a video appears a second before or after its scheduled time. On the other hand, for lip synchronization only a very small deviation is acceptable. Such tolerances can be specified in percentage or absolute terms.

When defining temporal relations, with or without tolerance factors, the precision of specification can also vary. For example a delay might be specified as an absolute value such as 3 seconds or as a relative value such as "shortly after."

For the case of spatial relations, these too could have associated tolerance and precision factors. The question is whether or not these are useful, since spatial relations are not constrained by processing power (as is the case for temporal relations), but by pixel resolution. Tolerance and precision measures may be more useful when scaling items, or when creating layouts automatically where trade-offs have to be made in how closely coupled items need to be.

Scaling

When incorporating images or video into a presentation the original size of the item may not be appropriate and a scaling operation is required, Fig. 2–10(a). This may be a statically defined size, such as "400 by 200 pixels," or may be relative, such as "increase to 200%." This deformation may take place as a function of time or be an attribute of the object. It may also be in relation to other objects, for example, increase font size until heading fits above image. This last case has not, to the authors' knowledge, been implemented in an authoring system.

In order to satisfy temporal constraints that involve deriving the durations of objects, or satisfying constraints such as those given in Fig. 2–9, individual media items need to be scaled in the temporal dimension. These can take the form of specifying a preferred duration, and allowing this to be deviated from by some amount (as illustrated in Fig. 2–10(b)). Another form of scaling, called temporal glue, [16] and [5], allows variable length delays to be inserted into a document, so that when a media item's duration is changed, the other constraints remain satisfied. When applying scaling factors to media items, the acceptable tolerance needs to be taken into account by the playing software.

Temporal scaling can be specified explicitly in the MET^{++} system [1], for single and composite objects, and in the CMIFed system [20], it is derived from the document structure. Spatial scaling is implemented in CMIFed for displaying different sized images using the same channel.

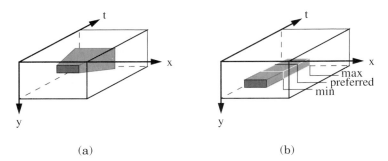

Figure 2-10 Scaling.
(a) Spatial scaling: media item can increase or decrease in size.
(b) Temporal scaling: media item has minimum, preferred, and maximum duration.

Interaction

The normal mode of operation with a multimedia presentation is that the timing relations within the presentation are calculated and the media items are displayed following the specifications. There are, however, a number of modes of interaction that can take place while the presentation is playing. These may be specified within the document, and may need the user to take an action.

A basic form of interaction is altering the speed, or direction, of the presentation as it plays. It may be played slower, faster, forwards, backwards, paused, continued, or stopped. This may be controlled by tools provided for the user, or specified as part of the document. Another common form of interaction is the hypermedia link. This specifies what happens to the currently playing presentation when the user selects to go to a different part of the presentation. This was discussed in more detail in the subsection Links on page 48.

A more general, and consequently more complex, form of interaction can take place through conditions. These may be specified via the link structure for user interaction, or among the items themselves. For example (taken from [13]), in a presentation where the duration of the items is not specified beforehand, a conditional action might be the following. Two media items are playing and when one of the items finishes playing the other one stops, and a then third item is played. Bordegoni [4] gives a further categorization of conditions as being deterministic or non-deterministic, and simple or compound.

The most general form of interaction can be specified with a full-blown programming language—often provided as a scripting language within a multimedia authoring system. This allows the creation of flexible and elaborate interactions, but with the consequence that they cannot be captured as part of a pre-defined document model.

Transportability

One of the goals for providing a document model for hypermedia is so that presentations can be created only once and played back on a number of different platforms, with little, or preferably no, further human intervention. This necessitates the capturing of sufficient information within the presentation description to guide the play-back process. As well as the need for a conceptual model, some way of describing the model is needed. This may be a proprietary data format, or an accessible standard, such as HyTime [11], [29] (based on SGML [33]), or MHEG [27], [28]. The scope of these standards varies. For example HyTime provides a language for expressing a hypermedia model but does not go any way towards building a system that could interpret a document description. MHEG, on the other hand, provides a set of tools for transporting packages of multimedia information.

Other work relevant to transportability is the notion of high-level resource descriptions, called channels in CMIFed [32]. When a document is played back on a particular platform, only the presentation attributes of the channel need be adapted to that platform and all the items played via the channel will conform to the attributes. Channels also allow alternative media items to be incorporated in a document description, so that when the document is played back on a particular platform one of these is chosen. For example, high-quality sound takes up unwanted network bandwidth and if it is to be played back on low-cost equipment a lower quality representation could be transmitted. While this example demands the existence of numerous data representations, this process may be carried out at run time [8]. If the user's hardware supports no sound at all then a text channel might be an acceptable (although undesirable) substitution.

Retrieval of Information

As more and more information becomes available on-line we need to find a way of finding relevant information. Classical databases are one approach, where the classification of the contained information is given beforehand by means of a schema. With widely distributed sources of multimedia information this approach is insufficient, and some other way is needed of labeling information so that it can be found again.

Multimedia information may be classified by having a library catalogue pointing at relevant items, but also by labeling items with entries from the library catalogue (similar to current book and article classifications). A hypermedia structure should not define what this labeling information should be, but should provide hooks for attaching classification information. Labeling can be carried out at the media item or even the anchor level. Burrill *et al.* [10], for example, define video anchors corresponding to real-life objects and these are annotated with a description of the objects they represent. It is not clear whether

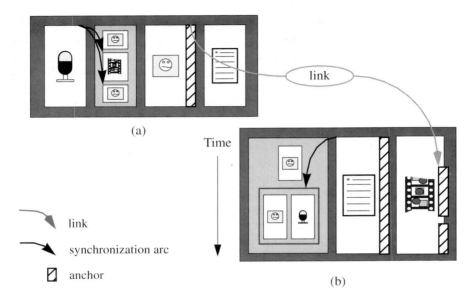

Figure 2-11   Amsterdam Hypermedia Model. The main components of the model are: *atomic component* (white box), *composite component* (shaded box), *link, anchor,* and *synchronization arc*. See text for explanations.

these annotations are part of an overall domain description. Work done by Davis [12], on the other hand, uses a rich domain description for annotating video clips for retrieval. These descriptions need not increase the storage problems significantly, since although for text nodes the amount of classification information may be larger than the text data, for video nodes this becomes an insignificant percentage.

2.4   The Amsterdam Hypermedia Model

The Amsterdam Hypermedia Model (AHM) [21],[2] is based on models for both hypertext and multimedia. The Dexter hypertext reference model, [15], developed by a group of hypertext system designers, describes the required structural relations. Our previous work on CMIF [9] describes a model for specifying timing relations between collections of static and dynamic media composed to form multimedia presentations. A diagrammatic impression of the AHM is given in Fig. 2–11, which we will refer to in the following subsections describing the main

---

[2] Note that the model described here has been updated since that published in [21].

elements of the model, discussing them in terms of the issues in the previous section.

Structural Information

The structure items of the model are composition, anchors, and links, illustrated in Fig. 2–11.

- *Components* can be atomic components, link components, or composite components. An atomic component, shown in Fig. 2–11 and specified in detail in Fig. 2–12(a), describes information relevant to a single media item. A link component, shown in Fig. 2–11 and Fig. 2–13, describes the relations between two components. A composite component, Fig. 2–11 and Fig. 2–12(b), is an object representing a collection of any other components.

- *Atomic component*, Fig. 2–12(a), includes the data needed for displaying the media item; information on how the media item is displayed (a default may come from a structure such as a channel with overrides per individual component); a duration calculated from the data type, assigned by an author or deduced from the structure, discussed in the section Media Items on page 44; semantic attributes enabling retrieval of a media item, discussed in the section Retrieval of Information on page 57; and a list of anchors.

- *Composition* (see page 45 and Fig. 2–12(b)) specifies the components belonging to the composite object and the timing relations among them.[3] For example, whether the grouping is time-dependent (parallel) or time-independent (choice), as discussed in the subsection Composition on page 45. For a time-dependent composition, obligatory timing relations are specified through a child's start time (relative to the parent component, or to a sibling component), and optional relations among any two descendant components using synchronization arcs. The range of expression of synchronization arcs is discussed in the section Temporal Layout Information on page 62. Other presentation information can be used to apply a transformation to all the components in the group, without having to alter the presentation specifications of the constituent components. This might, for example, be an increase in the rate of play. Attributes allow the attachment of semantic information to components for future retrieval.

- *Anchors* (see page 47 and Fig. 2–11) are a means of indexing into the data of a media item and are used for attaching links to components. The media-dependent data specification (the value) is specified as part of an atomic component, Fig. 2–12(a), and referred to from a composite anchor, Fig. 2–12(b), and from a link component, Fig. 2–13. Attributes can be attached to individual anchors

---

[3] The Dexter model also includes (a reference to) data in a composite component. This makes the presentation specifications (and other attributes) apply ambiguously to either the data in the current component or all the descendants of the component.

Component ID

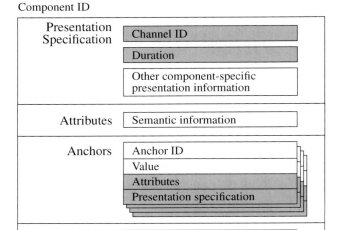

(a) Atomic component

Component ID

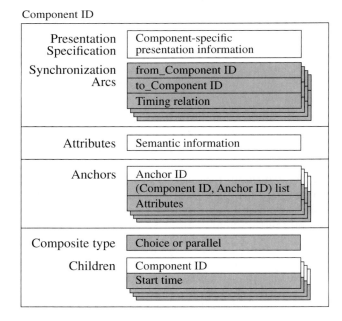

(b) Composite component

Figure 2-12 AHM atomic and composite components

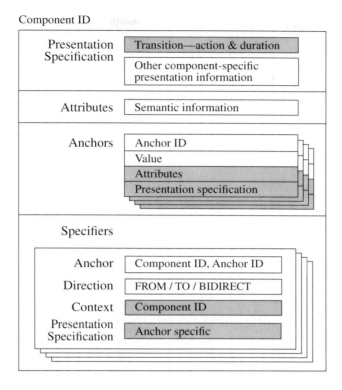

Component ID

Presentation Specification	Transition—action & duration
	Other component-specific presentation information
Attributes	Semantic information
Anchors	Anchor ID
	Value
	Attributes
	Presentation specification
Specifiers	
Anchor	Component ID, Anchor ID
Direction	FROM / TO / BIDIRECT
Context	Component ID
Presentation Specification	Anchor specific

Figure 2-13   AHM link component.

for information retrieval, as discussed in the section Retrieval of Information on page 57. A presentation specification per anchor allows, for example, different colors to be used for highlighting different anchor types, or for blinking an anchor of an author-specified "preferred link." Semantic information is also useful for a composite anchor, since it might represent a higher-level concept. For example, individual anchors labelled as "cat," and "dog" form a composite anchor labelled as "pet."

• *Links* (see page 48 and Fig. 2–11) enable an end-user to jump to information deemed by the author to be relevant to the current presentation. The link itself is a component, Fig. 2–13, with its own presentation specification, attributes, and anchors. The presentation specification can be used for recording transitions, see the subsection Links on page 48, where this may simply be *continue, pause,* or *replace* for the source context, or (in the replace case using the same screen area) a more complex specification of "dissolve to new context in 10 seconds." The attributes allow link typing to be stored, such as "is a generalization of," "is-a," or "is an example of." Since a link is also a component it too can have anchors referring to parts of the component.

The link component refers to a number of anchors in other components via a list of specifiers. Each specifier refers to an anchor in a component, states possible directions for following the link, and a context that is affected on leaving or arriving at the anchor. A link most commonly has two specifiers, with a FROM and a TO direction, allowing a traversal from the FROM context to the TO context. A link may have multiple specifiers, each with its own context, so that when the link is actioned a number of currently running presentations can be stopped and a new selection begun. A presentation specification in a specifier refers to the presentation of an anchor when the link is followed. For example the part of the media item referred to by the source anchor turns grey (to indicate that the interaction has been started) and that in the destination context blinks, to highlight specific information within the new context.

Temporal Layout Information

Timing relations in the AHM can be defined between atomic components, composite components or between an atomic component and a composite component. For example, in Fig. 2–11(a) both delays are specified between two atomic components where a video and image are timed to the spoken commentary. In Fig. 2–11(b) the delay is specified from a text item to the beginning of a composite component containing an image and spoken commentary. This timing information is stored either as the start time of a child component, or as a list of timing relations among the descendants of a composite component. This allows the timing of a presentation to be stored within the document structure itself and not as some unrelated data structure (such as a separate timeline). Note that the model specifies no boundaries on these timing relations—it is possible to specify a negative delay, so that an item can start before the whole group starts. These timing relations are specified in the model as *synchronization arcs*, Fig. 2–14. These can be used to give exact timing relations, but can also be used to specify tolerance and precision properties as discussed in the subsection Temporal Layout on page 52. The end of a synchronization arc may be a component, but may also refer to a (single) anchor within a component, allowing constraints to be specified within media items.

Synchronization arcs can be used to express all 13 timing relations from Fig. 2–9. These are illustrated in Fig. 2–15. Temporal glue, [16], can also be expressed in the form of sync arcs, illustrated in Fig. 2–16.

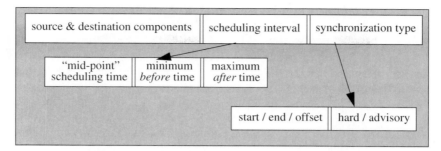

Figure 2-14   AHM synchronization arc.

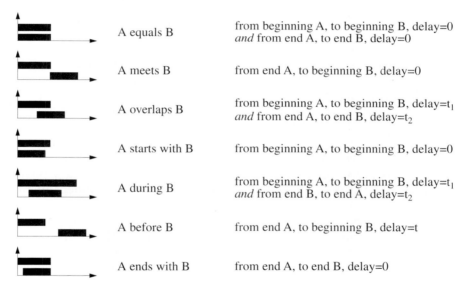

Figure 2-15   The "13" time relations expressed as synchronization arcs
$(t, t_1, t_2 > 0)$.

Spatial Layout Information

Layout information, such as that discussed on page 51, can be attached to each atomic component, but this can also be done through the use of *channels,* see page 52, allowing high-level presentation specifications to be defined. The model does not support explicitly the inclusion of spatial relations (as an analogue to synchronization arcs), but these could be included as a specialization of the presentation specification.

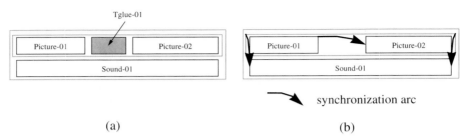

Figure 2-16   Temporal glue as synchronization arcs.
(a) Temporal composition with temporal glue as introduced object.
(b) Equivalent expressed as a number of synchronization arcs.

Summary

The Amsterdam Hypermedia Model has been designed to capture the elements of structure, timing, layout, and interaction that are needed to specify an interactive, time-based multimedia presentation. The model does not prescribe the form these relationships should take, but implies that they should exist, and proposes how to combine them with each other. Further work has been carried out on providing a formal description of the model [31].

Once a presentation has been described using our model, its description can be expressed in different intermediate forms suitable for multiple presentation environments. While we do not prescribe a language for specifying a presentation conforming to our model, it could be expressed in a system-independent language such as the HyTime (Hypermedia/Time-based Document Structuring Language) international standard [25], [29],[4] based on SGML (Standard Generalized Mark-up Language) [33]. Initial work on converting the CMIF document format to HyTime is reported in [17]. Similarly, transmission of (groups of) multimedia objects conforming to the model could be carried out using a standard such as MHEG [28].

2.5   Conclusions and Future Directions

A hypermedia presentation can be viewed as a collection of media items related by structural and presentation constraints. In order to capture the essence of a presentation for playback by systems other than that it was created for, we require some sort of model of the information structure. In this chapter, we have provided not only a particular document model, but have discussed the different components of the model and how they can be used for different purposes. For example, the model can be used to compare the expressive power of hypermedia

---

[4] Note that the details in the published standard, [25], have superseded those described in the journal article, [29].

authoring systems, and for transporting presentations from one platform to another. Components of the model discussed are the media items and their properties; document structure including composition, anchors, and links; spatial and temporal presentation issues, tolerance and precision, and scaling; reader interaction with the presentation; transportability of complete documents; and information retrieval.

An objective of the discussion on the model components is to give examples of their possible uses, for instance possible interpretations of an anchor's presentation specification. Another objective of the discussion was to understand the limits of our model and how it would relate to other possible models. The need for specifying a particular model comes from the desire to build a concrete authoring system (in our case CMIFed).

The Amsterdam hypermedia model combines the structural features of the Dexter model with the synchronization features of CMIF. The model is sufficiently powerful to describe the documents created by current multimedia and hypermedia authoring systems. Newer features not yet implemented in our own or other systems, such as spatial constraints between components, are not excluded from the AHM, but do not appear in the model explicitly.

The model enables document transportability by allowing the translation of the model to a particular language, for example HyTime or MHEG. An initial effort has already been carried out for the HyTime case. Attributes within the model allow for semantic labeling of media items, and larger structures, which can be used for multimedia information retrieval.

The limits of the AHM are reached in the case of interactivity, where links are the only means of specifying interactions. More complex interactions, such as conditionals, would require an extension to the model. Such interactions may, however, be regarded as outside the scope of a document model and more in the realms of generalized human computer interaction.

One of the directions in which we wish to continue this work concentrates on the semantic labeling not only of components but also of parts of components (via the anchor structures). This would firstly allow information retrieval for non-textual items. Building on such techniques, we would be able to go beyond pure searching and start combining the results of searches to produce new multimedia presentations—authoring using topic content rather than specifying explicitly every spatial and temporal constraint in the presentation. We have already carried out initial design work in this direction [19], [37].

Acknowledgments

Jacco van Ossenbruggen has stimulated a detailed examination of the Amsterdam Hypermedia Model and provided many useful comments on this chapter. Guido van Rossum, Jack Jansen, and Sjoerd Mullender designed and implemented the authoring environment CMIFed.

References

[1] Ackermann, P. "Direct manipulation of temporal structures in a multimedia application framework," in *Proceedings: Multimedia '94*, San Francisco, CA, Oct 1994, pp. 51–58.

[2] Allen, J.F. "Maintaining knowledge about temporal intervals," *Communications of the ACM*, Vol. 26, No. 11, Nov 1983, pp. 832-–843.

[3] Arons, B. "Hyperspeech: Navigating in speech-only hypermedia," in *Proceedings: ACM Hypertext '91*, San Antonio, TX, Dec 15-18, 1991, pp. 133–146.

[4] Bordegoni, M. "Multimedia in views." CWI Report CS-R9263, December 1992. <http://www.cwi.nl/ftp/CWIreports/AA/CS-R9263.ps.Z>

[5] Buchanan, M.C. and Zellweger, P.T. "Automatically generating consistent schedules for multimedia documents," *Multimedia Systems* Vol. 1, 1993, pp. 55–67.

[6] Buchanan, M.C. and Zellweger, P.T. "Automatic temporal layout mechanisms," in *Proceedings: ACM Multimedia '93*, Anaheim CA, Aug 1993, pp. 341–350.

[7] Koegel Buford, J.F. "Multimedia file systems and information models," in *Multimedia Systems*. J.F. Koegel Buford (ed.). New York: Addison-Wesley, 1994. ISBN 0-201-53258-1, pp. 265–283.

[8] Bulterman, D.C.A. and Winter, D.T. "A distributed approach to retrieving JPEG pictures in portable hypermedia documents," in *Proceedings of IEEE International Symposium on Multimedia Technologies and Future Applications*, Southampton, UK, Apr 1993, pp. 107–117.

[9] Bulterman, D.C.A., van Rossum, G., and van Liere, R. "A structure for transportable, dynamic multimedia documents," in *Proceedings of the Summer USENIX Conference*, Nashville, Tennessee, 1991, pp. 137–155.

[10] Burrill, V. A., Kirste T., and Weiss, J.M. "Time-varying sensitive regions in dynamic multimedia objects: A pragmatic approach to content-based retrieval from video," *Information and Software Technology Journal,* Special Issue on Multimedia, Vol. 36, No. 4, Butterworth-Heinemann, Apr 1994, pp. 213–224.

[11] Carr, L., Barron, D.W., Davis, H.C., and Hall, W. *Electronic Publishing*. Vol. 7, No. 3, 1994, pp. 163–178.

[12] Davis, M. "Media streams: An iconic language for video annotation," *Telektronikk* 5.93: Cyberspace Volume 89, No. 4, 1993, pp. 49–71, Norwegian Telecom Research, ISSN 0085-7130
<http://www.nta.no/telektronikk/5.93.dir/Davis_M.html>

[13] Erfle, R. "Specification of temporal constraints in multimedia documents using HyTime," *Electronic Publishing,* Vol. 6, No. 4, 1993, pp. 397–411.

[14] Eun, S., No, E.S., Kim,H.C., Yoon, H., and Maeng, S.R. "Eventor: An authoring system for interactive multimedia applications," *Multimedia Systems*, Vol. 2, 1994, pp. 129–140.

[15] Halasz, F. and Schwartz, M. "The Dexter hypertext reference model." *Communications of the ACM*, Vol. 37, No. 2, Feb 1994, pp. 30–39. Also NIST Hypertext Standardization Workshop, Gaithersburg MD, Jan 16–18, 1990.

[16] Hamakawa, R. and Rekimoto, J. "Object composition and playback models for handling multimedia data." *Multimedia Systems* Vol. 2, 1994, pp. 26–35.

[17] Hardman, L., van Ossenbruggen, J., and Bulterman, D.C.A. "A HyTime compliant interchange format for CMIF hypermedia documents." In press, 1995.
<http://www.cwi.nl/ftp/mmpapers/CMIF-HyTime.ps.gz>

[18] Hardman, L. and Bulterman, D.C.A. "Authoring support for durable interactive multimedia presentations," *Eurographics '95* State of The Art Report, Maastricht, The Netherlands, 28 Aug–1 Sep, 1995,
<http://www.cwi.nl/ftp/mmpapers/eg95.ps.gz>

[19] Hardman, L. and Bulterman, D.C.A. "Towards the generation of hypermedia structure," presented at the First International Workshop on Intelligence and Multimodality in Multimedia Interfaces, Edinburgh, UK, July 1995.

[20] Hardman, L., van Rossum, G., and van Bolhuis, A. "An interactive multimedia management game," *Intelligent Systems,* Vol. 5, Nos. 2–4, 1995, pp. 139–150.

[21] Hardman, L., Bulterman, D.C.A., and van Rossum, G. "The Amsterdam hypermedia model: Adding time and context to the Dexter model," *Communications of the ACM*, Vol. 37, No. 2, Feb 1994, pp. 50–62.

[22] Hardman, L., Bulterman, D.C.A., and van Rossum, G. "Links in hypermedia: The requirement for context," in *Proceedings: ACM Hypertext '93*, Seattle WA, Nov 1993, pp. 183–191.

[23] Hardman, L., van Rossum, G., and Bulterman, D.C.A. "Structured multimedia authoring," in *Proceedings: ACM Multimedia '93*, Anaheim CA, Aug 1993, pp. 283–289.

[24] Hjelsvold, R. and Midtstraum, R. "Modelling and querying video data," in *Proceedings of the 20th VLDB*, Santiago, Chile, 1994.

[25] HyTime. Hypermedia/Time-based structuring language. ISO/IEC 10744:1992.

[26] Little, T.C. "Time-based media representation and delivery," in *Multimedia Systems*, J.F. Koegel Buford (ed.). New York: Addison-Wesley, 1994. ISBN 0-201-53258-1, pp. 175–200.

[27] Meyer-Boudnik, T. and Effelsberg, W. "MHEG explained," *IEEE Multimedia*, Spring 1995, pp. 26–38.

[28] MHEG. Information Technology Coded Representation of Multimedia and Hypermedia Information Objects (MHEG) Part 1: Base Notation (ASN.1). Oct 15 1994. ISO/IEC CD 13552-1:1993.

[29] Newcomb, S.R., Kipp, N.A.,and Newomb, V.T. "'HyTime': The hypermedia/time-based document structuring language," *Communications of the ACM*, Vol. 34, No. 11, Nov 1991, pp. 67–83.

[30] Ogawa, R., Harada, H., and Kaneko, A. "Scenario-based hypermedia: A model and a system," in *Proceedings: ECHT '90* (First European Conference on Hypertext), Nov 1990, INRIA France, pp. 38–51.

[31] van Ossenbruggen, J., Hardman, L., and Eliëns, A. "A formalization of the Amsterdam hypermedia model." In press, 1995.
<http://www.cs.vu.nl/~dejavu/ahm-oz/index.html>

[32] van Rossum, G., Jansen, J., Mullender, K S., and Bulterman, D.C.A. "CMIFed: A presentation environment for portable hypermedia documents," in *Proceedings: ACM Multimedia '93*, Anaheim CA, Aug 1993, pp. 183–188.

[33] SGML. Standard Generalized Markup Language. ISO 8879:1986. Amendment 1: ISO 8879:1992/AM1:1992.

[34] Siochi, A., Fox, E.A., Hix, D., Schwartz, E.E., Narasimhan, A., and Wake, W. "The integrator: A prototype for flexible development of interactive digital multimedia applications," *Interactive Multimedia*, Vol. 2, No. 3, 1991, pp. 5–26.

[35] Smoliar, S.W. and Zhang, H. "Content-based video indexing and retrieval," *IEEE Multimedia*, Summer 1994, pp. 62–72.

[36] West, N. "Multimedia masters: A guide to the pros and cons of seven powerful authoring programs," *MacWorld*, Mar 1993, pp. 114–117.

[37] Worring, M., van den Berg, C., and Hardman, L. "System design for structured hypermedia generation," in *Visual Information Systems '96*, Melbourne, Feb 1996, pp. 254–261.

PART 2

Information Retrieval Techniques

C H A P T E R 3

Content-Based Indexing and Retrieval

H.V. Jagadish

AT&T Research
Murray Hill, New Jersey
jag@research.att.com

3.1 Introduction

Given a large set of objects (or records), selecting a (small) subset that meets certain specified criteria is a central problem in databases. In a multimedia database, the most common way to do this is to assign an alphanumeric "tag" to each object, and to retrieve objects based on their tags. The tags could even be structured into multiple attributes, with the object itself being treated as merely one very large attribute from a logical perspective. Traditional relational algebra is then applicable on all the attributes in the tag, and predicates on these can be used to retrieve the object. More often, the tag may not have as much structure as a typical relational database. The tag may comprise English descriptions of what the object is about. Standard keyword based indexing, used in document retrieval, can then be used to retrieve the tags relevant to a given query, and the associated objects.

The problem with such an approach, from a philosophical perspective, is that we have the tail wagging the dog. Logical prominence is given to the alphanumeric annotation, while the important real data in the object is not given the consideration it deserves. From a practical point of view this leads to two problems. The first problem is how to select what to put in the tag, given an object. Multimedia objects, such as images, have many different attributes that could be of interest—there is no way that any tag could hope to capture them all. The trick, in any application context, is to identify the commonly used characterizations and to build tags based on these. Even so, there is loss of information. Tags are often liable to subjective interpretation—is that a grin on the face, or a grimace? Do we trust the infallibility of the classification algorithm used to obtain the tag? What if there is a better way to separate grins from grimaces? The other problem is how to create the tags, even after the information required in the tag has been identified. Does a human have to look at the image and fill in the corresponding tag for each image in a database? If so, how severely does the cost of such tagging limit the potential size of such a database? In many situations, automated tagging is almost a necessity.

The solution to these difficulties lies in retrieval by content. Here the query is actually posed against the object rather than against the tag. The actual content of the object is analyzed and used to evaluate specified selection predicates. Thus no human need determine whether a particular facial image has a grin or a grimace. For that matter, nor does any algorithm need to make this determination in advance. The best known algorithm (the most accurate, the cheapest to evaluate, or the best based on some combined criterion) can be used as part of the predicate evaluated at query time.

The obvious concern with respect to retrieval by content as described in the preceding paragraph is performance. Complex predicates can be very costly to evaluate, and performing such an evaluation on every object in the database may be infeasible. The major concern of this chapter is how to provide access structures that can decrease this cost.

In Section 3.2 we introduce the central concept of a two-phase search. How this works for approximate rather than exact matches is discussed in "EXAMPLE: Shape Similarity" on page 76. Our retrieval techniques often require indexing a high-dimensional space. In "The Tree Structure" on page 85, one way to manage such high dimensionality is described. Obtaining a good multi-dimensional attribute space can itself be a challenge, and some help is provided in Section 3.5. Finally, Section 3.6 has some concluding remarks.

3.2 Two-Phase Search

Given that search predicates can often be complex, there is little hope of being able to develop index structures that can home in exactly on the set of objects in the database that satisfy any given search predicate. In fact, search predicates can often be sufficiently subtle that simply evaluating the predicate on a single object can sometimes require extremely sophisticated vision or pattern recognition techniques. For instance, it is not at all easy to match one view of a 3-dimensional object against a different view of a test object to determine whether the two images represent the same object.

On the other hand, given some relatively simple criteria, index structures may be constructed. The trick is to have a coarse definition of the predicate, which can be indexed, and then to perform the more sophisticated analysis object by object on the set of objects returned by the coarse selection. The difficulty is in taking the complex predicate of interest, and obtaining from it an indexable coarse predicate that introduces no false dismissals, and as few false positives as possible.

To understand this two-phase concept better, consider a traditional relational database, with a multi-attribute selection predicate specified in a query while only single-attribute indices are available. A query plan likely to be selected by the query optimizer would involve performing an indexed retrieval on one attribute (the one likely to provide the best selectivity from those in the query predicate), and then evaluating the rest of the predicate on the items selected by this coarse retrieval. Due to the precise Boolean semantics of logic, it is clear, if we retrieve objects that satisfy one conjunct in a conjunctive predicate, that we have included in the retrieved set all objects from the database that could satisfy the complex conjunctive predicate. If the complex predicate is not just a conjunction of simple predicates, then we have more work to do.

Consider a geographical database with objects such as counties, rivers, and forests. Consider a query, "Which counties does river Foo flow through?" Answering this query requires a "spatial join" between entities (the river and the county boundaries) that each have an involved shape. Finding intersections accurately can get particularly tricky when rivers demarcate county boundaries, or flow close to them. Rather than perform this careful intersection of the river with every county in the map, we can quickly identify a set of candidate counties by using rectangular bounding boxes for all entities. An index structure can be constructed to identify which bounding boxes of counties intersect with the specified bounding box for the river. While this technique will clearly result in no false dismissals of intersecting counties, there may be too large a set of candidates generated on account of "bends" in the river causing an excessively large rectangular bounding box for it. One can improve matters by defining a coarse rectangular grid, and marking which counties cover at least a portion of each grid square. Candidate counties for intersection with the river are only those with grid squares in common with the river. With this sort of a representation, not only are we guaranteed no false dismissals, we also have a trade-off between the amount of work done in the initial indexing versus the amount of work in the second phase. This trade-off is controlled by selecting the size of the grid square. Small grid squares mean more indexing work, and large squares mean less work but more false hits. These sorts of trade-offs have been studied extensively in the context of spatial databases, and a number of sophisticated versions of the coarse ideas presented above can be found in the literature.

EXAMPLE: Shape Matching

We now turn to a more detailed example with rectilinear shapes in two dimensions, that is, polygons, not necessarily convex, all of whose angles are right angles so that all edges are horizontal or vertical. Since any general shape can be approximated by a fine enough rectilinear "staircase," and since digitization produces this effect in any case, we believe that this restriction to rectilinear shapes is not too limiting. We study the two-dimensional case for its ease of exposition, and because it is by far the most important case in practice. Extensions to higher dimensions are conceptually straightforward.

Shape matching is an important image processing operation. Considerable work has been done on this problem, with different techniques being used to identify shapes, usually in terms of boundary information or other local features (cf. [22], [1]).

Our measure of similarity is "area difference." That is, two shapes are similar if the error area (where the two do not match) is small when one shape is placed "on top of" the other. In a digital domain, we obtain a pixel-wise exclusive OR of the two shapes, and pronounce the two shapes similar if the number of pixels ON in the result is small.

Rectangular Shape Covers

Rectangular covers for two-dimensional (rectilinear) shapes have been studied extensively (cf. [3], [4]). *Additive* rectangular covers are what we think of naturally: the given rectilinear shape is obtained as the union of several rectangles. *General* rectangular covers permit both addition and subtraction of rectangles, with subtraction treated as a pixel-wise set difference.

The benefit of a general rectangular cover is the possibility of considerably more succinct descriptions, as can be seen in Fig. 3–1. The drawback is that the process of obtaining good descriptions becomes more complex, as we shall see below.

Let C_i, with integer $i >= 0$, be the *current* (partial) cover after i rectangles have been included in the (prospective) cover. C_0 is the empty set (of pixels or points in the plane). In an additive rectangular cover, $C_{j+1} = C_j \cup R_{j+1}$, where R_j is the jth rectangle added. In a general rectangular cover, either $C_{j+1} = C_j \cup R_{j+1}$ or $C_{j+1} = C_j - R_{j+1}$, depending on whether the new rectangle is added or subtracted.

Call the shape to be covered S. For every finite rectilinear shape there exists an integer K such that we can find a $C_K = S$. No further rectangles need be added to C_K, so we define $C_j = C_K$ for $j >= K$.

In [9] it has been suggested that it may be possible to describe the features of an object "sequentially" so that the most important features are described first, and any truncation of the sequence is a "good" approximation of the shape.

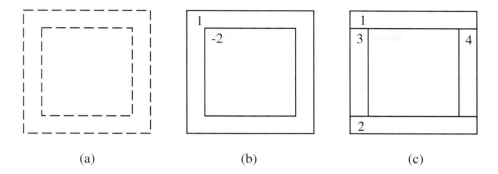

(a)   (b)   (c)

Figure 3-1   (a) An annular shape, (b) A general rectangular cover for it, and (c) An additive rectangular cover for it.

A description thus comprises a sequence of "units" of description, where each unit iteratively refines the information provided thus far. A "Cumulative Error Criterion" has been defined to identify the best possible sequential description. According to this criterion, the error after the first unit of description, after two units of description, and so on, is accumulated, until the complete description is obtained. Thus, the error in the last stages is counted many times, while the error in the first stages is counted only a few times, and there is an incentive to minimize the error early. A general technique has been provided to find the best sequential description of a given shape.

This idea of sequential description applies in particular to rectangular covers. Our notion is to obtain such a sequential description of an image and then truncate it to obtain an approximate description. The claim is that this approximation leaves out the less essential features of the image, and is likely to have a small error given the criterion used to obtain the sequential description in the first place. Moreover, the truncation is likely to get rid of high frequency noise, such as specks of dirt, and other low area artifacts.

Neither the additive rectangular cover nor the general rectangular cover for a given shape is unique. Fig. 3–2 shows some different ways that an "L" shaped object could be covered additively. Clearly, we prefer the covers shown in Fig. 3–2(b)–(e) to the cover shown in Fig. 3–2(a): the latter has an unnecessarily large number of rectangles in it. Even if we restrict ourselves to covers comprising exactly two rectangles, we still have many choices, even for as simple a shape as an L, as we can see from Fig. 3–2(b)–(e).

The specific algorithm used to obtain a good sequential description is immaterial as long as one has been agreed upon. As far as we are concerned, each shape in our database comprises an (ordered) set of rectangles (along with a positive or negative sign, if we use general rather than additive rectangular covers). The shape is described by means of the relative positions of these rectangles. In

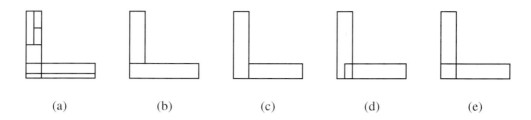

(a)   (b)   (c)   (d)   (e)

Figure 3–2   Some potential additive rectangular covers for an L shape.

the next section we describe a storage structure for such shapes, and show how an index structure may be constructed for matching shapes.

Storage Structure

For each rectangle one can identify a lower-left and an upper-right corner, which we shall call the L and U corner respectively. Each corner can be represented by a pair of X,Y coordinates in an appropriate coordinate system, such as position on the digitizing camera or screen pixels. Thus a set of K rectangles can be represented by a set of $4K$ coordinates (K rectangles times 2 corners each times 2 coordinates per corner).

To aid in the retrievals that we intend to perform, rather than store these coordinates directly, we apply a few transformations to them. First, rather than store the L and U corner points directly for each rectangle, we obtain distinct position and size values. The position of the rectangle is given in terms of the mean of the L and U corner points, i.e., the point $(x_L + x_U / 2, y_L + y_U / 2)$. Here x_L is the X coordinate of the L corner point, and so forth. The size of the rectangle is obtained as the difference between the L and U corner points, i.e., as the pair $(x_U - x_L, y_U - y_L)$. Thus, we still have four values, or two pairs of numbers, to store for each rectangle. However, after this transformation they represent the position and size of the rectangle rather than the locations of the corner points.

Second, the position of the first rectangle is used to normalize the positions of the other rectangles. That is, the center of the first rectangle is placed at the origin, and all coordinates are taken with respect to this origin. This transformation is represented by a shift, which is a pair of constants that has to be subtracted from all the X coordinates and all the Y coordinates respectively of the position values for each of the rectangles. Their size values remain unaffected. Since the center position of the first rectangle is 0,0 after the shift, we do not store it. Instead, we store the amount of the shift, which is given by the coordinates of this center point before the shift.

Third, the size of the first rectangle is used to normalize the positions and sizes of the other rectangles. For this, the X and Y size parameters of the first rectangle are used to divide the X and Y (both size and position) parameters respectively of all the other rectangles. (Note that the X and Y size parameters of the first rectangle are both strictly positive, and therefore can safely be used as divisors for this normalization). Further, we take the (natural) logarithms of the normalized size values, thus making them "additive" like the position values. (No logs are required for the position values.) After the normalization, the size of the first rectangle is 1,1 (and its logarithm is 0,0). Rather than store this value, we store the original size parameters of this rectangle, obtained after the first transformation, which were used as the constants for this third transformation. This pair of constants are scale factors in the X and Y dimensions for the other rectangles.

Finally, we make one additional change. Rather than retain two global scale factors, one for each dimension, we retain their product as "the scale factor" (this is the square of a linear scale factor, and is an area scale factor), and their ratio (the Y scale factor divided by the X scale factor) as a "distortion factor."

Thus, a shape, described by a set of K rectangles, can be stored as a pair of shift factors for the X and Y, a scale factor, and a distortion factor, all of which are stored as "part of" the first rectangle, and a pair of X and Y coordinates for the center point and a pair of X and Y size values for each of the remaining $K-1$ rectangles, after shifting and scaling.

The value of K, the number of rectangles required to describe a shape, could be very large for some shapes. However, we are guaranteed that "most" of the interesting shape information will be in the first few rectangles. So it suffices to index on a small number, k, of rectangles for the first phase of search. Our experience, in trying out various synthetic shapes, appears to indicate that a value of k, the number of rectangles indexed, of 2 to 5 suffices to provide only a few hits in a large database, even if K is an order of magnitude larger for many shapes in the database.

The shape description has, by this means, been converted into a set of coordinates for a point in 4k-dimensional space. We can now use any multi-dimensional point indexing method that we desire, such as grid-files [15], k-D-B trees [17], buddy trees [19], holey-brick trees [13], z-curves [16], etc.

Our mapping from objects to multidimensional space has the additional virtue that the more important attributes occur first and are distinguished from the less important attributes. In consequence, it is possible to use a multi-dimensional indexing structure specifically designed for large numbers of dimensions, such as the TV-tree described in Section 3.4, for this purpose.

3.3   Approximate Matching

In the case of multimedia objects, often not only do we want to retrieve objects that match the specified query criteria exactly, but often also those that match it approximately. The question then is what is similarity? One can conceive of many different dimensions along which one can measure similarity. (See [14] for an eloquent treatment of this subject.)

From the perspective of the database, one can represent similarity in terms of a *transformation function* with an associated transformation cost. The choice of language used to describe these transformation functions determines the notion of similarity in a particular application. This transformation language applies to a *pattern description language* in which the multimedia objects themselves are described, and can in turn be embedded in a general *query language* such as relational algebra. See [11] for details on this framework.

Given this conceptual machinery, the question we wish to address in this chapter is how to construct an index structure that can enable efficient retrievals by "similarity."

Our solution technique is, based upon the (application-specific) notion of similarity, to obtain an appropriate "feature vector" for each object. In other words, we map each multimedia object to a point in an attribute space. This mapping is carefully selected so that no two "similar" objects, (with a low cost of transformation from one to the other), can be mapped to distant points. (However, it is acceptable for two dissimilar objects to be mapped close, as long as this does not happen "too often.")

Now, given a query point, it can be expanded into a query region of appropriate size, depending on the approximation tolerance desired. A multi-dimensional index structure can be used to retrieve objects corresponding to data points from this query region. The retrieved objects may include some that do not satisfy the query, but many times can be guaranteed to include all that will satisfy the query. A more sophisticated matching algorithm, or a human, can then sort through these hits. Thus we are back to the two-phase solution technique described above.

EXAMPLE: Shape Similarity

Returning to the problem of shape matching, even a very simple notion of similarity, such as allowing a small difference in area covered, with dissimilarity measured as the area difference, causes some wrinkles in the techniques just described for shape similarity. This, in spite of the fact that the entire index structure has been developed based on the same area difference measure for selecting the optimal rectangle cover.

The obvious way to obtain objects of similar shape is to retrieve all objects whose shape descriptions have rectangles with similar, even if not identical, position and size as the query shape description. The way to do this is to "blur" the query point, by specifying a range along each attribute axis, corresponding to some flexibility with regard to the exact values for the position and size of each rectangle. The extent of this blurring can be determined independently for each attribute axis, by means of appropriate parameters. The larger the amount of blurring permitted, the weaker the search criterion, and the larger the set of objects selected as being "similar" to the given query shape. In most applications, rather than specify independent parameters for the blur permitted in the position and size of each rectangle, global parameters can be specified. These global parameters can, for example, define the blur permitted to be an affine function of the value. Thus larger position or size values will have proportionately larger error margins allowed, but with some error margin allowed even for small values.

Given that the shape descriptions being used are sequential rather than arbitrary, a more subtle way to obtain approximation is not to use all the rectangles in the description of the query shape. Since most of the key features of the shape are expected to have been defined in the first few rectangles, similar, but not identical shapes can be expected to differ only in the last few rectangles of their descriptions. Thus by controlling the number of rectangles of description used, one can choose how strongly a shape must be similar to a given query shape for it to be retrieved. In the extreme case, for example, one could use only the first rectangle, so that a match with uniform scaling, say, would retrieve all shapes the largest part of whose mass was proportioned (height to width) in roughly the same ratio as the query shape.

For any given query, the number of rectangles to include in the search is a parameter that must be selected carefully. Clearly, if the index structure in the shape database has been constructed on k rectangles, k is an upper limit on this parameter. To be more generous in interpreting similarity, we may wish to index based on fewer rectangles. However, if too few rectangles are used, then the retrieval may return shapes completely dissimilar to the query shape. One reasonable heuristic is to truncate the description when the error area becomes a small enough fraction of the total. Another heuristic is to truncate the description when the size of the error fixed by (or the size of) the next rectangle becomes a small enough fraction of the total area. Such heuristics are often reasonable, but one can always find cases where they are inappropriate. In fact, for a general (not additive) rectangular cover, it is even possible for the error not to decrease monotonically!

Multiple Representations

One potential problem with the similarity retrieval as suggested here is that some shapes may have two or more dissimilar sequential descriptions that are almost equally good, or equivalently that two fairly similar shapes may have very different sequential descriptions.

In Fig. 3–3, the optimal (sequential general rectangular cover) descriptions are presented for two familiar shapes (T and F). Observe how the optimal description changes as the relative sizes of the parts are changed. In both cases, there is some threshold where the switch-over occurs from one description to the other. Where a mathematical criterion would place a sharp dividing line, humans may have a fuzzy transition. Two shapes close to, but on opposite sides of, this dividing line may appear quite similar to a human eye, even though their optimal sequential descriptions are completely different. For example, a human

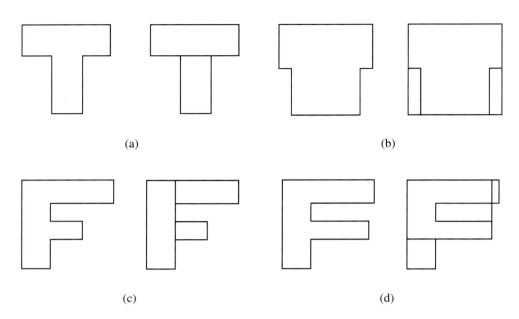

(a)   (b)

(c)   (d)

Figure 3-3   Similar shapes may have very different optimal (general rectangular cover) descriptions.

may consider the "F" in Fig. 3–3(c) quite similar to the one in Fig. 3–3(d). However, their descriptions are completely different.

This problem occurs not just for general rectangular covers, but for additive rectangular covers as well. Recall the additive rectangular covers for an "L" shape shown in Fig. 3–2. The cover of Fig. 3–2(b) is preferred if the horizontal arm of the shape has greater area, and Fig. 3–2(c) if the vertical arm has greater area.

Even worse, consider an "H" shape. In any properly balanced rendering of this letter, the left and right vertical strokes are both approximately as long and approximately as thick. Which gets selected to be the first rectangle in a sequential description is a matter of chance. The error criterion is likely to be almost identical either way. This sort of problem with multiple equally good descriptions almost always arises for symmetric shapes. The same (or almost the same) shape with two different choices of sequential description will map to two completely different points in the attribute space over which we index.

One way to resolve this problem if two or more sequential descriptions are almost as good is to keep all of them. Thus, unless the "T" shape is really skinny and definitely a "T," its sequential description may be stored both ways. Similarly, for an "H" shape, two sequential descriptions may be stored, with one having the left vertical stroke as the first rectangle and the right vertical stroke as the second, and the other having the two in reversed order. While this approach does solve the problem, it has the disadvantage of multiplying the size of the database. In the worst case, the number of different "reasonable" sequential descriptions could be exponential in the length of the description.

A better solution is to obtain multiple "good" sequential descriptions of the given query shape and then to perform a query on each of them, taking the union of the results obtained. This way, a little more effort is required at query time, but the database and index structure do not have to expand. Moreover, the number of different sequential descriptions that have to be tried is exponential in the length of the query description which is likely to be considerably shorter than the length of the full sequential description for the query shape (and for objects in the database). In practice, this number is typically smaller than this already acceptable worst case.

Dimension Mismatch

In general, the length of the sequential description of an object need not match the number of dimensions in the index. If an object in the database has a longer sequential description, only the first part of it is used in the index structure. This will usually be the case.

Consider, however, the case where there is an object in the database with a very short description. For example, there may even be a pure rectangular shape, which requires exactly one rectangle to describe it. For such shapes with a K (the number of rectangles in the sequential description) smaller than k (the number of rectangles over which an index structure is to be constructed) we have a problem because some of the rectangles over which the index structure is to be constructed do not exist.

This problem is solved by adding to such a description $k-K$ dummy "rectangles," all with one size parameter zero, but with the other size parameter and the position parameters (in the X and Y) that represent a range from $-\infty$ to ∞ instead of a single value. Thus, these objects become hyper-rectangles in attribute space rather than simple points. Most multi-dimensional index structures can handle such hyper-rectangles, in addition to points. Since there are two size parameters, there are two choices for each rectangle and 2^{k-K} choices for the sequence of $k-K$ dummy rectangles. Thus, 2^{k-K} entries, one corresponding to each possible choice, are required for such an object.

In the case of an exact match, this scheme works in a straightforward way. In the case of a similarity match, consider a query shape that has a few additional rectangles. If the query shape is similar to the object of concern in the database (with a short description), these additional rectangles must have a small area, and therefore for each additional rectangle at least one of the two size parameters must be small. Once "blurring" is introduced for similarity retrieval, the small size parameter of each additional rectangle maps to a range that includes zero. Irrespective of the position parameter and the other size parameter of these rectangles, they will intersect appropriate dummy rectangles in (at least one of the multiple representations of) the object of concern in the database.

Conversely, if a particularly simple query shape is supplied, the above procedure can be applied to extend the query shape description. However, we also have the alternative of simply ignoring the additional attribute axes, at the cost of potentially retrieving too many objects from the database.

As mentioned above, each object with too short a description requires multiple entries in the database with the number of entries being exponential in $k-K$. This may be acceptable, if $k-K$ is small (say, 1), and there are only a few objects with such short descriptions, which is usually the case. Otherwise, the database can be redesigned as follows:

Rather than have independent size values in the X and Y dimensions, we could obtain a single size value for each rectangle as the product of the two values. This number gives the area of that rectangle relative to the first rectangle. We also obtain the ratio of the X and Y sizes, giving the distortion of each rectangle relative to the first. Now, an object with a short description need only have the single size parameter set to zero for the dummy "rectangles" in the description, and the distortion parameter set to an infinite range. Thus each object requires a single entry in the database. The reason we have not selected this alternative is that after two ratios are taken, the value of the distortion parameter becomes sensitive to minor changes, and hence less useful as a metric for shape similarity.

3.4   Index Structures

To summarize, the two-phase technique, whether for exact or similarity retrieval, typically reduces each object to a point in some multi-dimensional attribute space. This space is then indexed by use of a multi-dimensional index structure.

There are a number of different multi-dimensional index structures described in the literature. See [16], [20], [7], [17], [8] to name a few. Almost all of these structures have hidden in them algorithms that require time or space that grows rapidly, often exponentially, with the number of dimensions in attribute space. Thus these techniques are great when used to index an attribute space with only a few dimensions, but perform poorly when used on an index space with hundreds of dimensions.

The solution proposed in [12] is to "contract" and "extend" the feature vectors dynamically, that is, to use as few of the features as necessary to discriminate among the objects. This agrees with the intuitive way that humans use to classify objects: for example, in zoology, the species are grouped in a few broad classes first, using a few features (e.g., vertebrates versus invertebrates). As the classification is further refined, more and more features are gradually utilized (e.g., the feature of warm-blood versus cold-blood, for the vertebrates; similarly, the feature of lungs versus branchia, etc.).

With this idea, define a TV-tree that, like any other tree, organizes the data in a hierarchical structure: Objects (i.e., feature vectors) are clustered into leaf nodes of the tree, and the description of their *Minimum Bounding Region (MBR)* is stored in its parent node. Parent nodes are recursively grouped, too, until the root is formed. Compared to a tree that uses a fixed number of features, the TV-tree provides a higher fanout at the top levels, using only a few, basic features, as opposed to many, possibly irrelevant, ones.

Furthermore, at the lower levels, all points in a node are likely to have certain feature values in common, and these need not be repeated for each of its children. Thus, even at the lower level, in spite of more dimensions being utilized, a high fanout can often be maintained.

The basic telescopic vector concept can be applied to a tree with nodes describing bounding regions of any shape (cubes, spheres, rectangles, etc.). Also, there is flexibility in the choice of "telescoping function," which selects the features on which to focus at any level of the tree. We discuss these design choices in the next two subsections.

Telescoping Function

In general, the telescoping problem can be described as follows:

Given an $n \times 1$ feature vector $\hat{x}$ and an $m \times n$ $(m \leq n)$ contraction matrix A_m, the $m \times 1$ vector $A_m \hat{x}$ is an m-contraction of $\hat{x}$. A sequence of such matrices A_m, with $m = 1,\ldots$ describes a telescoping function provided that the following condition is satisfied: If the m_1-contractions of two vectors, $\hat{x}$ and $\hat{y}$, are equal, then so are their respective m_2-contractions, for every $m_2 \leq m_1$.

While a variety of telescoping functions can be defined, the most "natural" choice is simple truncation. That is each matrix A_m has a 1 in positions $(1,1)$ through (m,m), along a diagonal, and 0 everywhere else. In this section we assume that truncation is the telescoping function selected.

Ordering of Dimensions   The proposed method treats the features asymmetrically, favoring the first few ones over the rest, when truncation is used as the telescoping function. For similarity queries, which are likely to be frequent in the application domains we have in mind, it is intuitive that a good ordering of the features will result in a more focused search. Even for exact match queries, since the depth of the tree will typically not be enough to have considered all features, a good choice of order will improve the response time of our method. Notice however that the *correctness* is not affected: The difference between a good ordering and a poor ordering is that the latter may make our method examine many "false alarms," and thus do more work, but it will never create "false dismissals."

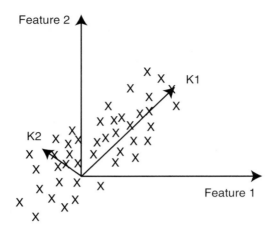

Figure 3–4 Illustration of the Karhunen-Loeve transform.

In most applications, it will be appropriate to "transform" the given feature vector to achieve such a good ordering. Ordering the features on "importance" order is exactly what the *Karhunen-Loeve* (K-L) transform achieves: Given a set of n vectors with d features each, it returns d new features, which are linear combinations of the old ones, and which are sorted in discriminatory power. Fig. 3–4 gives a 2-D example, where the vectors *k1* and *k2* are the results of the Karhunen-Loeve transform on the illustrated set of points. For more details on the Karhunen-Loeve transform, see [6].

The Karhunen-Loeve transform is optimal if the set of data is known in advance, that is, the transform is data-dependent. Sets of data with rare or no updates appear in real applications: for example, databases that are published on CD-ROM; dictionaries; files with customer mailing lists that are updated in batches; etc. The Karhunen-Loeve transform will also work well if a large sample of data is available in advance, and if the new data have the same statistical characteristics as the old ones.

In a completely dynamic case, we have to resort to data-independent transforms, such as the Discrete Cosine (DCT) [21] the Discrete Fourier (DFT), the Hadamard, the wavelet [18] transform etc. Fortunately, many data-independent transforms will perform as well as the Karhunen-Loeve if the data follows specific statistical models. For example, the DCT is an excellent choice if the features are highly correlated. This is the case in 2-D images, where nearby pixels have very similar colors. The JPEG image compression standard [21] exactly exploits this phenomenon, effectively ignoring the high-frequency components of the Discrete Cosine Transform. Since the retained components carry most of the information, the JPEG standard achieves good compression with negligible loss of image quality.

Shape of Bounding Region

As mentioned earlier, points are grouped together, and their minimum bounding region (MBR) is stored in the parent node. The shape of the MBR can be arbitrary, such as (hyper-)rectangle, cube, sphere, etc. The shape that is simplest to represent is the sphere, requiring only the center and a radius. A sphere of radius r is the set of points with Euclidean distance $\leq r$ from the center of the sphere. The Euclidean distance is a special case of the L_p metrics, with $p=2$:

$$L_p(\vec{x}, \vec{y}) = \left[\sum_i (x_i - y_i)^p \right]^{1/p} \tag{1}$$

For the L_1 metric (or *Manhattan*, or *city-block* distance), the equivalent of a sphere is a diamond shape; for the L_∞ metric, the equivalent shape is a cube.

Definition 1:   The L_p-*sphere* of center $\hat{c}$ and radius r is the set of points whose L_p distance from the center is $\leq r$.

The up-coming algorithms for the TV-tree will work with *any* L_p-sphere, without any modifications to the TV-tree manipulation algorithms. The only algorithm that depends on the chosen shape is the algorithm that computes the MBR of a set of data.

Minor modifications are required in the TV-tree algorithms to accommodate other popular shapes, like "rectangles" or "ellipses." Compared to L_p-spheres, these shapes differ only in the fact that they have a different "radius" for each dimension. The required changes in the TV-tree algorithms are in the decision-making steps, such as the criteria for choosing where to split, for choosing which branch to traverse during insertion, and so on.

For the rest of this paper, we concentrate on L_p-spheres as Minimum Bounding Regions.

Node Structure

Each node in the TV-tree represents the minimum bounding region (an L_p-sphere) of all its descendents. Each region is represented by a center, which is a "telescopic" vector, and a scalar radius. We use the term *Telescopic Minimum Bounding Region* (TMBR) to denote an MBR with such a "telescopic" vector as a center.

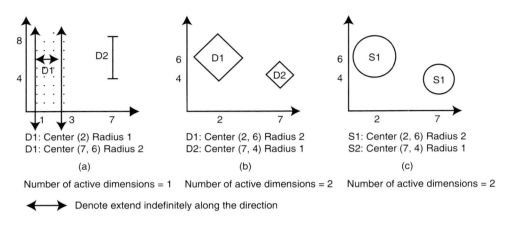

D1: Center (2) Radius 1   D1: Center (2, 6) Radius 2   S1: Center (2, 6) Radius 2
D1: Center (7, 6) Radius 2   D2: Center (7, 4) Radius 1   S2: Center (7, 4) Radius 1

       (a)   (b)   (c)

Number of active dimensions = 1   Number of active dimensions = 2   Number of active dimensions = 2

⟵⟶ Denote extend indefinitely along the direction

Figure 3-5   Example of TMBRs (diamonds and spheres).

Definition 2:   A "telescopic" L_p-sphere with center $\check{c}$ and radius r, with *dimensionality d* and with α *active dimensions* contains the set of points $\check{y}$ such that

$$c_i = y_i \quad i = 1, \ldots, d - \alpha \tag{2}$$

and

$$r^p \geq \text{sum}_{i=(d-\alpha+1)}^{d} (c_i - y_i)^p \tag{3}$$

The reason we need this concept is that, as the tree grows, some leaf node will eventually consist of points that all agree on their first, say, k dimensions. In this case, the TMBR should exploit this fact; its first k dimensions are *inactive* dimensions, in the sense that they are useless in distinguishing between the node's descendents.

For example, in Fig. 3–5(a), D2 has 1 inactive dimension, the first one, and 1 active dimension, the second one. D1 also has one active dimension, the first one. The dimensionality of D1 is 1 (only the first dimension has been taken into account in specifying D1) and the dimensionality of D2 is 2 (both dimensions have been considered).

According to the algorithms of the TV-tree, the active dimensions are always the last ones. Moreover, we can control the number of active dimensions α and ensure that all the TMBRs in the tree have the same α. This number is a design parameter of the TV-tree.

Definition 3:   The *number of active dimensions* (α) of a TV-tree is the (common) number of active dimensions that all its TMBRs have.

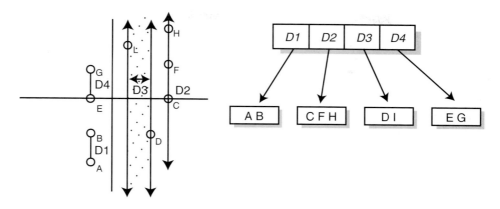

Figure 3–6   Example of a TV-1 tree (with diamonds).

The notation TV-1 denotes a TV-tree with $\alpha = 1$; Fig. 3–5 shows the TMBRs of TV-1 and TV-2 trees. Typically, α determines the discriminatory power of the tree. Whenever more discriminatory power is needed, new dimensions will be introduced to ensure the number of active dimensions remains the same.

The Tree Structure

The TV-tree structure bears some similarity to the R-tree. Each node contains a set of branches; each branch is represented by a TMBR denoting the space it covers; all descendants of that branch will be contained within that TMBR; TMBRs are allowed to overlap. Each node occupies exactly one disk page.

Examples of TV-1 and TV-2 trees are given in Figures 3–6 and 3–7. A-I denote data points (only the first two dimensions are shown).

In the TV-1 tree, the active dimension is 1, thus the diamonds extend only along 1 dimension at any time. As a result, the shapes are straight lines or rectangular blocks (extended infinitely). In the TV-2 case the TMBR resemble two-dimensional L_p-circles.

Algorithms

Search   For both exact and range queries, the algorithm starts with the root and examines each branch that intersects the search region, recursively following these branches. Multiple branches may be traversed because MBRs are allowed to overlap. The algorithm is straightforward and the pseudocode is omitted for brevity.

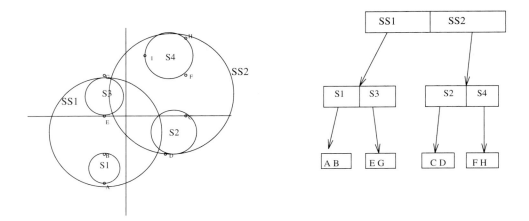

Figure 3-7 Example of a TV-2 tree (with spheres).

Spatial join can be handled as well. Recall that such a query requires all pairs of points that are close to each other (e.g., closer than a tolerance ε). Again, a recursive algorithm that prunes out remote branches of the tree can be used; efficient improvements on this algorithm have recently appeared [2].

Similarly, nearest-neighbor queries can be handled with a branch-and-bound algorithm, as in [5]. The algorithm works as follows: given a point, examine the top-level branches, and compute upper and lower bounds for the distance; descend the most promising branch, disregarding branches that are too far away.

Insertion   To insert a new object, traverse the tree, at each stage choosing the branch that seems most suitable to hold the new object. On reaching the leaf level, insert the object in the leaf. Overflow is handled by splitting the node, or by re-inserting some of its contents. After the insertion/split/re-insert, update the TMBRs of the affected parents. For example, the radius of a TMBR may be increased when its dimensionality is decreased to accommodate the new object (Fig. 3–8).

The routine *PickBranch(Node N, element e)* examines the branches of the node N and returns the one that is most suitable to accommodate the element (point or TMBR) *e* to be inserted. In choosing a branch, use the following criteria, in descending priority:

1. Minimum decrease in dimensionality. (That is, choose the TMBR with which the new object can agree on as many coordinates as possible, so that it can accommodate the new object by contracting its center as little as possible. For example, in Fig. 3–9(a), R1 is picked over R2 so to avoid folding of R2.)

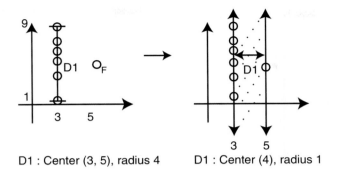

D1 : Center (3, 5), radius 4   D1 : Center (4), radius 1

Figure 3–8   Decrease in dimensionality during insertion.

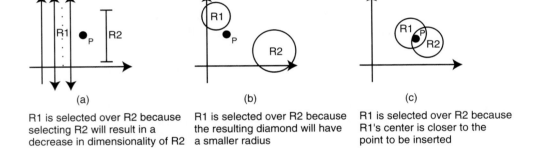

(a)   (b)   (c)

R1 is selected over R2 because   R1 is selected over R2 because   R1 is selected over R2 because
selecting R2 will result in a   the resulting diamond will have R1's center is closer to the
decrease in dimensionality of R2 a smaller radius   point to be inserted

Figure 3–9   Illustration of choose-branch criteria.

2. Minimum increase in radius.

3. Minimum distance from the center of the TMBR to the point (in case that the previous two criteria tie).

The motivation behind criterion (1) is to push new items towards low-dimensionality regions (TMBRs), to speed up their splitting into more, but higher-dimensionality regions. Fig. 3–9 shows the different instances of the branch selection.

Handling of overflowing nodes is another important aspect for the insertion algorithm. Here an overflow can be caused not only by an insertion into a full node but by an attempt to extend a "telescopic" vector as well. Splitting of the node is the most obvious way to handle overflow. However, reinsertion can also

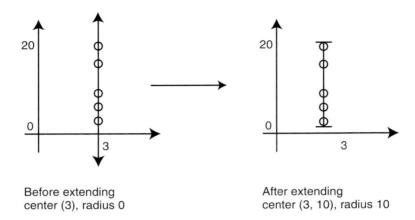

Before extending   After extending
center (3), radius 0   center (3, 10), radius 10

Figure 3-10   Unfolding of a TMBR (diamond), with $\alpha = 1$.

be applied, selecting certain items to be reinserted from the top. This provides a chance to discard dissimilar items from a node, usually achieving better clustering.

The insertion algorithm is summarized as follows:

Algorithm 1   Insert algorithm
begin
  /* Insert element e into tree rooted at N */
  Proc Insert(Node N, element e)
  1) *Use PickBranch() to choose the best branch to follow; descend the tree until the leaf node L is reached.*
  2) *Insert the element into the leaf node L.*
  3) *If leaf L overflows*
          If it is the first time during insertion
              Choose p_{ri} of elements in L and re-insert them from the top
          else
          Split the leaf into two leaves.
  4) *Update the TMBRs that have been changed (because of insertion and/or splitting). Split an internal node if overflow occurs.*
end

Splitting   The goal of splitting is to redistribute the set of TMBRs (or vectors, when leaves are split) into two groups so as to facilitate future operations and provide high space utilization.

There are several ways to do the split. One way is to use a clustering technique. The goal is try to group vectors so that similar ones will reside in the same TMBR.

Algorithm 2   Splitting by clustering
begin
  / assume N is an internal node; similar for leaf nodes */*
  Proc Split(Node N, Branch NewBranch, float min_percent)
  1) *Pick as seeds the branches B1 and B2 with the two most un-similar TMBRs (i.e., with the smallest common prefix in their centers; on tie, pick the pair with the largest distance between the centers). Let R1 and R2 be the groups headed by B1 and B2 respectively.*
  2) *For each of the remaining branches B:*
       Add B to that group R1 or R2 according to the PickBranch() function
end

Another way of performing the split is by ordering: The vectors (that is, the centers of the TMBRs) are ordered in some way and a "best" partition along the ordering is found. The current criteria being used are (in descending priority):

1. Minimum sum of radius of the two MBRs formed

2. Minimum of (sum of radius of TMBRs—Distance between their centers)

In other words, we first try to minimize the "area" that the TMBRs cover; and then to minimize the overlap between the diamonds.

Algorithm 3   Splitting by ordering
begin
  / assume N is a internal node; similar for leaf nodes */*
  / minfill is the minimum percentage (in bytes) of the node to be occupied */*
  Proc Split(Node N, Branch NewBranch, float minfill)
  1) *Sort the TMBRs of the branches by ascending row-major order of their centers.*
  2) *Find the best break-point in the ordering, to create two sub-sets: (a) ignore the case where one of the subsets is too empty (≤ minfill bytes) (b) among the rest of the cases, choose that one break-point that the TMBRs of the two sets will have the least total radius. Break ties by minimum (sum of radius of TMBRs – distance between the centers).*
  3) *If requirement (a) above leaves no candidates, then sort the branches by their byte size and repeat the above step, skipping step (a), of course.*
end

The last step in the algorithm guards against the (rare) case where one of the TMBRs has a long vector for center, while the rest have short vectors. In this case, a seemingly good split might leave one of the two new nodes highly underutilized. The last step makes sure that the new nodes have similar sizes (byte-wise).

Deletion   Deletion is straightforward, unless it causes an underflow. In this case, the remaining branches of the node are deleted and re-inserted. The underflow may propagate upwards.

Extending and contracting   As mentioned previously, extending and contracting of telescopic vectors is important. Unfolding is done at the time of split and reinsertion. When the objects inside a node are redistributed (either by splitting into two or removing at reinsertion), it may be the case that the remaining objects have the same values in the first few (or all) active dimensions. Thus during the recalculation of the new TMBR, unfolding will occur, meaning new active dimensions will be introduced and those on which all the objects agree will be rendered inactive.

An example on unfolding of diamonds is given in Fig. 3–10. After the unfolding, the diamond extends only along the y-dimension.

On the other hand, folding occurs during insertion. When an object is inserted into a TMBR such that the inactive dimensions of the TMBR do not agree completely with that of the object, the new TMBR will have to have some dimensions contracted, resulting in a TMBR with lower dimensionality.

Another issue involved is the unfolding of TMBRs. When objects are clustered during splits or when objects are removed during reinsertion, it may happen that the TMBR formed (with the current number of dimensions) will have zero radius. At that time new dimensions will need to be extended. This is done when the bounding regions is recalculated after each insertion or split.

3.5   Obtaining the Mapping

Thus far we have relied upon our understanding of the application semantics to come up with a multi-attribute vector that captures the notion of similarity we care about. This is often a daunting task. Where the application domain is not well understood, this task may well be impossible. One solution is to use clustering techniques, based purely on measures of distance given. We describe here the FastMap technique proposed in [12].

Suppose one is given a set of N objects, with pair-wise "distances" between the objects (for the similarity metric of interest) recorded in an $N \times N$ distance matrix. Our task is to map these N objects into a k-dimensional space, from some k, such that the distance between any two objects in the k-dimensional space is fairly close to, but always less than the actual distance between the objects as recorded in the distance matrix.

Such a mapping is accomplished, for $k=1$, as follows. Select two (distant) objects, O_a and O_b as "pivots"; assign a coordinate of 0 to O_a ($x_a = 0$) and a coordinate of $d_{a,b}$ to O_b ($x_b = d_{a,b}$), where $d_{a,b}$ is the distance between O_a and O_b. The value of the coordinate for all other objects is obtained by projecting them onto the line from O_a to O_b. By the cosine law, for object O_i, we obtain $x_i = d_{a,b}/2 + (d_{a,i}^2 - d_{b,i}^2)/2d_{a,b}$.

Now we can compute the "remainder" after this projection by applying Pythogoras' Rule. Between objects O_i and O_j, the remaining distance is $d'_{i,j} = sqrt(d_{i,j}^2 - (x_i - x_j)^2)$. (Some Euclidian assumptions are required to guarantee that the term inside the square root is positive. If this quantity turns out negative, then the FastMap technique proposed is not applicable).

To obtain a mapping to a space with dimensionality k greater than 1, simply repeat the two steps above. That is, first compute one coordinate using a pair of selected pivots. Then compute the remainder distance matrix. Now use this matrix to compute the next coordinate using exactly the same procedure as for the first one. Compute the remainder. Continue until a large enough number of dimensions have been created, or the remainder has become small enough.

The major question that remains is how to select the pivot objects. Ideally, these are the two objects that are farthest apart. Finding this pair of objects requires that every entry in the distance matrix be examined. Heuristics can be used to decrease the computational cost. One proposal is to select one object at random and find the object, O_a, farthest from it. Then find the object O_b that is farthest from O_a. Use O_a and O_b as the required pivots. Only twice the square root of the number of entries in the distance matrix need be examined by the heuristic.

One final note. In the discussion above, we suggested computing the "remainder distance matrix" after each pivot and projection. This is actually not necessary. It is enough to compute only the entries of the distance matrix necessary for the next stage of computation.

3.6   Discussion

The core concept presented in this chapter is the technique of mapping an object into a point in an appropriate multi-dimensional feature space, and then using an appropriate index structure on this multi-dimensional space to aid a rapid first-phase query response producing a superset of the required result. A second, application-specific compute-intensive phase can then analyze this search result. Similarity retrieval is performed by appropriately expanding the search region in feature space.

The hardest step in this process is the choice of an appropriate feature space. The mapping of objects into this space has to satisfy the requirement that no two similar objects be mapped into distance points in feature space. That is, given any two objects with a transformation cost of δ to go from one to another, there must exist an ε, monotonically non-decreasing function of δ, such that the two objects are guaranteed to map to points no more than a distance ε apart.

Further, if the index is to have reasonable selectivity, too many dissimilar objects should also not be clustered close together. The FastMap technique provides one automated way to obtain a reasonable choice of feature space.

If the dimensionality of the feature space is high, many traditional multi-dimensional index structures may perform poorly, since they were originally designed for 2- and 3-dimensional spaces. However, more recent index structures, such as the TV-tree discussed here, are capable of handling a very large number of dimensions adequately.

References

[1] Ayache, N. J. and Faugeras, O. D. "HYPER—A new approach for the recognition and position of two-dimensional objects," *IEEE Trans. on Pattern Analysis and Machine Intelligence*, Vol. PAMI-8, 1986, pp. 44–54.

[2] Brinkhoff, T., Kriegel, H.-P. and Seeger, B. "Efficient processing of spatial joins using R-Trees," in *Proc. of ACM SIGMOD*, Washington, DC, May 1993, pp. 237–246.

[3] Chang, S-K., Cheng, Y., Iyengar, S.S., and Kashyap, R.L. "A new method of image compression using irreducible covers of maximal rectangles.," *IEEE Trans. on Software Engineering*, Vol. 14, No. 5, May 1988, pp. 651–658.

[4] Franzblau, D. S. "Performance guarantees on a sweep-line heuristic for covering rectilinear polygons with rectangles," *SIAM J. Disc. Math.*, Vol. 2, No. 3, 1989, pp. 307–321.

[5] Fukunaga, K. and Narendra, P.M. "A branch and bound algorithm for computing K-nearest neighbors," *IEEE Trans. on Computers (TOC)*, Vol. C-24, No. 7, July 1975, pp. 750–753.

[6] Fukunaga, K. *Introduction to Statistical Pattern Recognition*, 2nd Ed. San Diego: Academic Press, 1990.

[7] Guttman, A. "R Trees: A dynamic index structure for spatial searching," in *Proc. ACM SIGMOD International Conference on the Management of Data*, Boston, MA, 1984, pp. 47–57.

[8] Jagadish, H.V. "Spatial search with polyhedra," in *Proc. Sixth IEEE International Conference on Data Engineering*, Los Angeles, CA, Feb 1990.

[9] Jagadish, H.V. and Bruckstein, A.M. "On sequential shape descriptions," *Pattern Recognition*, Vol. 25, No. 2, 1992, pp. 165–172.

[10] Jagadish, H.V. "A retrieval technique for similar shapes," in *Proc. ACM-SIGMOD International Conference on the Management of Data*, Denver, CO, May 1991.

[11] Jagadish, H.V., Mendelzon, A., and Milo, T. "Similarity-based queries," in *Proc. International Conference on the Principles of Database Systems*, San Jose, CA, May 1995.

[12] Lin, K-I., Jagadish, H.V., and Faloutsos, C. "The TV-tree: An index structure for high-dimensional data," *VLDB Journal*, Vol. 3, No. 4, 1994, pp. 517–542.

[13] Lomet, D.B. and Salzberg, B. "A robust multi-attribute search structure," in *Proc. Fifth IEEE International Conference on Data Engineering*, Los Angeles, CA, Feb 1989, pp. 296–304.

[14] Mumford, D. "The problem of robust shape descriptors," Center for Intelligent Control Systems Report CICS-P-40, Harvard University, Cambridge, MA, Dec 1987.

[15] Nievergelt, J., Hinterberger, H., and Sevcik, K.C. "The grid file: An adaptable symmetric multikey file structure," *ACM Trans. on Database Systems*, Vol. 9, No. 1, 1984.

[16] Orenstein, J.A. and Manola, F.A. "PROBE spatial data modeling and query processing in an image database application," *IEEE Trans. Software Engineering*, Vol. 14, No. 5, May 1988, pp. 611–629.

[17] Robinson, J.T. "K-D-B-tree: A search structure for large multidimensional dynamic indices," in *Proc. ACM SIGMOD Conference on the Management of Data*, Ann Arbor, WI, 1981.

[18] Ruskai, M.B., Beylkin, G., Coifman, R., Daubechies, I., Mallat, S., Meyer, Y., and Raphael, L. *Wavelets and Their Applications*. Boston, MA: Jones and Bartlett Publishers, 1992.

[19] Seeger, B. and Kriegel, H.P. "The buddy tree: An efficient and robust access method for spatial database systems." in *Proc. 16th International Conference on Very Large Databases*, Brisbane, Australia, Aug 1990, pp. 590–601.

[20] Sellis, T., Roussopoulos, N., and Faloutsos, C. "The R+ tree: A dynamic index for multidimensional objects," in *Proc. 13th International Conference on Very Large Databases*, Brighton, U.K., Sep 1987, pp. 507–518.

[21] Wallace, G.K. "The JPEG still picture compression standard," *CACM,* Vol. 34, No. 4, Apr 1991, pp. 31–44.

[22] Wallace, T.P. and Wintz, P.A. "An efficient three-dimensional aircraft recognition algorithm using normalized Fourier descriptors," *Computer Graphics and Image Processing*, Vol. 13, 1980, pp. 99–126.

Video and Image Content Representation and Retrieval

Nevenka Dimitrova and Forouzan Golshani

Philips Research
345 Scarborough Rd
Briarcliff Manor, NY 10510
nvd@philabs.research.philips.com

Department of Computer Science
Arizona State University
Tempe, Arizona 85287-5406
golshani@asu.edu

4.1 Introduction

*T*raditionally, in the context of multimedia information modeling, video has been considered as a kind of object that can be captured, stored, played back, or edited. All of these operations are done with almost no regard to the contents of the video—similar to a file that can be created, duplicated, relocated, and displayed without knowing what it actually contains. In this chapter, we address exactly this issue, and propose a setting for the recovery of the semantics of video data and for the modeling and classification of video streams based on the video contents.

One of the primary traits of video data is the fact that it can illustrate motion. This is precisely the difference between moving pictures and still images. Thus, one important step in the process of video content retrieval is the recovery of motion information. We will present an algorithm that achieves this. We will then show how this type of information can be used for classification and subsequent query processing in multimedia databases containing video.

A number of terms are often used in conjunction with video objects. The term *video sequence* refers to both the *video stream* as well as the *video information*, i.e. the bit stream which consists of physical video data plus the meaning of what the video stream conveys.

Our approach to video information modeling, representation, and querying is minimalist in nature. We extract as little information as possible in order to index the objects and their movements in video sequences. This is in contrast to the trend in computer vision research started by David Marr [41]. Marr's theory distinguishes three levels of representation, namely, an encoding of local boundary elements in an image, *primary sketch*, the viewer centered representation of visible surfaces, *2.5D sketch*, and an object centered representation of shape using hierarchical decomposition, *3D structure*. The basic insight in Marr's work is that it is crucial to identify the type of information the visual system delivers before concentrating on the real time details of how the visual information is processed and stored.

Marr's work and ours differ most significantly at the highest level of object representation. Marr introduced 3D structures for representation of objects. In the case of a human figure, at the broadest level of description the figure is represented as a cylinder whose axis is along the center. At the next level, the description is broken down into head, torso, and four limbs, which themselves are represented by cylinders. Each of these parts is considered at a finer level of detail. The 3D model is a hierarchical representation of the three-dimensional structure of objects in terms of hierarchical decomposition of the object into parts, whereas each part is described in terms of its own parts. Marr's representation does not account for the paths traversed by objects.

The model presented in this chapter adopts the view of multiple levels of representation, in which the recovery of 3D representation may not be necessary for the process of indexing, since features extracted from objects (including relevant motion descriptions) can give enough information about the contents of the video sequences. Our approach can be simplified as one that attempts to recover $(2+t)$D structures. Obviously, this is different from recovering 3D structures since we extract 2D representations of objects in time. This is a viable approach as evident from the studies conducted by Johansson [33] who in the early 1970s introduced the idea of object/event recognition regardless of the existence of object representations. The experiments consisted of attaching lights to the joints of a human subject dressed in dark cloths, and observing the motion of lights against a dark background. Not only the object (human being) could be recognized but the audience could describe the movements and the events taking place. Goddard introduced high-level representations and described the computational processes required for the recognition of human motion based on moving light displays in [21]. The idea is that recognition of any motion involves indexing into stored models of the movement. These stored models, called scenarios, are represented based on coordinated sequences of discrete motion events. The moving lights experiments clearly indicate that minimalist approach is viable for content representation and indexing.

This chapter attempts to illustrate how video content information can be used in multimedia query processing. As such, the chapter covers the two seemingly distinct areas of motion analysis in digital video and information modeling and retrieval. After a brief review of extant work, we present an algebraic framework for multimedia data modeling in Section 4.3. This section will demonstrate what can be done with each type of multimedia information. Particularly, it will show the extent to which we can deal with video data in the absence of content analysis and motion recovery. The following section, Section 4.4, introduces our motion recovery algorithms and the associated operators. We will then show in Section 4.6 how the semantic information can be combined with other types of data in such activities as classification and query processing.

4.2   Related Work

The topic of this chapter draws from a number of areas which have been investigated independently and for the most part in isolation. Without any claims to its completeness, in this section we highlight several experiments in each of the following areas: image analysis and classification, conceptual modeling of video data, motion analysis, and multimedia information modeling.

Image Analysis and Classification

Querying and retrieval in image information systems have been influenced by the language support from conventional (hierarchical, network, relational) databases [50]. Pictorial SQL (PSQL) [52] and Query by Pictorial Example (QPE) [9] are examples. The language of PSQL is an extension of SQL which supports user-defined abstract data types that are used for definition of pictorial domains. Spatial comparison operators and functions for computing attributes are defined on each domain. Retrieval is based on the associations between the pictorial and alphanumeric domain. In QPE, queries are specified using forms (tables) in the style similar to QBE (Query by Example). Another query language that has similar flavor to QBE is PICQUERY [34]. PICQUERY is built on top of a conventional DBMS. It provides support for a comprehensive set of data accessing and manipulation operators for image manipulation and pattern recognition as well as geometric operations.

The query processor of PROBE [46] supports point sets with a geometry filter which produces an approximate answer that is refined further by detailed manipulations on individual spatial objects, such as spatial join and spatial selection.

The Intelligent Image Database System (IIDMS) [7] offers several modes of querying images: query by the name of the image, query by keywords, query by a frame number, query by an iconic example, and query by 2D strings.

The VIMSYS project supports an iterative query model [27], [28]. The user first specifies a domain of interest and then uses an interactive graphical interface to choose and display the objects of interest and their attributes.

Image database must be capable of managing many types of information. Such information may be classified into: iconic data (the images themselves), image related data (resolution, format description), information extracted from processing images (numerical, structural features), image world relationship data, and world (application) related data [25]. In order to facilitate representation of these different types of data, most data models in image databases distinguish between logical and physical image representations [32], [43], [10].

The physical representation describes the raw image at a level higher than pixels independent of the semantics of an application. The physical image includes a representation of edges, loops, lines, or connected diagrams. The logical representation has associated semantics that depends on the actual application. The logical representation is normally what the user requires for image retrieval. In the model proposed by Chang [8], the physical image contains the raw image as well, and the logical image acquires several levels of semantic information as it passes through different stages of processing. The logical and the physical image constitute the so-called *generalized icon*. The generalized icon can contain active index cells as well. An *active index* means that the index:

1. can be imprecise and approximate,

2. can be used to initiate actions, and

3. can be dynamically changed.

This leads to the notion of *smart images*, which offers potential that has not yet been exploited in image retrieval.

A fast image indexing algorithm is proposed by Gong and others in [24]. Images are indexed by both the numerical index keys generated automatically from the captured primitive features using a set of rules and traditional descriptive keywords entered by users. The image features used for indexing are: color, shape features like circularity and major axis orientation, location of regions, as well as histogram content.

Gudivada [26] uses a representation of objects in 3D image databases by assigning a Spatial Orientation Graph (SOG) to each image. SOG contains the spatial relationships between objects in a scene expressed through *directional cosines*. The scheme is translation- and scale-invariant, but not rotation-invariant.

The QBIC system developed by IBM [19] addresses the issue of content based image and video retrieval by incorporating a variety of algorithms. The retrieval queries are composed using example images, user constructed sketches and drawings, selected color and texture patterns, camera motion, and other graphical information. However, motion is used only for reference frames and not for querying based on object motion.

Conceptual Modeling of Video Data

Object-oriented Video Information Database (OVID) is a database system that provides a mechanism to share common descriptional data among video objects, called "interval-inclusion based inheritance" [45]. The data model features schema-less description, i.e., it does not have a predefined class hierarchy. In OVID, the meaning of video objects is given by a set of attributes and their values, which are manually assigned. OVID does not involve processing of the frames or objects inside the frames. The retrieval is based on descriptional data given in text format. The attributes form a generalization hierarchy, and users can specify which of them are inheritable. OVID is one of the first attempts to represent the meaning of video objects using a generalization hierarchy. This approach is different from our spatiotemporal model because we also include the motion descriptions along with the other descriptions of video sequences.

Another system proposed by Little *et al.* [40] supports content-based video retrieval and playback. The authors define a specific schema composed of movie, scene, and actor relations with a fixed set of attributes. The system requires manual feature extraction. The features are then inserted into the schema. Querying involves the attributes of movie, scene, and actor. Once a movie is selected, a user can browse from scene to scene beginning with the initial selection. Querying in this system is limited to the predetermined attributes of the movies.

Media Streams is a visual language that enables users to create multi-layered, iconic annotations of video content [12]. The objects denoted by icons are organized into hierarchies. The icons are used to annotate video streams in what the author calls a "Media Time Line." The iconic primitives constitute a controlled vocabulary that can be extended by means of combination. The Media Streams interface helps to alleviate problems caused by divergence of description.

In [47], Otsuji and Tonomura propose a cut detection method which is useful in handling video information. The proposed mechanism for cut detection called *projection detection filter* is based on finding the highest difference in consecutive frame histogram differences over a period of time. A similar approach for automatic video indexing and full video search is presented by Nagasaka in [44]. This video indexing method relies on automatically selecting first frames within a shot for content representation. Although this method is useful in detecting shot boundaries, the most representative frames might not be always associated with the first or last frame of the shot boundary. Thus, more detailed analysis of the video sequences is needed.

In [57], Teodosio provides an approach to extracting a representative image called *salient video still* from a sequence of images. The methodology involves determining the optical flow between successive frames, applying affine transformations calculated from the flow warping transforms, like rotation and translation, and applying a weighted median filter to the high resolution image data resulting in the final image. Teodosio proposes another method for synthesizing panoramic overviews from a sequence of frames, described in [58]. Bobick presents two methods for extracting representational frames for annotation of video in [6]. The first method is to use multiple concurrent representations, and the second one is to transform the imagery into a frame which is natural for the domain and allows direct application of domain knowledge. However, extraction of representational frames (also called R-frames) is a time-consuming process, and we can not rely fully on extracting representational frames.

Swanberg and her colleagues introduce a method for identifying desired objects, shots, and episodes prior to insertion in video databases in [56]. During the insertion process the data is first analyzed with image processing routines to identify the key features of the data. In this model episodes are represented using finite automata. In this model, only video clips with inherently well defined structure which can be recognized by the automata can be represented. The model exploits the spatial structures of the video data without analyzing object motion. Zhang *et al.* present an evaluation and a study of knowledge-guided parsing algorithms [63]. Another model for automatically generating indexes without deep analysis by segmenting continuous audio and video is introduced by Gabbe [20].

A model-driven approach to digital video segmentation is presented by Hampapur *et al.* in [29]. The paper deals with extracting features that correspond to cuts, spatial edits, and chromatic edits. The authors present extensive formal treatment of shot boundary identification based on models of video edit effects. This work is important in the initial stages of video processing, since we need to identify shot boundaries before we can extract meaningful information within a shot.

An algebraic approach to content-based access to video is presented by Weiss [60]. Video presentations are composed of video segments using a *Video Algebraic Model*. The algebra contains methods for temporally and spatially combining video segments, as well as methods for navigation and querying. However, the algebraic operations are designed for compositing video presentations. In our model, the algebraic operations encompass editing (compositing) as well as content extraction and representation of video sequences.

A set of techniques for processing video data compressed using JPEG (Joint Picture Expert Group) compression at near real time rates is introduced by Smith in [54]. The amount of data processed is reduced by processing video data in compressed form, avoiding full decompression and compression. The paper shows how new algorithms can be devised which operate on semi-compressed video signal. These algorithms can be applied to compute linear *global digital special effects* such as scaling, rotation, and translation. The novel idea of this work is processing compressed video streams which results in faster video processing. In this chapter, we show how to extract motion descriptions from a compressed video stream. We believe that one of the natural extensions to our work is to incorporate algorithms for image processing and object recognition that will work in parallel with video encoding and motion extraction.

A content-based browsing method is introduced by Arman in [3], where each shot is represented by a frame called *Rframe*. A method for easy navigation is introduced that is superior to the current techniques of fast forward and rewind. The video sequences are preprocessed off-line in order to detect video scene changes. This is followed by very simple motion analysis on each video shot. The Rframes consist of a body, four motion tracking regions, and an indicator for the length of the shot. The four motion tracking regions trace the motion of boundary pixels through time. The motion tracking regions serve as an indicator of missed scene changes. The objects within the scene shots are represented using moment invariants, and the color representation is achieved using histogram methods.

Recently, the process of automatic video analysis has been extended to automatically recognize film genres as well as to automatic creation of digital video libraries. Fischer and his colleagues from the University of Manheim proposed a method for automatic recognition of film genres [18]. Their method consists of three steps. The first step is syntactic analysis of properties such as color statistics, cut detection, motion fields, and audio statistics. The second step is derivation of style attributes such as type of camera operations, scene transitions, and presence of speech vs. music. The last step is to map the detected style attributes to film genres such as newscast, commercials, cartoons, and sports. The Informedia project [11] at the Carnegie Mellon's speech, image, and natural language processing groups is concentrated on creating intelligent automatic mechanisms for populating a video library. An example of such techniques is the development of a *video skim* which is a short synopsis of the actual video [55]. A text transcript is created from the audio track by using the speech processing system Sphinx-II. Keywords are extracted from this transcript based on word frequency/ inverse document frequency weightings and separated from the audio track. The audio information is combined with the corresponding significant frames to produce a video skim.

Motion Analysis

Although motion plays an important role in visual recognition tasks, motion recognition, in general, has received little attention in the video representation and retrieval compared to the volume of work in textual annotation and image analysis for key frames. It has been shown that in some cases motion information alone is sufficient for human visual systems to achieve reliable recognition [33]. Our work relies on the recent trend in computational vision which promotes the idea that motion analysis should not depend on complex object descriptions [1], [21]. However, the idea of object/event recognition regardless of the existence of object representations can be traced back to the early seventies, when Johansson introduced his experiments with moving light displays. The idea is to attach lights only to the joints of a human subject dressed in dark and observe the motion of lights against a dark background. The audience can recognize not only the object (human being) but also can describe the kind of motion and the event taking place. The moving lights generate paths (trajectories) which are salient properties of the moving objects. These trajectories are spatiotemporal representations of the object's motion. The experiments with moving light displays have generated a number of research projects in computer vision which attempt to analyze motion without full recovery of the object structure.

In [2], [1], Allmen presented a computational framework for intermediate-level and high-level motion analysis based on *spatiotemporal surface flow* and *spatiotemporal flow curves. Spatiotemporal surfaces* are projections of contours over time. Thus, these surfaces are direct representations of object motion. Spatiotemporal surface flow is defined as a natural extension to optical flow. Spatiotemporal surface flow is used to recover spatiotemporal flow curves. Allmen equates these spatiotemporal curves to the paths described by the moving light displays. Using clusters of spatiotemporal flow curves, moving objects in the scene can be recognized. The problem of detecting cyclic motion is also considered.

In [21], Goddard presented the high-level representations and computational processes required for the recognition of human motion based on moving light displays. The idea is that recognition of any motion involves indexing into stored models of movements. These stored models, called scenarios, are represented based on coordinated sequences of discrete motion events. The thesis shows that the recognition of gait can be achieved directly from motion features without complex shape information. The algorithms are articulated in the language of structured connectionist models.

Motion-based recognition of activities is further developed in a system called EMo which automatically generates control functions for linked mechanisms that express specific emotions [30]. The EMo system relies on finding an evaluation function that determines how much of a certain emotion is being displayed based on a given set of physical characteristics. It takes advantage of the fact that evaluation functions, which take physical characteristics of a motion sequence of a stick figure as input, can be used as a filter on a set of motion sequences to choose one which expresses a desired emotion.

In the literature, there are general methods for object motion estimation and representation as well as domain restricted methods. A general architecture for moving object analysis is presented in [37]. The process of motion analysis is divided into three stages: detection of moving objects, object tracking, and final motion analysis. The architecture is tested on models for human motion. Another approach to interpretation of the movements of articulated bodies in image sequences is presented in [51]. The human body is represented by a three-dimensional model consisting of cylinders. This approach relies on modeling of the movement from medical motion studies. Koller and his colleagues [36] proposed a methodology for tracking vehicles in road traffic scenes. The motion of the vehicle contour is described using affine motion model with a translation and a change in scale. A vehicle contour is represented by closed cubic splines. We build on the research in all these domain specific motion analysis projects. A related line of research is in the area of robot path planning [17]. One of the future avenues for research in motion recognition is to exploit the knowledge of the geometry of the scene in order to restrict the set of possible paths for a moving object.

Multimedia Information Modeling

Extant work in this area is extensive and goes back to earlier attempts in complex data modeling. Proper organization and structuring of multimedia information help us better understand the impact of, and the value added by, each individual media type, as well as their collective effects. The key challenge in modeling is to find an appropriate logical representation for the entities of interest. Among many methodologies proposed for multimedia information modeling, the object-oriented approach has seen more attention, mostly due to the fact that it can hide the internal representation and implementation details and emphasize the interrelationships between entities. An example is the Description Based Media Object Data Model (DEMOM) which provides a uniform framework for managing different types of media data, i.e., images, text, sound, or graphics [31].

The model presented here is object oriented in essence. It attempts to unify a number of techniques for motion analysis as well as individual frame (image) analysis. As such, it has been influenced by a number of prior investigations. We adopt a spatiotemporal mechanism for motion representation similar to the one proposed by Allmen. For intermediate- to high-level translation, we have a model similar to Goddard's Shape-Motion-Scenario representation [21]. However, our model is not specific to recognition of human motion. We build on the experience from various research projects about domain-specific motion analysis in order to propose a generic model for motion recognition in video sequences. We use low- and intermediate-level motion analysis methods similar to those offered by [1] and others. Our object recognition ideas have been influenced by the work of Jain *et al.* [28], [27], Grosky [25], and the research in image databases. The work in algebraic formalization of video access is influenced by Weiss [60]. Several lines of research such as those in [40], [56], [63], [48] provided many useful ideas for the modeling aspects of our investigations. A short report of our work was presented in [14].

4.3 Video Information Model

Many multimedia applications can benefit from retrieval of the video information based on its visual content. However, the sheer volume of information generated by digital video applications requires new methods for video modeling. The problem is that any model for content retrieval has to have the capability of extracting image and motion features from massive amounts of data in video streams.

Currently, modeling methods for content-based retrieval of video information use one of the following: a) manual annotations for extracting descriptive information, b) iconic representations derived using automatic methods for detecting scene changes (also called *video cuts*), and c) static properties derived from extracted features of objects using image analysis techniques. However, derivation of manual annotations is extremely slow for large-scale applications. Automatic methods for iconic representations do not concentrate on extracting important features of moving objects. The methods that employ image analysis techniques concentrate on individual frame processing. However, what distinguishes one movie from another is the events in a sequence of frames which convey the story. Video modeling should take into account the temporal nature of video streams, the fact that recognized objects are obtained from coherently moving entities. The temporal nature of video sequences should be well understood and integrated with the static analysis of individual frames.

Video Information Characterization

The video data stream is complex from the aspects of storage, playback, and retrieval. There are various types of information associated with the storage of the physical video stream, such as the size, frame rate, compression method, etc.

The following types of physical information are associated with the video stream:

- Physical object—video stream
- Physical attributes (length, size, frame numbering)
- Video-related information (format resolution headers, frame rate)

Video carries much more complex information than any other media in multimedia systems. The *conceptual video data type* is derived using structures that represent spatial properties of objects as well as using structures that represent the temporal aspects of these objects, such as motion. The conceptual information that can be derived from a video stream can be categorized as follows:

- O—set of objects present in video.
- M—set of motion representations.
- Features, spatial relationships, derived from the set of objects O.
- Spatiotemporal information that can be derived only from O and M together.
- Domain related information which is supplied by the application designer.
- Temporal relationships which can be inferred from M.
- Image world information.

The queries on the contents of the video data are directed to the conceptual video data type.

With this categorization in mind, we will first present the general formal framework of our video information model, and then we will introduce the image data type as a basis for the video data type. Those aspects concerned with editing, delivery and simple querying of the video data type will be introduced in Section 4.4. We will delay the introduction of the retrieval aspects of the video data type because we need to unfold the stages of motion analysis.

A Framework for Information Modeling

In this section we present a formal foundation for the multimedia information model. It is based on an algebraic framework [22], [61] which has been used in many other areas including programming languages, software and hardware specifications, and object-oriented modeling. Algebraic specifications are developed in the following manner. Given an alphabet consisting of several classes of symbols for types and their associated operators, a schema is specified. (Formally, the schema corresponded closely to the notion of signature in the algebraic framework.) The schema has all the necessary syntactic information along with typing rules, i.e., the rules that determine what type of object(s) can be given to each operator and what type of object(s) it will return. In our system, the domain-dependent information, provided by the system developer, is combined with the application-independent constructs, provided by the system itself, in order to create the schema. In essence, the schema is a formal specification of all objects of interest, real or conceptual, and the relationships between them. Given a schema, the set of well-formed expressions is defined. These expressions are constructed by using the numerous powerful operators that are provided for each type. We will see that, despite a formalized underpinning, the language presented here is extremely simple. Strongly resembling conventional set theory, our language has a functional flavor, similar to Lucid [59]. For simplicity, a general overview of the model will be presented first.

The basic constructs of the model are *data types* and *functions* that operate on the data types. Two main kinds of data types that are used in this discussion are:

- System-defined, fixed data types, called "deliverable types," are: string, integer, boolean, text, image, audio, and video. The traditional data types integer, string, and boolean are known as printable objects. Analogously, we call audio and video deliverable (presentable) types, since they inherently contain a time component. These are the application-independent constituents of the system and are present in any specification.
- User-defined data types, called "entity types," such as "PERSON," or "STUDENT," are those that represent objects or concepts in the real world. These, generally, have properties that are embodied in deliverable types.

A data type may have any number of operators associated with it. Operators that are associated with user-defined types are called user-defined functions. User-defined functions describe the domain-related relationships, cross references between entity types, and the attributes of objects. Cross references typically represent multivalued relationships. Function types have the general form of:

$$\phi: \alpha_0 \times \ldots \times \alpha_{n-1} \to \alpha_n$$

where every α_i, called a type expression, is inductively defined as:

— a data type

— $\alpha_1 \cup \alpha_2$, $\alpha_1 \times \alpha_2$ or $\mathcal{P}(\alpha_1)$ where α_1 and α_2 are type expressions.

Note that the above definition will allow the functions to take as arguments: object types, their unions, cartesian products, and powersets.[1]

In addition to the user-defined functions, we need a collection of operators that are independent of the application domain, and as such operate on system defined data types. Each data type, such as text, graphics, scanned images, audio, and video, has a rich selection of operators associated with it. For example, the operator appendPar performs concatenation operation for the type *Text*. All set theoretical, boolean, and arithmetic operators are included. In addition, there are a number of variable binding operators. The main characteristic of these operators is that they cause a variable to range over the elements of its domain. An example is the set construction operator that has the form $\{f(x) \mid \mathcal{P}(x)\}$, where $f(x)$ denotes the desired output objects, and $\mathcal{P}(x)$ denotes the retrieval predicate that must hold for those objects. While x ranges over its domain, whenever $\mathcal{P}(x)$ is satisfied, $f(x)$ is added to the set. There are a number of other operators like this, including the logical quantifiers. We will see some examples when we introduce video operators.

A complete list of operators and their semantics are offered in [13], [23]. It is sufficient to mention the following operators:

- set operation symbols: isin, isSubsetOf, isTrueSubsetOf, union, intersection, difference, Union, Intersection, noOf
- equality operators: is, isnot
- temporal synchronization (for all media types): sim, before, meets, equals, starts at, finishes
- spatial composition (applied only to graphics, images and video): left, right, bottom, up, showIn, arrange
- integer operation symbols: +, −, *, /, <, >, <=, >=, min, max, ave, sum, prod
- string operation symbols: concat, strLen
- logical operation symbols: and, or, implies, not

---

[1] The powerset $P(A)$ of any set A is the set of all subsets of A.

- text: appendPar, cutPar, eqPar, keyword, isKeywordIn, parSim
- graphics: insPatch, pictureSum, fill, domain, colors, getPatch, getColor, restriction, scale, translate, dot, lineSeg, box, coincident, contains, disjoint, visible, bounded
- audio: intensity, extract, audioIns, audioLen, audioSim
- images: shift, zoom, superimpose, overlay, imageSim
- video: videoLen, pace, videoClip, videoIns

The above list of data types and their associated operators are all part of the schema (signature) of the multimedia information system. The syntax of the language is developed on the basis of this schema.

In the algebraic setting, the algebra associates with each type a set of objects that behave as mandated by the specification of that type. Thus, the set associated with the type *Integer* is, obviously, the set of integer numbers. Other data types denote objects that have the predefined properties. Objects of type *Text* are paragraphs. Data type *Audio* denotes signals of one dimension. The type *Image* contains signals of two dimensions, as elaborated below. Finally, *Video* has signals of three dimensions $F(x,y,i)$ represented as $F_i(x,y)$ where i represents the frame counter, and x and y are pixel coordinates. When no confusion is expected, we may omit the references to the coordinates x and y or to the frame counter i. When needed we will use superscripts to distinguish between different video streams, e.g. $F_i^1(x,y)$ and $F_i^2(x,y)$. The following notation will be used:

— $F_b(x,y)$ for the first frame of the video sequence

— $F_e(x,y)$ for the last frame of the video sequence

— $F_c(x,y)$ for the current frame of the video sequence

The algebra allows partial functions. Whenever the function is not defined over a certain part of the domain we use the symbol θ to denote the undefined values.

Since the focus of this paper is specifically on the *Image* and *Video* data types, in the next two sections we will describe the image data type and the video data type in detail.

Image Data Type

The image data type should be flexible enough to accommodate various stages of image interpretation. It should support general operations for extracting the semantics of the image as well as the associated domain-dependent and the user-dependent operations for extracting information. The image data type should also incorporate multiple views for various interpretations of the image, as well as evolving interpretations of the image.

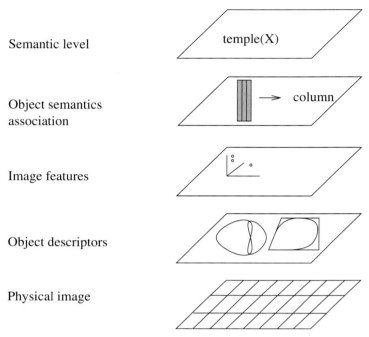

Semantic level

Object semantics
association

Image features

Object descriptors

Physical image

Figure 4-1   Multilevel representation of the image data type.

We consider the image to be a hierarchically structured data type. As illustrated in Fig. 4–1, the image data type includes the following:

1. Physical image, which refers to the digitized image representation. At the physical level this translates into an image stored (or compressed) in an image file format. Each image is a function that associates intensity values to pixels on a two dimensional (or multidimensional) grid.

2. Set of extracted boundaries of objects, regions, or chain codes (basically, object descriptors).

3. Identified image features, used for object recognition and subsequent classifications.

4. Object semantics association, which is the assignment of real world semantics to the objects or features identified in the image.

5. Real-world descriptions: These are better known as domain knowledge and are expressed using rules, predicates, semantic nets, or a scheme that will enable further reasoning about the content of the images. For example, the fact that bridges are found at the crossings of rivers and roads can be used in locating a bridge in the image. The task of identification is greatly simplified because we do not explore all the possibilities.

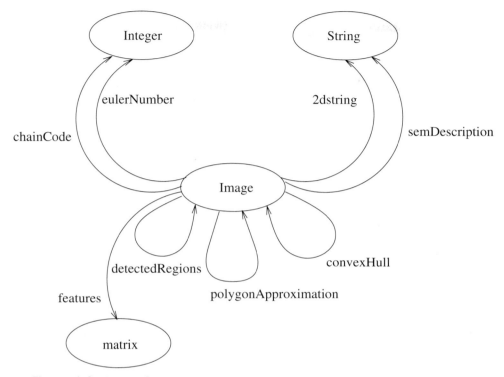

Figure 4-2   Image data type.

The objects at different levels of the image data type hierarchy are obtained by image analysis operators. The classification of the operators in our model is done with respect to the functionality of each particular operator and its purpose in the whole system. The operators that work between levels one and two in the image data type representation are basic enhancement/segmentation image processing operators. Cross-level operators at levels 3, 4, and 5 are the semantic-level operators. Fig. 4–2 illustrates an abstract view of the image data type and associated operators. The overall categorization of the operators is:

- Low-Level Operators: Image processing operators for image registration, image enhancement, salt and pepper noise removal, contrast operators, spatial filtering, i.e. the preprocessing operators, fall in this category. These operators return the physical image type, that is, the output is of the same type as the input image. The preprocessed image is then used for analysis and region/edge detection. Examples include the following:
  — Linear and non-linear filtering: for noise suppression, image smoothing/sharpening, and edge/feature enhancement.

— Image arithmetic and logical operators: to detect differences between images, filter out transient phenomena (video), and compensate for non-uniform illumination.

— Intensity mapping: for contrast stretching/compression.

- Object-Representation Operators: The object-representation/extraction operators serve for populating the higher levels of the image data type. These functions are useful for extracting the shape information, boundary, and skeleton of the objects inside the image, as well as for associating the world-related information with the extracted features and objects. Below are some examples and their associated tasks:

   — Area counting: to determine the presence or absence of an object, feature or flaw

   — Gray scale analysis: to detect surface features, roughness

   — Connectivity analysis: to determine how many objects, compute distances

   — Edge detection: to find features or objects

   —Template matching: to locate specified patterns of pixel intensities

   — Boundary detection: to detect partially visible or low contrast objects.

- Retrieval Operators: Operators in this category make use of all information stored at any level of the hierarchy. These operators are used for comparison of descriptor and feature values like perimeter comparison, signature comparison, moments comparison, region matching, etc. Their output is of type either boolean or integer, and indicates the similarity level between the input object and the found matching object.

Our approach to modeling image data is different from that of the VIMSYS data model (see [27], [28]) stemming from the fact that the foundation of our formalism is an algebraic one. We separate the image descriptors and the features of objects since features are represented by values of attributes which are derived from the object descriptors.

Video Data Type

Video data streams carry much more complex information than any other type of media. Operators on the video stream range from operators for delivery of video streams, editing operators, as well as operators for extracting motion for video

classification. With what we have presented so far, we can discuss video operators for editing and delivery. Operators for content classification will be presented in a later section since content analysis requires introduction of certain
operators that are essential for motion analysis and video indexing.

Editing Operators

The primitive operators for video editing are analogous to the list processing
operators. For list processing, first *head*, *tail*, and *append* (car, cdr, ... in Lisp) are
defined, and then, based on these more elaborate operators are introduced. A
similar process is followed for type video. The primitive video operators that are
defined first are (note the reversed Polish notation):

> — $\downarrow$ for obtaining the first frame of a video sequence. Thus
> $F(x,y) \downarrow = F_b(x,y)$

> — $\uparrow$ for obtaining the video sequence without its first frame.

Based on the above, we can define such operators as:

> — $\downarrow_a$ returns the first portion of the video sequence up to frame
> number a. We write $F \downarrow_a$ to indicate the first a frames of F.

> — $\uparrow_a$ returns the last portion of the video sequence starting with
> frame number a. Thus $F \uparrow_a$ denotes the last portion of F starting
> with frame number a.

> — circ which appends one video sequence to the end of another.
> Thus, concatenation of two video sequences is performed by this
> operator.

Many editing tasks can now be introduced via more elaborate operators,
including the following:

> — Inserting a video stream into another video stream:

$$v\_insert: Video \times Video \times Integer \rightarrow Video$$

where:

$$v\_insert(F^1, F^2, a) = \begin{cases} F^1 \downarrow_a \circ F^2 \circ F^1 \uparrow_a & \text{if } a \geq 0 \text{ and } F^1 \text{ has at least } a \text{ frames} \\ \theta & \text{otherwise} \end{cases}$$

> — Extract a video clip from a video stream:

$$v\_clip: Video \times Integer \times Integer \rightarrow Video$$

where

$$v\_clip(F, a_1, a_2) = \begin{cases} F - F \downarrow_{a1} - F \uparrow_{a2} & \text{if } a_1 \leq a_2 \text{ and } F \text{ has at least } a_2 \text{ frames} \\ \theta & \text{otherwise} \end{cases}$$

— Video cut extraction:

$$cuts\colon Video \to \mathcal{P} \ (Integer)$$

$$cuts(F) = \{i | difference(F_{i-1}^{\cdot}, F_i) > threshold\}$$

The operator *cuts* takes an input video stream and returns a set of frame numbers which correspond to a drastic scene change, i.e., video cut. Determining the difference between the frames F_{i-1} and F_i is not a straightforward task. Cut detection is important in the initial stages of video processing, since shot boundaries have to be identified to extract meaningful information within a shot. Otsuji and Tonomura [47] proposed a cut detection method which is based on finding the largest difference in consecutive frame histogram differences over a period of time. A similar approach for automatic video indexing and full video search is presented by Nagasaka [44]. Shot boundary identification based on models of video editing effects is presented by Hampapur [29]. The work by Zabih [62] focuses on detection and classification of scene breaks in image sequences. Classification is performed by detecting the appearance of intensity edges that are distant from edges in the previous frame.

— Extract a set of motion icons from a video stream:

$$micons\colon Video \to \mathcal{P} \ (Image)$$

where

$$micons(F) = \{F_i | i \in cuts(F)\}$$

This operator extracts frames in a video sequence that correspond to video cut changes. A *micon* is a visual representation of the most representative scenes of a video stream.

— Extract a still image from a video sequence:

$$still\colon Video \to Image$$

where

$$still \ (F) = F_c$$

This operator extracts the current frame c of the sequence.

Delivery Operators

Delivery operators take a video stream and present it at the user's request during the retrieval time. These operators do not change the content of the input video stream.

Consider the video stream $F_i(x,y)$. As before, we use $F_b(x,y)$, $F_e(x,y)$, and $F_c(x,y)$ to denote the beginning frame, the ending frame, and the current frame of the video stream, respectively.

The two primary delivery (playback) operators, *play* and *reverse*, are defined as follows:

$$play = \triangleright_{i\,=\,c}^{e} F_i(x, y)$$

$$reverse = \triangleleft_{i\,=\,c}^{b} F_i(x, y)$$

The operators $\triangleleft$ and $\triangleright$ are similar in nature to operators that force variables to range over their domain. Analogous to $\int$ in $\int_a^b f(x)dx$ which causes x to range over the interval $[a,b]$, $\triangleright$ and $\triangleleft$ force the frame counter to range from c (i.e., the current frame) to the end or to the beginning of the frame counter, respectively.

Video Attribute Operators

Finally, a host of operators for querying the physical attributes of video are included. For example, given a video clip, *v_length* returns a number representing the length of the sequence.

$$v\_length : Video \rightarrow Integer$$

Similar operators are introduced for querying other attributes of the physical video. The expected playback frame rate is given by the operator:

$$frame\_rate : Video \rightarrow Integer$$

The following operator gives the physical storage size of the video:

$$size : Video \rightarrow Integer$$

Another format related video information is the resolution of the individual frames:

$$resolution : Video \rightarrow String$$

The following operator gives back the compression scheme used for storing the video data:

$$compression : Video \rightarrow String$$

Fig. 4–3 contains a schematic description of the operators that apply to the physical video type. Single arcs denote that the returned object is a single element. Double arcs denote that the returned object is a set of elements.

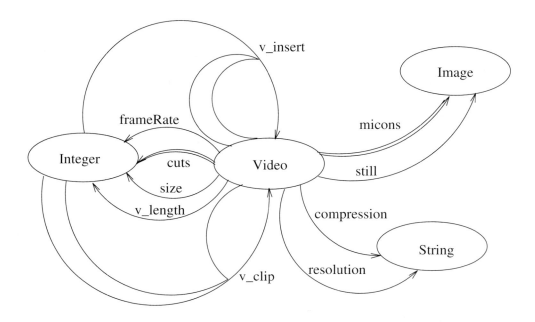

Figure 4-3   Video data type.

The Query Language EVA

A query language for multimedia information systems must provide a number of features that are not shared with ordinary query languages. One such feature is the ability to deal with spatial and temporal dimensions of multimedia objects. This capability ensures that, when presenting the query results, temporal precedence and spatial compositions of objects are exactly those requested by the user.

Defined within the algebraic paradigm described above, EVA is a query language that provides all the necessary constructs for retrieval and management of multimedia information [23]. The basis of the language is a schema (algebraic signature) which contains all the entity types (both user-defined and application-independent types) and the associated operators. By using these operators, the user can specify the desired objects in a simple way. EVA has a formal grammar by which the set of acceptable expressions can be generated. While EVA yields an attractive graphical language [42], writing queries in the formal notation of the language is just as simple.

The main construct in EVA is the set construction operator which has the form:

$$\{f(x)|P(x)\}$$

where $f(x)$ stands for the objects of interest, and $P(x)$ represents all the conditions that must be met. In general, f may be a complex structure consisting of objects of different types. For example, the desired answer to the query may consist of objects of type integer, text, audio, and video. In such cases, temporal coordination is necessary in order to ensure an understandable presentation. EVA provides a number of operators for temporal coordination or synchronization of results. The list includes: *at*, *sim* (simultaneously), *before*, *meets*, *starts*, and *finishes*. The semantics of these operators are defined formally in [23], and is omitted for brevity. The synchronization operators may be combined to generate the desired effects. For example, the expression

$$\{(f_1(x)sim\ f_2(x))before\ f_3(x)|P(x)\}$$

means: whenever the condition(s) $P(x)$ hold, first present $f_1(x)$ simultaneously with $f_2(x)$ and then present $f_3(x)$. In order to appreciate the necessity of the synchronization operators, one may think of f_1 as an audio clip that corresponds to the image f_2 and consider f_3 to be a video clip. Without the coordination, the semantics of the presentation may be distorted or completely lost.

Example: Consider a system for storing information on car racing in which information about race cars and drivers are stored. The user defined entity types and the associated operators for this application form a schema that is represented graphically in Fig. 4–4. The type expressions of some sample functions are:

nameOf	:	*Driver*	$\rightarrow String$
pictureOf	:	*Driver*	$\rightarrow Image$
drives	:	*Driver*	$\rightarrow Car$
racesIn	:	*Driver*	$\times Car \rightarrow Race$
coverage	:	*Race*	$\rightarrow Video$
yearOf	:	*Race*	$\rightarrow Integer$
winnerOf	:	*Race*	$\rightarrow String$
rnameOf	:	*Race*	$\rightarrow String$
announcement	:	*Race*	$\rightarrow Audio$
modelOf	:	*Car*	$\rightarrow String$
makeOf	:	*Car*	$\rightarrow String$

Below are two sample queries on this schema.

- Show the video of all races won by a **Ferrari**.

$$\{coverage(R)\ |\ winnerOf(R)\ \text{is "}Ferrari\text{"}\}$$

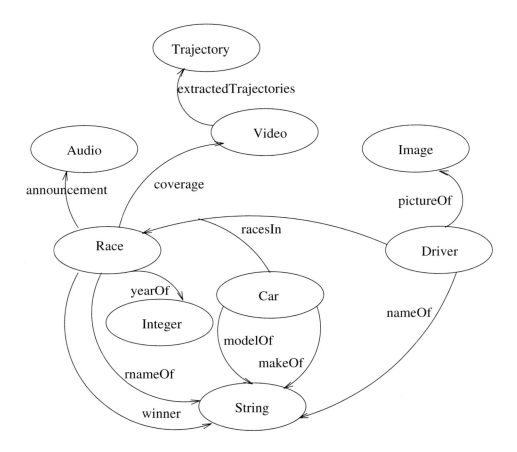

Figure 4-4   Car racing schema.

While R ranges over the elements of the object Race, the query checks if the winner is "Ferrari" and displays the respective video clip which contains the video coverage of the event.

- Show the video and simultaneously play the announcements of the PA system for all 1994 races.

$$\{coverage(R)\ sim\ announcement(R)\mid\ yearOf(R)\ is\ \textbf{1994}\}$$

For each race R, if the year in which the race occurred is 1994, the query processor displays the respective video coverage simultaneously with the announcements.

Limitations

The reader may have noticed that so far, although we addressed the physical aspects of video, we have not dealt with the contents of moving pictures. We treated video as a simple object that can be retrieved and displayed. However, video may contain much more information than what can be extracted automatically using techniques developed in dynamic scene understanding. Dynamic video content extraction requires the use of domain knowledge and smart tracing methods in order to interpret and describe events in video sequences. For example, we can automatically trace movements of basketball players and retrieve video sequences based on particular pattern of motion, or based on the specific path traversed by the player and the ball. Not only can dynamic motion analysis characterize the objects that are present in the video sequence, but it can also describe what is happening in the video sequence. In order to achieve the goal of recovering activities and events, we need to integrate the representation in space and representation in time into one coherent representation scheme.

One main requirement for meeting the above objectives is to bridge the gap between low-level computational processes and the high-level descriptions. This topic is still a research area in the area of computer vision. As discussed previously, we propose a representation scheme that renders multiple layers of descriptions. The querying process can involve the descriptions of objects in the video as well as description of movements and activities of objects in the video.

In the subsequent sections, we will focus on the contents of moving pictures and how the content information may be used to improve the process of classification and retrieval.

4.4   Motion Analysis

The purpose of motion analysis is to recover the structure of the objects and to recognize moving objects [35]. The process of motion analysis is divided into three stages: detection of moving objects, object tracking by determining motion characteristics, and final integration of motion features.

Motion Detection

Motion detection deals with the recognition of changes over time stemming from displacements of portions of video frames in a video sequence. The descriptions of motion at the lowest level consist of representation of displaced pixels from, say, position A to position B.

A number of methods exist for motion detection. In pixel-based methods, motion analysis begins with detection of displacements of individual pixels. In area-based methods, the detection of displacement is at a much more coarse level. In MPEG, for example, the detection of displacement is at the level of 16×16 pixel areas. The MPEG-based motion estimation uses the fact that a frame is very likely to be similar to the preceding frame [49], [38]. The temporal redundancy of the video signal gives a basis for the assumption that locally the current frame can be modeled as a translation of a previous and a future frame. Each motion vector is obtained by minimizing a cost function that measures the mismatch between a block and each predictor candidate. Each bidirectional (B) and predicted (P) frame is an abundant source of motion information. In fact, each of these frames might be considered a crude interpolation of the optical flow. Thus, the extraction of the motion vectors of a single macroblock through a sequence of frames is equivalent to a low-level motion analysis.

The algorithm for motion tracing of a single macroblock through one frame pattern takes the forward and backward motion vectors that belong to a particular macroblock and computes the macroblock's trajectory. The algorithm computes the macroblock's position in a B frame by averaging the positions obtained from: (i) the block coordinates in the previous reference frame and forward motion vectors, and (ii) next (predicted) block coordinates and the backward motion vector. The position of a macroblock in a P frame is computed using only block coordinates of the previous reference frame and forward motion vectors. If during this tracing procedure the initial macroblock moves out of its position completely, then we will have to extract additional motion vectors for the new macroblock position. Motion tracing continues by changing the focus on the macroblock whose position overlaps with another macroblock in the direction of motion of the initial macroblock. The detail version of the algorithm is given in [14].

The advantages of MPEG based motion analysis are:

- Small overhead: Since the motion vectors are already extracted during the encoding process, we are just introducing the overhead of collecting the motion vectors.

- Robustness: It is true that the motion estimation algorithm of MPEG is not estimating the motion of the macroblock that we are specifically looking for, but it gives the displacement to the "best match" macroblock. Considering that most objects are "immutable" and they consist of groups of macroblocks which obey the integrity assumption, we can integrate the motion vectors of a macroblock over time.

- Smaller set of data: MPEG has a large compression ratio, especially if the compression frame pattern contains multiples of B frames. The algorithms that work on the compressed stream will be looking into a data stream that might be 200 times less than the original stream.

- Smarter set of data: MPEG P and B frames already contain motion vectors. Motion recovery begins with "collecting" those vectors.

- "On-the-fly" processing: Motion analysis is performed during the compression of video stream.

Motion Tracing

A macroblock trajectory is the spatiotemporal representation of the motion of a macroblock. Before the motion tracing starts, the proper trajectory representation should be chosen. The simplest one is the point representation. A trajectory in this case is a set of points represented by the absolute or relative frame coordinates of the position of the object, say

$$\{(x_1, y_1), (x_2, y_2), \ldots, (x_n, y_n)\}$$

where (x_j, y_j) is derived by projecting (x, y, j) onto the image plane. (x, y, j) denotes the position of an object i.e., (x, y) at time instant j.

Given the initial point representation of a trajectory, a continuous representation can be derived using a suitable polynomial interpolation. Trajectories can also be represented using direction-oriented primitives, such as chain codes. The diversity of the trajectory representations makes the processes of motion tracing and querying more flexible. These processes rely on trajectory matching which computes distance measures between two trajectories.

In the motion tracing process, the individual trajectories are subsequently used for extracting object motion. This process is different for rigid and non-rigid bodies. A rigid object consists of one solid part to which motion trajectory is associated. If the object consists of several parts which themselves represent rigid objects, then, such a non-rigid object is represented as a set of rigid objects with their respective trajectories.

Rigid object motion is represented by a single trajectory. The trajectory is one common representation of the trajectories of all the component macroblocks. Finding the most representative trajectory is not a simple task. In the simplest case, the trajectory of the object centroid can be taken as the reference object trajectory. An alternative is to create a common trajectory by processing all trajectories created during motion of an object. If a pixel based method is used for motion detection, then we might want to examine only a subset of all trajectories. In the case of MPEG based motion detection, we use the trajectories of the macroblocks that "cover" the object. Thus, there is one trajectory per each 16×16 pixel block.

The following two assumptions make the object motion recovery feasible:

i. Integrity of objects: We consider objects to be rigid or consisting of rigid parts connected to each other. We do not consider situations in which objects disintegrate. This assumption is important because we only use object-trajectory representation.

```
Given set T = {t₁,t₂, … , tₙ}
Normalize T
For each i, cᵢ ← makeCluster(tᵢ)
C = {c₁, c₂, … , cₙ}
    For each cluster, cᵢ ∈ C
        Select cluster cⱼ ∈ C
            For trajectories tᵢ ∈ cᵢ  and tⱼ ∈ cⱼ
                if distance(tᵢ,tⱼ) < radius
                    cₖ = mergeClusters(cᵢ,cⱼ)
                    C = C \ {cᵢ,cⱼ} ∪ {cₖ}
            next j
        next i
    end
```

Figure 4-5 Algorithm for clustering of trajectories.

ii. Motion continuity: Each macroblock under consideration has continuous motion. This assumption is important for the trajectory representation, since every trajectory segment represents continuation of the previous trajectory segment.

When there is no a priori knowledge of the objects in a video sequence, we can apply a clustering mechanism for grouping the incoming trajectories. The clusters of trajectories should correspond to the rigid objects which are moving in the video sequence. The choices of a clustering mechanism, the trajectory representation, and the distance measure used to group the trajectories can influence the outcome of the trajectory clustering.

A hierarchical method for clustering of trajectories is used. The algorithm takes a set of trajectories as input. First, the trajectories are normalized so that each trajectory starts off at the coordinate beginning (0,0) (see Fig. 4–5). In the initialization step, all the trajectories are assigned to one cluster. Then, each cluster is compared to the rest of the clusters, and if a similar cluster is found, the current cluster will be merged with the matching cluster. During this merge, the new cluster will be assigned a trajectory which is an average between the two representative trajectories from the two merging clusters. The process will stop when there are no more clusters to merge. However, we can employ heuristics that will result in a different number of clusters.

A distance function is used to measure the similarity between two clusters. The clustering process can use a variety of functions for measuring the similarities between two trajectories. Two trajectories are considered similar if the perceived difference between them is bound by some tolerable measure.

There are various distance functions for measuring the similarity between two trajectories:

- Manhattan distance: Given points p=(x,y,t) and q=(s,r,t) from trajectories t_1 and t_2 at time t, we compute the distance using:

$$D(p,q) = |x - s| + |y - r|$$

- Chess distance: Given points $p=(x,y,t)$ and $q=(s,r,t)$ from trajectories t_1 and t_2 at the time t, we compute the distance using:

$$D(p,q) = max\{|x - s|, |y - r|\}$$

The chessboard distance is the closest distance between two points on a discrete grid. Manhattan distance, also called the city block distance, finds the points in the neighborhood of a certain point in a square fashion.

These distance functions are used for grouping of the trajectories into clusters of trajectories. While performing the clustering algorithm, we obtain a trajectory as a result of pairwise merging of given trajectories. Since the trajectories are normalized, each cluster forms a tunnel of trajectories around its own trajectory. Fig. 4–6 depicts the application of the clustering process for five trajectories. The trajectories are normalized so that their beginning point is the same. The measure for similarity is Manhattan distance, and the radius is one pixel. The outcome of the algorithm is two clusters: one represented by trajectory (1,1,1),(3,0,2),(5,4,3) and the second one represented by trajectory (1,1,1),(2,2,2),(3,3,3).

Instead of using the individual points in space at certain instants in time, we can use the characteristics of the curves that are fitted through the motion trajectories. These characteristics are velocity, curvature, and torsion and they are used frequently as measures for the shape of curves. Curvature at a point on a curve measures how fast the curve pulls away from the tangent vector at that point. Torsion at a point on a curve is a measure of twisting out of the plane formed by the tangent and the normal vector. A thorough treatment of motion analysis based on the characteristics of the flow curves is given in [1]. Flow curves correspond to the curve representations of trajectories in our research. The choices of the distance measure and clustering algorithm are left to the application.

We use the notation T to indicate the set of object trajectories. Each member of T is a sequence[2] whose range is the set of all motion vectors. As discussed previously, the actual appearance of the members of T depends on our choice of the representation scheme.

Fig. 4–7 illustrates the trajectory data type which captures the abstractions associated with motion tracing. Recall that this basic type is called *Trajectory*. Its associated functions are:

---

[2] A sequence is simply a function whose domain is natural numbers.

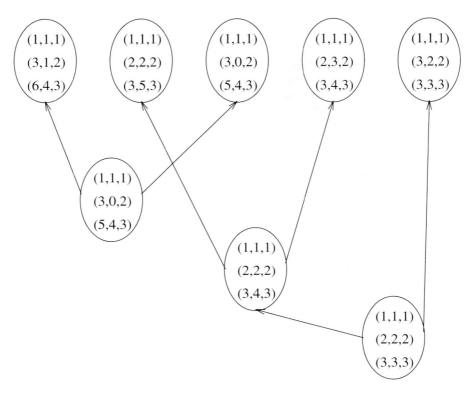

Figure 4-6   Application of the trajectory clustering algorithm.

— Trajectory representation functions *curve*, *description*, and *chainCode* corresponding to the three representations of a trajectory: interpolated curve, text description, and chain code representation.

— Trajectory attribute functions corresponding to the physical attributes of a trajectory: *path* which returns the path length, *velocity* which returns the average velocity for a particular trajectory, and *acceleration* which measures the acceleration.

— Trajectory comparison functions: *exactMatch* which compares two trajectories for exact match, *similar* which measures the similarity between two trajectories, and *cluster* which takes a set of trajectories, performs the clustering algorithm which we described previously.

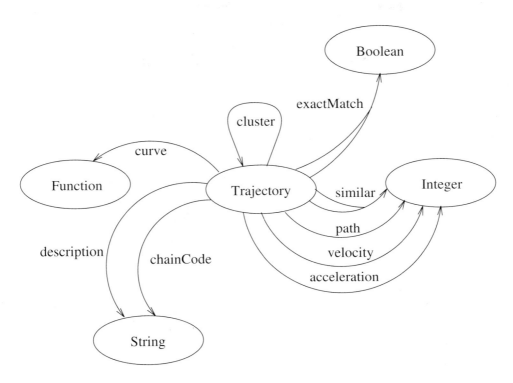

Figure 4-7   Trajectory data type.

Motion Understanding: A Minimalist Approach

One of the basic questions in motion recognition and understanding is how to incorporate the motion information into a more global generalized perception scheme of the whole scene/situation. The *Gestalt theory* offers an explanation in the field of psychology. Computational counterparts of the Gestalt theory are mostly based on the connectionist models. There are several methodologies for getting the overall meaning from a given scene, but a common successful computational theory has not been offered yet. We consider the high level motion analysis and understanding to be a problem that can be tackled using selected pieces of information derived from the motion tracing stage. However, we need additional domain dependent information in the form of constraints to synthesize the extracted motion information and possibly the object information into a high level description.

At the highest level of motion analysis, we associate domain-dependent "activities" with the object-trajectory representations. An activity can be recognized by the system based on a predefined set of procedures, or it can be

designated by the user. Note that recognizing activities is one of the most difficult tasks in any vision system. Such undertaking requires information on:

1. Relative positioning of rigid objects (subparts)

2. Relative timing of the parts' movements

3. Actual and perceived interaction of object parts.

The two main problems in recovering high-level motion representation are
(i) the fact that multiple sequences are occurring simultaneously (for example,
arm movements and leg movements in human motion) and in a coordinated fashion, and (ii) tempo changes are global (in the case of human body, the changes
apply to all four limbs and occur slowly).

An activity involves both spatial and temporal representations of the
objects of interest. We must identify the object components (shape and other features) and their respective trajectories (as we did in the previous section) at the
intermediate-level motion analysis, and then assemble activities. The time information is also needed for discrimination of activities of the same type, for example, strolling, walking, hurrying, etc. After assembling object activities, based on
additional knowledge, we can infer event information.

Let us use $\mathcal{A}$ to symbolize the set of activities. We assume that the existence
of a knowledge base $\mathcal{K}$ whose contents include all the necessary rules, constraints, and the procedures for deriving activities from lower level descriptions.

Each member a of $\mathcal{A}$ is a "composition" of t_1, t_2, ..., t_n, where for every
$1 < i < n$ we have:

- $t_i \in T$ and

- t_i satisfies every constraint in $\mathcal{C}_a$, where $\mathcal{C}_a \in \mathcal{K}$ represents the constraints
  governing the activity a.

To illustrate the process of object and motion analysis we present an example. Fig. 4–8 shows selected frames from the moving car video sequence. In this
case, we have a static camera, static background and a moving object which
appears to be rigid. The motion trajectories of the covering macroblocks are
extracted, and then, the common trajectory is extracted as a result of the clustering process. Fig. 4–9 shows the trajectories of the moving car. Fig. 4–10 shows
the whole process of recovering object and motion characteristics from the car
video sequence.

Figure 4-8   Selected frames of the car video sequence.

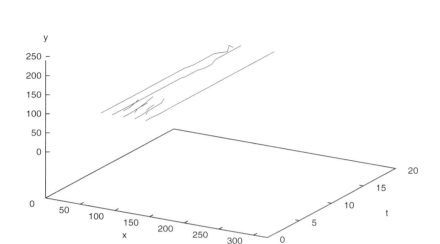

"plot.int41-61" ——

Figure 4-9   Extracted trajectories from the car video sequence.

4.5   Spatiotemporal Operators of the Video Data Type

The purpose of object analysis and motion analysis is to extract relevant properties of objects and their movements in order to represent the concepts emerging from the video sequences. In this section we bring together both aspects of video content analysis into a unique representation of the conceptual video data type. Fig. 4–11 contains a schematic description of the operators that apply to the conceptual video type.

Motion analysis begins with motion vector recovery followed by tracing of individual macroblock trajectories. Conceptually this process is captured by the operator:

$$extractedTrajectories : Video \rightarrow Trajectory$$

The data type *Trajectory* was described in a previous section.

The operator for feature extraction has the following signature:

$$features: Image \rightarrow featureMatrix$$

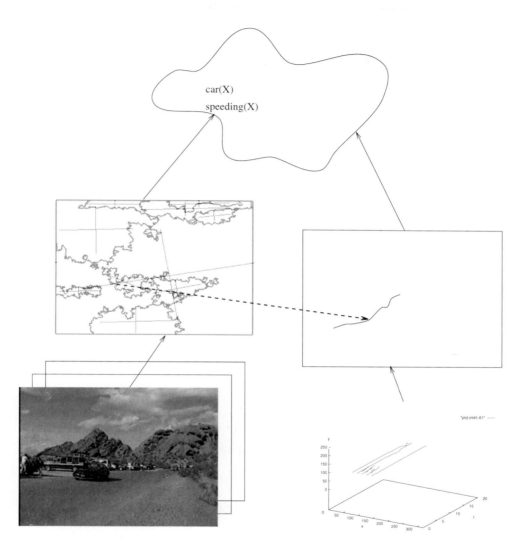

Figure 4-10   Spatial and temporal hierarchical representation of the car video sequence.

This operator takes an image and derives a set of features indexed into a feature matrix. The operator *leadsTo* which has the signature:

$$leadsTo \ : \ featureMatrix \rightarrow Object$$

takes the input feature matrix and performs a classification of the input features into a predefined set of object categories.

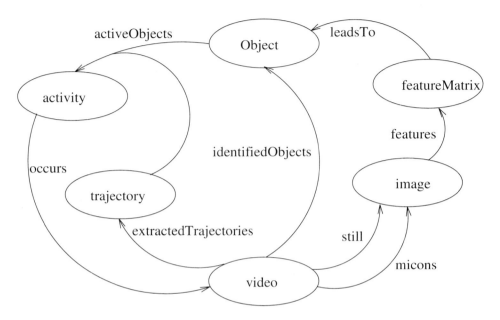

Figure 4-11 Conceptual video data type.

The process of feature selection and feature mapping is discussed extensively in the computer vision literature [53], [4]. The actual process of feature selection will be left to the specific domain implementation.

The operator *identifiedObjects* is abstracted as:

$$identifiedObjects : Video \rightarrow Object$$

where the *Object* is a union of all user defined data types. In addition, *Object* may contain other objects of interest. The operator *identifiedObjects* is representation of a composition of a series of other operators such as: *still, features*, and *leadsTo*.

By making use of object descriptions and their traversed trajectories, we can infer activities:

$$activeObjects : Object \times Trajectory \rightarrow Activity$$

Description of activities is derived from previously computed motion features. For example, if the object has been recognized as a car, then, associating a straight line with it as its trajectory, would result in an activity: *driveStraight*. Note that derivation of activities may be carried out even in cases where the object representation is an empty set.

The idea of derivation of activities directly from motion representation has been around for more than several decades. However, there are still numerous unanswered questions with its successful implementation.

Once the activities in a video sequence are described, we can pose the question: "What are the video sequences in which a particular activity occurs," by using the operator:

$$occurs : Activity \rightarrow Video$$

Occurs is an operator that delivers a video sequence which contains certain activity.

Fig. 4–11 represents the conceptual video operators described above. The figure is an attempt to synthesize all of the information derivable from the video sequences. We have already described those operators that are associated with the data types *Trajectory, Video,* and *Image.* Note that the operators for identification of objects are radically simplified in order to give the complete picture.

4.6   A Content Retrieval Scheme

The motion tracing and representation scheme introduced in previous sections serves as a basis for the retrieval of video sequences. Video sequences may be retrieved using the temporal (motion) characteristics, spatial characteristics, or using a combination of both representations. The *conceptual video data type* as presented in Section 4.5 is a basis for derivation of object-motion-video structures. The idea is that we can compute and retrieve the spatial and temporal features independently of each other. The retrieval functions augment EVA's retrieval capabilities since they turn the physical object *Video* into a conceptual one, i.e. an object with its own specific set of properties that can be incorporated into queries for more precise questions.

In order to establish a correspondence between the paths traversed by objects and their spatial descriptions we use a family of functions with the following signature:

$$Trajectory \times Object \rightarrow Activity$$

There are a variety of activities that can be inferred solely from trajectory description, but those activities would be the generic ones. For example, we may infer that whatever object had a trajectory congruent to a straight line, was performing "move straight" activity. Given a certain context, (for example in a situation where the only moving objects in the application domain are cars and we do not expect other moving objects) we can infer more specific activity *drive-Straight.*

The following activities are inferred from the set of video sequences in the car race schema:

- turnLeft (turnRight) is true if trajectory orientation changes to the left (right) with respect to the current direction
- driveStraight is true if trajectory orientation stays the same
- speedUp is true if velocity increases
- slowDown is true if velocity decreases
- collision is true if trajectory t_1 coincides with trajectory t_2 at a particular time instance

$$collision\colon Trajectory \times Trajectory \rightarrow Activity$$

For example: show all the video sequences in which John's Ferrari is speeding up:

$$\{speedUp(O)\ occurs\ in\ coverage(Race)\ |$$
$$exists\ Driver\ exists\ Car : (racesIn\ (Driver,\ Car)\ is\ Race\ and$$
$$nameof(Driver)\ is\ ``John"\ and\ makeof(Car)\ is ``Ferrari")\}$$

Using the derived descriptions, many new types of queries that refer to the contents of video sequences can be specified. Specifically, we can express queries that refer to the contents of video sequences. Examples include the following:

— Retrieve all the video sequences in which a red car is turning left.

— Retrieve all possible paths of John's Ferrari.

— Show all the video sequences in which John's car was slowing down.

The target language is a visual one that allows for specification of spatial properties, as well as exact and inexact specification of motion properties. In the rest of this section, we outline the design of a visual database language called VEVA [16], which has well-defined semantics in both character-based and icon-based paradigms.

Defined within the algebraic framework described above, VEVA is a visual query language that provides all the necessary constructs for retrieval and management of multimedia information. The basis for the language is a schema (algebraic signature) which contains entity types (both user-defined types and application-independent types) and the associated operators [23]. By using these operators, the user can visually specify a query for the desired objects in a simple way. VEVA has a formal grammar with which the set of acceptable expressions can be generated. The grammar for the visual language VEVA is given using visual rules in the style of a picture description language which was developed within the syntactic approach to pattern recognition [53]. The grammar rules contain nonterminal and terminal icons. The rules are given as graph rewriting rules where the left hand side is a nonterminal icon, and the right hand side is a graph containing nonterminal and terminal icons connected with customized links.

Parsing of visual expressions in VEVA is a process of determining the structure of the workspace. Note that parsing is the first step of the VEVA language processing, because lexical analysis is not necessary. All available icon symbols can be drawn from the given palette and connected by a set of permissible links. Thus, every expression that is drawn is lexically correct. The execution process begins by parsing the contents of the VEVA workspace. The algorithm finds the top-level set expressions which may contain other set expressions. Translated into visual terms, this algorithm finds the enclosed visual expressions or other iconic elements within a given oval. The algorithm recursively calls the set evaluation procedure for the sets that are contained in it, until there are single sets with simple function-predicate expressions left. The evaluated sets can be connected with temporal links which prescribe the order in which the resulting objects should be presented by the presentation manager. If the evaluated expression contains temporal links, then the parsed execution order is delivered to the presentation manager.

VEVA allows for visual queries in which we can specify the path of a moving object. An example query is shown in Fig. 4–12. The input trajectory can be given as a smoothed trajectory. The visual query given in Fig. 4–12 will select the make of those cars which in the given repository of video sequences perform a trajectory similar to the one drawn by the user. The result of this query is shown in Fig. 4–13.

4.7   Conclusions

The area of digital video processing has seen great improvements as evident by new capture boards and fast processors, but relatively little has been done on how best the information conveyed by video data can be recovered, analyzed, classified, and processed. The problem is that extraction of semantic information from video falls outside the general capabilities of the current machine vision techniques. It has been regarded as a time consuming process, particularly if one hopes to carry it out in an automatic fashion.

The goals of automatic content based modeling and retrieval of digital video are similar to the goals of image understanding. The difference however, is in the rate at which the incoming video signal needs to be processed and in the expected outcome. Decades of image understanding and scene analysis research have made only small steps in being able to describe a single picture. Current research in video modeling is attempting to describe what is happening in hundreds of images. As Bobick wrote in [6], "...one has to be crazy to pursue research in video annotation...," the task of near real-time processing and analyzing video data seems to be far fetched. At the same time, content-based retrieval of video seems to be so deceptively simple, since we humans perform it

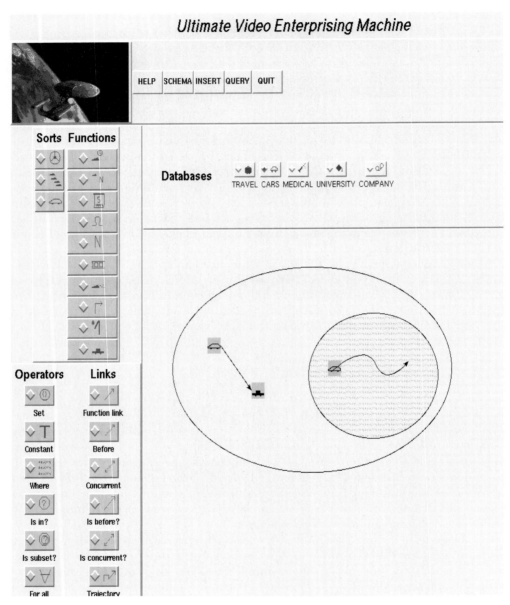

Figure 4-12   Visual query involving a trajectory description.

extremely well without any conscious effort. However, there is as much difference between content based video retrieval and image understanding as there is
between a database system and an intelligent knowledge base [39]. Providing a

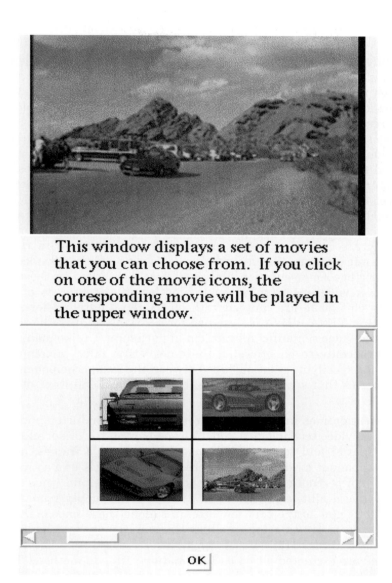

Figure 4-13   Result from the visual query.

means to model video data based on existing database and image understanding technologies is a viable goal, as opposed to pursuing research on a system that can perform the recognition task as well as humans do.

As a consequence, our guiding principle has been to let computers perform quantifiable measurements, and let the application designer attach semantic meaning to these measurements within a single video information model.

Our attempts to address the above needs must start with a modeling mechanism that allows for representing semantic knowledge from spatial and temporal features of the objects in video sequences. Computing high level motion descriptions can be done independently of recognizing objects [1]. More specifically, the recovery of object trajectories can be performed without any prior knowledge of objects undergoing motion. The goal is to have both independent retrieval along with the temporal and the spatial hierarchies as well as retrieval of combined features from the spatial and the temporal hierarchies. We treat motion vectors extracted during motion compensation phase of video encoding as coarse level optical flow that is further used for intermediate and high level motion description. Motion information extraction is then carried out at low level by motion vector detection, at the intermediate level by motion tracing, and the high level by associating an object and a set of trajectories with recognizable activities. In our object motion representations, we provide various levels of precision of trajectory representation. Retrieval functions based on these representations offer a wide spectrum of approximation in the process of matching. Motion representations are coupled with object representation for search and retrieval within VEVA. VEVA is designed for querying multimedia information in general, and video semantic information in particular. Unlike many other proposals that concentrate on browsing the data, VEVA offers a complete set of capabilities for specifying relationships between the image components and formulating queries that search for objects, their motions, and their other associated characteristics.

Our investigations in digital video retrieval were conducted and presented as if the digital video technology had not moved beyond the era of silent films. In addition to spatial and temporal characteristics of video frames, audio is an important component in identifying and recognizing objects and activities in the scene. In human perception, the auditory clues can be helpful when the images do not even give a hint (e.g., the sound of steps in an empty room indicates a walking person). One of the very few attempts along these lines is the Informedia project dedicated to creating intelligent automatic mechanisms for populating digital video library [11], [55]. A transcript is created from the audio track, and keywords are extracted based on information retrieval methods. The identified audio information is combined with relevant video segments to create video "paragraphs." The main idea is to extract relevant information such as specific objects, audio keywords, and relevant video structure which is made possible by integration of techniques in image and language understanding.

In future investigations, one should try to combine clues from various sources, such as text understanding, audio processing, and annotation as complimentary to computer vision and image processing techniques. So far, very little attention has been devoted to solving the video retrieval problem considering both the visual and the auditory domains. Speech recognition techniques and music representation and recognition techniques must be applied in conjunction with image understanding procedures.

References

[1] Allmen, M.C. "Image sequence description using spatiotemporal flow {curves: Toward motion-based recognition," PhD thesis, University of Wisconsin-Madison, 1991.

[2] Allmen, M. and Dyer, C.R., "Computing spatiotemporal relations for dynamic perceptual organization," *CVGIP Image Understanding*, Vol. 58, No. 3, 1993, p. 338.

[3] Arman, F., Depommier, R., Hsu, A., and Chiu, M-Y. "Content-based browsing of video sequences," in *Proceedings of ACM Multimedia '94*, Oct 1994, New York: ACM Press, 1994, pp. 97–103.

[4] Ballard, D.H. and Brown, C.M. *Computer Vision*. Englewood Cliffs, NJ: Prentice Hall, 1982.

[5] Ballard, D.H.,"Parameter nets," *Artificial Intelligence*, Vol 22, No. 3, 1984, pp. 235–267.

[6] Bobick, A.F., "Representational frames in video annotation," in Proceedings of the 27th Annual Conference on Signals, Systems, and Computers, Asilomar, CA, Nov 1993.

[7] Chang, S.K., Yan, C.W., Dimitroff, D.C., and Arndt, T., "An intelligent image database system, *IEEE Transactions on Software Engineering*, Vol. 14, No. 5, 1988, pp. 681–688.

[8] Chang, S.-K. and Hsu, A., "Image information systems: Where do we go from here?" *IEEE Transactions on Knowledge and Data Engineering*, Vol. 4, No. 5, 1992, pp. 431–442.

[9] Chang, S.K., "A methodology for picture indexing and encoding," in *Picture Engineering*, Fu, K.-S. and Kunii, T.L., Eds. Los Alamitos, CA: Springer-Verlag, 1982, pp. 33–53.

[10] Chien, Y.T., "Hierarchical data structures for picture storage, retrieval and classification," in *Pictorial Information Systems*, Chang, S.K. and Fu, K.S., Eds. Springer-Verlag, 1980, pp. 39–74.

[11] Christel, M.G., Stevens, S., Kanade, T, Mauldin, M., Reddy, R., and Wactlar, H., "Techniques for the creation and exploration of digital video libraries" in *Multimedia Tools and Applications*, Vol. 2, Dordrecht, Holland: Kluwer Academic Publishers, 1995.

[12] Davis, M., "Media streams: An iconic visual language for video annotation" in *Proceedings of IEEE Symposium on Visual Languages*, Bergen, Norway, 1993, pp. 196-202.

[13] Dimitrova, N., "An investigation in functional multimedia database languages," Master's thesis, Arizona State University, 1991.

[14] Dimitrova, N. and Golshani, F., "R_x for semantic video database retrieval," in *Proceedings of ACM Multimedia '94,* San Francisco, Oct 1994, New York: ACM Press, 1994.

[15] Dimitrova, N. and Golshani, F., "Motion recovery for video content classification," *ACM Transactions on Information Systems*, Vol. 13, No. 4, Oct 1995, pp. 408–439.

[16] Dimitrova, N., "Content classification and retrieval of digital video based on motion recovery," PhD thesis, Arizona State University, Mar 1995.

[17] Dorst, L., Mandhyan, I., and Trovato, K., "The geometrical representation of path planning problems," *Robotics and Autonomous Systems*, Vol. 7, 1991, pp. 181–195.

[18] Fischer, S., Lienhart, R., and Effelsberg, W., "Automatic recognition of film genres," in *Proceedings of ACM Multimedia '95,* San Francisco, Nov 1995, New York: ACM Press, 1995, pp. 295–304.

[19] Flickner, M. *et al.*, "Query by image and video content: The QBIC System," *IEEE Computer*, Vol. 28, No. 9, Sep 1995, pp. 23–32.

[20] Gabbe, J., Ginsberg, A., and Robinson, B., "Towards intelligent recognition of multimedia episodes in real time applications," in *Proceedings of ACM Multimedia '94,* San Francisco, Oct 1994, ACM Press, 1994, pp. 227–236.

[21] Goddard, N., "The perception of articulated motion: Recognizing moving light displays," PhD thesis, University of Rochester, 1992.

[22] Goguen, J.A., Thatcher, J.W., and Wagner, E., "An initial algebra approach to the specification, correctness and implementation of abstract data types," in *Current Trends in Programming Methodology, Vol. IV* (Yeh, R., Ed.) Englewood Cliffs, NJ: Prentice Hall, 1978, pp. 80–149.

[23] Golshani, F. and Dimitrova, N., "Retrieval and delivery of information in multimedia database systems," *Information and Software Technology*, Vol. 36, No. 4, May 1994, pp. 235–242.

[24] Gong, Y., Zhang, H., Chuan, H.C., and Sakauchi, M., "An image database system with content capturing and fast image indexing abilities," in *Proceedings of the International Conference on Multimedia Computing and Systems*, Boston, MA: IEEE Computer Society Press, 1994, pp.121–130.

[25] Grosky, W. and Mehrotra, R. "Image database management," *IEEE Computer*, Vol. 22, No. 12, 1989, pp. 7–8.

[26] Gudivada, V.N. and Jung, G.S., "Spatial knowledge representation and retrieval in 3-D image databases," in *Proceedings of the International Conference on Multimedia Computing and Systems*, Los Alamitos, CA: IEEE Computer Society Press, 1995.

[27] Gupta, A., Weymouth, T., and Jain, R., "Semantic queries with pictures: The VIMSYS model," in *Conference on Very Large Data Bases*, Barcelona, Sep 1991, pp. 69–79.

[28] Gupta, A., Weymouth, T., and Jain, R., "Semantic queries in image databases," in *Visual Database Systems II*, (Knuth, E. and Wegner, L.M., Eds) Elsevier Science Publishers (North-Holland), 1991, pp. 201–215.

[29] Hampapur, A., Weymouth, T., and Jain, R. "Digital video segmentation," in *Proceedings of ACM Multimedia '94*, San Francisco, CA, Oct 1994, New York: ACM Press, pp. 357–364.

[30] Herschaft, J., "E-Mo: A system for automatically generating emotive-motions," Master's thesis, University of Utah, Salt Lake City, March 1995.

[31] Holtkamp, B., Lum, V.Y., and Rowe, N.C., "DEMOM—A description based media object data model," in *Fourteenth Annual International Computer Software and Application Conference*, 1990, pp. 57–63.

[32] Jagadish, H.V. and O'Gorman, L., "An object model for image recognition," *IEEE Computer*, Vol. 22, No. 12, 1989, pp. 33–41.

[33] Johansson, G. "Spatio-temporal differentiation and integration in visual motion perception," *Psychological Research*, Vol. 38, 1976, pp. 379–393.

[34] Joseph, T. and Cardenas, A.F., "PICQUERY: A high level query language for pictorial database management," *IEEE Transaction on Software Engineering*, Vol. 14, No. 5, 1988, pp. 630–638.

[35] Kasturi, R. and Jain, R. "Dynamic vision" in *Computer Vision: Principles*, Los Alamitos, CA: IEEE Computer Society Press, 1991, Chap. 6.

[36] Koller, D., Weber, J., and Malik, J. "Robust multiple car tracking with occlusion reasoning," Tech. report csd-93-780, EECS Dept., University of California at Berkeley, Nov 1993.

[37] Kubota, H., Okamoto, Y., Mizoguchi, H., and Kuno, Y., "Vision processor system for moving-object analysis," *Machine Vision and Applications*, Vol. 7, 1993, pp. 37–43.

[38] LeGall, D., "MPEG: A video compression standard for multimedia applications," *Communications of the ACM*, Vol. 34, No. 4, 1991, pp. 46–58.

[39] Lenat, D.B. and Guha, R.V., *Building Large Knowledge Based Systems*, Reading, MA: Addison-Wesley, 1990.

[40] Little, T.D.C., Ahanger, G., Folz, R.J., Gibbon, J.F., Reeve, F.W., Schelleng, D.H., and Venkatesh, D., "A digital on-demand video service supporting content-based queries," in *Proceedings of ACM Multimedia '93*, Anaheim, CA, Aug 1993, New York: ACM Press, pp. 427–436.

[41] Marr, D., *Vision*, Cambridge, MA: MIT Press, 1978.

[42] Michael, N., "VEENA—A visual query language," Master's thesis, Arizona State University, 1994.

[43] Mohan, L. and Kashyap, R.L., "An object-oriented knowledge representation for spatial information," *IEEE Transaction on Software Engineering*, Vol. 14, No. 5, 1988, pp. 675–681.

[44] Nagasaka, A. and Tanaka, Y., "Automatic video indexing and full-video search for object appearances," in *Visual Database Systems, II*, (Knuth, E. and Wegner, L.M., Eds.) Elsevier Science Publishers (North-Holland), 1992, pp.113–127.

[45] Oomoto, E. and Tanaka, K., "OVID: design and implementation of a video-object database system," *IEEE Transactions on Knowledge and Data Engineering*, Vol. 5, No. 4, 1993, pp. 629–643.

[46] Orenstein, J.A. and Manola, F.A. "PROBE spatial data modeling and query processing in an image database application," *IEEE Transaction on Software Engineering*, Vol. 14, No. 5, 1988, pp. 611–629.

[47] Otsuji, K. and Tonomura, Y. "Projection detection filter for video cut detection," in *Proceedings of ACM Multimedia '93*, Anaheim, CA, Aug 1993, New York: ACM Press, pp. 251–257.

[48] Ozkarahan, E., "Multimedia document retrieval," *Journal of Information Processing and Management*, Vol. 31, No. 1, 1995, pp. 113–131.

[49] Patel, K., Smith, B.C., and Rowe, L.A., "Performance of a software MPEG video decoder," in *Proceedings of ACM Multimedia '93*, Anaheim, CA, Aug 1993, New York: ACM Press, pp. 75–82.

[50] Rabitti, F. and Stanchev, P., "GRIM DBMS: a GRaphical IMage DataBase Management System," in *Visual Database Systems*, (Kunii, T.L., Ed.) Elsevier Science Publishers, 1989, pp. 415–430.

[51] Rohr, K., "Towards model-based recognition of human movements in image sequences," *CVGIP: Image Understanding*, Vol. 59, No. 1, Jan 1994, pp. 94-115.

[52] Roussopoulos, N., Faloutsos, C., and Sellis, T. "An efficient pictorial database system for PSQL," *IEEE Transactions on Software Engineering*, Vol. 14, No. 5, 1988, pp. 651–658.

[53] Schalkoff, R.J., *Digital Image Processing and Computer Vision*. New York: John Wiley and Sons, 1989.

[54] Smith, B., "Fast software processing of motion JPEG video" in *Proceedings of ACM Multimedia '94*, San Francisco, Oct 1994, New York: ACM Press, pp. 77–88.

[55] Smith, M.A. and Christel, M.G., "Automating the creation of digital video library," in *Proceedings of ACM Multimedia '95*, San Francisco, Nov 1995, New York: ACM Press, pp. 357–358.

[56] Swanberg, D., Shu, C.-F., and Jain, R., "Knowledge guided parsing in video databases," in *Image and Video Processing Conference; Symposium on Electronic Imaging: Science & Technology*, IS&T/SPIE, Vol 1908, San Jose, CA, Feb 1993, pp. 13–24.

[57] Teodosio, L. and Bender, W. "Salient video stills: Content and context preserved," in *Proceedings of ACM Multimedia '93*, Anaheim, CA, Aug 1993, New York: ACM Press, pp. 39–46.

[58] Teodosio, L. and Mills, M., "Panoramic overviews for navigating real-world scenes," in *Proceedings of ACM Multimedia '93*, Anaheim, CA, Aug 1993, New York: ACM Press, pp. 359–364.

[59] Wadge, W.W. and Ashcroft, E.A., *Lucid: The Dataflow Language*. New York: Academic Press, 1985.

[60] Weiss, R., Duda, A., and Gifford, D.K., "Composition and search with a video algebra," *IEEE Multimedia*, Vol. 2, No. 1, Spring 1995, pp. 12–25.

[61] Wieringa, R.J., "Algebraic foundations for dynamic conceptual models, PhD thesis, Vrije Universiteit te Amsterdam, 1990.

[62] Zabih, R., Miller, J., and Mai, K., "A feature-based algorithm for detecting and classifying scene breaks," in *Proceedings of ACM Multimedia '95*, San Francisco, Nov 1995, New York: ACM Press, pp. 189–200.

[63] Zhang, H.J., Gong, Y., Smoliar, S., and Tan, S.Y., "Automatic parsing of news video," in *Proceedings of the International Conference on Multimedia Computing and Systems*, Boston, May 1994, Los Alamitos, CA: IEEE Computer Society Press, pp. 45–54.

Video Segmentation for Video Data Management

Nilesh V. Patel and Ishwar Sethi

Vision & Neural Networks Laboratory
Computer Science Department
Wayne State University
Detroit, Michigan 48202
{nip, sethi}@cs.wayne.edu

Mandala Sciences Inc. decides to produce a year video of NBA 1996 games showing best events of the play such as fascinating baskets and three pointers, rebounding, offensive, and defensive plays. There are 29 teams in the NBA playing 82 pre-season games and 91 playoff games. This adds up to 1280 total games per season. Counting approximate game times of 3 hours requires browsing of 3840 hours of video sequentially on a video player to locate exciting events of the year. If the random access facility is provided with a properly indexed search for the great plays of the games, the task could be completed in few days. However the later facilities are not completely available.[1]

This example just illustrates one of the applications which demand the need for a sophisticated *Video Data Management System* with an ability to retrieve a video based on its content. *Content-based search* is a frequently used term in visual data management system. It is the ability to recall events based on their content information. A computerized system with such a capability is called *Visual Information Management System (VIMS)*. Video information management is a member of the VIMS family. This chapter introduces the reader to

---

[1] Inspired by [1].

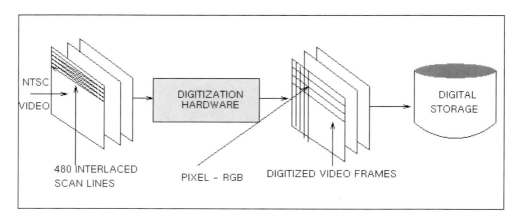

Figure 5-1   Video digitization process.

different issues in handling video data and discusses one of its component, *Video Segmentation*, in detail.

5.1   Digital Video Representation

Understanding of *Video Data Management System (VDMS)* requires knowledge of digital video representation in computer. The discussion can be divided into two parts: video digitization and digital video compression.

Digitization

Fig. 5–1 shows the basic digitization scheme for digital video. The digitization process uses specialized video grabber hardware to capture the analog video signal into digital form. The NTSC video standard provides 60 interlaced fields/ sec of analog video. Each field consists of 240 horizontal scan lines which in the interlaced mode produces 480 scan lines, 30 frame/sec video. The digitization hardware samples the scan line analog signal and produces a digital value. Every scan line is sampled for 640 times producing a 640×480 sample rectangular grid digital video frame. The sampling rate and frame rates are hardware dependent which again depends on the cost. The digitized samples are called pixels which represent the brightness and color information in the image. The detailed representation of digital video is shown in Fig. 5–2. It is clear that video consists of frames and a frame consists of pixels. Video frames are a function of time while the pixels are a function of spatial coordinates. This gives us two representations: $S_{x,y}(t)$ and $P(x,y)$ where $S_{x,y}$ is video frame at temporal position t

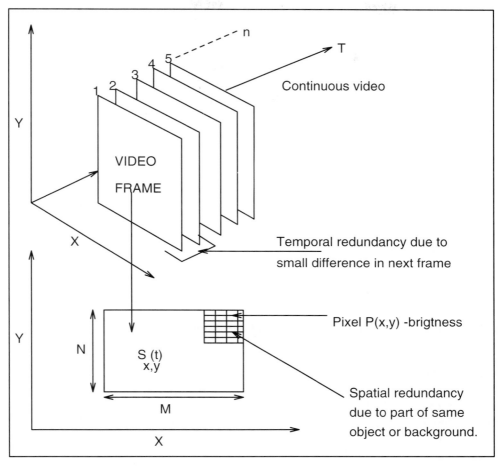

Figure 5–2 Representation of digital video.

and P is pixel at spatial position (x,y). Each pixel is defined by three color components for the color video or one brightness component for the gray (black and white) video. Each color/brightness component is enumerated in the range of 0–255, requiring eight bit or one byte representation. Considering a full frame rate (30 frame/sec), full resolution (640×480 pixels), and true color (RGB/pixel) video for digitization requires 27,648 Mbytes of memory per second. Such large and fast memory disk arrays are very expensive. A solution to the problem is provided by data compression techniques. Most of these exploit some characteristic of underlying data and remove the redundancy from it. Our next section on the MPEG compression standard describes these facts in more detail.

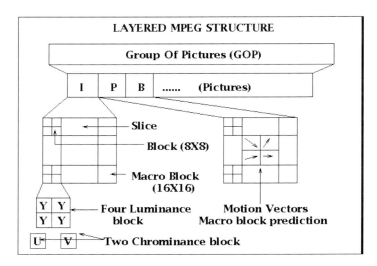

Figure 5-3   The layered structure of MPEG encoding

Compression

Digital compression technology has made a major contribution in the growth of multimedia information systems. Many video compression standards are accepted by the computer industry. These include the MPEG compression standard from the Motion Picture Expert Group, AVI from Microsoft Corp., QT from Apple Computer Inc., DVI from Intel Corp., and many more. The MPEG video compression standard is gaining more popularity due to its design based on the current needs and future developments in the video technology (HDTV). A brief review of the MPEG compression standard will enhance the following discussion and clarify underlying concepts.

MPEG Video Compression Standard

The MPEG[2] group was formed in 1988 to generate standards for digital video and audio compression. The MPEG standard defines a compressed bit stream, which implicitly defines a decompresser. All compression standards utilize the redundant information available in the data stream (video or audio) to aid compression and so does MPEG. Since audio compression is out of the scope of this chapter we will only concentrate on the MPEG digital video compression standard. Continuous motion video contains spatial as well as temporal redundancy. The spatial redundancy is characterized by neighboring pixels in a single frame, which is encoded by 8×8 DCT block coding followed by Huffman encoding in the MPEG standard. Temporal redundancy is due to the fact that the video is

---

[2] Consider MPEG I and II only.

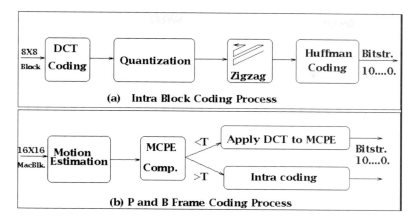

Figure 5-4   The coding scheme for I, P, and B frames.

composed of smaller clips, which are continuous in nature. The notion of block matching and motion vector estimation is used to avoid coding of temporally repeated blocks. The discussion in this section is limited to a brief overview of MPEG structure.

Structural Hierarchy of MPEG

The MPEG video stream has a hierarchical layered structure as shown in Fig. 5–3. The top level layer is denoted as Group Of Pictures (GOP), which consists of different types of encoded frames. These include one I (Intra), M number of P (Prediction), N number of B (Bidirectionally predicted), and D (DC) frames. The GOP is the basic chunk which provides random access to the video stream in MPEG. In turn, each I frame is the first frame available for random access. We will restrict ourself to I, P, and B types of frame encoding because most of the shareware and commercial software has I, B, and P frame encoding capability only.

The next level encoding is done for each individual frame. The first frame of each GOP is an I frame. It is followed by interleaved P and B frames until the end of the GOP. Better understanding of the encoding process of I, P, and B frames gives a greater insight on how one can utilize encoded information directly for processing purposes. The details of encoding of I, P, and B frames are shown in Fig. 5–4. Each individual color frame is first converted to YUV color space, where the first component (Y) gives the luminance information and the remaining two (U and V) give the chrominance information. The chrominance component of each frame is decremented by half in the X and Y direction. It has been shown that decimation of the chrominance channels does not reduce the image quality for natural scenes by a noticeable amount.

The I, P, or B frames are further decomposed into smaller units called macro blocks (16×16 pixels) and micro blocks (8×8 pixels). The horizontal stripe consisting of all aligned macro blocks is called a slice. A slice is used for predicting the DC component of each block in it. Each macro block in an image is composed of four micro blocks. All the blocks in an I type frame are encoded by Discrete Cosine Transformation (DCT). P and B frames are encoded at macro block level by estimating the motion vectors of individual macro blocks.

Intraframe Encoding

As discussed earlier, the spatial redundancy is organized by applying Discrete Cosine Transformation to each 8×8 size block in the image. Intra frame encoding is accomplish by dividing the entire image into 8×8 blocks. The basic schema for I frame encoding is shown in Fig. 5–4(a). The basic equation for the DCT is,

$$D_{u,v} = \frac{1}{4} C_u C_v \sum_{x=0}^{7} \sum_{y=0}^{7} D_{x,y} \cos\left[\frac{(2x+1)u\pi}{16}\right] \cos\left[\frac{(2y+1)v\pi}{16}\right]$$

where

$$C_u, C_v = \begin{cases} \frac{1}{2} & \text{if } (u,v) = (0,0) \\ 1 & \text{otherwise} \end{cases}$$

$D_{u,v}$ is a target cell of DCT coefficient, and $D_{x,y}$ is a target cell of a raw block.

The quantization and zigzag coding is applied to the transformed block to reduce the number of bits and organize the block in a way that it can be efficiently run length encoded [2]. The quantization converts most high-frequency components in the block to zero while maintaining the least error in encoding of low-frequency components. The zigzagging process organizes the quantized data suited for runlength encoding. The variable length coding (VLC) is done by Huffman encoding, using fixed tables. The DCT coefficients have a special two-dimensional Huffman table in that one code specifies a run-length of zeros and the non-zero value that ended the run.

P and B Frame Encoding

The P and B frames are encoded by motion prediction using the previous frame (in P type) or using previous and future frames (in B type). It is done at the macro block level in the luminance (Y) channel. Every macro block in the current frame is searched for the closest match in the previous or future frame. Many different search techniques have been proposed for this task. The Motion Compensated Prediction Error (MCPE) is then computed for each macro block. If MCPE exceeds a certain threshold, then all the blocks in that macro block are intra (I) coded as described earlier; otherwise difference is intra (I) coded and transmitted

Characteristic	Video data	Alphanumeric data
Symbol set	Finite	Infinite
Resolution	Low	High
Interpretation Ambiguity	Low	high
Interpretation Efforts	Low	High
Data Volume	Small	Large
Similarity Measure	Well Defined	Ill Defined

Table 5–1 Comparative characteristics of alphanumeric and video data.

along with motion vector. Motion vectors also provide intermediate information for many video parsing algorithms.

5.2   Video Databases

Organization of video information is a complex and challenging problem. The complexity of the problem arises from the fact that video is non-alphanumeric data with spatiotemporal structure. Besides this video information requires large storage capacity and fast processing facility. A comparative study of video and alphanumeric data will enhance our discussion on its management issues.

Characteristics of Video Data

A very informative discussion on the characteristics of video data can be found in [1]. A list of different features of video and alphanumeric data is given in Table 5–1 [1].

All the existing database systems deal with alphanumeric data which uses a finite symbol set for description of an object. On the other hand video uses virtually infinite symbols during its production process.

It is said that an image is worth 1000 words and a video is worth 1000 paragraphs. This illustrates the amount of information embedded in image and video data. Resolution of any media is defined as information included in its representation technique. Textual data, obviously, contains a very low resolution while the video contains high-resolution information.

Psychological studies have shown that content representation of visual information depends on human perception about that scene. It is true that a scene has more interpretation than the number of pixels composing the scene. In

Level	Granularity	Descriptive features
Video	meta	concept, producer, director...
Episode	macro	events description...
Clip or Shot	mini	action, talk, goal...
Frame	micro	object and its spatial relationship...

Table 5–2 Structural granularity of video data.

a nutshell, visual information contains lots of interpretation ambiguity than textual information. These also requires more effort in generating automatic content information from the visual media.

The size requirements for video information are already discussed in the Digitization section (page 140). A small video clip requires a large storage space which is not the case for alphanumeric data. But the most important difference between these two objects is similarity description. In cases of textual data, similarity is well defined and it is relatively easy to achieve. This is not the scenario for visual information due to the infinite symbol set. Exact similarity is impossible to achieve in a visual information search unless it is depicted in textual form through its content information and used as a search mechanism.

Video Databases: What Is Needed?

Any data management system requires two basic operations. The first is suitable data structuring for its representation and organization. The second is data indexing and retrieval. Every database application requires a choice of suitable data structures for its representation. Video databases also require an application-specific choice of data representation scheme. Indexing of the data objects deals with key feature identification and labeling of the objects. Content-based indexing has been shown great acceptance in video indexing techniques. Retrieval is a process of querying and accessing a particular object from a large collection.

Data Representation

The spatio-temporal nature of the video data requires spacial attention. The conventional data structuring methods are not readily applicable here. Video can be represented at multiple levels. Table 5–2 shows its granularity at different levels of representation. At the top level video can be seen as a single raw object which can be described through its concept, producer, director, musician, participants, type, etc. This is similar to keeping video as a book in the library database using some of its global characteristic features. The video as a whole can be accessed using one or more such features. It is useful to have a global description but not sufficient. The accessibility of internal events still requires sequential search. Episode level video structuring can provide such facility. Here temporal video can be divided along the time axis where different episodes or events occur. An episode of a video can be viewed as a chapter of a book which describes multiple events in a small chronologic era, i.e., a court drama of day one. This is a macro representational granularity of video data. The separation of video into such a meaningful episode is a difficult task. The best way to achieve such fragmentation is by first dividing it into atomic units called clips or shots. A clip or shot in a video refers to collection of contiguous video frames depicting the same action in time and space. A video clip provides a mini granularity of video data. The task of achieving such granularity is called video segmentation. Once the segments of video scenes are identified they can be indexed for a future search mechanism. Since video clips contains continuous recordings of a scene, the task of content identification is relatively easier than that of an episode. The video clips can be indexed using many characteristics and features. Further more similar indexed video clips can be grouped to generate an episode-level description also. The last level of granularity in video structuring is individual frames. No effort is needed to do frame separation in digital video. Such a separation is meaningful for indexing based on the presence of objects and their spatial relationship in the frame. For a video data what is happening in a clip is very important and hence object-level indexing can be combined with events to generate more precise object and related action indexing.

Video Data Indexing

Once the videos are decomposed into smaller atomic units, they require suitable labels for future search and retrieval process. The process of labeling the video clips based on their content information is called *Video Indexing*. It is a very important module of video database management systems. A hierarchical decomposition of video object and a partial list of indices for each level are shown in Fig. 5–5. The global indices such as type of the video (sports, movie, music, news etc.), cast (actors, players, singers, etc.), producer, and director can be used for searching an entire video from a large collection. The episode level indices such as content (drama, court scenes, climax) or intent can be used for an internal search of a video. The shot level classification can be utilized for video-editing-related queries or relational grouping of small clips. The frame classification provides very fine granularity which carries relatively less significance. Content- and similarity-based video indexing are the most popular techniques in video databases.

Content-based indexing   Content-based indexing is based on human psychology of remembering and recollecting information. Studies show that humans recall information through its content. For example, we try to recall a person by their description such as tall, gray hair, blue eyes, long nose, etc. Here

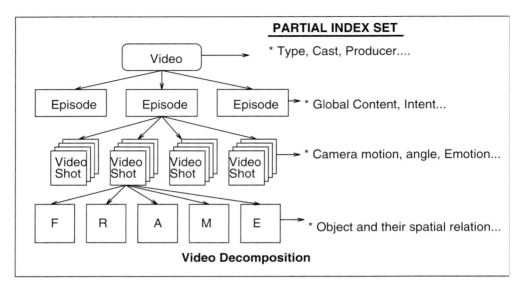

Figure 5-5 Hierarchical video decomposition and feature indexing.

the tallness, gray hair, or blue eyes are the content or features of the subject. Extraction of such descriptive contents from a video sequence is a called content identification and its use in the video labeling process is known as content-based indexing.

Content-based video indexing can be achieved using manual, semiautomatic, or fully automatic approach. Some example systems are: Athena Muse and Eva [3], [4], [5], [6], Virtual Video Browser [7], Video Database Browser [8], Media Stream [9]. The interactive video editing tools [3] provide tools to browse, search, select, and annotate the scenes, clips, and shots. The retrieved shots can be reorganized and reinserted in the database with new annotation and cross-referencing with the main database. Athena Muse was designed to create a highly interactive learning environment. Eva is a manual annotator system which allows researchers live annotation during an experiment. The label for annotations is generated prior to the experiment. Video annotations can be also done based on their temporal signature (Camera work) [10], [11], [12], [13], [14], [15], [16] or range of the shots (long- or short-distance camera shots) [17].

Similarity-based indexing   Similarity-based indexing and retrieval techniques in video databases are natural extensions to the image database's similarity retrieval research [18], [19], [20], [21], [22]. Video also inherits all the image properties and therefore work in image databases can be considered as a stepping stone towards video databases. Similar to image databases, many techniques have been proposed to accept visual queries in video databases [23],

ABRUPT SCENE CHANGE SEQUENCE

Figure 5–6   Frame sequence with abrupt scene change.

[15], [24], [25], [26], [27]. These indexing schemes make use of feature-based indexing, i.e., features of temporal activities such as track, shape, and color features of an object. The video database keeps feature information in a vector form. Any similarity query first extracts the relevant feature vector from the queried object and searches for the most closest feature vector in the database.

5.3 Video Segmentation

One way of finding video segments is by determining the boundaries between consecutive camera shots. A *shot* or *take* in video parlance refers to a contiguous recording of one or more video frames depicting a continuous action in time and space [28]. During a shot, the camera may remain fixed, or it may exhibit one of the characteristic motions: panning, tilting, zooming, or tracking. In recent years, methods for automatic determination of cut points to isolate shots in a video have received considerable attention due to many practical applications. As discussed earlier in video databases the isolation of shots is of interest because the shot level organization of video documents is considered most appropriate for video browsing and content-based retrieval [29], [3], [30]. Shots also provide a convenient level for the study of styles of different filmmakers. A statistical characterization of a video is also possible in terms of different attributes of a shot, for example, shot length, shot type—close shot, medium shot, and long shot, and camera movement in the shot. Such a characterization is useful to differentiate between the styles of different moviemakers [31]. A characterization of this nature can also provide a way of clustering video documents at a global level. Shot isolation is also needed in the coloration of black and white movies where each shot has its own gray-to-color mapping table.

The isolation of shots in a video is relatively easy when the transition from one shot to another consists of visually abrupt straight cuts or camera breaks as shown in Fig. 5–6. This can be accomplished by simply examining frame-to-frame intensity differences at the pixel level. However, this simple approach is susceptible to intensity differences caused by camera movement, noise, and illumination changes. A sample sequence of illumination changes and changes due to motion is shown in Fig. 5–7. In many cases, the transition between two shots is made through an temporal cut—a fade in, fade out, dissolve, or wipe as shown

SPECIAL EFFECT (FLASHING LIGHT OR CAMERA EXPOSER)

CHANGE DUE TO CAMERA MOTION

Figure 5-7   Effect of illumination and camera motion.

FADE IN BLACK SEQUENCE

FADE OUT FROM BLACK SEQUENCE

DESOLVE SEQUENCE

Figure 5-8   Video frames of different temporal scene transitions.

in Fig. 5–8. This is done to obtain a smooth visual transition which is considered more pleasing to the viewer. These temporal cuts, many times referred to as optical or gradual cuts, span several frames. Such cuts are difficult to isolate through the frame-to-frame intensity difference types of approaches and require some kind of global level characterization of each frame for comparison purposes.

The recent work on video segmentation, which has been driven by video databases and multimedia applications, can be grouped into two categories. The first category consists of video segmentation methods that use frame difference

[32], [14], and the second category consists of methods that detect scene changes using image histograms [33], [34].

Frame Difference Techniques

Work on frame difference signals can be tracked back to the pioneering work of Seyler [35] who first systematically studied the nature of frame difference signals and showed that the gamma distribution provides a good fit to the probability density function of frame difference signals. Following Seylor's work, Coll and Choma [36] performed an extensive experimental study of frame difference signals using four different types of videos: a sports video with lots of camera movement, an action video using a variety of camera techniques, a talk-show video with constant background and little camera motion, and an animated cartoon video with small figures moving against a fixed background.

A simple frame difference can be obtained by computing the pixel-to-pixel frame difference of two consecutive frames. Let the two adjacent video frames be $S_{xy}(t)$ and $S_{xy}(t+1)$. The difference frame $D_{xy}(t)$ can be computed as

$$D_{x,y}(t) = (\|S_{x,y}(t) - S_{x,y}(t+1)\|)\forall x, y \in S$$

Fig. 5–9 shows the pixel-to-pixel frame difference of two frames coming from the same scene and the frames coming from different scenes. The black portion in the image illustrates the small change in that part while the white region shows the large change. It is clear from Fig. 5–9 that a difference frame is a good measure of scene change detection. The use of frame differencing for scene change detection is motivated by the fact that neighboring video frames contain similar information until a scene changes. Many variants of the basic frame differencing scheme are used by researchers to segment the video. The difference measure is computed either with pixel-by-pixel comparison on entire frames or only on certain windows of interest in frames.

Otsuji, Tonomura and Ohba [32] utilized the number of pixels undergoing changes from one frame to the next for finding cut points. This can be achieved by taking the difference of sub-sampled images and thresholding at a suitable value. Let $S_{xy}(t)$ is a sub-sampled image at time t. The interframe difference coefficient, ID_{sum}, can be calculated as,

$$ID_{sum} = \sum_{\forall x, y \in S} 1, \text{ if } (\|S_{x,y}(t) - S_{x,y}(t-1)\| \geq T_d)$$

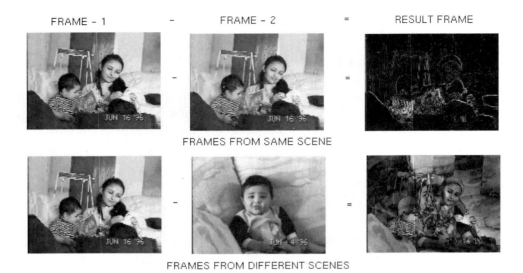

Figure 5-9   Frame differencing results.

The actual decision for cut point is taken by evaluating ID_{sum} quantity over three frames as,

$$Cut = \begin{cases} \text{True} & \text{if } (\|ID_{sum}(K) - ID_{sum}(K-1)\| \geq T_d) \\ & \text{and } (\|ID_{sum}(K) - ID_{sum}(K+1)\| \geq T_b) \\ \text{False} & \text{otherwise} \end{cases}$$

where T_a and T_b are suitable threshold quantities. The pure interframe difference cannot cope with noise, minor illumination changes, and camera motion. To improve performance, several modifications to the basic scheme of frame-by-frame comparison have been proposed. These include a five-frame comparison scheme [32] and a twin-comparison approach [14] which also performs motion analysis to check whether an actual transition has occurred.

Histogram Techniques

The interframe difference is susceptible to noise, illumination changes, and camera motion. Some global description of video frames is required to avoid such sensitivity. The histogram of a video frame provides a global description about the appearance of an image. Many video segmentation algorithms use this feature for finding the cut points in a video stream. A histogram can be computed by measuring probability distribution of pixel values in the entire image. Let us

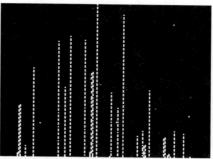

VIDEO FRAME AND ITS HISTOGRAM

Figure 5-10   Video frame and its histogram.

identify the pixel values by notation i, which ranges from 0–255. If there are total N pixels in the image I, the normalized histogram quantity, H_i, can be computed by the following expression

$$H_i = \frac{1}{N} \sum_{x, y \in 1} \delta(x, y)$$

$$\delta(x, y) = \left(\begin{array}{l} 1 \;\; \text{if } D_{x, y} = i \\ 0 \;\; \text{otherwise} \end{array} \right.$$

Fig. 5–10 shows the video frame and its histogram. Fig. 5–11 also shows histograms of the images used in the frame difference example of Fig. 5–8. The difference in the shape of the histogram is evident in different video frames coming from different scenes. The histogram of video frames are used in various ways to identify the changes in video frames.

In a work on shot detection, Tonomura [34] used the absolute sum of the difference of intensity histograms. The quantity is then compared to a suitable threshold for cut identification.

$$Cut = \left(\begin{array}{l} \text{True} \;\; \text{if} \left(\sum_{i = 0}^{255} \|H(t + \nabla t) - H(t)\| \geq T_h \right) \\ \text{False} \;\; \text{otherwise} \end{array} \right.$$

where $H(t)$ and $H(t + \nabla t)$ are histograms of the frame at time t and time $(t + \nabla t)$. He assumed that brightness distribution is related to the image, which only changes if the image changes. He also argued that small object motions gets suppressed by computing the histogram difference.

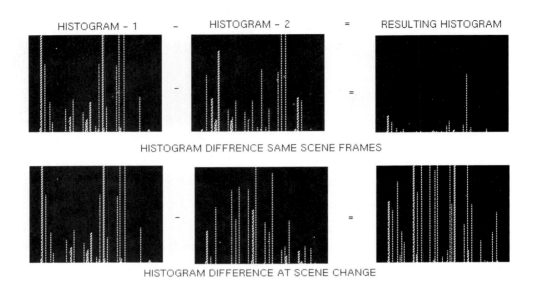

Figure 5-11   Frame histogram differencing.

In a different experiment use of color histograms has been explored by Nagasaka and Tanaka [33]. They used the color correlation between two frames in limited color space to identify scene change. The video frames are first divided into m square blocks of pixels. The video segment is detected by applying a suitable threshold to the block correlation. The correlation is established using the following expression,

$$C_m(t) = \frac{1}{K}\sum_{i=0}^{K}\frac{(H_{m,i}(t) - H_{m,i}(t-1))^2}{H_{m,i}(t-1)}$$

where m represents the block index, K is the number of colors used, and $H_{m,i}$ is the histogram for color i. Nagasaka's method then sorts all the correlation values and utilizes the first eight lowest values to get a summed correlation quantity, C_{SUM}. The cut point is detected if,

$$Cut = \left\{ \begin{array}{ll} \text{True} & \text{if } (C_{SUM} \geq T_H) \\ \text{False} & \text{otherwise} \end{array} \right.$$

Ueda *et al.* [37] use the same method by applying a threshold on 48 blocks and counting the number of blocks over the threshold. Methods using measures on intensity histogram differencing seem to perform relatively better but are still poor at detecting optical cuts. These modifications in the basic comparison scheme generally involve a fair amount of additional computation and thus limit the appeal of these methods for large video segments. Gargi and Devadiga [38], [39] tried to study the best color space suitable for video segmentation. They used the weighted summation of the difference of histogram difference and histogram intersection over a specified neighborhood in *RGB, HSV, YIQ, L*a*b*, L*u*v*,* and Munsell color space. Their computation is based on the following formula,

$$H_D(i) = H_1(i) - H_2(i)$$

$$H_I(i) = 1.0 - \sum \frac{MIN[H_1(i), H_2(i)]}{MAX[H_1(i), H_2(i)]}$$

$$T_C = \sum_i \sum_{j \in N(i)} W(j) * [H_D - H_I]$$

where H_1 and H_2 are the color histograms of two consecutive video frames, H_D is the histogram difference, H_I is the inverted histogram intersection and T_C is the cut coefficient. A suitable threshold was chosen to detect the cut points.

Aigrain and Joly [40] combined the knowledge of frame difference and histogram to identify different cut types. Their method is based on the modeling of the distribution of pixel differences. Using this model, they estimate the nature of the difference histogram for different kinds of cuts. These estimates are then used to locate cuts in a given video.

In addition to the above methods, some recent methods have shown the use of model-based schemes for improved shot detection. Swanberg, Shu, and Jain [41] used a model of the knowledge pertaining to video content that is created and used for cut detection. Zhang *et al.* [42] have also used this approach to parse news videos. In a similar work, Hampapur [1] used a different model of scene change to detect the shot boundary.

The enormous volume of the video data has also concerned many researchers about the video processing time. Many algorithms for video segmentation have used compressed video manipulation techniques. Patel and Sethi [43] have also shown the computation of basic features such as histograms and frame differencing directly from compressed video. Interested readers should consult [44], [45], [46], [47], [48], [49], and [50] for further reading.

5.4   Statistical Method for Video Segmentation

Our approach to scene change detection is based upon the following considerations:

- Within the same shot, a frame may differ from its neighboring frames due to one or more of the following factors: object movement, camera movement, focal length changes, and lighting changes. The scene change detection process should ignore, as far as possible, such frame-to-frame changes within a shot. One way to achieve this is to perform large spatial averaging on frame data prior to scene change detection.

- To minimize further the effect of frame-to-frame changes within a shot, the change detection process should be applied at a frame description level which takes into account information present in the entire frame. The intensity and color histograms of the entire frame provide such a descriptive level which is simple and easy to compute. Our experimental experience indicates that the intensity histogram representation of a frame is enough for scene change detection.

- To perform accurate shot boundary detection, the knowledge of the shot type is essential. A shot type refers to the gradation of distances between the camera and the recorded scene [28]. Although there are infinite gradations of distances between the camera and the recorded scene, each shot is generally considered to fit into one of the five basic gradations. These are: close up, close shot, medium shot, full shot, and long shot. These gradations do not imply a fixed measurable distance in each case but are rather defined with respect to the subject being recorded. For example, the close shot of a human subject implies entirely different distances than the close shot of a house. Since the magnitude of frame-to-frame changes within a shot is a function of shot type, e.g., an object movement in a close shot will induce more significant changes, say, in comparison with a medium or long shot, simply comparing the magnitude of changes is not an appropriate approach unless the comparison is normalized with respect to the shot type. Since shot type classification depends upon the distance between the camera and the subject being recorded, e.g., a person, a house, or an automobile, it is clear that this kind of normalization capability without a priori scene knowledge is impossible to achieve.

- Often during the editing process, a longer shot is cut into smaller strips to achieve either *intercutting* with shorter shots or parallel blending with another longer shot [28]. Effectively, such editing steps create false cuts in shots.

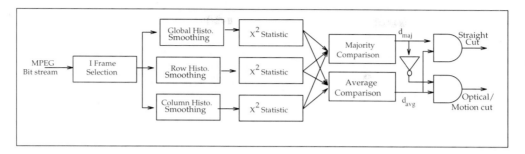

Figure 5-12   The video shot detection scheme.

- In view of above, it is safe to say that false cuts in a scene change detection procedure are natural. Furthermore, false cuts are harmless as the frames within such cuts are still coherent in action and satisfy all the requirements of a shot definition.

- Misdetection of an actual cut is a costly error that should be avoided since a missed cut makes a set of contiguous frames incoherent. Therefore, a scene change detection method should be primarily evaluated on missed cuts and not on false cuts.

- Since videos in digital form occupy an enormous amount of data, it is desirable to be able to detect scene changes in compressed video to reduce the overall processing time.

The block diagram of the shot detection scheme is shown in Fig. 5–12. The input to the system is a bit stream of MPEG video. This bit stream consists of three types of coded frames. These are: intraframes (I frames), predicted frames (P frames), and interpolated bi-directional frames (B frames). The I frames are coded independently of other frames in a video to provide random access to the MPEG bit stream. Each I frame is encoded in JPEG standard. The P frames are encoded relative to a prediction from a past frame—either an I frame or a P frame. The B frames provide the highest amount of compression as these are coded relative to prediction from a past and a future frame.

The first step in our shot detection scheme is the extraction of I frames from the encoded bit stream as we use only I frames for shot detection. This choice is based upon two considerations. First, I frames are the only accessible frames in MPEG video that can be processed independently of other frames. This makes the shot detection scheme fast. Second, I frames generally occur every 12 frames which provides an acceptable sampling rate for shot boundaries considering that the mean interval between shot boundaries varies from 5 to 23 seconds for different TV programs [36]. The downside of considering I frames only is that the shot boundaries are not localized with very high accuracy; however, this can be countered, if needed, by extra postprocessing once the I frames marking shot boundaries are detected.

The second step consists of computing intensity, row, and column histograms. These histograms are computed using the first coefficient of each 8×8 DCT encoded block which represents average block intensity. The row and the column histograms of an I frame with $M \times N$ DCT blocks are defined as:

$$X_i = \frac{1}{M} \sum_{j}^{M} b_{0,0}(i, j)$$

and

$$Y_j = \frac{1}{N} \sum_{i}^{N} b_{0,0}(i, j)$$

respectively, where $b_{0,0}(i,j)$ refers to the DC coefficient of a DCT block in row i and column j. As can be seen from the definitions of these histograms, they carry a certain amount of localized information unlike the intensity histogram which represents purely global information of an image. Thus using these three histograms to compare successive I frames provides a situation where global as well as local distribution of pixel intensity values is taken into account. This results in a high shot detection rate along with a small false alarm rate. To further enhance the shot detection performance, the Gaussian averaging is performed on histograms prior to their use in the chi-square test for comparison. This coupled with the existing block averaging in the DC coefficients of I frame blocks minimizes the sensitivity of our shot detection scheme to intensity changes due to illumination and small motion.

The next step consists of comparing the current I frame intensity, row, and column histograms with those of the previous I frame. This comparison is done by the chi-square test which is the most accepted test for determining whether two binned distributions are from the same source or not. Letting HP_j and HC_j, respectively, represent the jth bin of a histogram pair being compared, the chi-square statistic is given as

$$X^2 = \sum_{j} \frac{(HP_j - HC_j)^2}{(HP_j + HC_j)^2}$$

Applying the chi-square test on three pairs of histograms yields three coefficients which are used to calculate, for each pair, the significance probability that the histogram pair is drawn from the same distribution. This allows us to set decision thresholds at the same value in the interval of 0–1 irrespective of the number of bins in each histogram pair. The computation of significance probability is

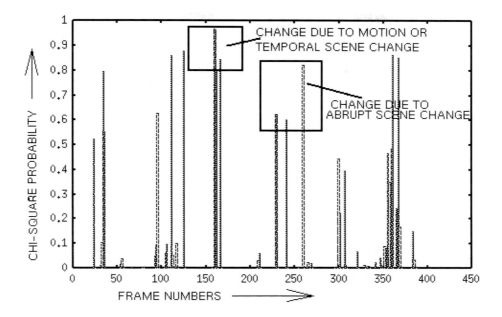

Figure 5-13   Plot of computed probability vs. frame.

done following the procedure given in [51]. The three significance probability values are then used to generate two comparison decisions to suit the differences in straight and optical cuts. First, each significance probability value is compared against a threshold to generate a binary decision. This gives rise to three binary decisions, one for each histogram pair. These are then combined using majority logic to generate the first comparison result. Let it be denoted by d_{maj}. The second comparison result is obtained by checking the average of the three significance probabilities against another threshold. Let this result be denoted by d_{avg}. A straight cut is then detected by the system whenever both d_{maj} and d_{avg} are 1. An optical cut is detected whenever d_{maj} is 0 but d_{avg} is 1. When both d_{maj} and d_{avg} are 0, no shot boundary is indicated at the I frame under consideration. Since an optical cut can span several frames or a shot with large motion over several frames can yield a cut decision spanning two or more I frames, the shot detection system waits for the next I frame before outputting the cut decision on the current I frame. This ensures that multiple cut decisions are not generated for shots with a large motion or a smooth optical cut. An example of this is shown in Fig. 5–13.

5.5   Performance Evaluation

Performance evaluation of video segmentation techniques is a difficult task as there is no standard video sequence extant for comparative study. The performance of segmentation very much depends on the choice of test video. The test videos must supply all possible video edit effects and scene categories. The criterion is difficult to meet, however one could try to make a complete set by including the following types of videos in the experiment.

- Video sequences with abrupt scene changes.
- Video sequences with different edit effects, i.e., fades, wipes, dissolves, etc.
- Video sequences with close-up moving camera/objects.
- Video sequences with moderate range shot and moving camera/objects.
- Video sequence with special effects such as lighting, interleaved shots etc.

Choice of Video

To evaluate the performance of the suggested shot detection scheme, we carried out a study using four different videos of varying characteristics. These videos consist of two music videos and two movie videos. Music video-1 has fast motion in close-ups with optical transitions and special effects. It has 3400 frames containing 60 cuts. Music video-2 is characterized by large camera motion shots. It is a fast-paced video with a variety of camera work and lengthy shots containing 4600 frames and 19 cuts. Movie video-1 contains all kinds of shots including stationary, camera motions, object motions, and smooth optical cuts. It has 7800 frames consisting of 71 cuts. Movie video-2 is a very long video consisting of 17,700 frames with 137 cuts. The video contains a large number of shots with multiple moving objects.

The MPEG encoding of the videos was done through a two-step process. The first step in the encoding process consisted of capturing the videos in DVM (motion JPEG) format on a PC equipped with a True Vision Targa 2000 board. These were then converted to MPEG format using the XingCD MPEG encoder. The MPEG encoding was done with a resolution of 320×240 pixels and an intraframe distance of 12 frames.

Evaluative Criterion

The scene change detection scheme can be evaluated using many parameters. These include shot detection success rate as percent correct detection, detection failure rate as percent miss detection, and over detection as percent false detection. Another way of evaluating the performance is by measuring precision and recall parameters. Let n_c, n_m, and n_f, respectively, be the number of correct,

Video	Total frames	Correct	False	Missed
Music Video-1	3400	57	9	3
Music Video-2	4600	16	4	3
Movie Video-1	7800	66	13	5
Movie Video-2	17700	130	11	7

Table 5–3 Performance of shot detection on different videos: best case results.

missed, and false cuts that are generated by a shot detection scheme. The precision and recall are then defined as

$$Precision = \frac{n_c}{n_c + n_f}$$

and

$$Recall = \frac{n_c}{n_c + n_m}$$

Ideally, both parameters should have a unity value for perfect recall and precision. However, in practice a balance between the two parameters is required.

Results

The performance of our shot detection scheme is shown in Table 5–3 and Fig. 5–14. Table 5–3 lists the best performance that was obtained by adapting the threshold value for each of the four videos. The aggregate performance on the total collection of 33,500 frames with 287 cuts in all is shown in Fig. 5–13 in a graphical form. This performance is given in terms of precision and recall parameters. Viewed from this perspective, we find that the suggested shot detection scheme performs well by balancing precision and recall.

5.6   Summary

In this work, the important problem of video databases is addressed and a solution based on information readily available in compressed video is presented. As the performance of the shot detection scheme suggests, it is possible to locate shot boundaries in MPEG video with a balanced precision and recall

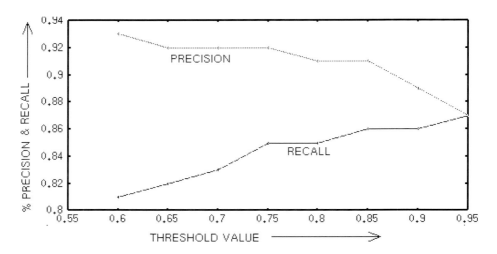

Figure 5-14 Performance of shot detection at various cut-off values for intraframe distance of 12 frames.

performance by making use of global and local histogramming of I frames. As indicated earlier, it is possible to perform additional processing once the I frames at shot boundaries have been detected to more accurately localize the shot boundaries. Furthermore, since all the results were obtained by using gray-level information only, we expect that these results can be improved by considering color information additionally.

Since video is truly a multimedia, we are currently investigating methods to process and incorporate compressed audio information for shot boundary detection as well as for shot indexing. Also, we are exploring the issue of shot characterization in terms of other attributes, such as shot range type and the underlying scene.

References

[1] Hampapur, A., "Designing video data management systems," PhD thesis, The University of Michigan, 1994.

[2] Tekalp, A.M., "Lossless compression" in *Digital Video Processing*, Upper Saddle River, NJ: Prentice Hall, 1995, pp. 348–366.

[3] Mackay, W.E. and Davenport, G., "Virtual video editing in interactive multimedia applications," *Comm. ACM*, Vol. 32, No. 7, July 1989, pp. 802–810.

[4] Hodges, M.E., Sasnett, R.M., and Ackerman, M.S., "A construction set for multimedia applications," *IEEE Software*, Vol. 6, Jan 1989, pp. 37–43.

[5]   Mackay, W.E., "EVA: An experimental video annotator for symbolic analysis of video data," in *SIGCHI Bulletin*, Vol. 21, Oct 1989, pp. 68–71.

[6]   Hodges, M.E. and Sasnett, R.M., "Plastic editors for multimedia documents," in *USENIX Summer*, June 1991, pp. 463–471.

[7]   Little, T.D.C., Ahanger, G., Folz, R.J., Gibbon, J.F., Reeves, F.W., Schellenge, D.H., and Venkatesh, D., "A digital on-demand video service supporting content-based queries," in *Proc. of ACM Multimedia*, San Francisco, Oct 1993, pp. 427–433.

[8]   Rowe, L.A., Boreczky, J.S., and Eads, C.A., "Indexes for use access to large video databases," in *SPIE Proceedings, Storage and Retrieval for Image and Video Databases II*, Vol. 2185, San Jose, CA, 1993.

[9]   Davis, M., "Media Stream: An iconic language for video annotation," in *IEEE Symposium on Visual Languages*, Bergen, Norway, 1993, pp. 196–202.

[10] Abe, S., Tonomura, Y., and Kasahara, H., "Scene retrieval method for video database applications using temporal condition changes," in *Proc. Conference on Machine Intelligence and Vision*, Tokyo, Apr 1989, pp. 355–359.

[11] Tonomura, Y., Akutsu, A., Otsuji, K., and Sadakata, T., "VideoMap and VideoSpace-Icon: Tools for anatomizing video content," in *Proceedings of ACM, INTERCHI'93*, Apr 1993.

[12] Tonomura, Y. and Abe, S., "Content oriented visual interface using video icons for visual database system," *Journal of Visual Languages and Computing*, Vol. 1, No. 1, Mar 1990, pp. 183–198.

[13] Tonomura, Y., Otsuji, K., Akutsu, A., and Ohba, Y., "Stored video handling techniques," *NTT Review*, Vol. 5, No. 2, Mar 1993, pp. 82–90.

[14] Zhang, H., Kankanhalli, A., and Smoliar, S.W., "Automatic partitioning of full-motion video," *Multimedia Systems*, Vol. 1, 1993, pp. 10–28.

[15] Ahanger, G., Benson, D., and Little, T.D.C., "Video query formulation," in *SPIE/IS&T Proceedings on Storage and Retrieval in Image and Video Databases*, Vol. 2420, San Jose, CA, Feb 1995, pp. 280–291.

[16] Mann, S. and Picard, R.W., "'Video Orbits': Characterizing the coordinate transformation between two images using the projective group," Tech. Report 278, M.I.T. Media Lab., 1995.

[17] Hampapur, A., Jain, R., and Weymouth, T.E., "Indexing in video databases," in *SPIE/IS&T Proceedings on Storage and Retrieval in Image and Video Databases*, Vol. 2420, San Jose, CA, Feb 1995, pp. 292–306.

[18] Chang, N.S. and Fu, K.S., "Picture query language for pictorial database systems," *Computer*, Vol. 14, No. 11, Nov 1981, pp. 23–33.

[19] Hamano, T., "A similarity retrieval method for image databases using simple graphics," in *IEEE Workshop on Languages for Automation, Symbolic and Intelligent Robotics*, Aug 1988, pp. 149–154.

[20] Hirata, K. and Kato, T., "Query by visual examples," in *Proc. of Third International Conference on Extending Database Technology*, Vienna, Mar 1992, pp. 56–71.

[21] Bimbo, A.D., Campanai, M., and Nesi, P., "A three-dimensional iconic environment for image database querying," *IEEE Trans. on Software Engineering*, Vol. 19, No. 10, 1993, pp. 997–1011.

[22] Niblack, W., Barber, R., Equitz, W., Flickner, M., Petkovic, D., and Yanker, P., "The QBIC project: Querying image by content using color, texture and shape," in *SPIE/IS&T Proceedings on Storage and Retrieval in Image and Video Databases*, San Jose, CA, Feb 1993.

[23] Arman, F., Depommier, R., Hsu, A., and Chiu, M-Y., "Content-based browsing of video sequences," in *Proc. of ACM Multimedia*, San Francisco, Oct 1994, pp. 97–103.

[24] Yeung, M.M., Yeo, B-L., Wolf, W., and Liu, B., "Video browsing using clustering and scene transitions on compressed sequence," in *SPIE / IS&T Proceedings on Storage and Retrieval in Image and Video Databases*, Vol. 2420, San Jose, CA, Feb 1995, pp. 399–413.

[25] Dimitrova, N. and Golshani, F., "R_x for semantic video database retrieval," in *Proc. of ACM Multimedia*, San Francisco, Oct 1994, pp. 219–226.

[26] Ioka, M. and Kurokava, M., "Estimation of motion vectors and their application to scene retrieval," *Machine Vision and Applications*, No. 7, 1994, pp. 199–208.

[27] Lee, S-Y. and Kao, H-M., "Video indexing—An approach based on moving object and track," in *SPIE Proceedings*, Vol. 1908, pp. 25–36, 1993.

[28] Arijon, D., *Grammar of the Film Language*. Los Angeles: Silman-James Press, 1976.

[29] Davenport, G., Smith, T.A., and Pincever, N., "Cinematic primitives for multimedia," *Computers and Graphics*, Vol. 15, 1991, pp. 67–74.

[30] Smoliar, S.W. and Zhang, H., "Content-based video indexing and retrieval," *IEEE Multimedia*, Vol. 1, No. 2, Apr 1994, pp. 62–72.

[31] Salt, B., "Statistical style analysis of motion pictures," *Film Quarterly*, Vol. 28, 1973, pp. 13–22.

[32] Otsuji, K., Tonomura, Y., and Ohba, Y, "Video browsing using brightness data," in *Proc. SPIE Conf. Visual Communications and Image Processing*, Boston, Nov 1991, pp. 980–989.

[33] Nagasaka, A. and Tanaka, Y., "Automatic video indexing and full-video search for object appearances," in *Proc. 2nd Working Conf. Visual Database Systems*, Budapest, Oct 1991, pp. 119–133.

[34] Tonomura, Y., "Video handling based on structured information for hypermedia systems," in *ACM, Proceedings of the International Conference on Multimedia Information Systems*, Singapore, 1991, pp. 333–344.

[35] Seyler, A.J., "Probability distributions of television frame differences," *Proc. IEEE*, Vol. 53, 1965, pp. 355–366.

[36] Coll, D.C. and Choma, G.K., "Image activity characteristics in broadcast television," *IEEE Trans. Communications*, Vol. 26, 1976, pp. 1201–1206.

[37] Ueda, H., Miyatake, T., Sumino, S., and Nagasaka, A., "IMPACT: An interactive natural-motion-picture dedicated multimedia authoring system," in *Proc. CHI'91,* New Orleans, Apr 1991, pp. 343–350.

[38] Gargi, U., Oswald, S., Cosiba, D., Devadiga, S., and Kasturi, R., "Evaluation of video sequence indexing and hierarchical video indexing," in *SPIE / IS&T Proceedings on Storage and Retrieval in Image and Video Databases—III*, Vol. 2420, San Jose, CA, Feb 1995, pp. 144–151.

[39] Devadiga, S., Cosiba, D., Gargi, U., Oswald, S., and Kasturi, R., "Semiautomatic video database system," in *SPIE / IS&T Proceedings on Storage and Retrieval in Image and Video Databases—III*, Vol. 2420, San Jose, CA, Feb 1995, pp. 262–267.

[40] Aigrain, P. and Joly, P. "The automatic real-time analysis of film editing and transition effects and its applications," *Computers and Graphics*, Vol. 18, 1994, pp. 93–103.

[41] Swanberg, D., Shu, C.F., and Jain, R., "Knowledge guided parsing in video database," in *Proc. IS&T SPIE's Symposium on Electronic Imaging: Science and Technology*, San Jose, CA, 1993.

[42] Zhang, H., Gong, Y., Smoliar, S.W., and Tan, S.Y., "Automatic parsing of news video," in *Proc. IEEE Multimedia Conf.,* Boston, 1994, pp. 45–54.

[43] Patel, N.V. and Sethi, I.K., "Compressed video processing for video segmentation," in *IEE Proceedings: Video, Image and Signal Processing*, in press.

[44] Smith, B.C. and Rowe, L.A., "Algorithms for manipulating compressed images," *IEEE Computer Graphics and Applications*, Vol. 13, No. 5, 1993, pp. 34–42.

[45] Arman, F., Hsu, A.,and Chiu, M-Y, "Image processing on compressed data for large video databases," in *Proc. First ACM International Conference on Multimedia*, Anaheim, CA, Aug 1993.

[46] Zhang, H., Low, C.Y., Gong, Y., and Smoliar, S.W. "Video parsing using compressed data," in *Proc. SPIE Conf. Image and Video Processing II*, Vol. 2182, San Jose, CA, 1994, pp. 142–149.

[47] Deardorff, E., Little, T.D.C., Marshall, J.D., Venkatesh, D., and Wlazer, R., "Video scene decomposition with the motion picture parser," in *IS&T SPIE Symposium on Electronic Imaging Science and Technology,* San Jose, CA, Feb 1994.

[48] Yeo, B-L. and Lui, B., "Rapid scene change detection on compressed video," *IEEE Transactions on Circuits and Systems for Video Technology,* in press.

[49] Juan, Y. and Chang, S-F., "Scene change detection in a MPEG compressed video sequence," in *IS&T SPIE Proceedings: Digital Video Compression Algorithm and Technology,* Vol. 2419, San Jose, CA, Feb 1995.

[50] Liu, H-C.H. and Zick, G.L., "Scene decomposition of MPEG compressed video," in *IS&T SPIE Proceedings: Digital Video Compression Algorithm and Technology,* Vol. 2419, San Jose, CA, Feb 1995.

[51] Press, W.H., Teukolsky, S.A., Vetterling, W.T., and Flannery, B.P., *Numerical Recipes in C*, 2nd Ed. Cambridge: Cambridge University Press, 1992.

Multimedia Interfaces

C H A P T E R **6**

Visual Interfaces to Multimedia Databases

S.K. Chang and M.F. Costabile

Department of Computer Science
University of Pittsburgh
Pittsburgh, PA 15260, USA
Phone +1-412-6248423
chang@cs.pitt.edu

Dipartimento di Informatica
Universitá di Bari
Via Orabona 4
70126 Bari, Italy
Phone +39-80-5443300
fcosta@iesi.ba.cnr.it

6.1 Introduction

Recent advances in storage technologies have made the creation of multimedia databases both feasible and cost-effective. Wideband communications also greatly facilitate the distribution of multimedia information across communication networks. Parallel computers lead to faster voice, image, and video processing systems. High-resolution graphics and dedicated co-processors enable the presentation of visual information with superior image quality. Multimedia information systems have found their way into many application areas, including geographical information systems [30], office

167

automation [40], distance learning [31], health care [41], computer-aided design [2], computer-aided engineering [28], and scientific database applications [1].

Wider applications also lead to both more numerous and more sophisticated end users. Multimedia information systems, like other types of information systems, have increasingly become knowledge-based systems, with capabilities to perform many sophisticated tasks by accessing and manipulating domain knowledge. The above mentioned technological advances dictate a better methodology to design knowledge-based, user-specific multimedia information systems. The design methodology, taking into consideration the diversified application requirements and users' needs, should provide a unified framework for multimedia representation, querying, indexing, and spatial/temporal reasoning.

Multimedia databases, when compared to traditional databases, have the following special requirements [20], [21]:

1. The size of the data items may be very large. The management of multimedia information therefore requires the accessing and manipulation of very large data items.

2. Storage and delivery of video data requires guaranteed and synchronized delivery of data.

3. Various query mechanisms need to be combined, and the user interface should be highly visual and should also enable visual relevance feedback and user-guided navigation.

4. The on-line, real-time processing of large volumes of data may be required for some types of multimedia databases.

The focus of this chapter is on the third requirement mentioned above. For multimedia databases, there are not only different media types, but also different ways to query the databases. The query mechanisms may include free text search, SQL-like querying, icon-based techniques, querying based upon the entity-relationship (ER) diagram, content-based querying, sound-based querying, as well as virtual-reality (VR) techniques. Some of these query mechanisms are based upon traditional approaches, such as free text search ("retrieve all books authored by Einstein") and SQL query language ("SELECT title FROM books WHERE author = Einstein"). Some are developed in response to the special needs of multimedia databases such as content-based querying for image/video databases ("find all books containing the picture of Einstein") [20], and sound-based queries that are spoken rather than written or drawn [48]. Some are dictated by new software/hardware technologies, such as icon-based queries that use icons to denote query targets ("a book") and objects ("a sketch of Einstein"), and virtual reality queries where the query targets and objects can be directly manipulated in a virtual reality environment. Except for the traditional approaches and those relying on sound, the other techniques share the common characteristic of being highly visual. Therefore, we will concern ourselves mainly with multiparadigmatic visual interface to multimedia databases.

A visual interface to multimedia databases, in general, must support some type of visual querying language. Visual query languages (VQLs) are query languages based on the use of visual representations to depict the domain of interest and express the related requests. Systems implementing a visual query language are called Visual Query Systems (VQSs) [3], [7]. They include both a language to express the queries in a pictorial form and a variety of functionalities to facilitate human-computer interaction. As such, they are oriented to a wide spectrum of users, ranging from people with limited technical skills to highly sophisticated specialists. In recent years, many VQSs have been proposed, adopting a range of different visual representations and interaction strategies. These interaction paradigms will be discussed in Section 6.4, but most existing VQSs restrict human-computer interaction to only one kind of interaction paradigm. However, the presence of several paradigms, each one with different characteristics and advantages, will help both naive and experienced users in interacting with the system. For instance, icons may well evoke the objects present in the database, while relationships among them may be better expressed through the edges of a graph, and collections of instances may be easily clustered into a form. Moreover, the user is not required to adapt his or her perception of the reality of interest to the different views presented by the various data models and interfaces.

The way in which the query is expressed depends on the visual representations as well. In fact, in the existing VQSs, icons are typically combined following a spatial syntax [13], while queries on diagrammatic representations are mainly expressed by following links and forms are often filled with prototypical values. Moreover, the same interface can offer to the user different interaction mechanisms for expressing a query, depending on both the experience of the user and the kind of the query itself [6].

To effectively and efficiently access information from multimedia databases, we can identify the following design criteria for the user interface: (1) various query mechanisms need to be combined seamlessly, (2) the user interface should be visual as much as possible, (3) the user interface should enable visual relevance feedback, and (4) the user interface should support user-guided navigation. Addressing these issues, this chapter explores the design of multiparadigmatic visual interfaces to multimedia databases. For the general issues and problem areas in multimedia interface design, the reader is referred to [5]. In Section 6.2, we discuss the visual representation of the information space. Strategies for visual reasoning are surveyed in Section 6.3. Section 6.4 gives a taxonomy of visual querying paradigms, and Section 6.5 deals with multimedia database interaction techniques. Finally, in Section 6.6 we describe an experimental prototype to illustrate the concept of multiparadigmatic visual interface for multimedia databases.

6.2   Representation of the Information Space

In a visual interface for multimedia databases, the information stored in the multimedia database needs to be visualized in an information space. This visualization can either be carried out by the user in the user's mind, in which case it is essentially the user's conceptualization of the database; or the visualization could be accomplished by the system, in which case the visualization is generated on the display screen. In this section we describe the different representations of the information space.

Database objects, in general, are abstracted from real-life objects in the real world. Therefore, we can distinguish the *logical information space* and the *physical information space*. In the logical space, the abstract database objects are represented. In the physical space, the abstract database objects are materialized and represented as physical objects such as images, animation, video, voice, etc. The physical objects either *mimic* real-life objects such as objects in a virtual reality, or *reflect* real-life objects such as diagrams, icons, and sketches.

The real world, from which the database objects are abstracted, is the environment that the database objects must relate to. The real world also is often abstracted in the information space. Only in the virtual reality information space will the real world be represented in a direct way (see later).

The *logical information space* is a multi-dimensional space, where each point represents an object (a record, a tuple, etc.) from the database. A database object, e_j, or an *example*, is a point in this space. Conceptually, the entire information space then corresponds to all the database objects in a database. The logical information space is thus a unified view of the database, i.e., a universal relation.

Each attribute of a database object represents one dimension in this multi-dimensional space. Therefore, in the logical information space, different dimensions actually have different characteristics: continuous, numerical, discrete, or logical.

A *query* q_i is an arbitrary region in this information space. A *clue* x_k is also an arbitrary region in the logical information space, but it may contain additional directional information to indicate *visual momentum*, such as the direction of browsing. Therefore, an example e_j is a clue. A visual query q_i is also a clue.

The information retrieval problem is to construct the "most desirable" query q_i with respect to the examples e_j and the clues x_k presented by the user. The "most desirable" query is one which will retrieve the largest number of relevant database objects and whose "size" in the information space is relatively small. The process of visual reasoning, which will be discussed in Section 6.3, may help the user find the most desirable query from examples and clues.

The logical information space may be further structured into a *logical information hyperspace*, where the *clue* becomes hyperlinks that provides directional information, and the information space can be navigated by the user by following the directional clues. Information is "chunked," and each chunk is illustrated by an example (the hypernode).

The *physical information space* consists of the materialized database objects. The simplest example is as follows. Each object is materialized as an icon, and the physical information space consists of a collection of icons. These icons can be arranged spatially, so that the spatial locations approximately reflect the relations among database objects. More recently, *intelligent visualization systems* are being developed for task-specific visualization assistance [27]. Such systems can offer assistance in deriving perceptually effective materialization of database objects.

In the physical information space, the objects reflect real-world objects, but the world is still an abstraction of the real world. One further step is to present information in a *virtual reality information space*. Virtual Reality allows the users to be placed in a 3D environment they can directly manipulate. What the users see on the screen will be the same as what can be experienced in the real world. 3D features can be used to present the results in a virtual reality (VR) setting. For example, the physical location of medical records can be indicated in a (simplified) 3D presentation of a Virtual Medical Laboratory by blinking icons. If the database refers to the books of a library, we can represent a Virtual Library in which the physical locations of books are indicated by blinking icons in a 3D presentation of the book stacks of the library. VR such as the Virtual Library or the Virtual Medical Laboratory can become a new query paradigm. For example, the user can select a book by picking it from the shelf, like in the real world.

It is worth noting that we are talking about "nonimmersive VR [44], i.e., the user is placed in a 3D environment he or she can directly manipulate without wearing head-mounted stereo displays or special gloves, but acting only with mouse, keyboard, and monitor of a conventional graphics workstation. This is an alternative form of VR that is being explored in several research laboratories. The use of 3D modeling and rendering is the same as in immersive VR, because the scene is displayed with the same depth cues: perspective view, hidden-surface elimination, color, texture, lighting, shading. Researchers working in nonimmersive VR report that the user is drawn into the 3D world, since mental and emotional immersion takes place, in spite of the lack of visual or perceptual immersion. Moreover, mouse/keyboard controlled interaction techniques are easy to learn and use and are often faster than Dataglove interaction techniques. Therefore, significant advantages come from using such familiar and inexpensive tools, that lower start-up costs. Indeed, immersive VR technology has still many limits and problems (producing and synchronizing stereo images, handling of immersive input devices, etc.), so that researchers spend much more time focusing on the devices rather than on applications and interaction techniques. As a further advantage, nonimmersive VR does not force office workers to wear special equipment that isolate them from their usual environment, minimizing psychological and physical stress that most users will not tolerate [4]. On the

Space	Objects	World
Logical Information Space	Abstract	Abstract
Logical Information Hyperspace	Abstract Clustered	Abstract
Physical Information Space	Real*	Abstract
VR Information Space	Real	Real

Table 6–1 Summary of information spaces.

*Real objects in the physical information space reflect real-life objects, rather than mimic real-life objects.

other hand, new approaches on using the immersive VR, such as interactive Worlds-in-Miniature (WIM) [47], may pave the way for more applications of the immersive VR.

Nonimmersive VR is a valuable interaction paradigm that will be fruitful in multimedia database applications, as well as in general business applications. When displays and input devices that are easily manageable and not intrusive will be available, immersive VR will become acceptable.

The above categorization can be summarized by Table 6–1.

6.3   Strategies for Visual Reasoning

Visual reasoning is the process of reasoning and making inferences, based upon visually presented clues. As mentioned in Section 6.2, visual reasoning may help the user find the most desirable query from examples and clues. In this section we survey strategies for visual reasoning.

Visual reasoning is widely used in human-to-human communication. For example, the teacher draws a diagram on the blackboard. Although the diagram is incomplete and imprecise, the students are able to make inferences to fill in the details, and gain an understanding of the concepts presented. Such *diagram understanding* relies on visual reasoning so that concepts can be communicated. Humans also use *gestures* [24] to communicate. Again, gestures are imprecise visual clues for the receiving person to interpret.

In human-to-computer communication, a recent trend is for the human to communicate to the computer using visual expressions. Typically, the human draws a picture, a structured diagram, or a visual example, and the computer interprets the visual expression to understand the user's intention. This has been called *visual coaching, programming by example* [36], or *programming by rehearsal* [22], [26] by various researchers.

Visual reasoning is related to spatial reasoning, example-based programming, and approximate/vague retrieval. *Spatial reasoning* is the process of reasoning and making inferences, about problems dealing with objects occupying space [17]. These objects can be either *physical objects* (e.g., books, chairs, cars, etc.) or *abstract objects* visualized in space (e.g. database objects). Physical objects are tangible and occupy physical space in some measurable sense. Abstract objects are intangible but nevertheless can be associated with a certain space in some coordinate system. Therefore, visual reasoning can be defined as spatial reasoning on abstract objects visualized in space.

Example-Based Programming refers to systems that allow the programmer to use examples of input and output data during the programming process [36]. There are two types of Example-Based Programming: *Programming by Example* and *Programming with Example*. "Programming by Example" refers to systems that try to guess or *infer* the program from examples of input and output or sample traces of execution. This is often called "automated programming" and has been an area of AI research. "Programming with Example" systems require the user to specify everything about the program (there is no inferencing involved), but the programmer can work out the program on a specific example. The system executes the programmer's commands normally, but remembers them for later re-use. Halbert [23] characterizes Programming with Examples as "Do What I Did" whereas inferential Programming by Example might be called "Do What I Mean." Many recently developed visual programming systems utilized the example-based programming approach [22], [37], [46]. The approach described in Section 6.6 combines presentation of visual clues (programming by example) with query augmentation techniques (programming with example).

We now discuss visual reasoning approaches for databases. Most research in database systems is based on the assumptions of precision and specificity of both the data stored in the database, and the requests to retrieve data. In reality, however, both may be imprecise or vague. Motro characterizes three categories of imprecision and/or vagueness: (1) the data stored in the database is imprecise; (2) the retrieval request is imprecise; and (3) the user does not have a precise notion of the contents of the database [35].

Imprecision in stored data can be dealt with by applying fuzzy sets theory to provide a linguistic description of the stored imprecise data. Fuzzy queries also allow the user to give imprecise retrieval requests. Such techniques are generally applicable when the source of imprecision is quantifiable into numbers, for example, "the age of a person is somewhere between 40 and 45" (imprecision in stored data), "retrieve all middle-aged employees" (imprecision in queries). However, when the source of imprecision is not easily quantifiable, for example, "find persons with faces similar to Einstein's face," the above techniques are less suitable. Recent research in content-based retrieval may lead to techniques to address such problems.

Imprecision in the user's model may be classified as follows [34]: incomplete knowledge of the data model, imprecise information on the database schema and/or its instance, vagueness of user goals, and incomplete knowledge about the interaction tools.

To deal with imprecision in user's model, several approaches have been investigated: (i) **browsing** techniques to provide different views of the database [34]; (ii) **heuristic interpretation of user's query** to transform the user's query by a connective approach [16], [49], [14]; (iii) **example-based techniques** to generalize from selected examples [51], or to modify the original query if the answer is not considered satisfactory [50], [35]. The modification is done either interactively or automatically.

Browsing is generally effective and widely used but may be very wasteful on the user's time. Heuristic interpretation of a user's query can lead to "false drops" or "false hits." Example-based techniques work well for some applications but are hard to generalize. In addition, two common limitations of these approaches [16] are worth mentioning here: (1) the browsing environment and the querying environment are usually distinct, thus separating the learning and the querying activities; (2) knowledge about the user must be gathered to build the user profile (user model). The approach described in Section 6.6 integrates the querying environment (using the visual query) and the browsing environment.

6.4 Taxonomy of Visual Querying Paradigms

As discussed in Section 6.2, the information stored in a multimedia database is organized in a logical information space. Such logical information needs to be materialized in the physical information space in order to allow the user to view it. We are particularly interested in materializations performed by using visual techniques. Therefore, visual query systems, as defined in Section 6.1, are needed. A survey of VQSs proposed in the last years is presented in [7]. In that paper the VQSs are also compared along three taxonomy criteria: 1) the visual representation that is adopted to present the reality of interest and the applicable language operators; 2) the expressive power that indicates what can be done by using the query language; 3) the interaction strategies that are available for performing the queries.

The query paradigm, which settles the way the query is performed and represented, is very much dependent on the way the data in the database (that are the query operands) are visualized. The basic types of visual representations analyzed in [3] are form-based, diagrammatic, and iconic, according to the visual formalism primarily employed, namely forms, diagrams, and icons. A fourth type is the hybrid representation, that uses two or more visual formalisms.

A form can be seen as a rectangular grid having components that may be any combination of cells or groups of cells (subform). A form is intended to be a generalization of a table. It facilitates the users by exploiting the usual tendency of people to use regular structures for information processing. Moreover, computer forms are abstracted from conventional paper forms familiar to people in their daily activities. Form-based representations have been the first attempt to provide users with friendly interfaces for data manipulation, taking advantage of the bidimensionality of the computer screen. QBE has been a pioneer form-based query language [51]. The queries are formulated by filling appropriate fields of prototypical tables that are visualized on the screen.

Representations based on diagrams are widely adopted in existing VQSs. We use the word diagram with a very broad meaning, referring to any graphics that encode information using position and magnitude of geometrical objects and/or show the relationships among components. Referring to the different types of visual representations analyzed in [32], our broad definition of diagram include graphs (such as bar, pie, histogram, scatterplot, etc.), graphic tables, network charts, structure diagrams, and process diagrams. An important and useful characteristic of a diagram is that, if we modify its expression by following certain rules, its content can show new relationships [18]. Often, a diagram uses visual elements that are one to one associated with specific concept types. Diagrammatic representations adopt as typical query operators the selection of elements, the traversal on adjacent elements, and the creation of a bridge among disconnected elements.

The iconic representation uses sets of icons to denote both the objects of the database and the operations to be performed on them. In an icon we distinguish the pictorial part, i.e., the image shown on the screen, and the semantic part, i.e., the meaning that such an image conveys. The simplest way to associate a meaning to an icon is by exploiting the similarity with the referred object. If we have to represent an abstract concept, or an action, that does not have a natural visual counterpart, we have to take into account different correlation modalities between the pictorial and the semantic part, like analogy, methonimics, convention, etc. (see [3] for more details). In iconic VQSs, a query is expressed primarily by combining icons. For example, icons may be vertically combined to denote conjunction (logical AND) and horizontally combined to denote disjunction (logical OR) [10].

All the above representations present complementary advantages and disadvantages. In existing systems, only one type of representation is usually available. This significantly restricts the database users that can benefit from the system. An effective database interface should supply multiple representations, in order to provide different interaction paradigms, each one with different characteristics. Therefore, each user, either novice or expert, can choose the most appropriate paradigm to interact with the system. Such a kind of multiparadigmatic interface for databases has been proposed in [6], where the selection of the appropriate interaction paradigm is made with reference to a user model that describes the user's interest and skills. Another interesting query paradigm is introduced in [12]. It is based on the idea that a Virtual Reality representation of the database application domain is available. An example will be presented in Section 6.6.

The research on multiparadigmatic visual interfaces is conceptually similar to the research on multimodal interfaces for multimedia databases [5]. *Multi-*

modal interfaces support multiple input/output channels for human-computer interaction. The rationale for providing different input and output mechanisms is to accommodate user diversity. Humans, by their very nature, have unpredictable behavior, different skills, and a wide range of interests. Since we cannot obtain a priori information on how each user wishes to interact with the computer system, we need to create customizable human-computer interfaces, so that the users themselves will choose the best way to interact with the system, possibly by exploiting multiple input and output media.

Effective user interfaces are difficult to build. Multimodal and multimedia user interfaces are even more difficult to build. They have further requirements that need to be fully satisfied. The qualities for multimodal and multimedia interfaces have been studied in [25], where the authors identified the following for consideration by the interface designer: (1) blended modalities, (2) appropriate resolvable ambiguity and tolerable probabilistic input capability such as whole sentence speech and gesture recognition, (3) distributed control of interaction among interface modules using protocols of cooperation, (4) real-time as well as after-the-fact access to interaction history, and (5) a highly modular architecture. In our view, one such quality, "blended modalities," requires special emphasis. Blending of modes means that at any point a user can continue input in a new, more pragmatically appropriate mode. The requirement "at any point" is not easy to achieve. In the multiparadigmatic interface described in [6], conditions for allowing a paradigm switch during query formulation are carefully demonstrated. The problem needs to be investigated both from the system's and from the cognitive viewpoint. Besides any model that can help predict user behavior, extensive experimentation is needed with users in order to make sure that the presence of several modes does not create mental overload.

Another issue of great importance to multiparadigmatic interface design is that the expressive power achievable in the different modes, i.e., the kind of database operations that can be performed, may not be the same. For the different visual paradigms analyzed above, form-based and diagrammatic paradigms often provide the same expressive power as the relational algebra [3], but VR only allows selection of objects and retrieval of objects for which similarity functions have been specified. This is even more evident when we consider interaction through different media. A database expert will be very comfortable when performing queries with SQL, which is even more powerful than relational algebra. The same expressive power cannot be achieved, with the current technology, if we use either speech or stylus-drawn gesture; such modes have the further disadvantage of providing ambiguous or probabilistic input. Until now the design of interfaces avoids the use of such kind of inputs, because their ambiguity is unmanageable. Next generation interfaces should include such input modes, if appropriate to the task the interface is for, and provide means to resolve specific ambiguities. One possibility is changing the interaction mode, so that in the new mode a certain operation is no longer ambiguous.

6.5   Multimedia Database Interaction Techniques

Computer technology is providing everybody with the possibility of directly exploring information resources. On the one hand, this is extremely useful and exciting. On the other, the ever-growing amount of information at disposal generates cognitive overload and even anxiety, especially in novice or occasional users. The current user interfaces are usually too difficult for novice users and/or inadequate for experts, who need tools with many options, and consequently limiting the actual power of the computer.

We recognize three different needs of people exploring information: 1) to understand the content of the database, 2) to extract the information of interest, and 3) to browse the retrieved information in order to verify that it matches what they wanted. To satisfy such needs, the user-interface designers are challenged to invent more powerful search techniques, simpler query facilities, and more effective presentation methods. When creating new techniques, we have to keep in mind the variability of the user population, ranging from first-time or occasional versus frequent users, from task-domain novices versus experts, from naive (requesting very basic information) versus sophisticated users (interested in very detailed and specific information). Since there is not a technique capable to satisfy the needs of all such classes of users, the proposed techniques should be conceived as having a basic set of features, while additional features can be requested as users gain experience with the system.

A user interacting the first time with an information system should be allowed to easily navigate into the system in order to get a better idea of the kind of data that can be accessed. Since the information systems become larger and larger, while each user is generally interested in only a small portion of data, one of the primary goals of a designer is to develop some kind of filters to reduce the set of data that needs to be taken into account. At Xerox in recent years a group of researchers has developed several information visualization techniques, with the aim of helping the users understand and process the information stored into the system [43]. They have created the "information workspaces," i.e., computer environments in which the information is moved from the original source, such as networked databases, and where several tools are at the disposal of users for browsing and manipulating the information. One of the main characteristics of such workspaces is that they offer graphical representations of information that facilitate rapid perception of the overall patterns. Moreover, they use 3D and/or distortion techniques to show some portion of the information at a greater level of detail, but keeping it within a larger context. These are usually called fish eye techniques, but it is clearer to call them "focus + context" that better gives the idea of showing an area of interest (the focus) quite large and with detail, while the other areas are shown successively smaller and in less detail. Such an approach is very effective when applied to documents, and also to graphs. It achieves a smooth integration of local detail and global context. It has more advantages of other approaches to filter information, such as zooming or the use of two or more views, one of the entire structure and the other of a zoomed portion. The former approach shows local details but looses the overall structure, the latter requires extra screen space and forces the viewer to mentally integrate the views. In the "focus + context" approach, it is effective to provide animated transitions when changing the focus, so that the user remains oriented across dynamic changes of the display avoiding unnecessary cognitive load.

Shneiderman points out that the perfect search paradigm that retrieves all and only all of the desired items is unattainable [45]. Still, he suggests some ways for achieving flexible search. A first possibility for searches within documents is to allow "rainbow search." It is based on the fact that most word processors support several features (different fonts, sizes, styles, etc.); and text attributes (footnotes, references, etc.), therefore it could be useful to allow a search of all words in italic or a search through only footnotes. Another new technique is "search expansion": when looking for documents using some term, the system can also suggest more general (or specific) terms, synonyms, or related terms from a thesaurus or a data dictionary in order to perform a more complete search.

Search techniques applicable to multimedia data are very interesting. For instance, sound is included among data types of multimedia databases, and it could constitute both an output (as a response of the system) or an input (as a query). Some existing electronic dictionaries already provide both the meaning of words as well as their pronunciation, so offering full information on every requested word. In [33] the authors present "sonification," i.e., the mapping of data to sound parameters, as a rich but still unexplored technique for understanding complex data. The current technology has favored the development of the graphical dimension of user interfaces while limiting the use of the auditory dimension. This is also because the properties of the aural cues are not yet as well understood as those of visual signals. Moreover, sound alone cannot convey accurate information without a visual context. The tool described in [33] uses sound to complement visualization, thus enhancing the presentation of complex data. Sound can be useful in some situations, for instance to set up an alarm when working with the computer to remember to do something at a certain time. The opposite is also true, i.e., visualization can help in analyzing sound. For example, it is useful for an expert performing a detailed analysis of a certain sound to look at the graphics of its amplitude in a given time interval.

We can think of a sound search in a music database. The user hums some notes and the system provides the list of symphonies that contain that string of notes. This is not difficult to achieve provided that the user inputs the notes in an unambiguous way (for example entering the notes on a staff connected to the computer) and the search is performed on the score sheets of symphonies stored with the music.

A system called Hyperbook uses sounds as an imitation of bird calls (either in the melody or in the tone) to retrieve specific bird families within an electronic book on birds [48]. The user can also retrieve a bird by drawing a silhouette of the bird. The descriptions provided by both techniques are incomplete since it is difficult for the user to give an exact specification. Hyperbook solves such queries on the basis of a data model, called metric spatial object data, which represents objects in the real world as points in a metric space. In order to select the candidate objects, distances are evaluated by the system, enabling the user to choose those objects (birds) which have a minimal distance from the query in the metric space.

Interesting and useful techniques can be exploited for searching images in a database on the basis of their pictorial contents. Given a sketch of a house, the user may want to find all pictures that contain that house. With the visual query system called Pictorial Query-By-Example (PQBE), Papadias and Sellis propose an approach to the problem of content-based querying geographic and image databases [39]. PQBE makes use of the spatial nature of spatial relations in the formulation of a query. This should allow users to formulate queries in a language close to their thinking. As in the case of the well-known Query-By-Example, PQBE generalizes from the example given by the user, but, instead of having skeleton relational tables, there are skeleton images.

Several researchers are proposing interaction environments exploiting different techniques than the visual ones. In [42], an interactive multimedia prototype is shown that allows users seated in front of a terminal to experience a virtual reality environment. The system integrates a number of key technologies and the purpose of the prototype is to experiment with such new interaction possibilities. The users communicate with each other and with artificial agents through speech. The prototype also includes audio rendering, hand gesture recognition, and body-position-sensing technology. The authors admit that their system is limited by the current technology, but they are confident that in a couple of years what is today expensive or yet impossible will be commonplace.

Traditional languages such as SQL allow the user to specify exact queries that indicate matches on specific field values. Non-expert and/or occasional users of the database are generally not able to directly formulate a query whose result fully satisfies their needs, at least in their first attempts. Therefore, the users may prefer to formulate a complex query by a succession of progressive simple queries, i.e., step by step, by first asking general questions, obtaining preliminary results, and then revisiting such outcomes to further refine the query in order to extract the result they are interested in. Since the results obtained up to a certain point may not converge to the expected data, a nonmonotone query progression should be allowed. During this process of progressive querying, an appropriate visualization of the preliminary results could give a significant feedback to the user. Moreover, it will provide hints about the right way to proceed towards the most appropriate final query. Otherwise, the user will immediately backtrack and try a different alternative path. Often, even if the user is satisfied with the result, he or she is also challenged to further investigate the database, and as a result may acquire more information from it.

The above-described advantages of performing a progressive query through visual interaction, also displaying, in a suitable representation, the obtained partial results, has lead to the Visual Querying and Result Hypercube (VQRH), which is a tool that provides a multiparadigmatic approach for progressive querying and result visualization in database interaction [12]. Using the VQRH tool, the user interacts with the database by means of a sequence of partial queries, each displayed, together with the corresponding result, as one slice of the VQR Hypercube. Successive slices on the Hypercube store partial queries performed at successive times. Therefore, the query history is presented in a 3D perspective, and a particular partial query on a slice may be brought to the front of the Hypercube for further refinement by means of a simple mouse click.

Another powerful technique for querying a database is "dynamic query," that allows a range search on multi-key data sets. The query is formulated through direct manipulation of graphical widgets such as buttons and sliders, one widget being used for every key. The result of the query is displayed graphically and quickly on the screen. It is important that the results fit on a single screen and that they are displayed quickly, since the users should be able to perform tens of queries in a few seconds and immediately see the results. Given a query, a new query is easily formulated by moving with the mouse the position of a slider. This gives a sense of power but is also fun for the user, who is challenged to try other queries and see how the result is modified. As in the case of the progressive query, the user can ask general queries and see what the results are; then he or she can better refine the query. An application of dynamic queries is shown in [45] and refers to real-estate database. There are sliders for location, number of bedrooms, or price of homes in the Washington, D.C. area. The user moves these sliders to find appropriate homes. Selected homes are indicated by bright points of light on a Washington, D.C. map shown on the screen.

6.6   An Experimental Multiparadigmatic Visual Interface

To test our ideas about a multiparadigmatic visual interface that allows progressive queries, we have developed a system called Visual Query and Result Hypercube (*VQRH*) [12]. A prototype of such a system has been implemented on a PC using Visual Basic. It runs under the Windows NT environment and can be easily interfaced with different commercial database systems. In the experiment, we use dBase IV, although other commercial database systems can also be used.

We have experimented with information retrieval using VQRH in two application domains: (a) the medical databases, and (b) the library databases. The subjects are students with no previous experience in using VQRH. We will not describe VQRH in details here. We just recall its basic features, namely: (1)

the screen is divided into two main windows, in the left one the user formulates its query, and the results are shown in the right window; (2) both query and results can be visualized in any of the available paradigms for query and data representation; (3) the queries formulated during an interaction section are stored, with the corresponding results, as successive slices of the Hypercube, so each slice can be easily recalled.

The preliminary experiments indicate that the users have little difficulty in learning VQRH, and they can formulate queries after half an hour of interaction. They generally like the idea of progressive querying, and find it useful to be able to recall any past query-and-result slice. From such experiments, it is already clear that the visualization of the retrieved result is very important for the success of this approach. While in the initial design of VQRH only physical information spaces were used for presenting the data, in a second version of the prototype a VR information space was added. VR is established as a query paradigm, that is, the user selects with the mouse the items of this 3D space he or she is interested in.

When performing a query, the admissability conditions to switch between a *logical paradigm* (our previous paradigms are all logical paradigms) and a *VR paradigm* (such as the Virtual Library) can be defined as follows. For a logical paradigm, a *VR-admissable query* is an admissable query whose retrieval target object is also an object in VR. For example, the VR for the Virtual Library contains stacks of books, and a VR-admissable query could be any admissable query about books, because the result of that query can be indicated by blinking book icons in the Virtual Library. Conversely, for a VR paradigm, an *LQ-admissable query* is a VR where there is a single marked VR object that is also a database object, and the marking is achieved by an operation icon such as *similar_to* (find objects similar to this object), *near* (find objects near this object), *above* (find objects above this object), *below* (find objects below this object), and other spatial operators. For example, in the VR for the Virtual Library, a book marked by the operation icon *similar_to* is LQ-admissable and can be translated into the following query: "find all books similar to this book." An example of a VR-admissable logical query is illustrated in Fig. 6–1. The query is to find books on bicycles. It is performed with the iconic paradigm. The result is presented as marked objects in a Virtual Library. The user can then navigate in this Virtual Library, and switch to the VR query paradigm. Fig. 6–2 illustrates an LQ-admissable query. The query is to find books similar to a specific book about bicycles that has been marked by the user. The result is again rendered as marked objects in a Virtual Library. If we switch to a form-based representation, the result could also be rendered as items in a form. This example illustrates progressive querying can be accomplished with greater flexibility by combining the logical paradigms and the VR paradigms. The experimental VQRH system supports VR paradigms, but the similarity function must be supplied for the problem domain.

The experiment was very useful for understanding the limitations of the screen design and their impact on the system's usability. Some interesting

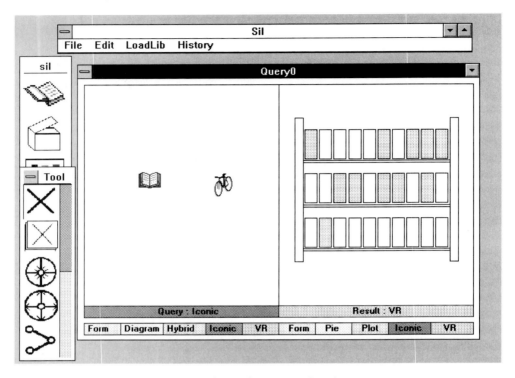

Figure 6-1   A logical query with result in virtual reality.

characteristics of the VR paradigm emerged, which led to a revised screen design. Indeed, the distinction between query space and result space does not make sense in VR, since a query is performed by acting, with either the mouse or another pointer device, in the environment the user is in. The result of the query usually determines some modification of such an environment, and this new situation is that one on which a successive request has to be performed. As a consequence, when working with the VR paradigm, the user gets confused by the separation of the query window and the result window. This is easily understandable by looking at Fig. 6–1 and Fig. 6–2. The situation depicted in Fig. 6–1 does not create any problem for the user, who is formulating a query in the iconic paradigm but wants to see the result in VR, since VR actually provides visual indication of where the requested books can be found. Moreover, showing the results in separate windows gives the user the possibility of viewing them in a different representation, providing the user the full advantage of viewing the data in different ways [7]. For example, while VR gives immediate indication about the physical location of a book, in a form-based representation more

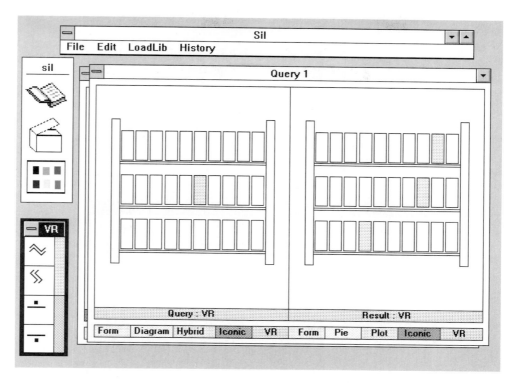

Figure 6-2   A VR query with results also in virtual reality.

details can be provided at once, such as title of the book, authors, exact number of pages, etc. Therefore, in a situation involving a change of paradigm between query and result representations, the user is perfectly comfortable with the two windows shown on the screen.

However, the user gets confused when working in VR, in the situation depicted in Fig. 6–2. The two windows both show the book shelf, but the left-side window shows the VR query and the right-side window shows the VR result. When the user is visualizing the VR result, it is unnatural to go to a different window to modify the query. There should be only one window, showing both the VR result and the VR query. Therefore, in the new version of the VQRH prototype, the computer screen appears as shown in Fig. 6–3 and Fig. 6–4. The user first navigates in the Virtual Library (Fig. 6–3), and clicks on a bookshelf. The bookshelf is shown in Fig. 6–4. The user then proceeds to click on individual books, and uses operators such as "near," "similar_to," "above," etc. to retrieve other books.

Figure 6-3   The Virtual Library.

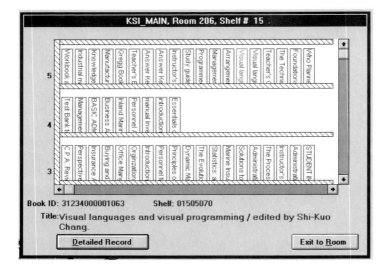

Figure 6-4   A VR query in the VR information space.

6.7 Conclusion

The use of visual interfaces combining different query mechanisms represents a step toward a truly effective utilization of multimedia information systems by large classes of users. The query mechanisms include speech, sound, gestures, etc., but the user interface should be highly visual to enable the user to gradually grasp the database contents, the navigation technique, the visual reasoning strategy, as well as the querying process. As it was pointed out in [7], in the last ten years the research on visual query systems passed from conceiving merely hypothetical and vague ideas to building real systems. Yet, much more needs to be done, both from the theoretical and the application-oriented point of view. Since the success of a complex application is largely due to the way it matches the users' expectations as well as their skills and learning ability, more efforts should be devoted to experimenting and validating the proposed interfaces, in order to provide an accurate evaluation of their usability, which is a crucial factor to the practical utilization of such interfaces for multimedia information systems.

References

[1] Ahmed, Z., Wanger, L., and Kochevar, P., "An intelligent visualization system for earth science data analysis," *Journal of Visual Languages and Computing*, Vol. 5, No. 4, Dec 1994, pp. 307–320.

[2] Anupam, V. and Bajaj, C.L., "Shastra: Multimedia collaborative design environment," *IEEE Multimedia*, Vol. 1, No. 2, 1994, pp. 39–49.

[3] Batini, C., Catarci, T., Costabile, M.F., and Levialdi, S. *Visual Query Systems*. Tech. Report 04.91, Dipartimento di Informatica e Sistematica, Universitá di Roma "La Sapienza," Italy, 1991 (revised in 1993).

[4] Beaudouin-Lafon, M. "Beyond the workstation: Mediaspaces and augmented reality," in *Proceedings of 1994 HCI Conference*, Boston, MA, 1994. pp. 9–18.

[5] Blattner, M.M. and Dannenberg, R.B., eds. *Multimedia Interface Design*. Reading, MA: Addison-Wesley, 1992.

[6] Catarci, T., Chang, S.K., Costabile, M.F., Levialdi, S., and Santucci, G. "A graph-based framework for multiparadigmatic visual access to databases," *IEEE Transactions on Knowledge and Data Engineering*, Vol. 8, No. 3, June 1996, pp. 455–475.

[7] Catarci, T. and Costabile, M.F., eds. Special Issue on Visual Query Systems. *Journal of Visual Languages and Computing*, Vol. 6, No. 1, 1995.

[8] Catarci, T., Costabile, M.F., Levialdi, S., and Santucci, G., "Visual query systems for databases: A survey," Technical Report 35/17, Departimento di Scienze dell'Informazione, Universitá di Roma "La Sapienza," 1995.

[9] Chang, H., Hou, T., Hsu, A., and Chang, S.K. "Tele-action objects for an active multimedia system," in *Proceedings of the Second International IEEE Conference on Multimedia Computing and Systems*, Washington, DC, May 15-18, 1995. pp. 106–113.

[10] Chang, S.K., "Visual reasoning for information retrieval from very large databases," *Journal of Visual Languages and Computing*, Vol. 1, No. 1, pp. 41–58, 1990.

[11] Chang, S. K. "Toward a theory of active index," *Journal of Visual Languages and Computing*, Vol. 5, pp. 101–118, 1995.

[12] Chang, S.K., Costabile, M.F., and Levialdi, S., "Reality bites—Progressive querying and result visualization in logical and VR spaces," in *Proc. of IEEE Symposium on Visual Languages*, St. Louis, Oct 1994, pp. 100–109.

[13] Chang, S.K., Costagliola, G., Pacini, G., Tucci, M., Tortora, G., Yu, B., and Yu, J.S. "Visual language system for user interfaces," *IEEE Software*, Vol. 12, No. 2, Mar 1995, pp. 33–44.

[14] Chang, S.K. and Ke, J.S., "Translation of fuzzy queries for relational database system," *IEEE Transactions on Pattern Analysis and Machine Intelligence*, Vol. PAMI-1, No. 3, July 1979, pp. 281–294.

[15] D'Atri, A., Di Felice, P., and Moscarini, M., "Dynamic query interpretation in relational databases," *Information Sciences*, Vol. 14, No. 3, 1989.

[16] D'Atri, A. and Tarantino, L., "From browsing to querying," *Data Engineering*, Vol. 12, No. 2, June 1989, pp. 46–53.

[17] Dutta, S., "Qualitative spatial reasoning: A semi-quantitative approach using fuzzy logic," in *Conference Proceedings on Very Large Spatial Databases*, Santa Barbara, CA, July 17–19, 1989, pp. 345–364.

[18] Eco, U., *A Theory of Semiotics*. Bloomington, IN: Indiana University Press, 1975.

[19] Faloutsos, C. *et al.* "Efficient and effective querying by image content," IBM Research Division Almaden Research Center, Technical Report RJ9543 (83074), Aug 1993.

[20] Faloutsos, C., Barber, R., Flickner, M., Hafner, J., Niblack, W., Petkovic, D., and Equitz, W. "Efficient and effective querying by image content," *Journal of Intelligent Information Systems*, Vol. 3, pp. 231–262, 1994.

[21] Fox, E. A. "Advances in interactive digital multimedia systems," *IEEE Computer*, Vol. 24, No. 10, pp. 9–21, Oct 1991.

[22] Gould, L. and Finzer, W., "Programming by rehearsal," *Byte*, June 1984, pp. 187–210.

[23] Halbert, D.C., "Programming by example," Xerox Office Systems Division, TR OSD-T8402, Dec 1984.

[24] Hanne, K. and Bullinger, H., "Multimodal communication: Integrating text and gestures," in *Multimedia Interface Design*. Reading, MA: Addison-Wesley, 1992, pp. 127–138.

[25] Hill, W., Wroblewski, D., McCandiess, T., and Cohen, R., "Architectural qualities and principles for multimodal and multimedia interfaces," in *Multimedia Interface Design*. Reading, MA: Addison-Wesley, 1992, pp. 311–318.

[26] Huang, K.T., "Visual interface design systems," in *Principles of Visual Programming Systems*. Englewood Cliffs, NJ: Prentice-Hall, 1990.

[27] Ignatius, E., Senay, H., and Favre, J., "An intelligent system for task-specific visualization assistance," *Journal of Visual Languages and Computing*, Vol. 5, No. 4, Dec 1994, pp. 321–338.

[28] Kawata, Y., Kawasaki, A., Udomkitwanit, W., Yabu, A., Kobayashi, H., Wijayarathna, P., and Maekawa, M., "EVE: A visual specification environment with support for formal descriptions of physical properties," in *Proc. of First International Conference. on Visual Information Systems*, Melbourne, Feb 5–6, 1996, pp. 518-529.

[29] Kovacevic, S., "A compositional model of human-computer dialogs," in *Multimedia Interface Design*. New York: Addison-Wesley, 1992, pp. 373–404.

[30] Lang, L., "GIS comes to life," *Computer Graphics World*, Vol. 15, No. 10, Oct 1992, pp. 27–36.

[31] Little, T.D.C. and Venkatesh, D., "The use of multimedia technology in distance learning," in *Proceedings of the IEEE International Conference on Multimedia Networking*, Aizu, Japan, Sep 1995, pp. 3–17.

[32] Lohse, G.L., Biolsi, K.A., Walker, N., and Rueter, H.H., "A classification of visual representations," *Communications of the ACM*, Vol. 37, No. 12, 1994, pp. 36–49.

[33] Madhyastha, T.M. and Reed, D.A. "Data sonification: Do you see what I hear?" *IEEE Software*, Vol. 12, No. 2, Mar 1995, pp. 45–56.

[34] Motro, A., "BAROQUE: An exploratory interface to relational databases," *ACM Trans. on Office Information Systems*, Vol. 4, No. 2, Apr 1986, pp. 164–181.

[35] Motro, A., "VAGUE: A user interface to relational database that permits vague queries," *ACM Trans. on Office Information Systems*, Vol. 6, No. 3, July 1988, pp. 187–214.

[36] Myers, B.A., "Visual programming, Programming by example, and program visualization: A taxonomy," *Proceedings of SIGCHI'86*, Boston, MA, April 13-17, 1986, pp. 59–66.

[37] Myers, B.A., *Creating User Interfaces by Demonstration*. Boston: Academic Press, 1988.

[38] Niblack, W. and Flickner, M., "Find me the pictures that look like this: IBM's image query project," *Advanced Imaging*, Apr 1993.

[39] Papadias, D. and Sellis, T., "Pictorial query-by-example," *Journal of Visual Languages and Computing*, Vol. 6, No. 1, 1995, pp. 53–72.

[40] Rau, H. and Skiena, S., "Dialing for documents: An experiment in information theory," *Journal of Visual Languages and Computing*, Vol. 7, No. 1, Mar 1996, in press.

[41] Reis, H., Brenner, D., and Robinson, J., "Multimedia communications in health care," presented at the New York Academy of Sciences Conference on Extended Clinical Consulting by Hospital Computer Networks, March 1992.

[42] Rich, C., Walters, R.C., Strohecker, C., Schabes, Y., Freeman, W.T., Torrance, M.C., Golding, A.R., and Roth, M., "Demonstration of an interactive multimedia environment," *IEEE Computer*, Vol. 27, No. 12, 1994, pp. 15–22.

[43] Robertson, G. G., Card, S.K., and Mackinlay, J.D. "Nonimmersive virtual reality," *IEEE Computer*, Vol. 26, No. 2, pp. 81–83, 1993.

[44] Robertson, G.G.,Card, S.K., and Mackinlay, J.D., "Information visualization using 3D interactive animation," *Communications of the ACM,* Vol. 36, No. 4, 1993, pp. 57–71.

[45] Shneiderman, B., *Designing the User Interface*. New York: Addison-Wesley, 1992.

[46] Smith, D.C., *Pygmalion: A Computer Program to Model and Stimulate Creative Thought*. Stuttgart: Birkhauser, 1977.

[47] Stoakley, R., Conway, M.J., and Pausch, R. "Virtual reality on a WIM: Interactive worlds in miniature," *Proc. of CHI-95*, Denver, Colorado, May 7–11, 1995, pp. 265–272.

[48] Tabuchi, M., Tagawa T, Fugisawa, M., Negishi, A., Kojima, K., and Muraoka, Y., "Hyperbook," in *Proc. of International Conference on Multimedia Information Systems,* Singapore, 1991, pp. 3–16.

[49] Wald, J.A. and Sorenson, P.G., "Resolving the query inference problem using Steiner trees," *ACM Trans. on Database Systems*, Vol. 9, No. 3, 1984, pp. 348–368.

[50] Williams, M.D., "What makes RUBBIT run?" *International Journal on Man-Machine Studies*, Vol. 21, No. 4, Oct 1984, pp. 333–352.

[51] Zloof, M.M., "Query by example," *IBM Systems Journal*, Vol. 16, No. 4, 1977, pp. 324–343.

Multimedia Interfaces—Multimedia Content Indication

Yoshinobu Tonomura

NTT Human Interface Laboratories
Kanagawa, Japan
tonomura@nttvdt.ntt.jp

7.1   Introduction

*M*ultimedia is becoming richer in the types of information possible due to continued advances in technology. Various interfaces for interacting with multimedia are now possible for various applications. However, it is not easy to design an effective and easy-to-use multimedia interface that allows us to make full use of such rich information. This issue is becoming more and more important because digital multimedia libraries [1] are being established over networks.

Many multimedia handling systems have been developed so far for applications such as multimedia presentations, authoring, and video editing systems. In the earlier systems, computers were used to perform the basic functions such as controlling peripheral devices, and not much importance was placed on content indication to enhance the user's comprehension. As more computer power is now available for user interfaces, it is more important to concentrate on content indication in system design. Effective representations of multimedia contents appropriate for the applications are desired. Representation means presenting some extraction of the content in a form that supports the user's understanding. Examples include visualization and vocalization.

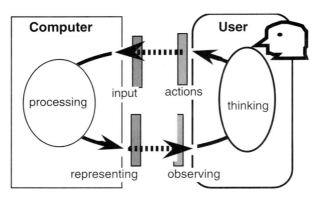

Figure 7-1 Multimedia interface cycle.

This chapter focuses on the issues and techniques of creating and using multimedia content indication. Video which is one of the most promising media is especially focused on.

7.2 Issues

A simple model of interactions between a user and computer in multimedia handling is shown in Fig. 7–1. There is an interaction cycle which is repeated. In the cycles, the decisions of the human and the responses from the computer should be rapid for continuous and smooth human thinking without losing ideas and without increasing the stress involved. Note that the information representation is the key factor for human action decisions.

We sometimes encounter problems in the cycles. For example, it is not easy to get the idea of each content especially when it comprises multiple media with temporal factors such as video. What we want to see most from the content is different for different purposes. The important technical issues in coping with such problems are summarized as follows.

- Interface design that realizes intuitive and effective interactions appropriate for the application and usage. It should follow our information comprehension style.
- Structure in data description and processing which realizes the above interface design with high flexibility and efficiency.
- Processing algorithms that support the efficient data handling in computers.

Among these issues, the interface design issue is mostly focused on in this chapter. Before going into details about our approaches, let's see several related works in the video handling field.

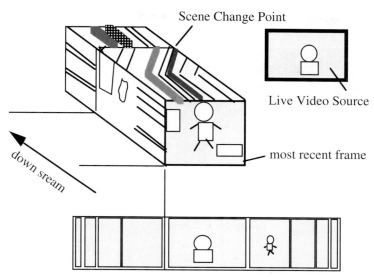

Scene Change Point

Live Video Source

most recent frame

down sream

Figure 7-2   Video Streamer [2].

7.3   Related Work

In the research on interface for video handling in computers, video content indication, video semantics representation, and database visualization are the major topics.

A tool for real-time streaming video content indication called Video Streamer by Elliot and Davenport offered a very intuitive interface [2]. It was a pioneering work in designing a tool for interacting with real-time video content. The Video Streamer shows spatio-temporal video streams in a three-dimensional block of images (Fig. 7–2).

You can see the flows of the objects in a video from the patterns on the side of the volume. Scene change points can be visually discerned from the patterns' discontinuities. One of the nice things here is that it is a real-time video indicator with the very recent past stream. Of course, it can handle stored video in the same manner. The lower image in Fig. 7–2 is called the micro-viewer. It presents a series of frames side by side with the center frame representing the user selected part. The frame image width is shortened in a fish eye manner the further it is in time from the central frame. The Video Streamer can be one module of a new style video editing tool.

As a more complex example, Fig. 7–3 shows a browser by Arman *et al.* that displays a sequence of representative images (Rframes) with motion tracking

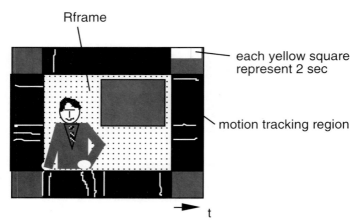

Figure 7-3   Video browser [3].

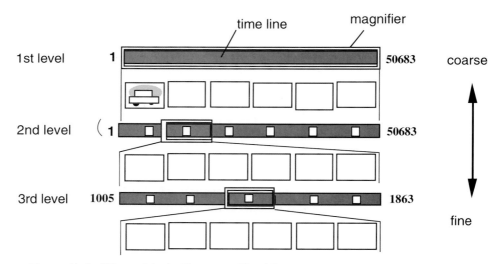

Figure 7-4   Hierarchical video magnifier [4].

stripes [3]. Each Rframe consists of a body, four motion tracking regions, and shot length indicators. The body of the Rframe can be chosen using the rule used to extract representative frame images. The four motion tracking regions trace the motion of boundary pixels through time, and act as guides to camera or global motion. You need a little experience to comprehend what the tracking stripes mean, but it is an interesting interface displaying "motion" information in still images.

A magnifier tool for video browsing by Mills *et al.*, shown in Fig. 7–4, proposed a tool that offers a range of views from wide to close [4]. It allows a user to recursively magnify the temporal resolution of a video source while preserving the levels of magnification in a spatial hierarchy. The tool is simple and it does not use any video features, but it is effective in supporting actual video manipulation.

Media Streams by Davis is an iconic visual language for video annotation [5] which is a creative work on video semantics representation. Media Streams enables users to create multi-layered, iconic annotations of video content. It has three main interface components: the Director's Workshop, Icon Palettes, and Media Time Lines. The user first creates iconic descriptors using iconic primitives which cover various cinematic primitives and accumulates the descriptors on Icon Palettes. Then, by dragging iconic descriptors from Icon Palettes and dropping them onto a Media Time Line, the user annotates the temporal media represented in the Media Time Line. Media Streams, which is an iconic visual language for video annotation, is an eloquent video content indication.

As for a visual database visualization, FilmFinder by Ahlberg and Shneiderman is an interface to movie databases and is an example of the visual information seeking method [6]. The information used is explicitly represented and stored in the database. The user can narrow the search areas by visually selecting category, title, actor or actress, or rating. A typical interface of this tool has the X axis representing time and the Y axis of the popularity measure. Different kinds of information can be used on the axes to segregate the movies. When the number of filtered movies is small, the granularity can be fine, and a browser indicator with rich information can be used.

These tools on multimedia content indication exhibited interesting approaches. Although they were designed for each specific purpose or usage, they tackled common interface issues raised earlier.

7.4 Multimedia Content Indication

Content indication is the process of explicitly presenting some part of the content for its better comprehension by the user. This section covers several topics of content indication: requirements, a content information model, indication styles, and indication processes. Among several kinds of multimedia, we focus on stream media such as video which convey messages in continuous or continual streams of media data.

Requirements

A user has only vague ideas about represented information in the early stages of interactions with a computer, and the goal is gradually formed and actions are

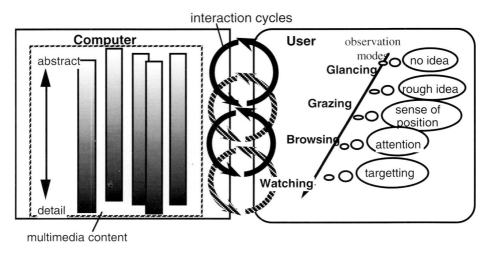

Figure 7–5   Interfacing multimedia contents.

specified during repetitions of the interaction cycle already shown in Fig. 7–1. Here, we extend the model into more detail processes in dealing with multimedia contents (Fig. 7–5). The model includes the human's observation modes: Glancing, Grazing [7], Browsing, and Watching. These modes correspond to details the user gets about the contents.

The user starts to "understand" the represented contents at the glancing stage. At the grazing stage, by roaming around and peeking at the contents, the user gets "a sense of positioning" in the information-represented world. After browsing several contents, the user may begin to pay special attention to a specific content. In the process of forming a goal, the user accesses several contents and gets some knowledge of them. At the watching stage, detailed information is observed.

Considering this model, the following characteristics are important things and should be offered in interfaces for multimedia content indication.

Smooth Stage Transition

The transition between observation stages should be as smooth as possible because the corresponding human thinking process is continuous. Therefore, the computer must be able to represent each content from abstract to full detail according to the observation mode of the user, hopefully seamlessly.

Sense of Overview

In order to offer the sense of overview of the represented information, the interface should cover a wide range of, or all of, the related contents. Represented information should also convey at least a vague idea about the coverage of the represented contents to the user.

Sense of Positioning

A sense of positioning with regard to the contents, which is useful in the user's early content exploration, should be given. For example, if contents are arranged in a chronological order, the user has a better feel for content position given some idea about time information.

Effective Representation

Each content should be represented in the most effective way to let the user know what it is about. Therefore, highly intuitive representations are needed. This is not easy when the content involves temporal material such as video.

Responsiveness

In order to make the multimedia interface cycles smooth and rapid, user action should immediately impact the content representation so that the needed information is instantly available. For example, more detailed information appears when clicked.

Attractiveness

The interface should be fun to use to arouse the user's interest and actions. A content oriented interface would reserve the original indication style as much as possible and avoid abstract representations as a central indication. The above issues also have something to do with this attractiveness.

Content Indication Basics

In realizing content indication considering the requirements, the indication process must be flexible. Therefore, the description of multimedia content should be separated into the content itself and attribute information. A simplified model of content information description is shown in Fig. 7–6.

The core part of multimedia content is the actual media information such as text codes for texts and compression-coded data for audio and video. The attribute information is, for example, coding information, content structure information, content profile information, and link relations, which can be used for content processing. The coding information, such as coding method used and the parameters, is used for decoding the core information. The content structure information includes structural information of the content such as the story outline of a video. The profile information is general information about the content such as authoring information, comments, or any other information that would be useful for handling the content. The attribute information enriches content representation styles.

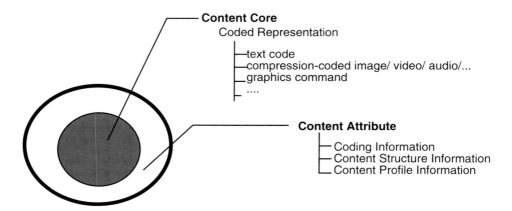

Figure 7–6   Content information.

Multimedia applications require a variety of indication styles to make content viewing appropriate for the usage. Represented information is also dependent on each application. However, considering the requirements and content information model above, there are three common factors important in content indication: indication granularity, multi-dimensional information relief, and indication style base. Here, we describe a content indicator in a combination of these three factors.

Content Indicator ::= (Granularity, Information Relief, Style Base)

Indication Granularity

In accordance with the user's observation mode, the user should be able to vary his/her viewpoint of the content from macro to micro level. The indication granularity [8], that is the granularity of the represented information, is rough in macro-view and fine in micro-view. The granularity and the user's observation modes are shown in Fig. 7–7.

The normal granularity is used for normal content indication such as normal-speed video playing in the case of video content. A content indication should trigger a user's attention and should help understanding at the rough granularity level. In other words, the indication should be successful as a clear identifier of the content. It should be highly representative and intuitive enough to permit the user's instant recognition. At the middle granularity level, some kind of content summary is provided. In this sense, how representative the indication is of the content is important especially at the rough and middle levels. This sort of granularity control is needed for the interactive viewing of multimedia content.

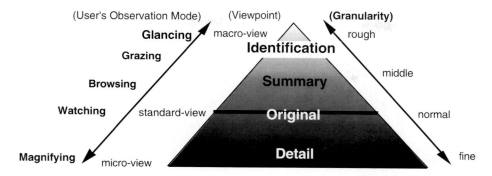

Figure 7-7   Indication granularity and user's observation modes.

Indicators corresponding to various granularity levels are shown in Fig. 7–8. They include poster, browser, viewer, and magnifier. These indicators do not always need to be separate, sometimes one indicator that can be controlled from rough to fine granularity is preferred.

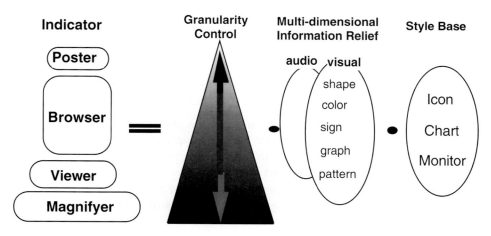

Figure 7-8   Indication basic factors.

Poster   Poster is the most macro-indicated and iconic representation. It uses the essential part of the content as an identifier of the content. The simplest poster is a miniature or reduced content representation. If the content is an image, the poster can be just a shrunk image of the original. In the case of video content, it can be a spatial and temporal miniature. The composite poster consists of several parts of the content (Fig. 7–9).

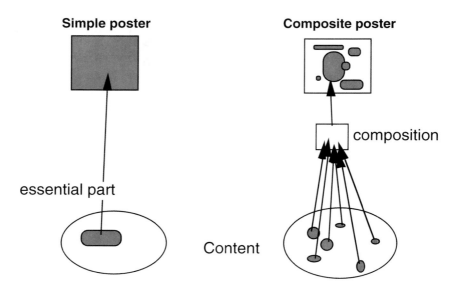

Figure 7-9   Poster.

One of the central issues in poster making is how the essential parts are extracted from the original content and represented. The method depends on the application. Poster type film advertisements are good examples of a composite poster. They are well designed to display the main cast and catchwords. When the content is a book, the cover design is a good candidate for the poster.

Browser   Browser indication should give an overview of the content in an effective manner considering the media and the application. It is desirable that the indication granularity be changeable. It is also important to give a sense of positioning of what is where to the user.

An at-a-glance-type browser needs much space to display but needs less user control. An interactive-type browser needs frequent user control to browse but needs less space to display. Trade-off must be set for the actual application.

Viewer   A viewer indicates the content at the normal granularity level. The position of the current viewing point should be indicated when the viewer indicates only a part of the entire content. Switching to the browser or the magnifier should be possible and the transition should be as smooth as possible. Displaying additional information related to the current part of the content such as camera conditions for video is an important function.

Magnifier   The magnifier indication is the detailed representation and focuses on certain parts of the content. Fine granularity control inside the magnifier, which varies the magnifying factor, should be available.

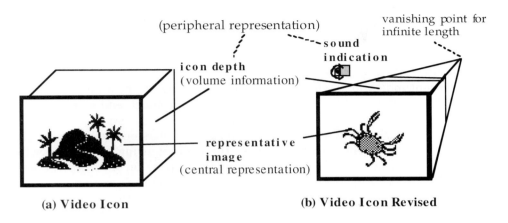

Figure 7–10   Video icon [10], [12].

Examples based on these indicators corresponding to these four types of indication modes are shown later.

Multi-Dimensional Information Relief

Rich information is contained in multimedia content and it is inherently multi-dimensional. It is sometimes useful to focus on the specific information and indicate it by using the feature of relief. In order to do that, attribute information of the multimedia content needs to be effectively used. Extraction of implicit information contained in the content core and its indication is needed.

The central issue here is to find effective indication methods using the multi-dimensional processing of the contents. The content attribute which is explicit information in the content structure directly helps in the processing. If the attribute needed is implicitly contained in the content, it has to be extracted from the content for utilization.

There are two indication styles: modification of the central content representation and peripheral representation. For example, shape or color of the central content representation can be modified according to a certain feature of the content. Attaching symbolic information as peripheral representations is sometimes useful. In the video content indication shown in Fig. 7–10(b), a speaker-style iconic indication is attached to the central representation to show that the content includes sound.

Among the information to be shown in content indication, media kind and content volume information are important. In the case of an image or video, content-oriented central representation, i.e., shrunk images, implies the indication of the kind of media. The number of pages for text-based content, the temporal length of audio or video content, and image size for still image content, are examples of volume information indication. Of course, numeric representation of such information is possible, however, intuitive graphic representation is more effective.

Style Base

Various content indication styles are possible depending on the applications and situations [9] but three basic styles are important: icon, chart, and monitor.

The icon style is a compact representation which also can be a target for user operation. It is used to show, as a minimum, the existence of content. The chart style is used to show more detail of the content using a wide area for information representation. The rule governing the conversion of the logical position of content information into a geographical position on the screen depends on the application. The monitor style is an original indication of the content for content viewing. It is used to show the content in the most natural manner. For example, replaying video content in a relatively large window at normal speed is one case.

In the case of voluminous contents which have temporal factors or many pages of texts, the function of immediate access to specific parts should be possible for the user's fast trial and selection. This accessibility improves user's comprehension of the content through interaction. These basic styles are modified with actual parameters in indication processing.

Basic Content Indicator

In this section, basic types of content indicators are introduced with examples. In order to indicate content to users, content information stored in a computer must be converted into easily perceived forms. The content indicator is the module and interface that realizes this indication.

The content oriented representation preserves the original content style so that users can easily catch the content. This representation is important because it takes advantage of the excellent ability of humans in catching the essential information of the content. Some examples of content-oriented representation as content indicators for video are provided below.

The simplest video content indicators include the Video Icon [10] and Micon (movie icon) [11] which works as a poster. Fig. 7–10(a) is an example of a Video Icon. The depth of the icon indicates the duration of the video. As a general description, this indicator can be described as follows.

$$\text{Video Icon} ::= (\ \text{poster}\ (\ \text{miniature}\ ),\ \text{shape}\ (\ \text{length}\ )\ ,\ \text{icon}\ )$$

Here, the granularity is the poster level with a content miniature, the shape of the representation provides length information, and the indication is based on the icon style. In the revised version of Video Icon in Fig. 7–10(b), the depth

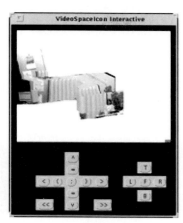

(a) Front View   (b) Top-left View

Figure 7-11   VideoSpaceIcon [13].

indication reaches a fixed point, that is a vanishing point for infinite length video using nonlinear conversion rule, which saves display space [12]. In these cases, the central representation is a miniature image or short movie.

One advanced indication of video content is provided by the VideoSpaceIcon [13], which is a three-dimensional representation of spatial and temporal video features as a poster in icon style (Fig. 7–11).

VideoSpaceIcon :: = (poster (miniature) , shape (camera work) , icon)

It is created by changing the image size and position to match the camera work parameters of zooming and panning or tilting for each frame. You can interactively rotate the VideoSpaceIcon to see any side; the top view indicates horizontal camera works such as panning, while the side view shows vertical camera operations such as tilting. The three-dimensional form of the icon allows us to grasp how the camera was operated at a glance while maintaining temporal context. As shown by these examples, intuitive representation of attribute information is effective for the user's content comprehension.

Switching to the browser is done by an operation such as clicking on the icon. In the case of the video browser, the basic structure is the shot sequence. An example of chart-based browsers which represent information spatially for browsing is shown in Fig. 7–12. Video Icon is used in the browser to represent the different video segments in the sequence. Each icon represents a shot or a scene. In the case of Fig. 7–12, their position implies the sequence order.

Video Browser ::= (browser (Video Icon), sequence (linear order), chart)

Live Video Monitor   Video Icon   Video Browser Window

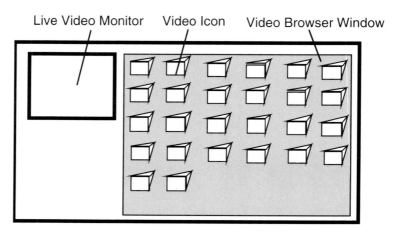

Figure 7-12 Chart-based video browser

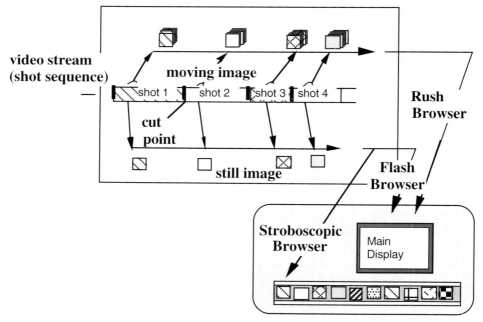

Figure 7-13 Video browsers [20].

By using an automatic video segmentation algorithm [14], [15], [16] [17], the segmentation needed in this browser can be performed automatically. Motion vectors caused by camera operations can be displayed over the icons [18].

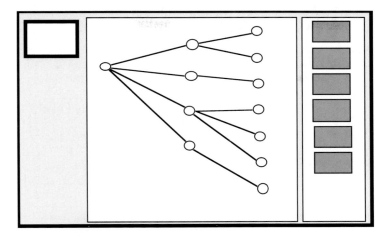

Figure 7-14   Link-indication video browser.

Some examples of the monitor-based fast video browsers using the shot sequence are illustrated in Fig. 7–13: flash and rush [10]. The flash browser displays a representative frame image for each shot in a sequence, while the rush browser shows representative moving images instead of still images. The stroboscopic browser, also shown in Fig. 7–13, is a kind of chart-based browser, and displays representative frame images spatially in a row. It is possible that when the user wants to see more detail of the specific part, the mouse indicated shot is sampled and displayed in a new row, in which the granularity gets finer. In this browser indication, which is a form of time-to-space conversion, the screen memorizes the sequence of the video content for the user.

For a video that is not linearly structured but has links between video segments, those links should be indicated for structure comprehension. Fig. 7–14 shows the link-indication browser. It can be used to represent hierarchically structured movies. In this kind of hierarchical structured representation, story granularity is rough in the upper levels and fine in the lower ones.

Structured Content Processing

In order to realize effective indication and interactions, content and related information should be structured as much as possible. Efficient processing is needed if the interface is to be very responsive. Therefore, the interface should handle only essential information and not process content data.

One solution is to store the information useful for handling multimedia content as middle-level descriptions called content indexes. The content indexes are compact descriptions of content features. The processes such as content

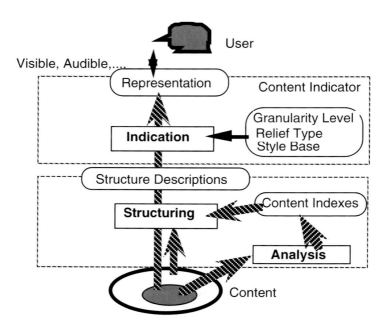

Figure 7-15   Structured content processing.

representation, reactions to user operations, and positioning of content related icon objects, can be realized with these indexes. Structure information included in the attribute information is treated as a content index for processing.

Structured content processing, as explained in Fig. 7–15, is comprised of three important modules: analysis, structuring, and indication. The analysis is performed to extract essential information from the content and make implicit information explicit. In the case of video content, for example, video features useful for cut detection and camera operation detection are extracted from the video content and are described as video indexes. The video indexes can be further processed such as selecting representative frames for the content browser. This kind of structure processing using indexes is called index-based processing. The representation process is based on the indication styles and the desired granularity.

As higher-level descriptions of structured video, algebraic expressions for video composition and search, which realize video handling with abstract video data, was proposed [19]. When the indexed-based video handling and algebra-based video handling is combined, structured content processing would be dramatically enhanced.

Content Indicator for Video Handling

In this section, our approaches to the content indicator for video handling are introduced. Multimedia applications using videos are, for example, video editing, video on demand, presentation, and viewing.

PaperVideo [20]: Video information fixed on paper

As a paper-based video browser, PaperVideo is a new video interface concept in that video information is fixed on paper. Paper is a basic and familiar material and tool for human life and will continue to be so in the future. Various kinds of video information can be represented automatically on paper based on image analysis such as Content Overviewer and Direct Shot Map as follows.

Content Overviewer   The primary function of PaperVideo is to make paper work as a photo album and provide a visual index to video. The visual index should offer a clear idea about the temporal context of the video to the user. An example of the Content Overview is shown in Plate 1. It is a kind of chart-based video browser. Each image is obtained by sampling at the shot change point which is automatically detected. The time sequence runs from left to right and is carriage-returned to left down as in texts. The layout style and image size can be freely modified. The time code is the index determining image position. You can easily get the idea of this video and what happened. Of course, it means more to the person who took the video.

Direct Shot Map   In the Content Overview, no images between representative images are shown. Considering the need to point out a specific part of the video, another style of video image representation was developed called Direct Shot Mapping. It fills the gap between the Content Overview and the original video.

The method of realizing this function is simple. The representative image used in the Content Overview is placed at the left of the column and the images equally sampled (in this case one per second) in each shot are arranged on its right sequentially over time (Plate 2). In this case one of two columns is shown. When the number of images in one shot exceeds fifteen, the image position is carriage-returned to the left down.

Direct Shot Map allows shot length to be discerned at a glance from the length of the row. The rough layout of the images provides a clue as to the "rhythm" of the video. This is one of the basic scene structure visualization methods made possible by the cut detection technique.

Video Panorama [21]: Video space reconstruction

We often want to widen our view of a video when a shot is panned. This is possible with the automatic video space creation method used in VideoSpaceIcon.

The VideoSpaceIcon, which is a three dimensional representation, offers a panoramic view of the video space when it is seen from the front. The panoramic front view, called Video Panorama, is obtained by reducing the temporal axis of the video space. The video panorama is an indication of the video space captured. Since panning operations to cover wide panoramic view are sometimes performed, this is a useful function in visualizing what can not be directly seen in the original.

An example of the Video Panorama is shown in Plate 3. The example was created from a video of an ski jump. The camera is panned to the right. The shape of the Video Panorama reflects the camera operations. A very wide area can be displayed at very high resolution when printed on paper. Teodosio's Salient Video Stills method can also create a panoramic view from video by using optical flow analysis [22].

A video panorama with motion trace is an expanded application of the video panorama in which movement is fixed within the video space. In general, video contains object movement. In many cases, a video is taken to catch a certain object motion. It is useful to visualize object motion on paper especially when the motion trace has some important meaning as in a sport video. It is not easy to create a motion trace when the camera is panned, tilted, or zoomed because the absolute position and size of the object changes with the camera operation. But the video space creation method used to create the video panorama overcomes this problem. First, the video space is created. In the video space, every static object remains in the same position and generates parallel lines over time axis, while a moving object generates non parallel lines. Therefore, object movement can be followed automatically. By intensifying object images at certain intervals, the Motion Trace is created. The example shown in Plate 4 was created based on Plate 3.

VideoScope [20]: Visualizing analysis

Like an oscilloscope analyzing an electronic device or a spectro-analyzer, the video content analyzer called VideoScope can show many different types of video features simultaneously. This kind of analysis tool may not be used in normal video viewing situations, but it is important for future digital video engineering.

A typical VideoScope interface is shown in Plate 5. It provides a kind of multidimensional information relief with the focus on video features. The top-left image is a live video window, the top-right one displays sampled reference images in equal intervals, the second graph displays average intensity of current video frame, the third graph shows first and second representative hue values, the fourth indicates the rate of changes of the hue histogram, and the bottom shows video X-ray images. Video X-ray images are the patterns indicating camera operations. The hue histogram shown at the left-bottom is quite lively.

These graphs show the features extracted from the input video in real time. VideoScope allows us to see how each feature behaves and how it relates to the other features at a glance.

Movie Spiral: Movie Structure Representation

Movie Spiral is not a direct video application but is an indication method which represents video structure in a very unique manner.

A movie is a linearly edited sequence but it has a hierarchical structure consisting of story, scenes, and shots. Assuming that a movie has a three-level hierarchy as shown in Fig. 7–16(a), the video spiral shown in Fig. 7–16(b) is created from the linear movie string by making a first order circle at each cut point and a second order circle at each scene change point.

The size of each shot (scene, movie) loop represents the length of the corresponding shot (scene, movie). The appearance represents the movie features (for example, structure, rhythm, length, and color) and this appeals to the user's intuition. An actual movie spiral is shown in Fig. 7–16(c) for a two-level hierarchy. The original movie sequence string is a sequence of frames sampled at equal intervals.

Sound Browser [23, 24]: Detecting the Presence of Music

Sound plays a very important role in video. In most methods to indicate the content of sound parts, the sound amplitude is displayed to represent the existence and the level of sound. However, it is not easy to "see" the kind of sound from the displayed pattern only.

A sound browser automatically extracts and differentiates music and human voices at regular intervals in a video sequence. Plate 6 shows one result possible with the sound browser. The note symbol indicates music and the lips indicate voices. It is very effective to grasp the video from the view point of the audio track and then focus on a specific part.

TVRam [24]

TVRam is an interface that indicates incoming video content in a chart-based browser using automatic real-time cut detection. The system also stores incoming video for later access. The iconic images are placed in temporal order like a program timetable.

An example of the TVRam interface is shown in Plate 7; the video source is a TV channel and the interface covers the last 24 hours of programming. All processes are automatic and the memory for video storing and the screen space is cyclically used. By clicking an iconic image, the corresponding video starts playing. This interface helps the user to comprehend the TV programs and offers a very speedy access method.

7.5   Summary

The issues and techniques of multimedia content indication were discussed. Granularity control based on structured multimedia processing is the key to useful multimedia content indication. Automatic processes that support various

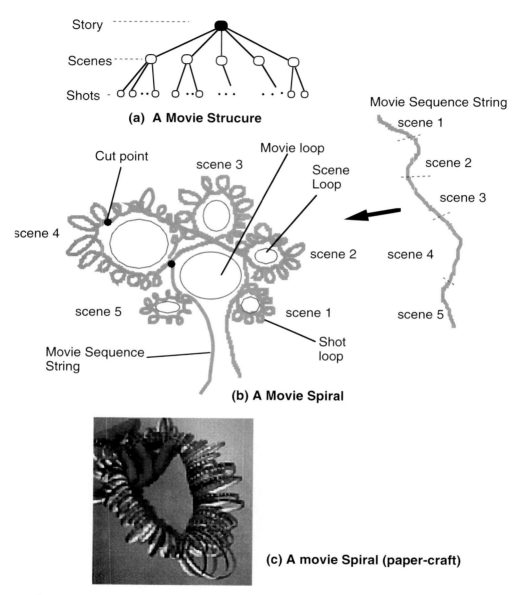

(a) A Movie Strucure

(b) A Movie Spiral

(c) A movie Spiral (paper-craft)

Figure 7-16   Movie spiral.

kinds of multimedia applications and situations are necessary, especially for temporal media such as video. Application examples that have unique features were introduced.

I hope this chapter arouses the imagination of the reader and leads to the invention of new styles of content indication that will enrich our multimedia life.

Acknowledgments

I would like to thank my colleagues, Akihito Akutsu, Yukinobu Taniguchi, Kenichi Minami, and Hiroshi Hamada for their helpful information and advice.

References

[1] Fox, E.A., Akscyn, R.M., Furuta, R.K., and Leggett, J.J., eds., "Digital libraries," *Communications of the ACM*, Vol. 38, No. 4, April 1995.

[2] Elliot, E. and Davenport, G., "Video streamer," in *Conference Companion for Interactive Experience, CHI'94*, Boston, 1994, pp. 65–66.

[3] Arman, F., Depommier, R., Hsu, A., and Chiu, M-Y., "Content-based browsing of video sequences," in *Proceedings of ACM Multimedia'94*, San Francisco, 1994, pp. 97–103.

[4] Mills, M., Cohen, J., and Wong, Y., "A magnifier tool for video data," in *Proceedings of CHI'92*, Monterey, CA, 1992, pp. 93–98.

[5] Davis, M., "Media Streams: An iconic visual language for video annotation," in *Proceedings of IEEE Symposium on Visual Languages*, CS Press, 1993, pp. 196–202.

[6] Ahlberg, C. and Shneiderman, B., "Visual information seeking: Tight coupling of dynamic query filters with starfield displays," in *Proceedings of CHI'94*, 1994, pp. 313–317.

[7] Lambert, S. and Ropiequet, S., eds., *CD-ROM: New Papyrus*. Microsoft Press, 1986.

[8] Davenport, G., Aguierre, S. and Pincever, N., "Cinematic primitives for multimedia," *IEEE Computer Graphics and Applications*, Vol. 11, No. 4, 1991, pp. 67–74.

[9] Lohse, G., Biolsi, K., Walker, N., and Rueler, H., "A classification of visual representations," *Communications of the ACM*, Vol. 37, No. 12, 1994, pp. 36–49.

[10] Tonomura, Y. and Abe, S, "Content oriented visual interface using video icons for visual database systems," *Journal of Visual Languages and Computing*, Academic Press, Vol. 1, 1990, pp. 183–198.

[11] Brondmo, H.P. and Davenport, G., "Creating and viewing the Elastic Charles—A hypermedia journal," in *Hypertext: State of the Art* (McAlesse, R. and Greene, C., eds.) Oxford, UK: Intellect Ltd., 1990.

[12] Tonomura, Y. and Akutsu, A., "A structured video handling techniques for multimedia systems," *IEICE Transactions on Information and Systems*, Vol. E78-D, No. 6, 1995, pp. 764–777.

[13] Tonomura, Y., Akutsu, A., Otsuji, K. and Sadakata, T., "VideoMAP and VideoSpaceIcon: Tools for anatomizing video content," in *Proceedings of INTERCHI'93*, Amsterdam, 1993, pp. 131–138.

[14] Nagasaka, A. and Tanaka, Y., "Automatic video indexing and full-video search for object appearances," in *Proceedings of 2nd Working Conference on Visual Database Systems*, Budapest, 1991, pp. 119–133.

[15] Otsuji, K. and Tonomura, Y., "Projection-detecting filter for video cut detection," *ACM Multimedia Systems*, Vol. 1, 1994, pp. 205–210.

[16] Zhang, H., Kankanhalli, A., and Smoliar, S., "Automatic partitioning of full-motion video," *ACM Multimedia Systems*, Vol. 1, 1993, pp. 10–28.

[17] Hampapur, A., Jain, R., and Weymouth, T., "Digital video segmentation," in *Proceedings of ACM Multimedia'94*, 1994, pp. 357–364.

[18] Ueda, H., Miyatake, T., and Yoshizawa, S., "IMPACT: An interactive natural-motion-picture dedicated multimedia authoring system," in *Proceedings of CHI'91*, 1991, pp. 343–350.

[19] Weiss, R., Duda, A., and Gifford, D., "Composition and search with a Video Algebra," *IEEE Multimedia*, Vol. 2, No. 1, 1995, pp. 12–25.

[20] Tonomura, Y., Akutsu, A., Taniguchi, Y., and Suzuki, G., "Structured video computing," *IEEE Multimedia*, Vol. 1, No. 3, 1994, pp. 34–43.

[21] Akutsu, A. and Tonomura, Y., "Video tomography: An efficient method for camera-work extraction and motion analysis," in *Proceedings of ACM Multimedia*, 1994, pp. 349–356.

[22] Teodosio, L. and Bender, A., "Salient video stills: Content and context preserved," in *Proceedings of ACM Multimedia'93*, 1993, pp. 39–46.

[23] Minami, K., Akutsu, A., Tonomura, Y., and Hamada, H., "An interface for sound browsing in video handling environment," in *Proceedings of HCI'95*, Elsevier Science B.V., 1995, pp. 55–60.

[24] Taniguchi, Y., Akutsu, A., Tonomura, Y., and Hamada, H., "An intuitive and efficient access interface to real-time incoming video based on automatic indexing," *ACM Multimedia'95*, 1995, pp. 25–33.

Multimedia Presentation

C H A P T E R **8**

Composition Models

R. Hamakawa and A. Atarashi

C&C Research Laboratories
NEC Corporation
1-1 Miyazaki 4-Chome
Miyamae-ku, Kawasaki
Kanagawa 216, Japan
{rei, atarashi}@mmp.cl.nec.co.jp

8.1 Introduction

Multimedia applications need to be able to handle a variety of multimedia objects,[1] such as video and audio, simultaneously. That is to say, while a simple VCR application might only require

---

[1] Since the object-oriented approach has a special suitability to multimedia, we view all sets of multimedia data here as objects.

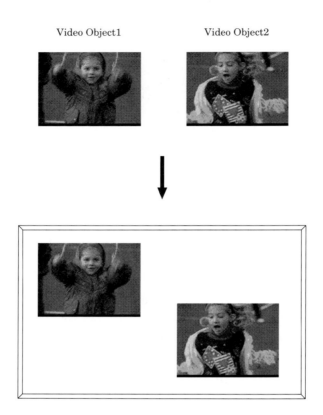

Figure 8-1   An example of spatial composition.

simultaneous playback of audio and video objects, a more useful application would be able to handle such other complicated combinations, as

- playing multiple video objects in a predetermined sequence
- playing a video object with a selection of audio objects, each of which represents the narration in a different language
- simultaneously playing two video objects, each of which represents the recording of a scene from a different camera angle
- etc.

A sophisticated mechanism for creating complex composition multimedia objects by combining individual multimedia objects is necessary. Such a mechanism may be referred to as a "composition model." Composition models employ two basic types of composition: **spatial** and **temporal**.

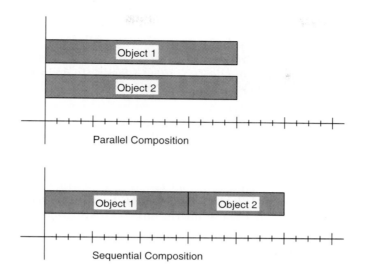

Figure 8-2   Examples of temporal composition.

Spatial composition defines the spatial relationships among the components of a composite multimedia data object (see Fig. 8–1), i.e., the layout of components in a display.

Temporal composition defines the temporal relationships among the components of a composite multimedia data object (Fig. 8–2).

While in a very small number of models these two types of composition may be seen to operate together in a "unified" fashion, in most composition models they function entirely independent of one another.

Temporal composition is the key process in creating complex multimedia objects. The most important variations among composition models result from different approaches to temporal composition.

There are basically two types of temporal composition. One is by *absolute* positioning of objects along a temporal coordinate. In this case, temporal composition is the process of preparing a temporal coordinate for the new composite multimedia object and then placing multimedia objects on it.

The other type of temporal composition is by *relative* positioning of objects. In this case, temporal composition is the process of defining relative relationships (such as before, after, etc.) among multimedia objects.[2]

---

[2] More details can be seen in [1].

A typical example of the use of absolute positioning may be seen in the model proposed by Gibbs *et al.* in [2][3].

Little *et al.* have proposed a conceptual model for composite objects which applies Allen's notion of interval-based temporal logic [9].

Hamakawa *et al.* have proposed a model based on relative positioning in which they extended the idea of the T_EX *glue* to facilitate defining flexible relationships among multimedia objects [6].

Another factor of great importance in composition models is the need to keep the amount of data contained in objects as small as possible while making data retrieval as fast as possible. This calls for an extremely efficient data arrangement scheme, one which makes full use of the logical advantages of object inheritance.

Weiss *et al.* have proposed a model for creating, searching, and playing back digital video presentations [13][14]. Oomoto *et al.* have proposed a video-object data model, and have defined three operations, *interval projection, merge,* and *overlap* for composing new video objects in the model [11].

In the sections which follow, we discuss each of these models in some detail.

8.2   Composite Multimedia Object Model by Gibbs *et al.*

Gibbs *et al.* have presented a class hierarchy for multimedia objects and a composite multimedia object model based on it [2][3]. They view multimedia objects as active objects [12] that produce and/or consume multimedia data values via ports. Multimedia objects are classified into three separate categories: 1) **source** objects, which have only output ports and produce multimedia data values; 2) **sink** objects, which have only input ports and consume multimedia data values; and 3) **filter** objects, which have both input and output ports, and both produce and consume multimedia data values.

Gibbs *et al.* have also introduced a graphical notation system in order to facilitate representing dataflow relationships between objects and to provide a basis for visually composing and editing composite objects (Fig. 8–3). Multimedia objects are denoted by circles, to which boxes representing ports are attached. External boxes represent output ports; internal boxes represent input ports. Dataflow is represented by arrows.

Temporal Transformations to Multimedia Objects

The Gibbs model contains two temporal coordinate systems: *world time* and *object time*. World time is the temporal coordinate common to all multimedia objects in an application, and it dominates their temporal behavior.

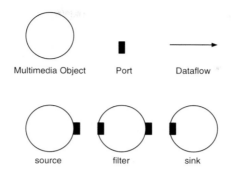

Figure 8-3   Multimedia objects.

Object time is specific to a given multimedia object. Each object can specify: 1) the origin of its object time with respect to world time, 2) its speed for processing multimedia data values, and 3) the orientation of its object time with respect to world time. These specifications are implemented with the following three temporal transformations: **Translate**, **Scale**, and **Invert**.

- **Translate** shifts the multimedia object in world time.
- **Scale** scales the overall duration of the object by a given factor.
- **Invert** flips the orientation of object time back and forth between "forward" and "reverse."

The effect of applying these temporal transformations to a multimedia object is illustrated in Fig. 8–4.

Composite Multimedia Objects

A composite multimedia object contains a set of component multimedia objects and specifications for their temporal and dataflow relationships. Temporal relationships define the synchronization and temporal sequencing of component objects. Dataflow relationships define the connections between the input and output ports of components.

Let us consider the example of creating a new composite object, c_1, which performs the following operations:

> Presentation of a video object, $video_1$, begins at time t_0. At time t_1, a fade is begun from $video_1$ to a second video object, $video_2$. The transition is completed at time t_2 and at time t_3 $video_2$ is stopped.

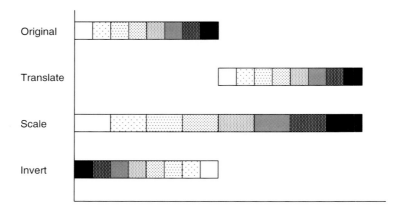

Figure 8-4 Temporal transformations.

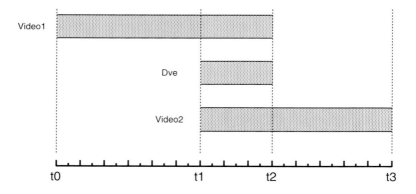

Figure 8-5 A composite timeline.

The temporal relationships among the component objects of the new composite object can be illustrated with a *composite timeline diagram*, such as that seen in Fig. 8–5.

The dataflow relationships among component objects can be defined with the previously introduced graphical notation, as seen in Fig. 8–6, which illustrates the dataflow relationship for object c_1 for the time interval $[t_1, t_2]$. During the interval, video frame sequences from $video_1$ and $video_2$ are processed by the digital video effect object dve, which produces a new sequence of video frames and sends it to the video display object.

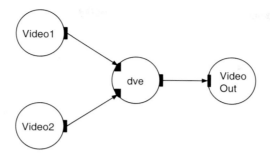

Figure 8-6   Examples of temporal composition.

Creating Composite Objects from BLOB

Gibbs *et al.*, have also proposed a model for creating composite objects from BLOBs (Binary Large OBjects) stored in multimedia database systems [3]. The model includes *interpretation* and *derivation*.

BLOBs, which are essentially sequences of bytes, are often used in storing large amounts of multimedia data within database systems. A BLOB can be an MPEG video stream, an audio stream, or an audio-video interleaved stream such as an MPEG system stream.

An *interpretation* gives a mapping from a BLOB to a meaningful media object. Examples include a mapping from a Motion JPEG stream to a sequence of JPEG frames, mappings from an MPEG System stream both to an MPEG video stream and to an MPEG audio stream, etc.

A *derivation* is a mapping from a set of media objects, and a set of parameters that govern the derivation, to a new media object. One example of derivation is a video transition, which implements a special effect, such as fade or wipe.

Fig. 8–7 illustrates an example creation of a composite multimedia object out of a BLOB.

8.3   Interval-Based Temporal Composition

Little *et al.* have shown that Allen's interval-based temporal logic [1][3] can be applied with great effect to the conceptual modeling of composite multimedia objects. They view multimedia presentation as composed of temporal intervals, with each interval representing the presentation of some specific multimedia

---

[3] This important logic was originally proposed as a method of formalizing temporal knowledge in the field of Artificial Intelligence.

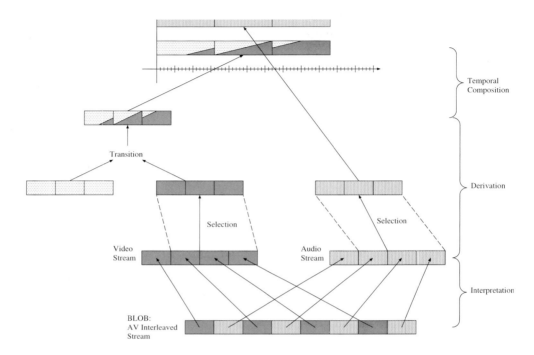

Figure 8-7   Creating a composite multimedia object out of a BLOB.

data element, such as a still image or an audio segment. In Allen's logic, there are thirteen distinct ways that any two intervals can be related. These thirteen can be expressed in terms of just seven relationships, however, since six of the thirteen represent no more than simple inverses of others (Fig. 8–8).

Little *et al.*, in an extension of Allen's logic, express the temporal constraints between two intervals (e.g. α and β) in terms of the following parameters: 1) start times (π_α, π_β) and durations (τ_α, τ_β) of the two intervals; 2) delay from the beginning of the first interval (τ_δ) to the beginning of the second; and 3) their overall duration (τ_{TR}).[4] They further show that these constraints are useful for: 1) identifying a temporal relation for given parameter values; 2) verifying that the parameters satisfy a temporal relation, TR; and 3) identifying overall interval duration, τ_{TR}, given a temporal relation TR.

Little *et al.* have also introduced *n*-ary temporal relations and *reverse* temporal relations. *n*-ary temporal relations are useful in simplifying the expression of relationships among multiple temporal intervals. Reverse temporal relations

---

[4] For example, if α *before* β, then $\tau_\alpha < \tau_\delta$, $\tau_\delta \neq 0$, $\tau_{TR} = \tau_\beta + \tau_\delta$, $\tau_{TR} > \tau_\alpha + \tau_\beta$.

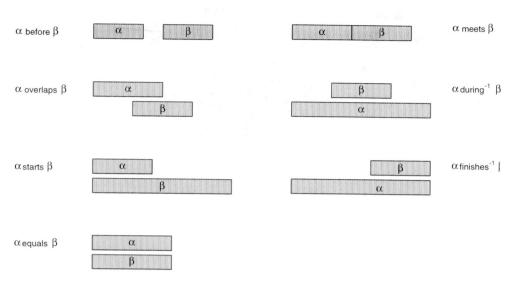

Figure 8-8 Binary temporal relations.

are useful in providing a basis for reverse playback of composite multimedia objects.

n-ary temporal relations

An *n*-ary temporal relation defines a single temporal relationship linking multiple intervals. A common characteristic shared by multiple intervals (e.g. stopping at the same point etc.) is easy to express with an *n*-ary temporal relation. While it could also be expressed with multiple binary relationships, to do so would be needlessly complex. Little *et al.* give the following formal definition of the *n*-ary temporal relation: Let P be an ordered set of n temporal intervals such that $P = \{P_1, P_2, ..., P_n\}$. A temporal relation, tr, is called an *n*-ary temporal relation, denoted tr $_n$, if and only if:

$$P_i \text{ TR } P_{i+1}, \forall i (1 \le i < n)$$

As in the case of binary temporal relations, there are essentially seven distinct representations of *n*-ary relations (Fig. 8–9). Little *et al.* express similar temporal constraints among intervals in terms of start time (π_i), duration (τ_i), and delay (τ_δ^i) of each interval, as well as of the overall duration (τ_{TR}^n) of the temporal intervals. They have also shown, using these parameters, how to determine the relative playing time for any object (i.e. *deadline determination*) as well as

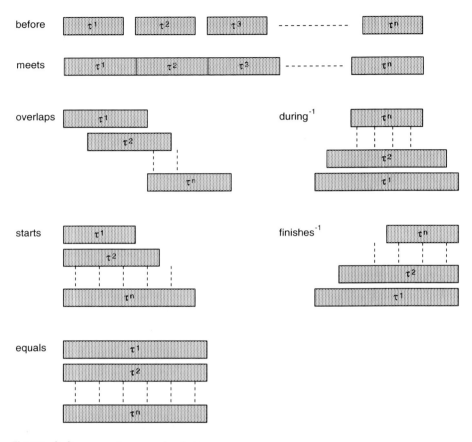

Figure 8-9 *n*-ary temporal relations.

how to determine where to begin play when only a fraction of an *n*-ary related object is intended for such play (i.e., *partial interval evaluation*).

Reverse Temporal Relations

Little *et. al* employ reverse temporal relations and define their *n*-ary extension in order to provide a basis for reverse playback of composite objects.

They define a reversal interval as the negation of a forward interval, i.e., if $[a,b]$ is an interval, then $[-b,-a]$ is its reversal interval. A reverse temporal relation TR_r is defined as the temporal relation formed among reverse temporal intervals. Let $[a,b]$ and $[c,d]$ be two temporal intervals related by TR, then the

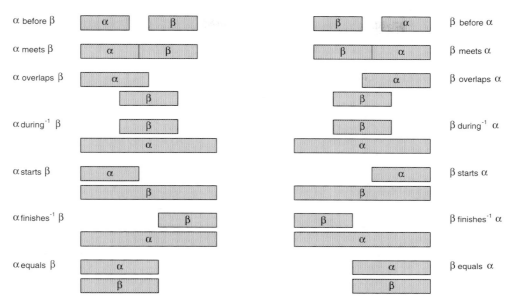

Figure 8–10   Forward and reverse temporal relations.

reverse temporal relation TR$_r$ is defined by the temporal relation formed between [-*b*,-*a*] and [-*d*,-*c*]. Since a reverse relation is a temporal relation, all the properties that are true for forward temporal relations are also true for reverse temporal relations. Reverse relations are summarized in Fig. 8–10.

Temporal Object Composition with *n*-ary Relations

Little *et al.* have introduced a temporal data model in order to express the semantics of *n*-ary temporal relations, which groups multimedia objects and provides them with temporal parameters.

They have introduced two types of nodes, *terminal* and *nonterminal*. *Terminal* nodes contain information with regard to media type (e.g. text, image, video, etc.) and a pointer for locating the actual data in storage. *Nonterminal* nodes are used to represent groupings of other nodes. A *nonterminal* node contains 1) an *n*-ary temporal relation used for grouping other nodes, 2) references to the nodes in the grouping, and 3) temporal parameters (forward and reverse delay as well as overall temporal duration) among the nodes.

The "*meets*" node in Fig. 8–11 is especially well suited to the task of representing a composite object for a movie segment composed of successive pairs of

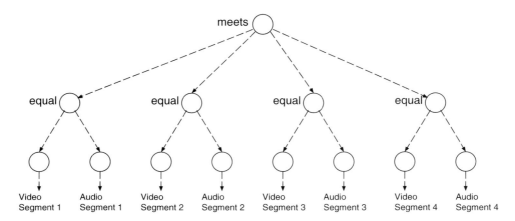

Figure 8–11   Conceptual model for a movie object.

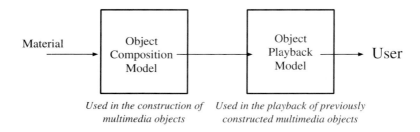

Figure 8–12   Multimedia object models.

equal length video and audio segments. The process of creating such a composite object is as follows: 1) create *terminal* nodes for all video objects and audio objects; 2) create a *nonterminal* node with an *equals* relation for each pair of video and audio objects; 3) create a *nonterminal* node with a *meets* relation for the video and audio pair nodes.

8.4   Object Composition and Playback Models by Hamakawa *et al.*

Object composition and playback models (Fig. 8–12) have been proposed by Hamakawa and Rekimoto in [6]. Their object composition model dealt with the static aspects of multimedia objects, such as name, duration time, etc., while

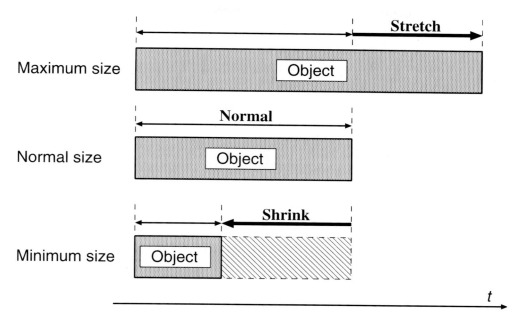

Figure 8-13   Temporal glue.

their object playback model dealt with the dynamic aspects of multimedia objects, such as play, stop, etc. In this section, we describe their object composition model.

Object Composition Model

The object composition model proposed by Hamakawa and Rekimoto has three distinctive features:

Temporal Glue   As in T_EX [7], the typesetting system intended for the creation of beautiful books, glue is an object which can stretch or shrink in two dimensional positional space. This glue can be extended into temporal space, making it "temporal glue," and introduced into multimedia object models (see Fig. 8–13). Each multimedia object will then have glue attributes (normal, stretch, and shrink) in three-dimensional space (2-dimensional position and time). It is also possible to provide a special object, called a *Glue* object, which does not exist as an entity in itself, but which has only glue attributes.

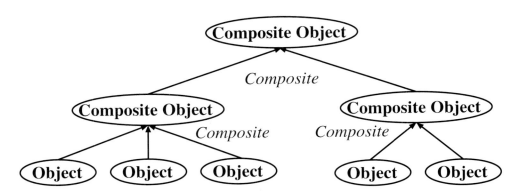

Figure 8-14   Object hierarchy.

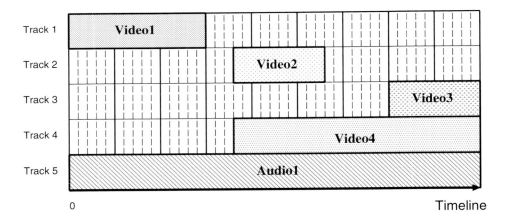

Figure 8-15   Timeline model.

Object Hierarchy   The object composition model employs a hierarchical structure composed of multimedia objects (Fig. 8–14). The complete layout of composite objects, such as the time length of each object, is determined when the highest ranking composite object is determined. When any multimedia object is edited, the attributes of all related composite objects are automatically recalculated to conform to the change.

Relative Location   In one common approach to constructing multimedia objects, the timeline model, individual multimedia objects are located on an absolute timeline scale (see Fig. 8–15). The object composition model differs from the timeline model in that it is not necessary to decide a precise timeline location

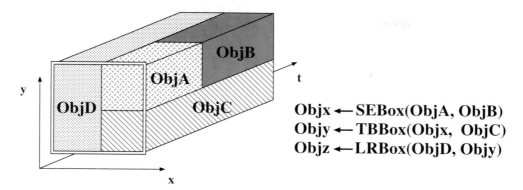

$$Objx \leftarrow SEBox(ObjA, ObjB)$$
$$Objy \leftarrow TBBox(Objx, ObjC)$$
$$Objz \leftarrow LRBox(ObjD, Objy)$$

Figure 8-16   Box example.

for each object. Only the relative locations among objects in time and space need be defined. Once objects are composed, their absolute locations (in both time and space) are calculated automatically.

Each multimedia object has a number of different attributes. Such attributes can be divided into the following three types:

Properties
> General information about multimedia data, such as data type, location, etc.

Hierarchy
> Information about how objects are combined.

Glue Attributes
> Values of temporal glue (i.e., normal, stretch, and shrink sizes), as well as spatial glue attributes.

We may note here that the concepts which most lend this model its characteristic nature are the concepts of relative location and temporal glue.

Constructing Composite Objects

Composite objects are constructed by arranging and modifying multimedia objects along designated dimensions. Control objects used to help in this construction include the following:

Box   This is used to arrange an object group along a designated dimension. There are three types; TBBox, LRBox, SEBox. They correspond, respectively, to an arrangement of Top-Bottom (space), Right-Left (space), and Start-End (time). Fig. 8–16 shows a basic example of Box.

$$Obj_{new} \leftarrow TBBox(Obj_1, Obj_2, ..., Obj_N)$$

$$\text{Obj}_{new} \leftarrow \text{LRBox}(\text{Obj}_1, \text{Obj}_2, ..., \text{Obj}_N)$$

$$\text{Obj}_{new} \leftarrow \text{SEBox}(\text{Obj}_1, \text{Obj}_2, ..., \text{Obj}_N)$$

Time-section This is used to create an object which initially has no attribute values of its own other than its representing a given time-section.

$$\text{Obj}_{new} \leftarrow \text{Section}(\text{Obj}, \text{from}, \text{to})$$

This value-less object can be referenced to any existing object so as to create a new object which contains the attribute values of the specific time-section of the object to which it has been referenced.

Overlay This is used to overlay one object with another object in the time-dimension.

$$\text{Obj}_{new} \leftarrow \text{Overlay}(\text{Obj}_1, \text{Obj}_2, ..., \text{Obj}_N)$$

When playing a video object and an audio object simultaneously, the operation is as follows:

$$\text{Obj}_{new} \leftarrow \text{Overlay}(\text{Video Obj, Audio Obj})$$

Loop This is a type of glue used to repeat an original object for a designated length of time.

$$\text{Obj}_{new} \leftarrow \text{Loop}(\text{Obj}, \text{normal}, \text{shrink}, \text{stretch})$$

In this model, because such static media as texts, still pictures, etc., do not contain information regarding the temporal dimension, loop is used to add temporal glue attributes to their other attributes when they are employed with dynamic media (audio, video etc.) in composite objects.

Position This is used to locate objects on a specific section of an absolute time-scale, as it would be if employed in a timeline model.

$$\text{Obj}_{new} \leftarrow \text{Position}(\text{Obj}, \text{StartTime}, \text{EndTime})$$

Additionally, the following two methods are provided to facilitate working with objects:

Mark This function serves to mark an object at a certain point in time, and to add to the object a title which indicates some feature of object-content relevant to that point in time.

$$\text{Mark}(\text{Obj}, \text{Time}, \text{Title})$$

Constraint This function attaches constraints to objects and is used primarily for synchronization, so as, for example, to ensure that a given audio object always ends at the same instant as a given video object, etc.

$$\text{Constraint}(\text{Condition})$$

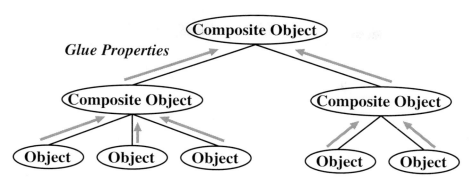

Figure 8–17   Glue property propagation.

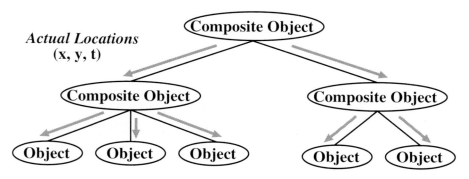

Figure 8–18   Determination of actual location.

A constraint may be attached to an object with regard to its start, to its end, or to a point marked on it. For example, `Constraint(Obj1.start=Obj2.start)`, `Constraint(Obj1.mark1=Obj2.end)`.

Glue Calculation and Determination of the Time Length of Each Object

Since each of the different objects comprising a composite object has glue attributes, the composite object itself has glue attributes (Fig. 8–17). The time length of each object is determined when the highest ranking composite object has been determined (Fig. 8–18). The time length of this highest ranking composite object is the normal time length of its glue attributes.[5]

---

[5] See [6] for a more detailed description of calculation methods.

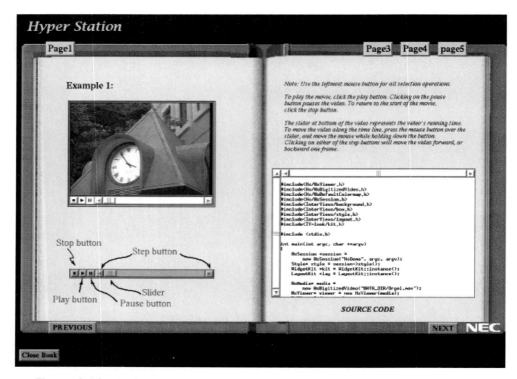

Figure 8-19 Multimedia presentation system.

To implement the above model on a computer, Hamakawa and Rekimoto constructed an audio and video extension library, called *Xavier*,[6] using Inter-Views [8]. Fig. 8–19 shows a multimedia presentation system using *Xavier*.

8.5 VIdeo Algebras by Weiss *et al.*

Weiss *et al.* [13][14] have proposed a data model called *algebraic video* which is used for composing, searching, and playing back digital video presentations. They have also demonstrated a prototype system which can create new video presentations with algebraic combinations of video segments. Their algebraic video data model consists of hierarchical compositions of video expressions

---

[6] *Xavier* can be obtained via anonymous ftp from interviews.stanford.edu in /pub/ contrib

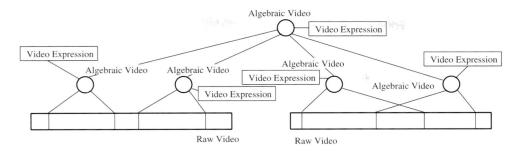

Figure 8-20   Algebraic video's structure.

created and related to one another by the following four categories of video algebra operations:

1. **Creation**: defines the construction of video expressions from raw video.

2. **Composition**: defines temporal relationships among component video expressions.

3. **Output**: defines spatial layout and audio output for component video expressions.

4. **Description**: assigns content attributes to a video expression.

   Simple video expressions can be used to create a single-window presentation from a raw video segment, which is specified by the name of the full raw video and the relevant range within it. Compound video expressions can be constructed from simpler ones using video algebra operations. In this construction, the simpler expressions may share the same video data (see Fig. 8–20).

   Weiss *et al.* specified 18 video algebra operations in all (two for Creation, 12 for Composition, two for Output, and two for Description). Below are some example operations, followed by a simple example of the creation of a sample presentation, as illustrated by Weiss *et al.* in [14].

	Usage	Function
Creation		
Create	create *name begin end*	Creates a presentation from a range within the identified raw video segment
Composition		
Concatenation	$E_1 \circ E_2$	Defines a presentation where E_2 follows E_1
Union	$E_1 \cup E_2$	Defines a presentation where E_2 follows E_1 and common footage is not repeated

Intersection	$E_1 \cap E_2$	Defines a presentation where only common footage of E_1 and E_2 is played
Difference	$E_1 - E_2$	Defines a presentation where only footage of E_1 that is not in E_2 is played
Parallel	$E_1 \parallel E_2$	Defines a presentation where E_1 and E_2 are played concurrently and start simultaneously
Parallel-end	$E_1 \; \wr\wr \; E_2$	Defines a presentation where E_1 and E_2 are played concurrently and terminate simultaneously

Description

| Description | description E content | Specifies that E/is described by *content* |

Example

C_1	= **create**	News.1995.1.1 10 25
C_2	= **create**	News.1995.1.1 20 30
C_3	= **create**	News.1995.1.1 30 40
C_4	= **create**	News.1995.1.1 40 50

| D_1 | =(**description** | C_1 "Anchor speaking") |
| D_2 | =(**description** | C_3 "Question") |

| C_5 | = | $C_3 \circ C_4$ |

| D_3 | =(**description** | C_5 "Question from audience") |

| C_6 | = | $C_2 \circ C_5$ |

| D_4 | =(**description** | C_6 "Smith") |

| C_7 | = | $C_1 \cup C_6$ |

| D_5 | =(**description** | C_5 "Smith on economic form") |

The results of these operations are depicted in Fig. 8–21.

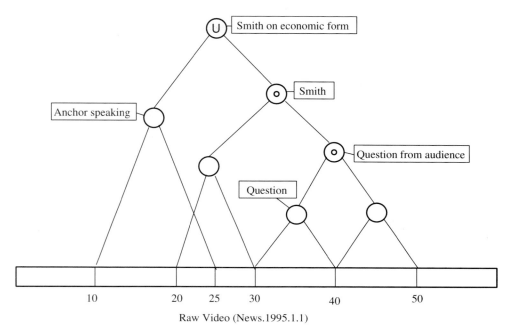

Figure 8-21   Sample presentation.

8.6   Ovid by Oomoto *et al.*

Oomoto *et al.* [11] have proposed a video-object data model, and have demonstrated on it a prototype video-object database system referred to as the Object-oriented Video Information Database (OVID) system. They have defined three operations, *interval projection, merge,* and *overlap,* for composing new video objects in the model. They have also introduced the concept of "interval-inclusion inheritance," which describes how a video object inherits attribute/value pairs from another video object.

Video Object Data Model

In their model, *video-objects* consist of

- Object identifiers
- Intervals (represented by pairs of frame numbers: starting and ending)

- Collections of attribute/value pairs

  In their definition, *video-object* may be represented as (*oid, I, v*) where

1. *oid* is an object identifier which is an element of $\mathcal{ID}$ (a set of identifiers)

2. *I* is a finite subset of $\mathcal{I}$ (a set of intervals)

3. *v* is an n-tuple $[a_1 : v_1, ..., a_n : v_n]$, where each a_i $(1 \le i \le n)$ is an attribute name, and v_i is a value defined recursively in the following manner:

   a. each element $x \in \mathcal{D}$ (a set of atomic values (numbers, strings, and special symbol top (*unknown*) and $\perp$ (*undefined*))) is a value

   b. each interval $i \in \mathcal{I}$ is a value

   c. for values $v_1, ..., v_n$, $\{v_1, ..., v_n\}$ represents a value referred to as a *set value*.

   d. each video-object is also a value

For a given video-object, $o = (oid, I, v)$ with its value $v=[a_1:v_1,...,a_n:v_n]$, $attr(v)$ denotes the set of all the attributes in v, and $value(o)$ denotes the value v. Also, value v_i is denoted by $v.a_i$. They have also introduced an inheritance mechanism by which some attribute/value pairs of a video-object are inherited by another video-object if the former video-object's interval contains the latter video-object's interval. For two given interval sets, I_1 and I_2, the *inclusion relationship* between them is defined as:

- For each $i \in I_1$, if there exists $i´ \in I_2$ such that $i \subseteq i´$, then I_1 is said to be *included* by the interval set I_2, denoted by $I_1 \sqsubseteq I_2$.

Composition Operations for Video-Objects

Oomoto *et al.* have introduced three basic operations, fundamentally similar to those used in ordinary video editing, to compose new video-objects from existing video-objects.[7]

Interval Projection

This is an operation which creates a new object by copying a portion of an existing object. The operation is efficient because only the descriptional data required for the copied portion is inherited.

---

[7] Each definition here is very rough. See [11] for a complete definition.

$$\left\{ \begin{array}{ll} o = & (oid, I, v) \\ I' & (I' \sqsubseteq I) \\ A & \text{a set of inheritable attributes} \end{array} \right\}$$

$$\Downarrow$$

$$\left\{ \begin{array}{ll} o' \quad = & (oid', I', v') \\ attr(v') = & attr(v) \cap A \\ v'.a \quad = v.a\,(\text{for each attribute } a \text{ in } attr(v')) \end{array} \right\}$$

Merge

This is an operation which creates a new object by concatenating two existing objects.

$$\left\{ \begin{array}{l} o_1 = (oid_1, I_1, v_1) \\ o_2 = (oid_2, I_2, v_2) \end{array} \right\}$$

$$\Downarrow$$

$$\left\{ \begin{array}{ll} o \quad = & (oid, I_1 \sqcup I_2, v) \\ I_1 \sqcup I_2 : & \text{the minimal set of intervals} \\ v \quad = [a_1 : v_1, ..., a_n : v_n] \text{ where each } a_i \text{ is in } attr(v_i) \cap attr(v_2) \end{array} \right\}$$

Overlap

This is an operation which creates a new object by copying a segment which two existing objects have in common.

$$\left\{ \begin{array}{l} o_1 = (oid_1, I_1, v_1) \\ o_2 = (oid_2, I_2, v_2) \end{array} \right\}$$

$$\Downarrow$$

$$\left\{ \begin{array}{ll} o \quad = & (oid, I_1 \sqcap I_2, v) \\ I_1 \sqcap I_2 : & \text{the maximal subset of } i_1 \cap i_2 \\ v \quad = [a_1 : v_1, ..., a_n : v_n] \text{ where each } a_i \text{ is in } attr(v_i) \cup attr(v_2) \end{array} \right\}$$

Fig. 8–22 shows simple examples of merge and overlap operations.

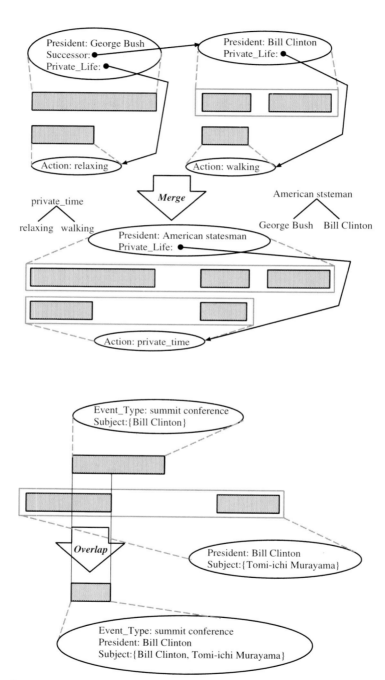

Figure 8-22 Operation examples in OVID.

8.7 Conclusion

We have described here the basic concepts at work in composite object models and introduced recent important research activities in the field.

We must note, however, that any composite object model will be of no use without proper implementation, and for that, the following considerations are especially important:

- Integration with playback models: Composite objects are first useful when they are played back. This means that a composite model must be integrated with a playback model, and the most important issue here is synchronization, both within element objects and among the element objects comprising composite objects.

- Integration with multimedia database systems: As we use more and more multimedia data, we will need to create multimedia database systems capable of more efficient data storage and retrieval, and composite models will need to be able to handle the multimedia objects stored in such databases.

- Good editing environment: Creating a composite object often requires repeated editing and playback. A well-designed editing environment will take full advantage of any superior characteristics in the underlying model so as to reduce as far as possible the time spent repeating this editing/playback cycle [5][10].

References

[1] Allen J.F., "Maintaining knowledge about temporal intervals," *Communications of the ACM*, Vol.26. No.11, 1983, pp. 832–842.

[2] Gibbs, S. "Composite multimedia and active objects," in *Proceedings of OOPSLA '91 (Conference on Object-Oriented Programming Systems, Languages, and Applications)*, Phoenix, AZ, Oct 1991, pp. 87–112.

[3] Gibbs, S., Breiteneder, C., and Tsichritzis, D., "Data modeling of time-based media," in *Proceedings of the ACM-SIGMOD 1994, International Conference on Management of Data*, Minneapolis, MN, May 1994, pp. 91–102.

[4] Hamakawa, R., Sakagami, H., and Rekimoto, J., "Audio and video extensions to graphical user interface toolkits," in Third International Workshop on Network and Operating System Support for Digital Audio and Video, La Jolla, CA, Nov 1992, *Lecture Notes in Computer Science*, Vol. 7, No. 12, Berlin: Springer-Verlag, 1992, pp. 399–404.

[5] Hamakawa, R., Sakagami, H., and Rekimoto, J., "Mbuild—Multimedia data builder by box and glue," presented at International Conference on Multimedia Computing and Systems, Boston, May 1994.

[6]   Hamakawa, R. and Rekimoto, J., "Object composition and playback models for handling multimedia data," in *Multimedia Systems*, Vol. 2. Berlin: Springer-Verlag, 1994, pp. 26–35.

[7]   Knuth, D.E., *The T$_E$X Book*. Reading, PA: Addison-Wesley, 1984.

[8]   Linton, M., Vlissides, J. and Calder, P., "Composing user interfaces with *InterViews*," *Computer*, Vol. 22, No. 2, Feb 1989, pp. 8–22.

[9]   Little, T. and Ghafoor, A. "Interval-based conceptual models for time-dependent multimedia data," *IEEE Transactions on Knowledge and Data Engineering*, Vol. 5, No. 4, 1993, pp. 551–563.

[10] de Mey, V. and Gibbs, S. "A multimedia component kit," in *Proceedings of ACM Multimedia '93*, Anaheim, CA, Aug 1993, pp. 291–300.

[11] Oomoto, E. and Tanaka, K., "OVID: Design and implementation of a video-object database system," *IEEE Transactions Knowledge and Data Engineering*, Vol. 4, No. 4, Aug 1993, pp. 629–643.

[12] Wegner, P., "Concepts and paradigms of object oriented programming," *OOPS Messenger*, Vol. 1, No. 1, Aug 1990, pp. 7–87.

[13] Weiss, R., Duda, A., and Gifford, D.K., "Content-based access to algebraic video," in *Proceedings of the International Conference on Multimedia Computing and System*, Boston, May 1994, pp. 140–151.

[14] Weiss, R, Duda, A., and Gifford, D.K., "Composition and search with a video algebra," *IEEE Multimedia*, Vol. 2, No. 1, Spring, 1995, pp. 12–25.

C H A P T E R   **9**

Memory Management: Codecs

Bhaskaran Vasudev and Wei Li

Hewlett-Packard Laboratories
Palo Alto, CA 94302
bhaskara@hpl.hp.com

Logitech Inc.
Fremont, CA 94555
Wei_Li@logitech.com

9.1   Introduction

*I*n recent years, there have been significant advancements in algorithms and architectures for the processing of image, video, and audio signals. These advancements have proceeded along several directions. On the algorithm front, new techniques have led to the development of robust methods to reduce the size of the image, video, or audio data. Such methods are extremely vital in many applications that manipulate and store digital representations of image, video, and audio signals. On the architecture front, it is now feasible to put sophisticated compression processes on a relatively low-cost single chip; this has spurred a great deal of activity in developing codecs for multimedia systems for the large consumer market.

One of the exciting prospects of such advancements is that multimedia information comprising image, video, and audio has the potential to become just another data type. This usually implies that multimedia information[1] will be digitally encoded so that it can be manipulated, stored, and transmitted along with other digital data types. For such data usage to be pervasive and to enable cost-effective codecs, it is essential that the data encoding be standard across different platforms and applications. This will foster widespread development of applications and will also promote interoperability among systems from different vendors. Furthermore, standardization can lead to the development of cost-effective codec implementations, which in turn will promote the widespread use of multimedia information. This is the primary motivation behind the emergence of image and video compression standards.

In this chapter we will describe the compression methodology that is used in the codecs. Our discussion will be from an algorithmic and architectural viewpoint and we will focus primarily on standards-based codecs for image and video data. We will not discuss audio codecs. We will also discuss some of our work in object-based compression techniques. Such techniques may form the basis of future compression standards for image and video.

9.2 Background

There are many broad definitions for what is meant by a codec; however, in this chapter, we restrict the definition of a **codec** to be an algorithm or method to **co**mpress and **dec**ompress a signal. Thus, in the cases where the signal is defined as an image or a video stream, the basic task of a codec is to compress the signal so as to yield a compact representation. There are many applications that benefit when image and video signals are available in compressed form. Without compression, most of these applications would not be feasible. Table 9–1 lists a representative set of such applications for image, video, and audio data, as well as typical data rates of the corresponding compressed bit streams. Typical data rates for the uncompressed bit streams are also shown.

Image, video, and audio signals are amenable to compression due to these factors:

- There is considerable statistical redundancy in the signal.

  a. Within a single image or a single video frame, there exists significant correlation among neighbor samples. This correlation is referred to as *spatial correlation*.

---

[1] A system that will encode and decode the multimedia information is usually referred to as a codec (**co**mpressor and **dec**ompressor).

Application	Data Rate	
	Uncompressed	**Compressed**
Voice 8k samples/s, 8 bits/sample	64 kbps	2–4 kbps
Slow-motion video (10 fps) framesize 176×120, 8 bits/pixel	5.07 Mbps	8–16 kbps
Audio conference 8k samples/s, 8 bits/sample	64 kbps	16–64 kbps
Video conference (15 fps) framesize 352×240, 8 bits/pixel	30.41 Mbps	64–768 kbps
Digital audio (stereo) 44.1k samples/s, 16 bits/sample	1.5 Mbps	128–1.5 Mbps
Video file transfer (15 fps) framesize 352×240, 8 bits/pixel	30.41 Mbps	384 kbps
Digital video on CD-ROM (30 fps) framesize 352×240, 8 bits/pixel	60.83 Mbps	1.5–4 Mbps
Broadcast video (30 fps) framesize 720×480, 8 bits/pixel	248.83 Mbps	3–8 Mbps
HDTV (59.94 fps) framesize 1280×720, 8 bits/pixel	1.33 Gbps	20 Mbps

Table 9–1   Applications for image, video, and audio compression.

b. For data acquired from multiple sensors (such as satellite images), there exists significant correlation amongst samples from these sensors. This correlation is referred to as *spectral correlation*.

c. For temporal data (such as video), there is significant correlation amongst samples in different segments of time. This is referred to as *temporal correlation*.

- There is considerable information in the signal that is irrelevant from a perceptual point of view.
- Some data tends to have high-level features that are redundant across space and time; that is, the data is of a fractal nature.

For a given application, compression schemes may exploit any one or all of the above factors to achieve the desired compression data rate. A systems view of a codec is depicted in Fig. 9–1.

The core of the encoder portion of the codec is the source coder. The source coder performs the compression task by reducing the input data rate to a level that can be supported by the storage or transmission medium. In a practical system, the source coder is usually followed by a second level of coding in the

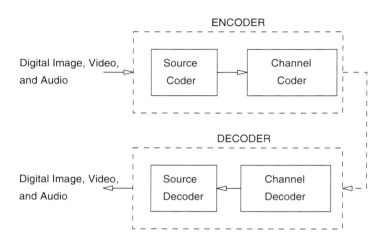

Figure 9-1   Generic codec system.

encoder, namely, the channel coder (Fig. 9–1). The channel coder translates the compressed bit stream into a signal suitable for either storage or transmission. In most systems, source coding and channel coding are distinct processes. In recent years, methods to perform combined source and channel coding have also been developed. Design trade-offs between source and channel codecs can often lead to a simpler overall system design; we illustrate this later in this chapter in our discussion of the H.324 videoconferencing compression standard. Note that, in order to reconstruct the image, video, or audio signal, one needs to reverse the processes of channel coding and source coding. This is usually performed at the decoder subsystem of the codec. From a systems design viewpoint, one can restate the codec design problem as a bit rate minimization problem, where several constraints may have to be met, including the following:

- Specified levels of signal quality. This constraint is usually applied at the decoder.

- Implementation complexity. This constraint is often applied at the decoder, and in some instances at both the encoder and the decoder.

- Communication delay. This constraint refers to the end to end delay, and is measured from the start of encoding a sample to the complete decoding of that sample.

Note that these constraints have different importance in different applications. For example, in a two-way teleconferencing system, the communication delay

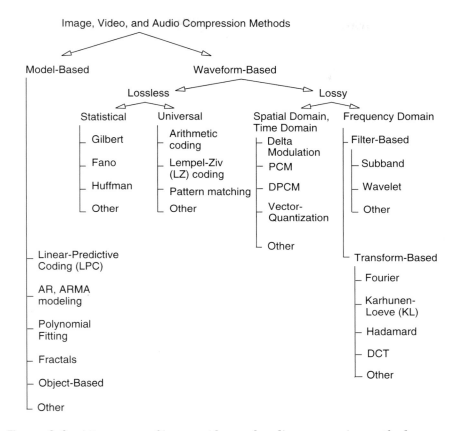

Figure 9–2 A taxonomy of image, video, and audio compression methods.

might be the major constraint, whereas, in a television broadcasting system, signal quality and decoder complexity might be the main constraints.

Codec Classification—Algorithm Viewpoint

From an algorithm viewpoint, it is the underlying compression method that distinguishes one codec from another. There is a wide range of compression methods that have been employed to compress image and video signals and a typical classification of these methods is shown in Fig. 9–2.

Lossless compression

In many applications such as in archiving of digital X-ray images, the decoder has to reconstruct without any loss of the original data. For a lossless compression process, the reconstructed data and the original data must be identical in

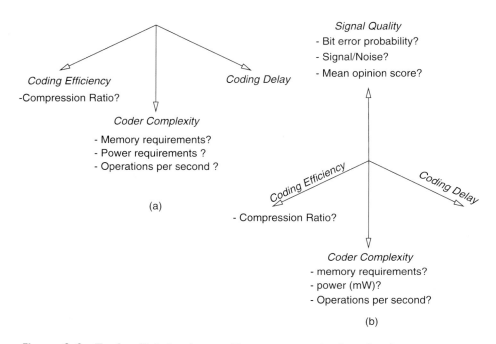

Figure 9-3 Trade-offs in lossless and lossy compression based codecs.

value for each and every data sample. This is also referred to as a reversible process. The choice of a compression method in codecs requiring lossless compression involves a trade-off along the three dimensions depicted in Fig. 9–3(a); namely, coding efficiency, coding complexity, and coding delay.

Lossy Compression

The majority of the applications in image or video data processing do not require that the reconstructed data and the original data be identical in value. Thus, some amount of loss is permitted in the reconstructed data. A compression process that results in an imperfect reconstruction is referred to as a lossy compression process. This compression process is irreversible. In practice, most irreversible compression processes degrade rapidly the signal quality when they are repeatedly applied on previously decompressed data. The choice of a specific lossy compression method in codecs involves trade-offs along the four dimensions shown in Fig. 9–3(b). Due to the additional degree of freedom, namely, in the signal quality, a lossy compression process can yield higher compression ratios than a lossless compression scheme.

Lossless and lossy compression methods fit within the general model depicted in Fig. 9–4. Most of the codecs that are presently used fit within this

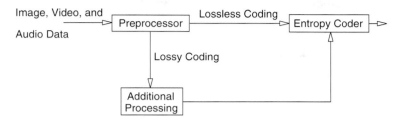

Figure 9-4   Lossless and lossy compression coding framework.

framework and employ both lossy and lossless compression schemes to achieve high coding efficiency. These compression methods will be described in detail in a later section.

Codec Classification—Implementation Viewpoint

For each compression algorithm that is adopted by the codec to achieve compression, one can envision two potential implementations for the codec, namely *software-only* or *hardware-assisted* implementations. The choice of which implementation is preferred is largely dependent on the compression algorithm. Presently, due to the limited computation capability of microprocessors, *software-only* implementations have been adopted only for the decoder portion of a codec and such implementations have low complexity but trade-off quality of the decoded image/video against the picture rate. Hardware-assisted codecs can offer higher decoded image/video quality but at the expense of additional cost [1]. In recent years the codec implementations have tried to achieve a balance between a purely software-only implementation and a hardware-assisted implementation. This hybrid approach is found in various multimedia instruction-set enhanced CPUs [2] such as HP's PA7100LC, Sun's UltraSparc, or Intel's MMX. We will provide examples for the *software-only, hardware-assisted,* and the hybrid approaches when we discuss some of the compression methods that are used in today's codecs.

Codec Classification: Sample Based or Block Based

Regardless of whether the codecs adopt lossless compression or lossy compression techniques, these codecs achieve data compression by exploiting redundancies in the data across space, time, or frequency. These codecs fall into two classes, (a) pixel based and (b) block based. Pixel-based codecs employ compression techniques that achieve compression by operating on one pixel at a time; for such codecs, there is no inherent bit savings if frequency domain approaches are adopted. Block-based codecs employ compression techniques that achieve compression by operating on many samples at a time and such codecs belong to these three categories: spatial-domain-based, temporal-domain-based, or frequency-domain-based. If a group of samples is highly correlated in the spatial domain, then it tends to also have a very compact frequency-domain representation; thus, a frequency-domain-based compression process is preferred for such datasets. For multidimensional data, such as video that have both spatial and temporal components, a hybrid spatial- and frequency-domain approach is adopted. Such hybrid techniques are the basis of all the image and video compression standards which will be discussed in this chapter.

Issues in Compression Method Selection in a Codec

When choosing a specific compression method for the codec, one should consider the following issues:

- Lossless or lossy. This is usually dictated by the coding efficiency requirements.

- Coding efficiency. Even in a lossy compression process, the desirable coding efficiency might not be achievable. This is especially the case when there are specific constraints on output signal quality.

- Consistency in coding efficiency. In some applications, large variations in coding efficiency among different data sets may not be acceptable.

- Resilience to transmission errors. Some compression methods are more robust to transmission errors than others. If retransmissions are not permitted, then this requirement may impact on the overall encoder-decoder design.

- Complexity trade-offs. In most implementations, it is important to keep the overall encoder-decoder complexity low. However, certain applications may require only a low decoding complexity.

- Nature of degradations in decoder output. Lossy compression methods introduce artifacts in the decoded signal. The nature of artifacts depends on the compression method that is employed. The degree to which these artifacts are judged objectionable also varies from application to application. In communication systems, there is often an interplay between the transmission errors and the coding artifacts introduced by the coder. Thus, it is important to consider all types of error in a system design.

- Data representation. In many applications, there is a need to support two decoding phases. In the first phase, decoding is performed to derive an intelligible signal; this is the case in data browsing. In the second phase, decoding is performed to derive a higher quality signal. One can generalize this notion to suggest that some applications require a hierarchical representation of the data. In the compression context, we refer to such compression schemes as *scalable compression methods*. The notion of scalability has been adopted in the compression standards that are described later in this chapter.

- Multiple usage of the encoding-decoding tandem. In many applications, such as video editing, there is a need to perform multiple encode-decode operations using results from a previous encode-decode operation. This is not an issue for lossless compression; however, for lossy schemes, resilience to multiple encoding-decoding cycles is essential.

- Interplay with other data modalities, such as audio and video. In a system where several data modalities have to be supported, the compression methods for each modality should have some common elements. For instance, in an interactive videophone system, the audio compression method should have a frame structure that is consistent with the video frame structure. Otherwise, there will be unnecessary requirements on buffers at the decoder and a reduced tolerance to timing errors.

- Interworking with other systems. In a mass-market environment, there will be multiple data modalities and multiple compression systems. In such an environment, transcoding from one compression method to another may be needed. For instance, video editing might be done on a frame by frame basis; hence, a compression method that does not exploit temporal redundancies might be used here. After video editing, there might be a need to broadcast this video. In this case, temporal redundancies can be exploited to achieve a higher coding efficiency. In such a scenario, it is important to select compression methods that support transcoding from one compressed stream format to another. Interworking is important in many communications environments as well.

In this section, we have briefly reviewed some of the basic concepts associated with the codecs for compression of image, video, and audio signals. In subsequent sections we will examine some of the algorithms that are used in the codecs.

9.3   Standards-Based Codecs

Since the mid-1980s, members from both the International Telecommunication Union (ITU) and the International Organization for Standardization (ISO) have been working together to establish a joint international standard for the compression of multilevel *still* images. This effort has been known as *JPEG*, the Joint Photographic Experts Group. Officially, JPEG corresponds to the ISO/IEC international standard 10918-1, *Digital Compression and Coding of Continuous-Tone Still Images* or to the ITU-T Recommendation T. 81.

In the digital video arena, in response to a growing need for a common format for coding and storing digital video, ISO established the Moving Pictures Expert group (MPEG) in 1988 with the mission to develop standards for the coded representation of moving pictures and associated audio information on digital storage media. The first phase of its work was completed in 1991 with the development of the ISO standard 11172, *Coding of Moving Pictures and Associated Audio—For Digital Storage Media at up to about 1.5 Mbit/s*. This standard is also known as *MPEG-1*.

In 1990, MPEG started the second phase of its work, namely, to develop extensions to MPEG-1 that would allow for greater input-format flexibility, higher data rates (as needed by high-definition TV), and better error resilience. That work led to the ISO standard 13818 (or ITU-T Recommendation H.262), *Generic Coding of Moving Pictures and Associated Audio* and this standard is also known as *MPEG-2*.

MPEG has already started working on developing new coding standards for very low bit rates. This activity is known as *MPEG-4* and the standard is expected to be defined by 1998.

The MPEG standards were essentially developed with a one-way video delivery model in mind; the codecs were not meant for two-way interactive applications such as videoconferencing. In the late 1980s, collaboration among telecommunication operators and manufacturers of videoconferencing equipment led to the development of the *H.320* video conferencing standard by the ITU (the video component of this standard is known as H.261). H.261 is also known as the $P \times 64$ standard because it describes video coding and decoding methods at the rates $p \times 64$ kbits/s, where p is an integer from 1 to 30. H.261 was ratified in Geneva in December of 1990. H.320 compliant codecs are intended to operate in a ISDN environment. ITU is presently developing a video conferencing standard for the general switched telephone network (GSTN) and mobile radio. This standardization effort is referred to as H.324 and is expected to be approved later in 1995. The H.324 suite is a recommendation for real-time voice, data, and video over V.34 modems on the GSTN telephone network. The video component of this standard is known as H.263. H.261 provides coded video at bit rates 64 kbits/s and above, whereas the H.263 video coding standard proposed for H.324 will provide coded video around 26 kbits/s.

Generic Model

The image/video coding standards JPEG, MPEG-1, MPEG-2, H.261, and H.263 use the same basic methodology for compressing image or video data and the method consists of a spatial redundancy reduction scheme and a temporal redundancy reduction scheme. Note that the latter is used only in MPEG-1, MPEG-2, H.261, and H.263 standards.

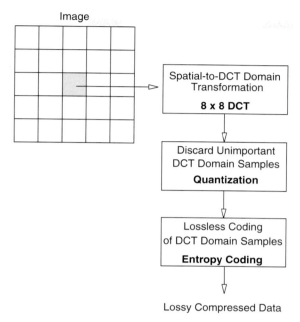

Figure 9-5   Generic DCT-based coding system.

Spatial Redundancy Reduction Scheme

The generic form of the spatial redundancy reduction scheme is shown in Fig. 9-5.

Denote the spatial-domain samples in the 8×8 block shown in Fig. 9-5 as (x_{ij}). The spatial-to-DCT domain transformation expressed in Equation (1) yields an 8×8 block (y_{kl}) in the DCT domain.

$$y_{kl} = \frac{c(k)c(l)}{4} \sum_{i=0}^{7} \sum_{j=0}^{7} x_{ij} \cos\left(\frac{(2i+1)k\pi}{16}\right) \cos\left(\frac{(2j+1)l\pi}{16}\right), \tag{1}$$

where $k, l = 0, 1, \ldots, 7$ and

$$c(k) = \begin{cases} \dfrac{1}{\sqrt{2}} & \text{if } k = 0 \\ 1 & \text{otherwise} \end{cases}. \tag{2}$$

An 8×8 blocksize is chosen for several reasons. From a hardware or software implementation viewpoint, an 8×8 blocksize does not impose significant memory requirements; furthermore, the computational complexity of an 8×8 DCT is manageable on most computing platforms. From a compaction efficiency viewpoint, a blocksize larger than 8×8 does not offer significantly better compression; this is attributable to the significant dropoff in spatial correlation which in turn lowers compression efficiency when a pixel neighborhood is larger than eight pixels. The choice of the DCT is motivated by the many benefits it offers:

- For highly correlated image data, the compaction efficiency due to the use of a DCT is close to that obtained with the optimum transform, namely, the Karhunen-Loeve Transform (KLT).
- The DCT is an orthogonal transform. Thus, if in matrix form the DCT output is $Y = TXT^t$, then the inverse transform is $X = T^tYT$. Since many codecs need to include a compression unit as well as a decompression unit, it needs to perform the forward transform as well as the inverse transform and orthogonality of the transform greatly reduces the complexity of the codec.

If say an 8×8 block in the spatial domain is

$$X = \begin{bmatrix} 168 & 161 & 161 & 150 & 154 & 168 & 164 & 154 \\ 171 & 154 & 161 & 150 & 157 & 171 & 150 & 164 \\ 171 & 168 & 147 & 164 & 164 & 161 & 143 & 154 \\ 164 & 171 & 154 & 161 & 157 & 157 & 147 & 132 \\ 161 & 161 & 157 & 154 & 143 & 161 & 154 & 132 \\ 164 & 161 & 161 & 154 & 150 & 157 & 154 & 140 \\ 161 & 168 & 157 & 154 & 161 & 140 & 140 & 132 \\ 154 & 161 & 157 & 150 & 140 & 132 & 136 & 128 \end{bmatrix} .$$

After subtracting 128 from each element of X (this is done in the JPEG, MPEG-1, MPEG-2, H.261, and H.263 standards), the 8×8 DCT output block as computed by (1) is given by,

$$Y = \begin{bmatrix} 214 & 49 & -3 & 20 & -10 & -1 & 1 & -6 \\ 34 & -25 & 11 & 13 & 5 & -3 & 15 & -6 \\ -6 & -4 & 8 & -9 & 3 & -3 & 5 & 10 \\ 8 & -10 & 4 & 4 & -15 & 10 & 6 & 6 \\ -12 & 5 & -1 & -2 & -15 & 9 & -5 & -1 \\ 5 & 9 & -8 & 3 & 4 & -7 & -14 & 2 \\ 2 & -2 & 3 & -1 & 1 & 3 & -3 & -4 \\ -1 & 1 & 0 & 2 & 3 & -2 & -4 & -2 \end{bmatrix} .$$

At this point, no compression has been achieved. Note that, compared to X, the DCT-transformed data Y has large amplitudes clustered close to y_{00}, commonly referred to as the DC coefficient. It is the process of quantization which leads to compression in DCT domain coding. The quantization step of Fig. 9-5 is expressed as

$$z_{kl} = round\left(\frac{y_{kl}}{q_{kl}}\right) = \left\lfloor \frac{y_{kl} \pm \left\lfloor \frac{q_{kl}}{2} \right\rfloor}{q_{kl}} \right\rfloor, k, l = 0, 1, \dots, 7 , \tag{3}$$

where q_{kl} denotes the kl^{th} element of an 8×8 quantization matrix Q. ($\lfloor x \rfloor$ denotes the largest integer smaller or equal to x.) The output of the quantization module yields the $8 \times$ block

$$
Z = \begin{bmatrix}
13 & 4 & 0 & 1 & 0 & 0 & 0 & 0 \\
3 & -2 & 1 & 1 & 0 & 0 & 0 & 0 \\
0 & 0 & 1 & 0 & 0 & 0 & 0 & 0 \\
1 & -1 & 0 & 0 & 0 & 0 & 0 & 0 \\
-1 & 0 & 0 & 0 & 0 & 0 & 0 & 0 \\
0 & 0 & 0 & 0 & 0 & 0 & 0 & 0 \\
0 & 0 & 0 & 0 & 0 & 0 & 0 & 0 \\
0 & 0 & 0 & 0 & 0 & 0 & 0 & 0
\end{bmatrix}.
$$

The process of quantization has resulted in the zeroing out of many of the DCT coefficients y_{kl}. The specific design of Q depends on psychovisual characteristics and compression-ratio considerations. All compression standards provide default values for Q. At this point, the quantized DCT domain representation, Z, has resulted in significant savings, since only 11 values are needed to represent Z compared to the 64 values needed to represent X; this represents a compression ratio of 5.8. The matrix Z can be efficiently represented using a combination of a run-length coding scheme and a Huffman coding scheme; we will describe the specifics of Huffman coding later. We will discuss the implementation issues and the compression capabilities for this approach when we discuss the JPEG standard in a later section.

Temporal Redundancy Reduction Scheme

In image sequences, there is significant spatial and temporal correlation. The DCT coding scheme of Fig. 9-5 exploits on the spatial redundancies within an image. In order to exploit both the spatial and the temporal redundancy, one might suggest using a 3-D DCT instead of the 2-D DCT. This approach has been shown to be quite effective from a compression viewpoint; however, the excessive complexity of a 3-D DCT renders this approach impractical. Instead, most video coders use a two-stage process to achieve good compression. The first stage uses a method that exploits the temporal redundancy between frames. The output of this stage is followed by a coding method that exploits spatial redundancy within the frame. The basic two-stage process is illustrated in Fig. 9–6. In order to create the difference frame of Fig. 9–6, the temporal redundancy processor may have to track the pixels from frame to frame. This is computationally intensive; hence, in the compression standards such as MPEG-1, MPEG-2, H.261, and H.263, only 16×16 pixel regions are tracked from frame to frame and this process is referred to as motion estimation. The temporal redundancy processor essentially performs the following steps:

1. Motion estimation is first performed. The process of motion estimation consists of finding for each 16×16 pixel region (referred to as a macroblock in the

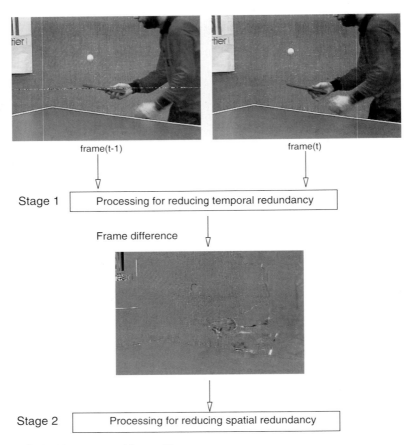

Figure 9-6   Two-stage video coding process.

compression standards) in frame(t), the corresponding region in say, frame($t-$ 1). Denote I(x,y,t) as the 16×16 pixel region in frame(t) (x,y are the top left-corners of the 16×16 block). Let the corresponding region in frame($t-1$) be at say ($x-u$, $y-v$). (u,v) is the motion-vector for the block at location (x,y) in frame(t).

2. The 16×16 motion-compensated difference block is then computed as I(x,y,t)$-$ $I(x-u,y-v,t-1)$.

   The motion-compensated difference is the output of the temporal redundancy reduction processor. Note that the main complexity is in the motion estimation stage. We will address this issue in a later section. DCT coding as shown in Fig. 9-5 is then used to reduce the spatial redundancy.

■ Plate 1

First frame image of each shot

One shot

Shot number

■ Plate 2

■ Plate 3

■ Plate 4

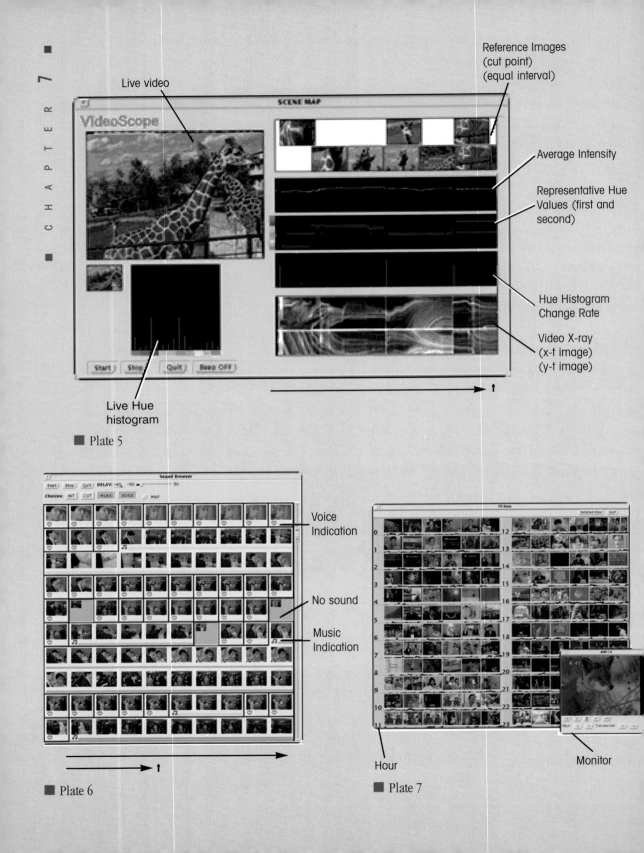

Live video

Reference Images
(cut point)
(equal interval)

SCENE MAP

VideoScope

Average Intensity

Representative Hue
Values (first and
second)

Hue Histogram
Change Rate

Video X-ray
(x-t image)
(y-t image)

Start   Stop   Quit   Beep OFF

t

Live Hue
histogram

■ Plate 5

Sound Browser

Start   Stop   Quit   DELAY: -40   -50   50

Choices: INT   CUT   MUSIC   VOICE   MAP

Voice
Indication

No sound

Music
Indication

t

■ Plate 6

TV Ram

Detailed View   Quit

0   12
1   13
2   14
3   15
4   16
5   17
6   18
7   19
8   20
9   21
10   22
11   23

Hour

Monitor

■ Plate 7

■ Plate 8

■ Plate 9

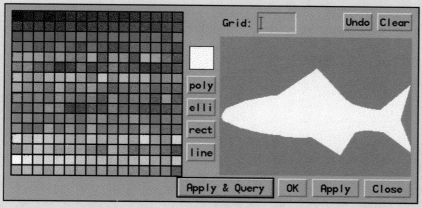

■ Plate 10

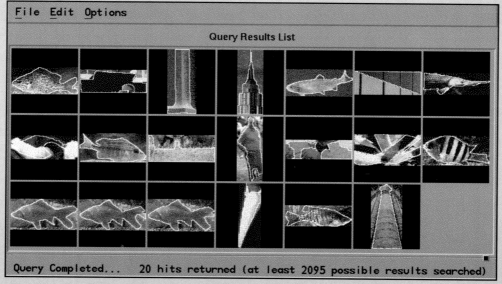

Query Completed...   20 hits returned (at least 2095 possible results searched)

■ Plate 11

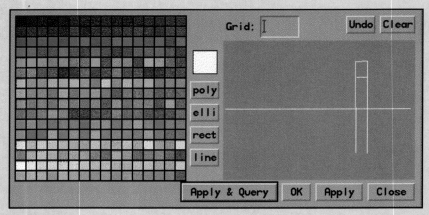

■ Plate 12

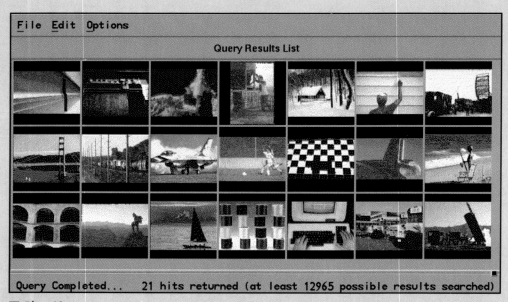

■ Plate 13

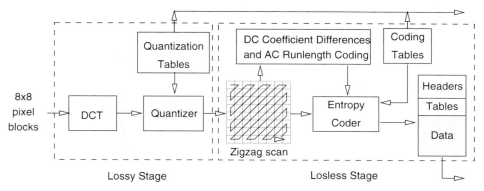

Figure 9-7   Block diagram of a JPEG encoder.

Still-Image Codecs Based on JPEG Standards

JPEG includes two basic compression methods: a DCT-based lossy compression method and a predictive method for lossless compression. In order to facilitate the acceptance of JPEG as an international standard and because of the various options available during JPEG encoding, the JPEG committee also defined an interchange format. This interchange format embeds image and coding parameters (type of compression, coding tables, quantization tables, image size, etc.) within the compressed bit stream. This allows JPEG compressed bit streams to be interchanged among different platforms and to be decompressed without any ambiguity.

JPEG Encoding

The basic computation pipeline for the DCT-based lossy compression scheme in JPEG is similar to that depicted in Fig. 9-5. Fig. 9–7 shows a block diagram of the DCT-based JPEG encoder for an image with a single color component (gray-scale). For color images, the process is repeated for each of the color components.The entropy coder consists of two stages. The first stage is either a predictive coder for the DC (or [0,0]) coefficients or a run-length coder for the AC coefficients. The second stage is either a Huffman coder or an arithmetic coder. Arithmetic coding provides better compression than Huffman coding; however, there are very few JPEG implementations that support arithmetic coding. There are three main reasons for this. First, the improvement in compression (2 percent to 10 percent) does not justify the additional complexity (especially for hardware implementations). Second, many of the algorithms on arithmetic coding are covered by patents in the United States and Japan. Therefore, most implementors are reluctant to pay license fees for minimal gains in performance. Third,

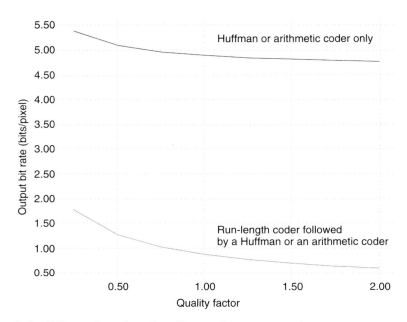

Figure 9–8   Effects of run-length coding on data compression.

the *baseline implementation*, that is, the implementation with the minimum set of requirements for a JPEG compliant decoder, uses only Huffman coding.

Lossless Coding Stage: JPEG

Due to the high correlation of DC values among adjacent blocks, JPEG uses differential coding for the DC coefficients. Each DC differential can be described by the pair (size, amplitude), where *size* defines the number of bits required to represent the amplitude, and *amplitude* is simply the amplitude of the differential. From this pair of values, only the first (the size) is Huffman coded. The AC coefficients in the 8×8 block are traversed in a zigzag order as $(0,1),(1,0),(1,1),(2,0),\ldots$ and this zigzag ordering allows for a more efficient operation of the run-length coder. A run-length coder yields the *value* of the next nonzero AC coefficient and a *run*; that is, the number of zero AC coefficients preceding this one. Each nonzero AC coefficient is then described by the pair (run/size, amplitude). The value of run/size is Huffman coded, and the value of the amplitude (computed as in the case of the DC differentials) is appended to that code.

To illustrate the benefits of run-length coding, Fig. 9–8 shows for a typical grayscale image the output bit rate with and without a run-length coder. The top plot shows the output bit rate when an ideal Huffman or arithmetic coder is applied directly to the output of the DCT quantizer in Fig. 9–7. The bottom plot shows the output bit rate when the ideal Huffman or arithmetic coder is preceded by a run-length coder. Bit rates are measured for various settings of the quality factor used to scale the quantization table. For a quality factor of one, the bit rate with a run-length coder is nearly four bits per pixel lower than the bit rate of an entropy coder alone. This is largely attributable to the efficient run-length representation of the zig-zag ordered AC coefficients. As the quality factor increases, more of the quantized AC values will be zero, and as expected, the benefits from a run-length coder are even higher.

Processing of Color Images

Thus far, we have considered JPEG compression of images with a single component. In practice, images may be represented by multiple color components, each at a different resolution. For example, most color scanners generate images with red, green, and blue color components (RGB). JPEG sets no restrictions on the type of the input color space. Instead, it views each image as a collection of image components. The maximum number of color components in JPEG is 255. Each sample may be represented by P-bits of precision. In JPEG, P can be either 8 or 12 for DCT-based coders and from 2 to 16 for lossless coders. Images with other pixel resolutions can still be coded using JPEG; however, pixel values have to be shifted to be within the resolutions supported by JPEG.

Implementation Issues

The specific implementation of the JPEG standard depends on the application requirements and whether a software or a hardware implementation is adopted. In this section, we will address several issues relevant to the implementation of the *baseline* JPEG standard.

The primary computation cost of JPEG encoding or decoding is in the calculation of the 8×8 DCT or inverse DCT which requires nearly 45 percent of the overall compression time. Several fast algorithms have been developed to reduce the computation complexity of the DCT. Recently a DCT algorithm due to Feig [3] has found great use in software implementations of the DCT since it requires only 54 multiplications and 464 additions for each 8×8 block. In a hardware implementation, due to its more regular dataflow, the DCT scheme developed by Chen [4] is used even though the Chen approach requires 192 multiplications and 416 additions for each 8×8 block. If the codec is implemented on a digital signal processor that has a multiply-accumulate unit, it is possible to modify the Chen DCT such that only 416 multiply-accumulate operations [2] are needed for a 8×8 block. Some general purpose microprocessors such as the HP PA7100LC [2] do not have a integer multiply unit. Recently several multiplication-free DCT algorithms have been proposed [5] and such techniques are good candidates for JPEG codecs implemented on low-power processors.

IDCT Sparseness: Note that an 8×8 inverse DCT (IDCT) requires the same number of operations as the DCT. However, for most JPEG compressed images, the 8×8 block that is input to the IDCT is quite sparse. The sparseness can be exploited to reduce the number of multiplies or adds since a full 8×8 inverse DCT need not be computed for such cases.

Arithmetic Precision Requirements: For eight bits per pixel data, the output of the 8×8 DCT will yield DCT coefficients that have a dynamic range between $-1,023$ and $1,023$. Determining the requirements for arithmetic precision in the DCT requires a careful study of the flowgraph associated with the specific DCT method. In general, using 12 bits of precision for the constants in the DCT flowgraph and 16 bits of precision for all arithmetic operations yields the same output quality as 32-bit floating-point arithmetic.

JPEG Extensions and Applications

Part 3 of the JPEG standard (ITU-T Recommendation T.84 or ISO/IEC 10918-3) specifies requirements and guidelines for encoding and decoding extensions to the processes defined in Part 1. It is currently a draft international standard and is expected to become an international standard by the end of 1995. There are four major extensions defined in this part: variable quantization, selective refinement, tiling, and a new image-interchange format. Extensions such as tiling and variable quantization will be quite useful when compressing mixed-mode documents wherein the image includes text images and natural imagery.

Video Codecs Based on MPEG-1 Standards

The MPEG standards are published in four parts: systems, video, audio, and conformance testing. The systems part specifies the system coding layer of the standards and defines how data, audio, and video streams can be multiplexed. For example, in MPEG-1, the systems layer provides sufficient information for synchronization of multiple video streams, random access to the data, and buffer management. In MPEG terminology, the video, audio, and data streams are generically referred to as elementary streams. Note that, in a system layer stream, more than one audio, video, and data stream can be included. A detailed discussion of the system stream is beyond the scope of this chapter. The video part specifies the coded representation of video data and a decoding process for reconstructing MPEG coded pictures. Audio is an integral part of the MPEG standards. The audio part specifies the coded representation of audio coded data and a decoding process. Finally, the fourth part of the standards provides guidelines for conformance testing.

The MPEG-1 video coding algorithm is a lossy compression scheme that can be applied to a wide range of input formats and applications; however, it has been optimized for applications that support a continuous transfer bit rate of about 1.5 Mbits/s (such as a CD-ROM).

MPEG-1 uses deliberately the term *picture* and not *frame* because it does not recognize interlaced sources. MPEG-1 resorted to a combination of

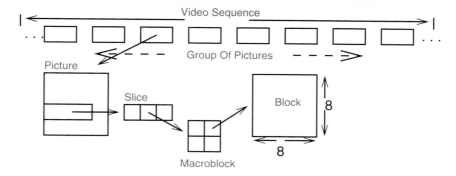

Each GOP is (typically) compressed independently
Slice - coding parameters (typically) adjusted at slice level.
Macroblock - motion estimation is done at this level.
Block - DCT coding at this level.

Figure 9-9   MPEG data hierarchy.

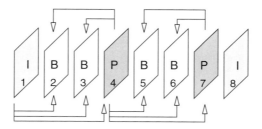

Figure 9-10   Example of inter-dependence among I, P, and B pictures in a video sequence.

intraframe and interframe coding techniques to achieve high compression. The intraframe technique is essentially the same as that employed in JPEG, whereas the interframe technique is the JPEG approach applied on the output of the temporal redundancy processor of Fig. 9–6.

MPEG-1 views the video data within a hierarchical structure as depicted in Fig. 9–9.

The video sequence is a collection of **group of pictures** (GOPs) and within each GOP, the pictures are intra (I) pictures, predictive (P) pictures and bidirectionally (B) predicted pictures. Fig. 9–10 shows the relationship among the three main picture types in a video sequence with eight pictures.

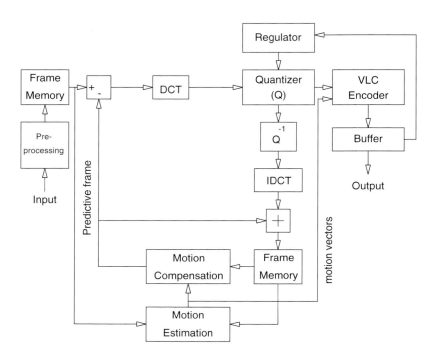

Figure 9-11   Block diagram of an MPEG encoder.

I pictures are not dependent on other pictures and are compressed using a method similar to that used for JPEG. They provide for fast random access, but offer only moderate compression. This situation is similar to applying lossy JPEG on individual pictures. Many hardware/software vendors offer a JPEG-based video compression scheme referred to as MJPEG (motion JPEG) which is essentially the use of JPEG on each picture of the video sequence. In MPEG, P pictures are coded using motion-compensated prediction from previous P pictures or I pictures. B pictures are coded using motion-compensated prediction from previous I or P pictures and provide the highest degree of compression.

MPEG Encoder

Fig. 9–11 shows the block diagram for the MPEG-1 and MPEG-2 encoder. Note that the basic computation pipeline consists of the DCT, Quantizer, and VLC (entropy) encoder—this is the JPEG computation pipeline.

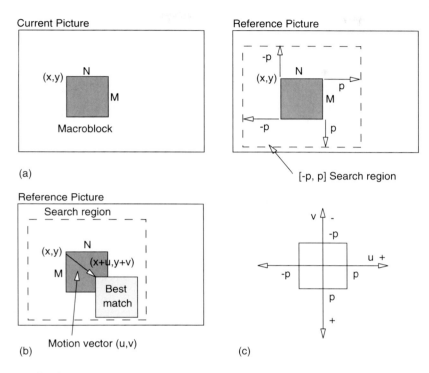

Figure 9-12 Motion-estimation process.

The most compute intensive task in the MPEG encoder is the motion estimation stage (temporal redundancy reduction process) which accounts for nearly 60–75 percent of the overall computations.

Motion Estimation

Note that the temporal redundancy reduction processing that is used for P and B pictures are at the macroblock (16×16) level, i.e. to compute the difference frame, we compute the motion-estimation for each macroblock. Fig. 9–12 illustrates the motion-estimation problem as it is posed in the video coding standards. Given a reference picture and an $N \times M$ macroblock in a current picture, the objective of motion estimation is to determine the $N \times M$ block in the reference picture that better matches (according to a given criterion) the characteristics of the block in the current picture. This implies that the motion model assumed for the compression standards is the translatory model, i.e., objects are assumed to undergo only x and y direction translations from picture to picture. Transformations such as warping and zooming are not accounted for in this model; this is the main cause of failure of the motion estimation in the MPEG-1,

MPEG-2, H.261, and H.263 compression standards. As the current picture, we define a picture at time t. As a reference picture, we define a picture either at past time $t–n$, for forward motion estimation, or at future time $t+k$, for backward motion estimation.

For each macroblock in a P or B picture that is to be coded, the process of finding a matching 16×16 region in a previously encoded (and hence decoded) I or P picture is computationally intensive. An exhaustive search strategy wherein each search location in Fig. 9–12 is used leads to a computation complexity of $(2p + 1)^2 \times MN \times 3$ operations for each macroblock. For $N = M = 16$ and typical values for broadcast TV (picturesize = 720×480, picture rate = 30 pictures/sec), the exhaustive search strategy needs a processor operating at 29.89 GOPS (giga operations per second) for $p = 15$.

Several suboptimum search strategies have been developed to reduce the computation complexity of motion-estimation. One such approach is the hierarchical motion-estimation approach depicted in Fig. 9–13.

For $N = M = 16$ and typical values for broadcast TV (picturesize = 720×480, picture rate = 30 pictures/sec), the hierarchical approach only needs 507.38 MOPs (million operations per second) for $p = 15$. This is a substantial reduction over the exhaustive search strategy. Other search strategies can lower the complexity even further [6].

MPEG Decoder

Fig. 9–14 shows the block diagram for the MPEG-1 and MPEG-2 decoder. As in the encoding case, the basic computation pipeline includes a stage similar to that used in JPEG. Since motion estimation need not be performed, the decoder is much simpler than the encoder.

Implementation Issues

MPEG decoding is substantially less complex than encoding by a factor of nearly five. Thus, MPEG-1 or MPEG-2 unlike JPEG is an asymmetric compression method wherein the computation complexity is substantially high at the encoder. Thus MPEG is well suited for applications that require primarily video playback and less of content creation.

A typical load distribution for MPEG-1 decoding is as shown in Table 9–2.

Recently many general purpose processor architectures such as the PA7100LC, Sun's UltraSparc, and Intel's MMX have added specific instructions to reduce the computation load due to the IDCT and motion compensation. Several system vendors have also developed MPEG-1 playback systems wherein the color transformation function is moved to the graphics display unit (as in HP's PA7100 LC), thereby significantly lowering the computation load on the CPU and also reducing the bandwidth on the CPU bus and main memory requirements since only the subsampled YUV data is transferred from the CPU to the graphics processor.

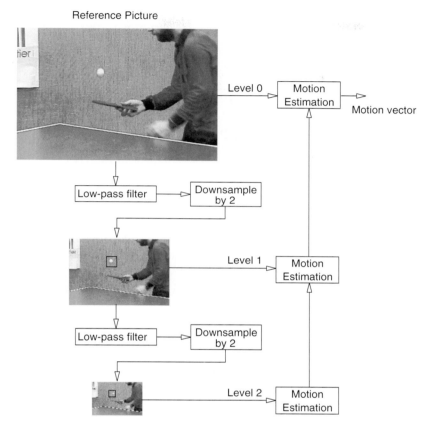

Figure 9-13   A generic hierarchical motion vector search strategy.

Video Codecs Based on MPEG-2 Standards

MPEG-2 is the outcome of the second phase of work by MPEG. MPEG-2 defines a generic standard that could be applied to as wide a class of applications as possible and to support a wide range of compressed bit streams and is also backward compatible with MPEG-1. The MPEG-2 encoding and decoding method is similar to that described earlier for MPEG-1. Here, we will describe the key differences with respect to MPEG-1.

Profiles and Levels

Since MPEG-2 is intended to support video at several bit rates and at several resolutions, for ease of implementation, MPEG-2 defines *profiles* and *levels*. A

Decoding Function	Load (%)
Bit stream header parsing	0.44
Huffman decoding and inverse quantization	19.00
Inverse 8×8 DCT	22.10
Motion compensation	38.64
Color transformation and display	19.82

Table 9-2 Example of the distribution of the computational load in MPEG-1 decoding.

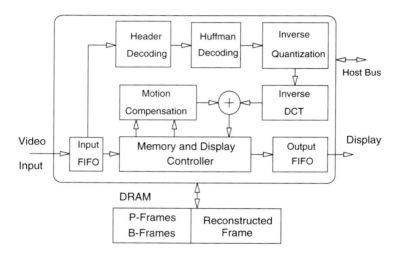

Figure 9-14 Block diagram of an MPEG decoder.

profile is a defined subset of the entire bit stream syntax specified by MPEG-2. The four profiles are Simple, Main, Main+, and Next. Within a profile, a level is defined as a set of constraints imposed on the parameters of the bit stream, such as picture resolution or maximum bit rate. Table 9–3 summarizes the key characteristics of the profiles and levels defined by MPEG-2. Picture resolution is given as pixels per line multiplied by the number of lines. The *Bit rate* data refer to the maximum compressed bit rate supported by the input buffers of a decoder. Areas with "N/A" indicate that there are no conformance restrictions for these variables. Most codecs in the market today implement only the Main profile at the Main level.

Levels		Profiles			
		Nonscalable		Scalable	
		Simple 4:2:0	Main 4:2:0	Main+ 4:2:0	Next 4:2:0
High	Max resolution/ rate (Hz)	N/A	1920 × 1152/60	N/A	1920 × 1152/60
	Min. resolution/ rate (Hz)	N/A	N/A	N/A	960 × 576/30
	Bitrate (Mbits/s)	N/A	80	N/A	100 (all layers) 80 (base+mid) 25 (base layer)
High-1440	Max resolution/ rate (Hz)	N/A	1440 × 1152/60	1440 × 1152/60	1440 × 1152/60
	Min. resolution/ rate (Hz)	N/A	N/A	720 × 576/30	720 × 576/30
	Bitrate (Mbits/s)	N/A	60	60 (all layers) 40 (base+mid) 15 (base layer)	80 (all layers) 60 (base+mid) 20 (base layer)
Main	Max resolution/ rate (Hz)	720 × 576/30	720 × 576/30	720 × 576/30	720 × 576/30
	Min. resolution/ rate (Hz)	N/A	N/A	N/A	352 × 288/30
	Bitrate (Mbits/s)	15	15	15 (all layers) 10 (base layer)	20 (all layers) 15 (base+mid) 4 (base layer)
Low	Max resolution/ rate (Hz)	N/A	352 × 288/30	352 × 288/30	N/A
	Min. resolution/ rate (Hz)	N/A	N/A	N/A	N/A
	Bitrate (Mbits/s)	N/A	4	4 (all layers) 3 (base layer)	N/A

Table 9–3 Profiles and levels in MPEG-2 video coding. N/A indicates no conformance restrictions for these variables.

Scalable Syntax

The MPEG-2 syntax has two categories: (1) Nonscalable syntax which is a super-set of the coding syntax for MPEG-1, with additional extensions that support the coding of interlaced signals; and, (2) scalable syntax, which allows for a layered coding of the video stream. Decoders can either decode the basic stand-alone layer for a signal of lower quality or use the additional layers to increase the quality of the decoded signal.

Support for Interlaced Pictures

MPEG-1 encoder assumes the input to be a progressive scan image whereas MPEG-2 encoders can treat the data as a progressive scan image or an interlaced scan image. Essentially this results in many modes for the motion-compensated prediction stage in MPEG-2 unlike the single motion-compensated prediction process in MPEG-1.

Color Subsampling

As in MPEG-1, input pictures are coded in the YCbCr color space; however, in addition to the 4:2:0 format used in MPEG-1 (each macroblock comprises of four 8×8 blocks of Y and one 8×8 block of Cb and Cr color components), MPEG-2 also supports the 4:2:2 (two 8×8 blocks of Cb and Cr color components) and 4:4:4 color subsampling formats. In the 4:2:2 format (also known as CCIR 601 format), the chrominance components have the same vertical resolution as the luminance component, but the horizontal resolution is halved. In the 4:4:4 format, all components have identical horizontal and vertical resolutions.

In summary, MPEG-2 is a superset of MPEG-1 and some of the features in MPEG-2 that are not found in MPEG-1 are shown below:

- Support for both interlaced and noninterlaced pictures.

- Support for 4:2:0, 4:2:2, and 4:4:4 subsampling schemes.

- Motion compensation based either on interlaced frames or noninterlaced fields and frames.

- Improved picture quality through new options for the quantization of the DCT coefficients and alternate zigzag ordering.

- New syntax for scalable bit streams.

The MPEG-2 standardization process is still evolving. It is now proceeding along two directions:

- Extensions to MPEG-2. These extensions include video coding with 10 bits per pixel, higher-quality audio coding, and specifications for interacting in real-time, as well as specifications that will allow applications to interact directly with MPEG compressed bit streams.

- Development of a coding standard for very low bit-rate applications (MPEG-4). It is a common belief that the techniques that have been the basis for MPEG-1 and MPEG-2 may be inadequate for MPEG-4, since the bit-rate targets for MPEG-4 will be around 8 to 64 kbits/s. The MPEG-4 standard is expected to be completed by November of 1998.

Videoconferencing Codecs Based on H.320 Standard

H.320 is a suite of standards and was developed for videoconferencing over ISDN lines. The H.320 standards suite includes:

- H.261: A video coding algorithm for compressing signals at data rates from 64 kbits/s to 1,920 kbits/s.
- G.722, G.726, and G.728: A series of algorithms for the compression of audio signals at data rates from 16 kbits/s to 64 kbits/s.
- H.221: This Recommendation specifies the frame structure for multiplexing video, audio, and data into a single bit stream.
- H.230 and H.242: These Recommendations specify the handshaking protocols between H.320 compliant equipment.
- H.233: This Recommendation allows manufacturers to select from three methods of encryption in their H.320 compliant equipment: DES, used in the United States; SEAL used in Japan; and BCRYPT, used in the United Kingdom. The H.233 Recommendation has not yet resolved the issue of how to pass the encryption keys from one location to another.

Here, we will discuss only the H.261 codec. The H.261 codec is similar to an MPEG codec in that compression is achieved in two stages, (a) temporal redundancy reduction using motion-estimation and motion-compensated prediction, and (b) spatial redundancy reduction using DCT coding. Unlike an MPEG codec, in most videoconferencing, the picture resolution will be CIF (common interchange format, 352×288). The computation complexity of a H.261 codec is shown in Table 9–4. Decompression requires approximately 200 MOPS and that is now easily achievable by several general-purpose RISC or DSP (digital signal processing) processors. However, an encoder requires more than 1,000 MOPS of processing power, which is outside the capabilities of a general-purpose processor at this time. Recently many vendors offer a hybrid solution, wherein, the encoding is done in dedicated hardware and decoding is done in software.

H.261 shares much functionality with the MPEG video coding standards. However, even though the key coding algorithms are the same, the two standards target different applications with different requirements in data rates, picture quality, and end-to-end coding delay. Table 9–5 shows the main differences between H.261 and MPEG.

Videoconferencing Codecs Based on H.324 Standard

ITU is presently developing a video conferencing standard for the general switched telephone network (GSTN) and mobile radio. This standardization

Compression	MOPS
RGB to YCbCr	27
Motion estimation (25 searches in a 16×16 region)	608
Inter-/Intraframe coding	40
Loop filtering	55
Pixel prediction	18
2-D DCT	60
Quantization, zig-zag scanning	44
Entropy coding	17
Frame reconstruction	99
Total	**968**
Decompression	
Entropy decoder	17
Inverse quantization	9
Inverse DCT	60
Loop filter	55
Prediction	30
YCbCr to RGB	27
Total	**198**

Table 9–4 Millions of operations/sec (MOPS) requirements for
H.261 compression and decompression.

effort is referred to as H.324 and was approved in November 1995. The H.324
suite is a recommendation for real-time voice, data, and video over V.34 modems
on the GSTN telephone network and this standards suite includes: (1) H.324 systems, (2) H.223 multiplex, (3) H.245 control, (4) H.263 video codec, and (5) G.723
speech codec. H.261 provides coded video at bit rates 64 kbits/s and above,
whereas the H.263 video coding standard proposed for H.324 will provide coded
video around 8–64 kbits/s.

In a practical videoconferencing application, there is a need for data sharing in addition to voice and video. The T.120 standard has been proposed for this
(e.g., shared whiteboard applications).

The basic configuration of the video source coding algorithm is an extension
of the methods used in H.261. The source coder can operate on five standardized

MPEG	H.261
Uses CIF, SIF, or higher spatial resolutions.	Uses QCIF or CIF spatial resolutions.
Variable image aspect ratio (defined in the header).	Fixed 4:3 aspect ratio.
Uses groups of pictures.	No notion of GOPs.
I, P, and B macroblocks.	No B macroblocks.
Typical bit rates are around 1.1 Mbps (MPEG-1).	Typical bit rates are around 384 kbps. Max. bit rate is 2 Mbps.
No restrictions on skipped pictures.	Only 1, 2, or 3 skipped pictures allowed.
Subpixel accurate motion vectors.	Pixel accurate motion vectors.
Typical motion vector range is +/− 15 pixels.	Typical motion vector range is +/− 7 pixels.
The end-to-end coding delay is not critical.	Used mostly in interactive applications. End-to-end delay is very critical.

Table 9–5   Main differences between the MPEG and the H.261 standards.

picture formats: sub-QCIF (88×72), QCIF(176×144), CIF (352×288), 4CIF (704×576) and 16CIF (1408×1152).

The decoder has motion compensation capability, allowing optional incorporation of this technique in the encoder. Half-pixel precision is used for the motion compensation, as opposed to H.261 where full pixel precision and a loop filter are used. Variable length coding is used for the symbols to be transmitted. Unlike H.261, wherein the motion is tracked on 16×16 regions, finer tracking (which leads to more efficient temporal redundancy reduction and hence lowering of the overall bitrate) is possible with H.263 since one can specify motion vectors for 8×8 regions. H.263 also includes the more efficient arithmetic coder as the entropy coder instead of the huffman coder that is used in H.261.

Implementation Issues

H.263 is primarily targeted to low bandwidth communication links such as wireless links. For such links, the objective is to design a complete codec namely a source and a channel codec, and not just the source codec. A joint source and

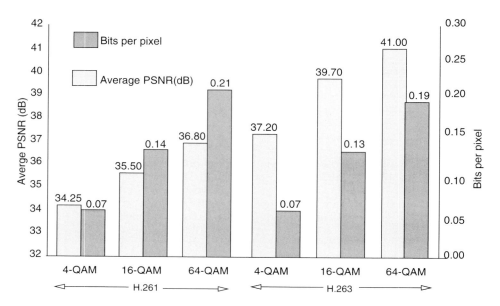

Figure 9-15 Performance comparison for H.261 versus H.263 video source codec in conjunction with 4,16,64-QAM channel codecs.

channel codec system design can lead to a simpler design for the overall codec. We illustrate this idea by comparing the performance of H.261 and H.263 video codecs over wireless links as shown in Fig. 9–15. Note that for the same compression ratio (or bit rate) of say 0.07 bits per pixel and the same channel codec (4-QAM), an H.263 codec yields better video quality (37.20 dB) compared with a H.261 codec (34.25 dB). In general for the same video quality, H.263 codecs require 30-40 percent lower bitrate than H.261 codecs. In Fig. 9–15, we also observe that a more efficient source codec can lead to a simpler channel codec; e.g. an H.263 codec yields 37.20dB at 0.07 bits per pixel using a simple 4-QAM channel codec, whereas an H.261 source codec yields nearly the same video quality (36.80 dB) at 0.21 bits per pixel using a more complex 64-QAM codec.

9.4 Non-Standards-Based Codecs

Codecs based on standard compression schemes, such as JPEG and MPEG, have been widely supported by the industry; however, this has not stopped the development and marketing of several proprietary image and video compression codecs. Examples of such schemes include the Kodak Photo-CD compression and storage format, the QuickTime environment from Apple, Indeo technology from Intel, or the Truemotion compression method from Horizons Technology. These proprietary schemes were developed to work within the limited computation capabilities that are available on low-end desktop PCs. Recently, with the development of the World Wide Web, several video delivery systems have been proposed as an alternative to MPEG video delivery; the primary motivation for developing alternate technologies is that the current networking protocols such as TCP/IP are not well matched to the MPEG compression method. The compression methodology within these proprietary schemes seem to fall into one of three classes, (a) hierarchical coders such as wavelet or subband decomposition methods, (b) vector-quantization (VQ) based approaches that are used directly on the spatial-domain video data or used in conjunction with the hierarchical coders, and, (c) fractal coders—these codecs have been quite popular for compressing still imagery and the authors are not aware of widely available fractal codecs for video.

VQ schemes   The basic idea in vector quantization is to segment the image/video into a sequence of M-dimensional vectors and compare each vector against a dictionary of patterns. The position of the pattern in the dictionary that closely matches the input M-dimensional vector is the output of the VQ-based compressor. Most of the VQ coders incorporate a Huffman coder to code the positions of the patterns to yield further compression. Decoding is relatively simple; the position data is used to index the dictionary and the corresponding pattern is then output as the representation for the encoder's input M-dimensional vector. Thus, VQ decoding in its most primitive form is a lookup table operation and can be performed extremely fast even on low-end computing platforms. Codecs such as the Cinepak coder (under Microsoft Windows), Apple's Quicktime, and earlier versions of Intel's Indeo employ VQ as one of the compression stages.

Wavelet schemes   In wavelet- or subband-based codecs, the first step is to decompose the image/video into a hierarchical, multiresolution representation, e.g., a low-pass image, followed by images of increasing spatial resolution that contain the detail information of the original image. Each of the subimages within the hierarchical representation can then be coded by an appropriately designed codec. The primary advantage of wavelet-based schemes is that the user can select portions of the compressed bitstream to decode the picture at any desired resolution. The resolution scalability allows a single bitstream to be retrieved by a range of devices. For example, a mobile video telephone may be able to get data only at say 26 kbps whereas a desktop PC connected to the local-area network can retrieve video at say 1.5 Mbps. In the standards-based approach, one may have to use a H.261 or H.263 codec for the mobile video telephone and a MPEG-1 codec for the desktop PC video delivery. With a wavelet-based approach only one bitstream need be maintained at the video server and the video server can extract the portions of the bitstream that are most

Codec vendor	Method	Framerate, Bitrate	Codec sweetspot
Cinepak	Hybrid VQ	30,250 KB/sec	135–185 KB/sec
Indeo 3.2	Hybrid VQ	30,250 KB/sec	85–225 KB/sec
IVI	Wavelet	13,250 KB/sec	145–185 KB/sec
Truemotion-S	Unknown	30,250 KB/sec	280–450 KB/sec
Mediamatic MPEG	MPEG-1	17,150 KB/sec	150 KB/sec

Table 9–6 Decoding frame rate for video using software codec implementations on a 133-MHz Intel Pentium PC. Frame rate data is for 10 percent CPU utilization.

appropriate for the video delivery system it is connected to. The Indeo Video Interactive (IVI) codec uses a wavelet-based compression method.

In Table 9–6, we compare the performance of several codecs based on non-standard compression methods [7]. In this table, the sweetspot column indicates the bit rate of the compressed video for which these codecs were originally optimized for. Note that the hybrid, VQ techniques can yield real-time performance (for video sequences that were encoded at 30 frames/sec). The Indeo Video Interactive codec yielded poor performance; future generation of these codecs is expected to yield better performance. We also note that software-only MPEG solutions yield unacceptable performance on current generation of PCs (many vendors quote 24 frames/sec performance for their software MPEG solutions; however, this performance is attainable only at very high CPU utilization).

9.5 Object-Based Codecs

In the previous sections of this chapter, we examined some of the approaches adopted by the current generation of image and video codecs. These codecs have been developed for a restricted set of information modalities, namely that the information is described in a two-dimensional space and they may have a temporal component. For these restricted information modalities, as we have observed in this chapter, compression standards such as JPEG, MPEG-1, MPEG-2, H.261, and H.263 are basically pixel-oriented approaches. Recently, it has been observed that higher-level representations of the data which is described in two-dimensional space and time may lead to a richer set of codecs and MPEG4 is evolving in this direction. In the context of MPEG-4 and very low bitrate video coding, the object-based compression techniques have gained popularity because of their ability to achieve extremely high compression ratios and the potential ease of content manipulation in the compressed domain. A number of methods have been reported [8], [9], and [10]. Willemin [8] proposed a pure 3-D split and merge method without considering the motion information. Musmann's system [9] depends on a reliable motion estimation and updates the textures in the motion failure region which is confined to be very small. The robustness of this system has been widely questioned. Salembier [10] described in an excellent paper their system based on the three dimensional recursive morphological segmentation with motion compensation. The unsatisfactory texture rendition with polynomial approximation is the major problem associated with the technique.

In this section, we will present a system based on the morphological segmentation of the Displaced Frame Difference (DFD). The basic idea is to segment the DFD into large zones where uncovered background lies or the block translational motion model fails, hoping deliberately that the ignored small regions will be less noticeable. The DFDs possess little correlation which makes the nonlinear morphological segmentation an appropriate choice. Although both our technique and that proposed in [10] employ the morphological operators, they are quite different. The segmentation of DFD in our technique is performed on a thresholded image, only binary morphological operators are used. The segmentation criterion is the surface of the aggregate pixels rather than the smoothness of the region. The interior content of the segmented region is coded in pixel domain, which results in a better texture rendition.

The next section describes the various functional blocks of the system. Then the section Segmentation-Based DFD Coding on page 270 presents the DFD segmentation and coding algorithm in detail. The section Coding Performance on page 273 deals with the simulation results. Finally, the section Next Step on page 276 concludes the chapter and points out future research directions.

System Description

A hybrid motion-compensating coding system is proposed. Intraframes are coded using wavelet transform. A multigrid motion estimation algorithm is used for motion compensation. The DFD is coded using morphological segmentation. Since coding artifacts are unavoidable at high compression ratios, a post-processing procedure is proposed to partially reduce the artifacts, hence improving the visual quality of the reconstructed sequence. The proposed approach combines the waveform–based technique and a segmentation-based technique; this leads to a codec which is less sensitive to the video content than model-based codecs.

Fig. 9–16 illustrates the block diagram of the system. It operates in two modes: intraframe mode and interframe mode. The first frame is always coded as intraframe. Subsequent frames are coded in interframe mode unless a scene change occurs or a maximum number of successive frames coded in interframe mode is reached. In intraframe mode, the frame is coded using the wavelet transform. The wavelet is specially designed for image coding [11] and performs far better than the classic QMF filers. In interframe mode, motion vectors are

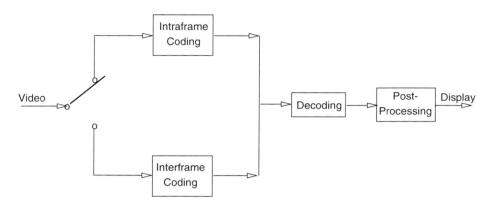

Figure 9–16   Block diagram of the codec.

computed between the current original frame and the previous reconstructed frame using a multigrid motion estimation algorithm. In order to improve the uniformity of the motion vectors, they are processed by checking the mean and variances of the direct frame difference for each block; this reduces the cost to code the motion vectors. Displaced frame differences are computed using the processed motion vectors. DFDs are then segmented into active regions of high energy using morphological operators. Contours of the active regions and their interior contents are coded separately. An edge-preserving post processing is performed at the receiver end in order to remove some annoying coding artifacts. In the next section, we concentrate on the DFD segmentation algorithm.

Segmentation-Based DFD Coding

Basic operations of the segmentation algorithm are shown in Fig. 9–17.

The main idea is to segment a DFD into regions of high energy, and then encode the contours and the interior contents separately. Fig. 9–18 shows an example of the segmentation algorithm. Fig. 9–18(a) is the original frame. Fig. 9–18(c) is the original DFD obtained from motion compensation. The major steps of the DFD segmentation algorithm of Fig. 9–17 are as follows:

1. Dynamic thresholding: The threshold is determined dynamically by computing the histogram of a DFD and fixing the threshold to separate the pixels into high energy part (β %) and low energy part. A marker image is produced where pixels marked by "1" (white) correspond to those with absolute value larger than the threshold and pixels marked with "0" (black) correspond to those with absolute value smaller than the threshold (Fig. 9–18(d)). The threshold is also used to control the bitrate.

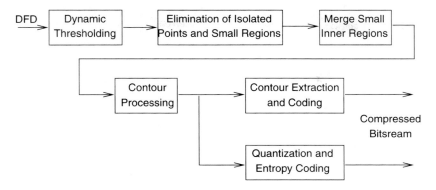

Figure 9–17   Major steps of the segmentation algorithm.

2. Elimination of small high energy regions: Median filters are applied to aggregate the white and the black pixels. n successive erosions with a structuring element of size 3×3 are applied on white regions followed by a geodesic reconstruction[serra82] operation. Thus small high energy regions are eliminated while large ones are kept intact.

3. Merging of small inner low energy regions: A contour pixel position is generally more expensive to code than a pixel value "0." Small inner low energy regions are thus merged with their surrounding high energy ones. This is achieved by applying m successive erosions on the black regions followed by geodesic reconstruction of the unremoved black regions.

4. Contour processing: The form of the marker image (Fig. 9–18(e)) is further processed to assure 4–connected closed contours after contour extraction. Contours (Fig. 9–18(f)) are extracted by computing the morphological gradient of the marker image.

   On the receiver end, the DFD is reconstructed as is shown in Fig. 9–18(h). The final reconstructed frame is shown in Fig. 9–18(b) side by side with the original frame for comparison.

   Simulations have shown that the proposed segmentation algorithm can capture accurately the uncovered background (e.g. tree outside the window in *Car Phone*) and regions of failure of the motion model (e.g. mouth, eye in *Miss America*). For more details of the segmentation algorithm, interested readers can refer to [13], [14], [15]. For this DFD segmentation approach, the total bits needed to code a DFD can be expressed as

$$R_{dfd} = R_s + R_c + I \times b \tag{4}$$

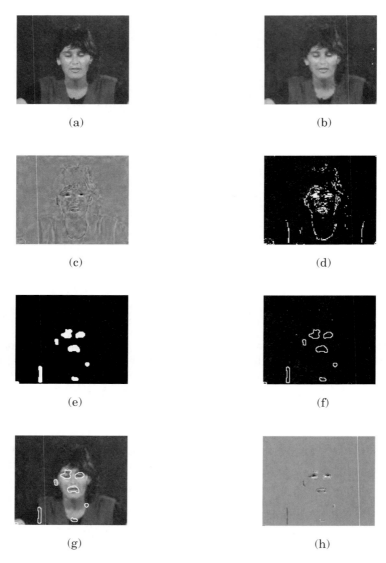

Figure 9-18   The major steps of segmentation: (a) Original frame. (b) Reconstructed frame. (c) Original DFD. (d) After thresholding. (e) Final marker image. (f) Contour image. (g) Contour image overlapped with reconstructed frame. (h) Reconstructed DFD.

where R_s is number of bits to code the interior pixel values of the segmented regions, R_c is the number of bits to code contour points' relative positions, I the number of contours, and b the number of bits to code a contour's first point

sequence	Miss America		Car Phone	
	16 kbps	32 kbps	16 kbps	32 kbps
R_b(bit)	8200	13152	17984	26808
R_{mv}(bit)	9088	8808	17664	18384
R_{dfd}(bit)	47664	109624	29656	85944
R_{tot}(bit)	64952	131584	65304	131136
bitrate (kbps)	15.9	32.2	16.0	32.1
overline $PSNR$	35.11	37.49	26.51	28.88

Table 9-7 Summary of simulation results at 16 kbps and 32 kbps.

position. For a typical head-and-shoulders video sequence, R_s requires around 1000 bits/frame and $R_c + I \times b$ requires 400 bits/frame. In a codec in which during each second of video, only 12 frames are coded, the average bit rate attainable with this codec employing DFD segmentation is 18 kbps.

Coding Performance

Various video sequences have been used to evaluate the performance of our proposed video coder. The simulation results of the sequences *Miss America* and *Car Phone* will be reported here. The sequence *Miss America* is a simple head-and-shoulder sequences with still and uniform backgrounds. The *Car Phone* sequence has a complex background and has global motion (camera pan and zoom). Coding is performed at QCIF resolution (176×144) on the luminance component. In the simulations 100 frames are taken from each of the test sequences and the coder employs a fixed frame skipping of two frames thus resulting in only 34 frames being coded. Assuming a 25 frames/sec rate for the original video sequence, the actual frame rate for the coder is 8.3 frames/sec. A standard procedure is used to convert the original CIF sequences to the QCIF format for coding.

The proposed coding system involves the following parameters: quantization stepsizes for each level of wavelet transform including DC in intraframe coding; quantization stepsize for DFD coding; percentage of the pixels kept in DFD segmentation; and thresholds for motion vector processing. These parameters can be regularized to obtain the desired bitrate for each sequence.

Let R_b be the number of bits to code an intraframe, R_{mv} the number of bits to code motion vectors, R_{dfd} the number of bits to code DFDs, and R_{tot} be the total number of bits. Then, we have

$$R_{tot} = R_b + R_{mv} + R_{dfd} \qquad (5)$$

Table 9-7 summarizes the total number of bits spent to code intraframes, motion vectors and DFDs, as well as the average PSNR value for each sequence.

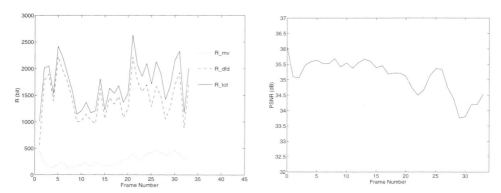

Figure 9-19 *Miss America* coded at 16 kbps. (a) Number of bits for motion vectors, DFDs and total number of bits. The number of bits for the intraframe is not shown. (b) PSNR as a function of frame number.

In our simulation with 100 frames for each sequence, only the first frame is coded as intraframe; in a practical implementation, one should periodically refresh the coder with intraframes (a typical period could be 100–120 frames). Due to the simple motion and still background of the sequence *Miss America*, the motion vectors cost fewer bits than the other two sequences. In case of the sequence *Car Phone*, due to the moving background, motion vectors cost many more bits, and not enough bits are left to code the DFDs. This explains the much lower PSNR values for *Car Phone*.

Fig. 9–19 shows the result for the sequence *Miss America* coded at 16 kbps. Fig. 9–19(a) shows the number of bits to code DFD and motion vectors for each frame. It can be observed that motion vectors are less expensive to code than DFDs because of the motion vector processing. The number of bits to code DFDs fluctuates from one frame to another. This is a characteristic of the proposed segmentation algorithm. The algorithm will code high-energy regions only when such a region is considered to be large. The PSNR value of each frame is depicted in Fig. 9–19(b). A difference of 2 dB exists between the intraframe and the worst quality interframe.

Figures 9–20, 9–21, and 9–22 show similar results for *Miss America* coded at 32 kbps and *Car Phone* coded at 16 and 32 kbps. Several general remarks can be given. (1) The number of bits to code DFDs oscillates much more than the number of bits to code motion vectors. (2) Complex sequences such as *Car phone* show less uniform quality, especially at low bitrate (see Fig. 9–20(a)). A difference of 4–5 dB exists between the intraframe and the worst coded interframe. (3) By doubling the bitrate from 16 kbps to 32 kbps, about 2 dB is gained on the average PSNR. The quality of the reconstructed sequences is more uniform at higher bitrates. (4) No explicit rate control is presently employed. However, we

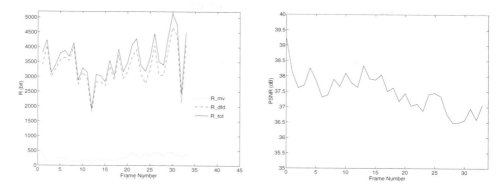

Figure 9-20 *Miss America* coded at 32 kbps. (a) Number of bits for motion vectors, DFDs and total number of bits. The number of bits for the intraframe is not shown. (b) PSNR as a function of frame number.

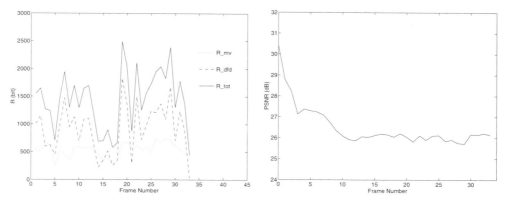

Figure 9-21 *Car Phone* coded at 16 kbps. (a) Number of bits for motion vectors, DFDs and total number of bits. The number of bits for the intraframe is not shown. (b) PSNR as a function of frame number.

have fixed the coding parameters(e.g., quantizer stepsize, number of segments to code) for all frames. Thus, it is unlikely that the PSNR will stabilize. (5) In a practical implementation of this coder, we propose refreshing the coder after every 100–120 frames. Thus periodic intraframe based refreshing is expected to prevent PSNR degradations across frames. (6) In a practical coder the chrominance components would also be coded. In the proposed coder, a simple vector-quantization extension of our scalar quantization scheme for coding the DFD pixel values can be used to code jointly the luminance and chrominance pixel values within a contour of the DFD.

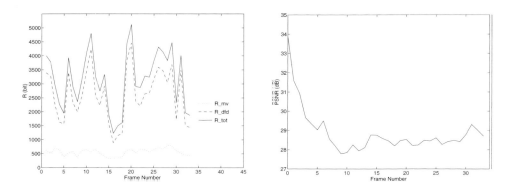

Figure 9–22 *Car Phone* coded at 32 kbps. (a) Number of bits for motion vectors, DFDs and total number of bits. The number of bits for the intraframe is not shown. (b) PSNR as a function of frame number.

Next Step

Presently MPEG4 is considering various object-based codecs for its standardization work. As we have demonstrated here, object-based codecs such as the one described here can yield good performance with modest complexity compared with a H.261 codec. The coding scheme as proposed here is a variable rate coder. Incorporation of a rate control mechanism coupled with an adaptive quantization strategy so as to yield constant bitrate with maximally uniform visual quality needs to be addressed. Further work also needs to be done to improve the error resiliency. As increased computation power becomes widely available and memory costs continue to decline, object-based techniques may well be the basis of image and video codecs for the 21st century.

9.6   Future Directions

Codecs have evolved from viewing the image or video data as pixels in a 2-D space to a dataset that can be described in higher dimensions. One view of the evolution of codecs is as depicted in Fig. 9–23.

As silicon and display technologies mature, the current generation of codecs that exploit the 2-D space and time representation of information will evolve accordingly. For instance, with the lowering cost of display technologies, we expect video information to be widely available in the HDTV format and the MPEG-2 compression standard can support such information. However, as multimedia information becomes widely available, there is a need to present infor-

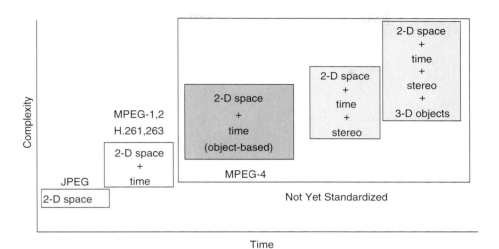

Figure 9–23   Codec evolution over time.

mation to the user in a richer format. For instance, a videoconferencing application might be greatly enhanced using stereoscopic representation of the video, so as to create a lifelike presence of the person in the virtual conference room. The codecs of today do not handle the stereoscopic information efficiently. Another axis along which the underlying information itself may evolve is in the combination of information from multiple sources. For instance, in computer games and scientific visualization applications, there will be a need to mix the synthetic rendered scenes with the traditional video information. The addition of stereoscopic representation or the combining of synthetic information requires a new breed of codecs which may not be simple extensions of the codecs based on the currently evolving standards of JPEG or MPEG.

References

[1] Rodriguez, A.A. and Morse, K., "Feasibility of video codec algorithms for software-only playback," in *Digital Video Compression on Personal Computers: Algorithms and Technologies, Algorithms and Architectures, Proceedings of SPIE,* Vol. 2187, pp. 130–139, Jan 1994.

[2] Bhaskaran, V. and Konstantinides, K., *Image and Video Compression Standards: Algorithms and Architectures.* Boston, MA: Kluwer Academic Publishers, Sep 1995.

[3] Feig, E. and Winograd, S., "Fast algorithms for the discrete cosine transform,"*IEEE Transactions on Signal Processing,* Vol. 40, No. 9, pp. 2174–2193, Sep 1992.

[4] Chen, W.H., Smith, C.H., and Fralick, S.C., "A fast computation algorithm for the DCT," *IEEE Transactions on Communications,* Vol. COM-25, pp. 1004–1009, 1977.

[5] Blonstein, S.M. and Allen, J.D., "The multiply-free Chen transform—A rational approach to JPEG," in *Visicom '91: Picture Coding Symposium,* Tokyo, Japan, Sep 1991, pp. 237–240.

[6] Konstantinides, K., Natarajan, B., and Balas, B. "Low-complexity algorithm and architecture for block-based motion estimation via one-bit transforms," in *IEEE International Conference on Acoustics, Speech and Signal Processing,* Vol. 6, May 1996.

[7] Ozer, J., "Software video codecs: the search for quality," *NewMedia Magazine,* Vol. 6, No. 2, pp; 46–52, Jan 29, 1996.

[8] Reed, T., Willemin, P., and Kunt, M., "Image sequence coding by split and merge," *IEEE Trans. Commun.,* Vol. 39, pp. 1845–1855, Dec 1991.

[9] Hotter, M., Musmann, H.G., and Ostermann, J., "Object-oriented analysis—synthesis of moving images," *Signal Processing, Image Communications,* Vol. 1, No. 2, pp. 117–138, Oct 1989.

[10] Meyer, F., Salembier, Ph., Torres, L., and Gu, C. "Region-based coding using mathematical morphology," *Proc. of IEEE,* Special Issue on Digital Television, Vol. 83, No. 6, pp. 843–857, June 1995. Invited paper.

[11] Egger, O. and Li, W. "Subband coding of images using asymmetrical filter banks," *IEEE Trans. on Image Processing,* Vol. 4, No. 4, pp. 478-485, Apr 1995.

[12] Serra, J., *Image Analysis and Mathematical Morphology.* London: Academic Press, 1982.

[13] Li, W. and Mateo, F.X., "Segmentation based coding of motion compensated prediction error images" in *IEEE International Conference on Acoustics, Speech and Signal Processing,* Vol. V, Minneapolis, MN, 1993, pp. 357-360.

[14] Li, W. and Kunt, M., "Morphological segmentation applied to displaced frame difference coding," *Signal Processing,* Special Issue on Mathematical Morphology and Its Applications to Signal Processing, Vol. 38, No. 1, pp. 45-56, July 1994.

[15] Reusens, E., Ebrahimi, T., and Li, W., "New trends in very low bitrate video coding," *Proceedings of IEEE,* Special Issue on Digital Television, Vol. 83, No. 6, pp. 877–891, June 1994.

Design of Large-Scale Multimedia-on-Demand Storage Servers and Storage Hierarchies[1]

Milind M. Buddhikot, Srihari Sampath Kumar, Guru M. Parulkar, and P. Venkat Rangan

Washington University
St. Louis, Missouri
{milind, srihari}@dworkin.wustl.edu
guru@arl.wustl.edu
314 935 {4203, 7541, 4621}

University of California at San Diego
San Diego, California
venkat@cs.ucsd.edu
619 534 7029

10.1   Introduction

*R*apid advances in communication, high-speed packet switching, mobile data communications, media compression, and processor and memory design will make a distributed multimedia computing infrastructure akin to that shown in Fig. 10–1 feasible in the near future. Exciting interactive applications such as multimedia mail, orchestrated presentations, high quality on-demand audio and video, collaborative multimedia document editing, large digital libraries or multimedia archives, and virtual reality environments will become widespread in this infrastructure. A user may want to access these applications from a variety of end systems such as a Personal Digital Assistant (PDA), a set-top box with a television set, a high-end

---

[1] This work was supported in part by the ARPA, National Science Foundation, and an industrial consortium of Ascom Timeplex, Bellcore, BNR, Goldstar, NEC, NTT, SynOptics, and Tektronix.

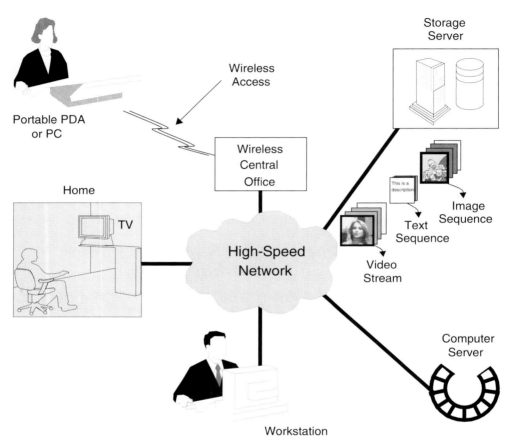

Figure 10-1   Future distributed multimedia infrastructure.

personal computer at home, or a workstation in the workplace. The interactive nature of these applications requires that the user be able to control playout or content of multimedia streams such as video, audio, and graphics. Specifically, a user may perform playout control commands such as *fast forward, rewind, pause/resume, fast-search,* and *random access search,* or may request media editing functions such as *clip, enhance, filter, restore,* etc. Also, most of these applications handle multimedia information in stored or static form. Therefore, the performance of such applications directly depends on the performance of storage servers that store such multimedia information.

The requirements of such Multimedia-On-Demand (MOD) storage servers are uniquely different than those of the existing network-based servers. First, the real-time nature of multimedia data requires QOS guarantees in the form of guaranteed periodic retrieval and transmission of data. Such guarantees can be provided by performing admission control and resource reservation. The layout of data on storage devices used at the server and the algorithms used to schedule retrievals from the server must be designed to ensure that such resource reservation is valid throughout the duration of an admitted client session. Clearly, *admission control, data layout,* and *storage access scheduling* are important design problems.

A MOD server that stores a large number of long multimedia documents must manage tera-/peta-bytes of storage systems that will be constructed in hierarchical fashion using storage devices of various types. The server must support potentially hundreds or thousands of concurrent clients independently. This, directly translates to a storage and network throughput requirement in excess of tens or hundreds of gigabits. Also, it is important that the server architecture be scalable in terms of throughput and number of clients.

The large system scale and expanse of the geographical distribution of the future multimedia computing infrastructure pose scalability problems. Specifically, such an infrastructure has to support millions of concurrent users that communicate with each other across the continents and access information streams originating at locations on the other side of the globe. Clearly, networking and storage systems that attempt to meet such requirements must be hierarchical and distributed. In general, in such an hierarchy, guaranteed high-performance accesses to data are inexpensive and easy to support only over short distances. Therefore, to alleviate the cost and performance penalty incurred in very remote data accesses, information caching must be explored at all possible levels in the system.

In this chapter, we present design of scalable storage server architectures and their hierarchies. First, we present essential background material required to understand the rest of the chapter (Section 10.2). We then describe various storage server architectures. Specifically, we cover three different architectures: one, the distributed storage server architecture called the Massively parallel And Real-time Storage (MARS) server currently under development at Washington University [2] and the alternate architectures based on MIMD and SIMD multiprocessor machines (Section 10.3). The data layouts for large-scale servers, specifically layouts in clustered MOD servers and layouts on storage devices such as disks are presented (Section 10.4). The admission control problem and possible solutions to it in the context of storage server design are also covered (Section 10.5). In the end, we describe the problem of *information* or *program caching* in a storage server hierarchy and present a near-optimal algorithm for computing a caching schedule for an interactive movies-on-demand application.

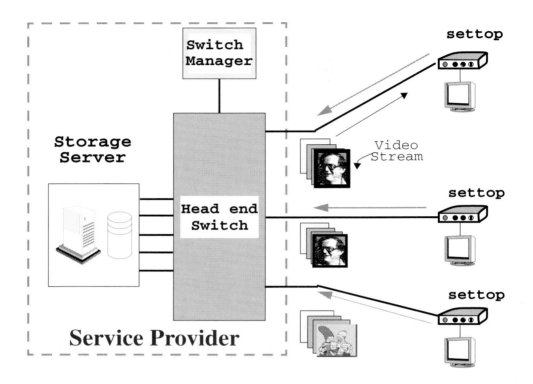

Figure 10-2   A typical Video-on-Demand (MOD) application.

10.2 Essential Background

We will first present some essential background to help the reader understand the research issues in design of large-scale MOD systems and services.

Application Scenarios

The two common emerging scenarios in which the future applications will be run are illustrated in Fig. 10–2 and Fig. 10–3. In the first scenario, commonly termed as **Video-on-demand**, as conceived by telephone companies, cable operators, and content providers like Time-Warner, the client accesses the multimedia data using a set-top box which replaces the VCR and a remote control device used to

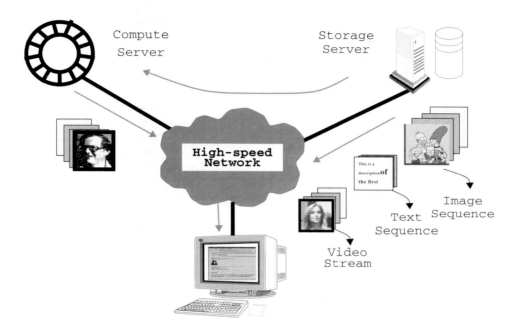

Figure 10-3 A World Wide Web-based Multimedia-on-Demand (MOD) application.

communicate control commands. This infrastructure primarily suites on-demand entertainment programs, news, home shopping, travel information, and network-based game applications.

In the second scenario which is popularly known as **World Wide Web,** millions of computers interconnected into a tangled web by the ever-increasing *Internet*, act as information servers and/or clients. The client is typically a browser program such as *Netscape* or *XMosaic* with a point-and-click interface. These clients access multimedia information in the form of text, images, audio, and video from the Web servers in the Internet via a special protocol called *HyperText Transfer Protocol* (HTTP) that employs the TCP/IP protocol stack for communication.

The client end systems in these two scenarios differ in capabilities such as amount of local buffers, compute power, and availability of specialized media processing. For example, a hand-held PDA, or a set-top box, will have small local buffers and minimal compute power compared to workstations or PCs. A storage server must provide interactive access to real-time and non-real-time data stored in multitudes of formats to such heterogeneous clients. To accomplish this, a clear definition of the service model that will be used by the server is essential.

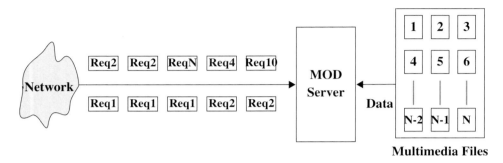

Figure 10-4   MOD server request-response model.

Properties of Request Arrival Process

Fig. 10–4 shows the model of a MOD server in a MOD retrieval environment. Each MOD server has N multimedia files, each of which has two attributes associated with it. The first attribute, duration D_k for the kth multimedia file, is the length of the time that would be required to play the file at standard playout rate, whereas the demand Q_k for the kth multimedia file measures the number of simultaneous connections the server can support for the file. The clients can access the multimedia file(s) by sending requests to the server. The server performs an admission control, which, based on the existing load and the resource usage admits or rejects the client request. The request arrival process at the MOD server may exhibit spatial and temporal locality as described below.

- **Spatial Locality:** The spatial locality property signifies that some of the data items are likely to be accessed more frequently than the others. If the multimedia documents, indexed 1 to N_{max}, are ordered in decreasing order of demand (i.e., if $i < j$, then $Q_i > Q_j$), the probability that the incoming request is for document p is higher than the probability that it is for document q, if $p < q$. For example, in case of an on-demand movie application, a large fraction of requests received are likely to be for certain popular and recently released movies and relatively less for old movies. Empirically, the arrival process at a movie rental shop can be modeled using Zipf's law [10]. Similarly, in the case of a tele-shopping mall, some stores would be more popular than the others and would therefore receive more requests. In case of a digital lecture archive, lectures on difficult topics and those given by laconic faculty members are likely to be accessed more often. However, some of the applications may exhibit less spatial locality than the others, for example, all contemporary publications in an on-demand digital library or radiological images in a patient information database are likely to be uniformly accessed.

- **Temporal Locality:** Depending on the application, the request arrival process at a MOD server will be temporally clustered to various extents. For example, in case of on-demand movies, the request rate for a set of popular movies would be higher during the evening time period of a weekend than on the weekdays and more requests would be received during the 6 to 9 PM than any other period of the day. On the other hand, in the case of a digital library or a radiological database, the request arrivals would be Poisson or slightly bursty.

The spatial locality is exploited in placement of multimedia data in a storage hierarchy consisting of different storage types. Clearly, frequently requested data should be assigned to faster storage devices that are typically more expensive. The temporal locality property is important in deciding the service and network model for the server.

On-Demand Service Types

An on-demand service type decides the method of data and control command exchange between the client and the storage server. It, thus, determines the extent of interactivity and personalization available to the client. The multimedia-on-demand services can be classified into following three types:

Pay-Per-View (PPV) service   Analogous to the existing PPV channels on cable networks, the time of access for a multimedia document in this service is decided by the server rather than the client. The MOD server multicasts the multimedia program at fixed times and any clients interested in receiving the program tune in to the server at those fixed times. Clearly, a client of such a service cannot control the stream playout and also has minimal freedom as to when the multimedia stream will be available to him. Implementing such a server hardly presents any technological challenges.

Near Video-on-Demand (NVD)   This service is motivated by the observation that for certain applications such as on-demand movies, request arrivals are likely to exhibit significant temporal and spatial locality. The Near Video-on-Demand service, sometimes called **Shared Viewing with Constraints** (SVC) exploits these properties of request arrivals. In this service, the client accesses the multimedia documents at any time it desires by sending request to the MOD server. The server processes and accepts such requests in groups to exploit the clustering properties of the arrival process. A new client request may face a variable admission latency, after which the client becomes a part of a multicast group, all members of which are connected to the server by a single multicast connection.

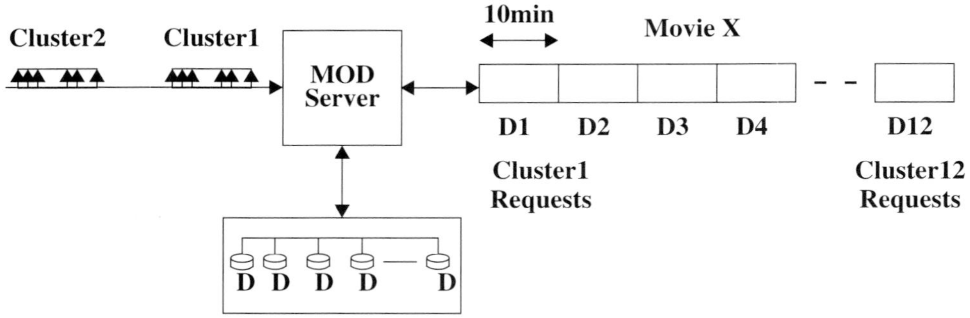

Figure 10–5 Shared viewing with constraints (SVC).

Consider the example of on-demand movies with a typical movie of two hour duration. As shown in Fig. 10–5, the server may decide to cluster requests received in a 10-minute duration and service all such clients as a single multicast group. Thus, in the worst case a client will face an admission latency of 10 minutes. Also, the maximum number of retrievals required at any given time will be 12, unlike only one in PPV service. One advantage of this scheme is that the movie can be divided into twelve independent units and stored on separate storage nodes, each of which can service a multicast group at a given instant as the movie playout progresses. For example, for clients belonging to cluster 1, the first 10 minutes of the movie are played out from one storage node and at the end of this duration, the cluster is switched to another storage node for the next 10 minutes of the movie. Thus, under busy conditions there can be as many as 12 multicast groups, each being serviced by one storage node and switched to an appropriate storage node at the end of a ten-minute duration. However, any kind of interactivity is clumsy to support. First of all, excessive interactivity such as rewind and fast forward requires frequent switching of clients to different multicast groups. Also, given that all the clients that are grouped and serviced together have the same "view" of the movie, any fast forward/rewind by any member will alter this "view" for all members of the group which is undesirable. If fast forward and rewind from each member are to be treated independently, multicast can't be used to realize any bandwidth saving.

The NVD represents incremental improvement over the PPV service, as it allows users to access the multimedia documents at arbitrary instances, unlike the fixed instances in PPV service and for this reason it is sometimes called near-video. However, supporting independent interactive operations is difficult in this service. Thus, the NVD service is unsuitable for applications where request clustering is difficult to achieve and interactivity is important.

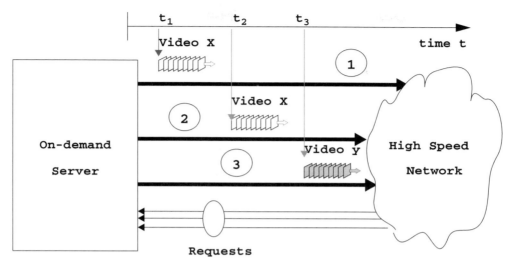

Figure 10-6 MOD server for a Dedicated Viewing service (DV).

True-Multimedia-On-Demand (TMOD) Fig. 10–6 illustrates this service model, in which each access request from the same or different clients is treated independently at the server. For example, in Fig. 10–6, even if two requests received at time t_1 and t_2 are close in time and for the same video sequence X, if admitted, the server will perform separate retrieval and transmissions for these requests. Due to this independence of requests, TMOD service model is sometimes referred to as Dedicated Viewing (DV). Consider an example of a neighborhood on-demand movie server connected to a head-end switch which connects to maximum 1000 users (households); all 1000 users might watch the same movie independently using DV service and would therefore require 1000 independent retrievals and deliveries. The primary advantage of this service is that it is a natural paradigm for personalized, interactive multimedia delivery, as streams received by multiple clients are independent and do not have any temporal relationship between them. Clearly, it is the appropriate service model for the future distributed multimedia on-demand applications. However, TMOD service has serious implications on the throughput. Consider an example of a storage server serving HDTV quality movies to 200 customers. Each HDTV stream requires 20 Mbps on the average. So in the worst case the aggregate network and storage throughput requirement is in excess of 4 Gbps.

Network Model

If we assume the true-on-demand service model for all future applications, the aggregate throughput requirements for the global networking infrastructure can be overwhelming. Consider an example scenario in which each active user is provided with an independent 20-Mbps HDTV connection. In the continental US alone, during the prime time, approximately 150 million users in 77 million households will require an aggregate network bandwidth of 1.54 terabits/sec [38],[24]. Ideally, if bandwidth and storage were free, a centralized superserver that stores all possible programs can serve all the clients. In an alternate scenario, if the storage costs were negligible, one can place as many programs close to the client premises as possible. Clearly, both these scenarios are unrealistic.

Though storage technology improvements have lead to remarkable increases in the storage capacities of devices and show every sign of continuing to do so [39], the storage costs will still be the major component of the total cost of a MOD system. In fact growing concern is being voiced that the enormous network and storage costs in design of large-scale storage systems and network infrastructure may far outweigh the amount of revenue it may generate. A survey [21] shows that while MOD has a high appeal among 44 percent of the respondents who were willing to pay for it, only a minuscule 14 percent were willing to pay *more* than the existing cable rates for it. Nearly two-thirds of the respondents owned a personal computer, with nearly half of them equipped with a modem; hence, we can infer that they were technology savvy and very much knew the difference multimedia-on-demand would make in their lives. Given this, minimizing network and storage costs is very important to make future MOD services affordable.

The three main ways to meet network and storage costs in scalable fashion are: *hierarchical solutions, caching,* and *sharing.* The consensus among the research community is that the network infrastructure that will support future interactive MOD services will be hierarchical in nature and will look somewhat like Fig. 10–7. As shown there, it will consist of an international backbone network connecting several national backbone networks which in turn interconnect numerous regional networks. Each regional network may interconnect several access networks through which broadband network access is provided to the homes. The technology of choice for a backbone network will be ATM over multiple high speed SONET links. In the short term, the access network, typically provided by a local phone exchange or a cable operator, will be based on one of the several technology proposals such as the *Subcarrier Modulated Fiber-Coax Bus* (SMFCB)[2] or *Baseband Modulated Fiber Bus* (BMFB)[3] [29]. This access network will connect the user equipment such as a set-top box to the rest of the network via the **headends**. In the long term, the headends may be replaced by an ATM switch of reasonable size such as $1K \times 1K$. A local MOD server will be connected to each headend. The higher levels in the hierarchy will have increasingly large scale storage servers.

---

[2] Also called Hybrid Fiber Coax (HFC).
[3] Also called Switched Digital Video (sdv).

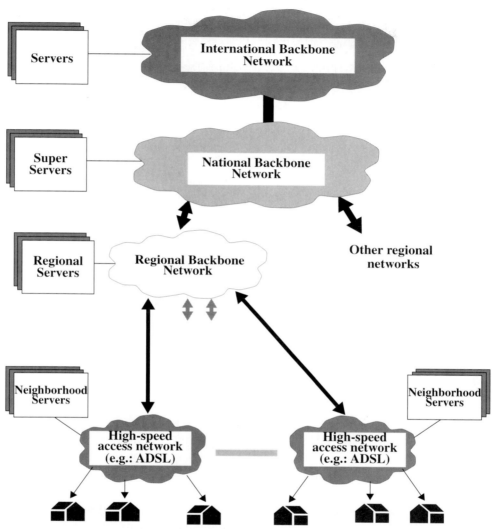

Figure 10-7   Hierarchical network model.

In fact, as shown in Fig. 10–8, the system will evolve from a synergy between various enterprises: *Storage Providers* that manage information storage at multimedia servers (a role akin to that of video rental stores and libraries in today's context), *Network Providers*, that are responsible for media transport over integrated networks (a role akin to that of cable and telephone and cable companies of today), and *Content Providers* such as entertainment houses, new producers, etc., that offer a multitude of services to subscriber homes using multimedia servers and broadband networks.

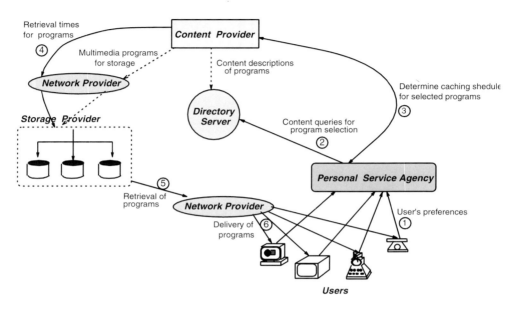

Figure 10-8   Service architecture.

The storage costs and network traffic in this hierarchy can be reduced by exploiting the spatial and temporal locality property of multimedia document accesses. Studies [5] have shown that the patterns of viewership are very much dependent on the time of the day. Akin to the telephone network, there are peak hours during which the traffic is maximum and the majority of the titles demanded is a small subset of the most recent set of hit movies. If the profile of user requests for various multimedia documents is available a priori, only those documents that are likely to be requested with high probability should be stored on the neighborhood servers and less frequently requested documents should be stored on servers in the higher levels in the hierarchy. This technique, commonly called **Info/program caching** [26], [24], also minimizes accesses to the servers in the higher levels of the hierarchy and reduces upstream bandwidth requirements in peak hours.

Performance Metrics for a MOD server

In order to compare and classify storage server architecture, we define the following set of performance metrics.

- **Concurrency:**   The server may have to support thousands of concurrent clients, each with a number of active media streams and each independently accessing the same or different data. The concurrency metric captures this requirement and is defined as the maximum number of clients that can independently access a multimedia document in any playout control state. Thus, in case of an on-demand movie server that can support at maximum 1000 clients, potentially all 1000 clients should be able to access the same copy of the movie independently at any time. Higher concurrency minimizes the need for document replication and storage costs.

- **Access Latency and Operation Latency:**   The access latency metric is defined as the amount of time a client has to wait after sending a request to the MOD server to receive the requested multimedia document. It mostly depends on the service model and the round-trip network latency is a minimal part of it. The access latency should be typically less than a few seconds. The operation latency metric is defined as the time required to effect an interactive operation such as *ff, rw, pause, stop, random access,* etc. Highly interactive MOD applications will typically require an operation latency of less than a second. It is desirable that the playout and operation latency be independent of the load on the server. Clearly, these two metrics characterize how effectively the server provides the QOS guarantees in the form of bounded delay.

- **Storage Capacity and Storage, Network Throughput per Dollar:** Given the storage intensive nature of multimedia data, the storage requirements for a large-scale server can be in excess of tens of terabytes. For example, a lecture archive in a small-sized academic department offering 50 classes in a semester, each with 50 1-hr lectures archived as MPEG video streams would require approximately 5.8 Tbs. The independent retrievals and transmissions for each active client in the TMOD service model demands large amounts of network and storage system throughput. For example, a movie server that supports one thousand users with HDTV quality movies will require network and storage bandwidth in excess of 20 Gbps. This metric defines the cost-effectiveness of the storage server in meeting the requirement of large storage capacity and the large throughput. It must be small for the MOD services to be affordable.

- **Scalability:**   It is desirable that a server architecture that supports say 100 clients and an aggregate throughput of 500 Mbps should be easily extendable to 1000 clients and a tenfold increase in network/storage throughput without significant modifications. In other words the server

Scale	Number of Clients	Concurrency	Access Latency	Throughput
Small	25	25	≈ < 1 sec	155 Mbps (OC-3)
Medium	100	100	≈ < 1 sec	622 Mbps (OC-12)
Large	1000	1000	≈ < 1 sec	0.5 Gbps
Super	10, 000	10, 000	≈ < 1 sec	50 Gbps

Table 10–1 Taxonomy of storage servers.

architecture should scale with number of clients. In addition, the server must support heterogeneous clients, multimedia data and access networks.

- **Extendibility:** The server must be able to support the multiple application scenarios and must be extendable to support different service models.

Taxonomy and Hierarchy of Storage Servers

Using the performance metrics described above (the section Performance Metrics for a MOD server on page 290), the storage servers can be classified as shown in Table 10–1. Since video is the most demanding of all the multimedia streams, in the classification the term client is synonymous with a video connection. Though the average rate of a video connection depends on various factors such as the size of the image, resolution, and the type of compression used, in the following description, we assume a standard NTSC quality video connection to be a 5-Mbps MPEG compressed stream. For HDTV quality compressed video streams the storage and network bandwidth will be even higher. It must be noted that the storage capacity and storage bandwidth (throughput) are two attributes of a storage system that are independent of each other. Given that the advances in storage technology have almost always improved the storage capacity more than the storage throughput, extracting higher throughput from a storage system is a more challenging task than providing a large storage capacity. Also, as a general case, the storage in all classes of servers will be hierarchical consisting of magnetic Direct Access Storage Disks (DASDs), magneto-optic devices like optical disks and magnetic and optical tapes. Therefore, the classification below does not include any reference to the storage capacity.

Note that the throughput requirements increase dramatically for large storage servers. With the advances in fast packet switching, providing an increased amount of network bandwidth is feasible. However, due to the modest rate of improvements in the speed of storage devices such as magnetic or optical disks, the same is not true of the storage throughput. Also, note that the access and operation latency requirements remain the same irrespective of the size of the server. Satisfying these throughput and latency requirements together can be very difficult.

10.3   Multimedia Storage Server Architectures

We will first motivate the need for new architectures for high-performance large-scale storage servers and then present a new architecture called *Massively parallel and Real-time Storage* (MARS) architecture. We will then discuss alternate storage server architectures and their advantages and disadvantages.

Large-Scale Servers: What Is the Problem?

The network-based storage servers in their present form suffer from serious storage and network I/O bottlenecks. The storage I/O bottleneck results primarily due to performance gap between the storage and processor-memory systems. It manifests itself by restricting the rate (the requests per second and the throughput in Mbps) at which storage devices can handle read/write operations to two orders of magnitude smaller than the maximum rate at which an application can issue requests. This performance gap will continue to worsen as the processor, memory and network speeds keep improving faster than that of on-line secondary storage, which is limited largely by the transfer rate of direct access magnetic disks. In spite of the promise of all-optical technologies such as holographic storage, inexpensive availability of high throughput secondary storage in the near future is unlikely. On the other hand, the rate of improvement in the storage density of magnetic disks [20],[39] indicates that magnetic storage will be cost-effective in meeting the storage capacity requirements of future multimedia applications. However, as reported in [8], the rate of improvements in seek time (8 percent a year), rotational latency (practically no improvements), and transfer speeds (22 percent a year) will be very modest. This suggests that a large-capacity disk storage used naively will not deliver the throughput required by future applications. To make matters worse, the traditional operating systems (such as UNIX) used in existing servers suffer from several drawbacks, such as random placement of data, mixing of the meta-data and data on the storage devices, excessive copying of data between the storage devices and the network interface, and the lack of real-time scheduling support. This mismatch between the requirements of multimedia and the traditional operating system support for secondary storage devices aggravates the storage I/O bottleneck even further. Clearly, the high-performance storage I/O will be critical to successful deployment of multimedia applications.

The network I/O bottleneck can be defined as the phenomenon that restricts the application level throughput for network-oriented tasks to a small fraction (20 to 30 megabits/sec (Mbps)) of the gigabits/sec (Gbps) network bandwidth. It results from a lack of integration of operating systems, network protocol processing, host architecture and network interface. However, several recent ideas, such as zero-copy or minimal copy host-network interfaces and efficient protocol processing have alleviated the network I/O bottleneck significantly.

However, existing servers still do not support direct movement of data between the storage and network devices with minimal copying and guaranteed delay.

Also, existing network servers are exclusively bus-based single processor or multiprocessor workstations. Since the bus-based interconnects do not scale well, large-scale servers cannot be built out of such machines. Also, the workload these servers support typically consists of online transaction processing, or bulk general purpose computing which do not need any soft-real-time guarantees necessary for future multimedia applications. In short, requirements of future MOD storage servers are radically different, and therefore designing such servers is a challenging task that requires significant architectural innovation.

The architectures of large-scale servers that attempt to meet these challenges can be classified into three categories:

1. **Distributed storage-based clustered multimedia servers**
2. **Shared memory MIMD multiprocessor machines**
3. **Massively parallel SIMD machines**

We will now discuss each of these in greater detail.

Massively-Parallel And Real-Time Storage (MARS) Architecture

The *Massively-parallel And Real-time Storage* (MARS) is a representative example of the first of the three categories namely the *Distributed-Storage*-based architecture. It is an ongoing project at Washington University in St. Louis funded by the NSF National Challenges Award (NCA) grant, aimed at prototype development and deployment of scalable multi-gigabit throughput media servers in a metropolitan area network.

The MARS architecture, shown in Fig. 10–9, consists of a set of independent storage nodes that are connected together by a fast packet-based interconnect and managed by a central manager. The high-speed interconnect which can be in the form of a high-speed packet switched bus, a ring, or even a general purpose multicast switch, directly interfaces the server to the external network. For example, an ATM interconnect would directly interface the server to an external ATM network. The interconnects such as ATM switches are already available off-the-shelf and are quite inexpensive. In the foreseeable future, the interconnect speeds will increase and costs continue to decrease as they become commodity items. Thus, the high-speed interconnect employed in MARS will be scalable and inexpensive.

Fig. 10–10 shows a prototype MARS server architecture that uses a 2.4-Gbps ATM cell-switched interconnect based on a ASIC called the *ATM Port Interconnect Controller*. The three main components of this architecture: the **central manager**, the ATM interconnect, and the storage nodes are described in greater detail below.

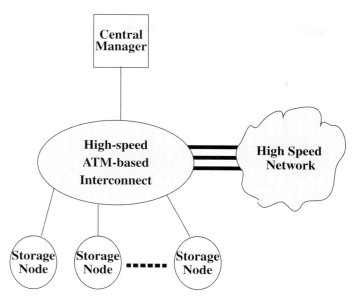

Figure 10-9   Massively parallel and real-time storage (MARS) system.

Central Manager

The central manager is responsible for data distribution, data retrievals, admission and access control, and billing functions. The MARS is a stateful server and stores the state information for every active stream. It follows a connection-oriented approach with resource reservations to provide QoS guarantees required by the media streams. Before a client can access a multimedia stream, the MARS server checks if it can reserve resources required to guarantee QoS for the new connection without affecting any of the existing active connections, and accordingly accepts or rejects the connection. The central manager performs this admission control in consultation with storage nodes. Typically, the central manager receives the connection requests from the remote clients. It uses an admission control procedure that runs entirely locally or in consultation with the node-level admission procedure to admit or reject the new request. Once admitted, the MARS server reserves resources such as the network bandwidth, storage bandwidth, compute support, and I/O scheduling at each node to provide statistical or deterministic guarantees for the stream retrieval.

For every document, the central manager also decides how to distribute the data over the storage nodes and manages the associated metadata information. The metadata information associated with the data is also distributed among various storage nodes and the central manager. Such data and metadata distribution (striping) depend on various factors, such as length of the document, demand in terms of the number of concurrent clients, degree of interactive

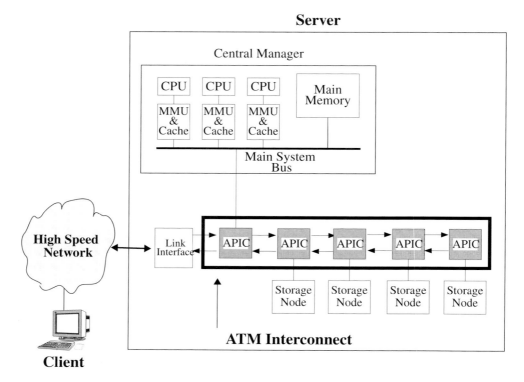

Figure 10-10 A prototype implementation of a MARS server.

behavior, and design of the data layout. Typically, the storage manager decides this distribution at the time the document is stored on the server.

For every active connection, the central manager schedules the data read/ write from the storage nodes by exchanging appropriate control information with the storage nodes. Note that the central manager only sets up the data flow to and from the storage devices and/or the network and does not participate in actual data movement. This ensures a high bandwidth path between the storage and the network.

APIC Based Interconnect

The packet switched interconnect in our prototype MARS architecture is constructed out of an ASIC called APIC (ATM Port Interconnect Controller) that is currently being developed as a part of an ARPA-sponsored gigabit local-area ATM testbed. The APIC chip is the basic building block for a high bandwidth *net-worked-I/O subsystem* that provides a direct interface to the network for the host (workstations as well as servers) and a variety of I/O devices.

In its simplest form, the APIC behaves like a 3×3 switch, two of whose ports can be treated as ATM ports and the remaining one as a non-ATM port. Using one of the ATM ports and a line interface, APIC can be directly interfaced to the input port of an ATM switch. As shown in Fig. 10–10, using the ATM ports, multiple APIC chips can be connected in a bidirectional daisy chain. Since each port is designed to operate at full 1.2-Gbps (SONET) rate, the aggregate data rate on the interconnect is ≈ 2.4 Gbps. The non-ATM port of an APIC can be looked upon as a read/write port to a data source, such as a memory or an I/O device. The APIC performs incremental AAL5 segmentation and reassembly of ATM cells through this port.

Each APIC manages a set of connections by maintaining certain state information for each active connection in a Virtual Circuit Translation Table (VCXT). The APIC also performs a simple single parameter (such as average bandwidth) based rate control or source pacing for each connection, which is important in scheduling multimedia streams from storage node to the network. The APIC also provides several dma mechanisms, such as *Simple DMA, Pool DMA, Protected DMA* aimed at allowing efficient transfer of data between various devices and memory with minimal copying. The discussion of these APIC internals is beyond the scope of this text, but can be found in [13],[14].

Storage Node

The capability of the MARS architecture to provide massive parallelism and support large number of concurrent accesses strongly depends on the functionality provided at the storage nodes.

Each storage node provides a large amount of storage in one or more forms, such as large high-performance magnetic disks, large disk arrays, or a high-capacity fast optical storage. The storage system collectively formed by all storage nodes may be homogeneous or hierarchical. If all storage nodes provide identical storage, such as disk arrays, the system will be homogeneous. On the other hand, a hierarchical storage can be constructed by assigning storage of different types to subsets of storage nodes. A client can be served the required data, either directly from the particular storage node (level) or by a staging mechanism, in which data is first moved to a node with faster storage (higher level) and then served from that device. For example, the nodes that use optical storage and robotically controlled tapes can be considered as off-line or near-line tertiary storage. When a client attempts to access the data stored on these devices, it is first cached on the magnetic disks at the other nodes and then served at full stream rate. Thus, the collective storage in the system can exceed a few tens of terabytes and still allow a large number of concurrent clients to access documents at the standard stream rate.

In addition to providing a storage facility, each storage node supports one or more of the resource management functions outlined below.

- **File System Support:**   Each storage node performs typical file system functions such as data and metadata management, metadata and data cache management, and data buffer management. In addition, it may support advanced database functions for efficient browsing and content-based searching of multimedia information.

- **Admission Control:** Each storage node keeps track of usage of local resources such as storage and interconnect bandwidth and performs local admission control.

- **Scheduling Support:** Each node, completely manages real-time scheduling of local data read and write functions for each active stream.

- **Compute Support:** A large amount of computing power can be provided by using sophisticated media processors such as the MVP [18] at each storage node. Such processors will be embedded on the path between the storage and the network, and can be used to perform media processing functions such as transcoding, speech recognition, image processing, and character recognition required by future multimedia applications.

The main objective in the design of the storage node is to provide a high-bandwidth, efficient data path between the external network and the storage devices. The architecture of the storage node described here assumes the storage in the form of a RAID; however it can be extended easily to accommodate other forms of storage such as a set of independent high-capacity optical and magnetic disks. A RAID storage node is illustrated in Fig. 10–11. Each storage node is constructed out of a high-performance processor subsystem such as a Pentium PC. The disk array at the node is constructed out of a set of *Small Computer System Interconnect* (SCSI) strings, with a fixed number of disks per string or a SCSI compatible disk array per string. In the case of commercial RAID disk arrays, an on-board processor performs disk array control functions. The same processor can serve as a local CPU at a storage node. The multiple SCSI strings interface to the APIC through a dual-ported memory, such as a video RAM (VRAM).

In order to understand the requirements that must be satisfied in the design of such a storage node, we examine the data and control path within the storage node. Fig. 10–11 illustrates the data path between the VRAM, the disk array, and the APIC. As shown there, the disk array controller writes the data prefetched from the disk array into the preallocated buffers in the VRAM using the direct access port. The APIC reads this prefetched data using the serial port of the VRAM. Both these accesses are arbitrated by the control logic. The node CPU issues control commands required for controlling prefetch and transmission activities by writing the memory mapped registers of the APIC and disk controller. These accesses through the control logic constitute the control path. Clearly, the node CPU is not involved in the high-speed data movement between the storage devices and external network.

The data is typically prefetched and stored in a buffer before it is transmitted on to the network. The commercial RAIDs commonly provide up to 40 Mbps or 320 Mbps throughput. The APIC is being designed for 1.2 Gbps throughput

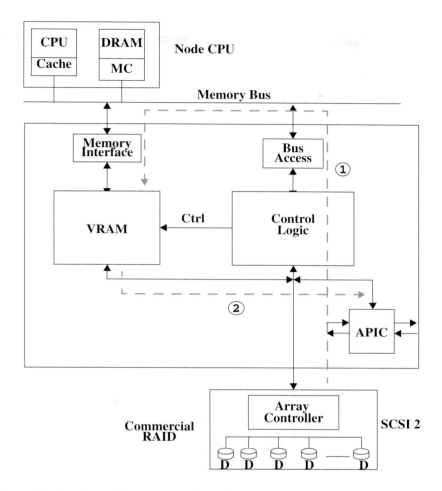

Figure 10-11   Example storage node architecture.

per port. Thus, in the worst case, the total throughput in and out of the buffering system must be of the order of 2 Gbps. However, memory systems constructed out of commercial DRAMS can provide a peak bandwidth of 500 Mbps. Given this, avoiding data copying and use of high bandwidth memory alternatives such as VRAM provides significant performance advantage.

A rough estimate of the size of such a memory system is also in order. If the average BW requirement of an MPEG stream is assumed to be 5 Mbps, the interconnect BW of 1.2 Gbps can accommodate roughly 240 clients. If the storage node prefetched 1 GOP of typically 9 frames, each connection prefetch buffer is roughly 0.2 Mbs, and over all 240 connections it is about 48 Mbs. Clearly,

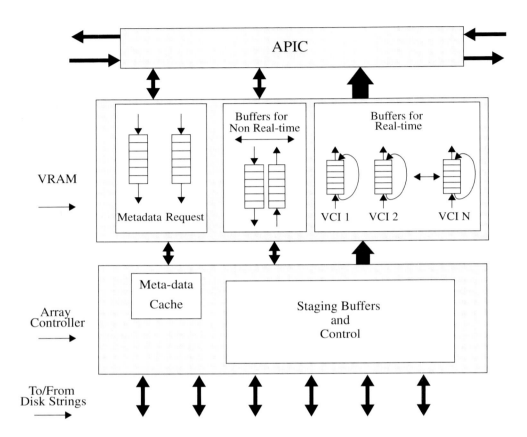

Figure 10–12 Details of node-APIC interface.

increasing this prefetch granularity increases the required buffer size. Also, as much as twice the size of prefetch buffers may be required to ensure smooth playout and playout control operations. In short, the data path must provide high capacity memory on the order of a few hundred megabytes and must sustain throughput of the order 2 Gbps.

The control path is responsible for admission control as well scheduling of prefetches from disk arrays and transmissions by the APIC. These tasks involve allocating/deallocating the data buffers, and scheduling related data structures, periodically updating scheduling information, and retrieving and managing the metadata. Such operations will typically be implemented in software as a part of a node level operating system and will require periodic timely access to the memory, storage, and network system to guarantee overall correctness of scheduling operations. Clearly, in addition to the aforementioned data path throughput, this added load must be sustained. As shown in Fig. 10–12, in a read-only environment, the local node OS asynchronously writes the data in the VRAM and the APIC consumes it to transfer it to the network. The vram is shared by the following buffers:

- **Buffers for Periodic Streams**: A set of circular buffers serve as the prefetching buffers for the data from periodic streams retrieved off the disk array. These buffers can be statically reserved on a per connection basis at the connection setup time or dynamically allocated during every cycle of the scheduling scheme described earlier. The size of allocated buffers depends on the media type as well as the playback rate. For example, the buffer requirement of a video stream is much larger than that of an audio stream. Also, a video stream played at 15 frames/sec needs much smaller buffers than the one played at the standard 30 frames/sec.

  The data compression techniques have implications for the buffer allocation policy as well as the buffer requirements. For example, the buffer required for a JPEG encoded stream is significantly larger than its MPEG encoded counterpart. Another characteristics of the compressed streams is that the size of successive frames in the media streams varies significantly, causing a frame-to-frame variability in the buffer requirements. For example, empirical evidence has shown a factor of four to five variability in the data content of single frame of MPEG compressed video streams. Thus, the static allocation of buffers, though simple, requires more memory because the size of the buffer allocated at the connection setup time has to be the maximum expected size of a frame.
- **Buffers for Non-Real-Time Tasks**: A set of buffers are used for read/ writes of non real-time streams, such as still images, text, and progressive image transmissions.
- **Request Buffers**: The storage node operating system sends control commands for read and write schedule management in a request queue in the VRAM (Fig. 10–11). The disk array controller reads these commands to initiate appropriate SCSI transactions to retrieve data from the storage devices. The request queue is partitioned based on the connection identifier or the VCIs.
- **Positional Metadata Buffers**: The positional metadata is the information about the location of the data on the storage devices. This data is provided by the central manager and used by the array controller to read (write) disks in the array. Like the request queue, the metadata queue is also partitioned based on VCIs.

These buffers are allocated and managed by the local operating system at the storage node. In the prototype architecture, each node runs a NETBSD UNIX operating system enhanced to handle multimedia data. Specifically, the filesystem and buffer management function in this OS have been modified to

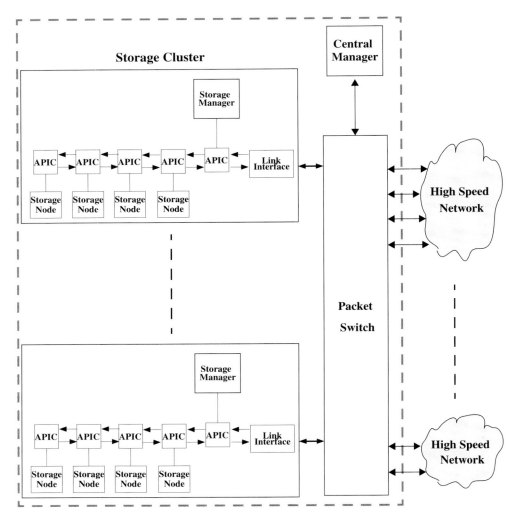

Figure 10-13   Cluster-Based Storage (CBS) architecture for MARS.

allow periodic retrieval of data and minimize buffer copying [11],[12]. Also, a new process scheduling technique called *Real-Time Upcalls* (RTU) is employed to support periodic event processing required to provide QoS guarantees [16], [15], [17].

A Scalable Extension

The Cluster-Based Storage (CBS) architecture, which is a scalable extension of the prototype implementation discussed earlier, is illustrated in Fig. 10–13. It consists of a set of independent clusters interconnected through a fast multicast ATM switch, such as [36], [37]. The ATM switch interfaces the server to the external network. Each of the clusters resemble our prototype implementation architecture. The APIC at the end of the daisy chain in a cluster transparently interfaces to one port of an ATM switch. Each cluster has a local cluster manager. The central manager in this architecture manages the switch, performs the network signaling operations, and cooperates with the cluster level storage managers to perform admission control.

Two types of information flows between the CBS server and the external network: one type is the control information such as the client requests for multimedia streams, stream manipulation commands such as fast forward, reverse, pause etc., server responses, and the network signaling information. The other type of information is the actual multimedia data for all active connections. Depending upon the implementation, the CBS architecture may reserve certain switch ports for control information and the rest of the ports for data traffic.

The scalability of this architecture accrues from increasing the number of ports and the bandwidth per port of the ATM switch, a trend supported by advances in the field of ATM switching. Note that the availability of multiple clusters provides a greater number of options for data distribution. For example, popular documents can be replicated in multiple clusters and incoming requests for them can be assigned to one of these clusters. If the number of documents is very large, a subset of them can be assigned and served from each cluster. Also, the documents of very long duration can be conveniently split into smaller parts, each of which can be stored independently on a separate cluster. Note that the packet switch in this architecture allows a connection from any input port to be switched and remapped to a different network level connection at any output port. This allows multimedia data to be striped not only over the storage nodes in a cluster, but over multiple clusters as well. The increased parallelism that results from the greater degree of data distribution in turn can support a larger number of concurrent accesses to the same document. In short, the CBS architecture is truly scalable in terms of number of clients, storage capacity, and storage and network throughput.

Shared Memory MIMD Multiprocessor-Based Storage Servers

Use of shared memory MIMD multiprocessor machines as MOD represents another architectural approach to design of large scale MOD servers. The proposed MOD servers from vendors like Silicon Graphics, and Whittaker Communications, Inc. are examples of this approach. Here we will briefly describe the Silicon Graphics server architecture shown in Fig. 10–14 [34].

The architecture consists of several R4400 CPU boards, I/O subsystems in the form of HIO boards, and interleaved memory boards interconnected by a 1.2 GBps *PowerPath-2* bus with separate 256 bit data and 64-bit address paths.

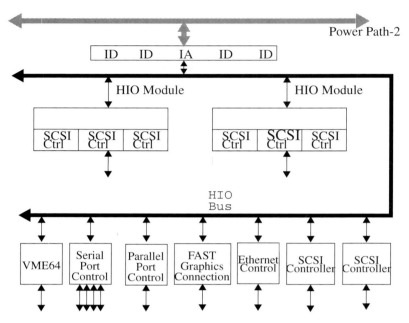

Figure 10-14   Details of the power channel board.

Each HIO board uses a internal proprietary HIO I/O bus rated at 320 MBps throughput. At present, maximum four such boards are allowed in the high-end configuration, theoretically providing a 1.280 GBps of I/O throughput.

Each HIO board, shown in Fig. 10–16, contains an intelligent Ethernet controller, serial RS-232/422 and parallel port controllers, VME64 controller, and a graphics connection. The storage I/O capability is provided in the form of two SCSI-2 controllers, each capable of 20 MBps rated throughput. Each I/O board has slots for two HIO modules, each of which can be populated with up to three SCSI-2 modules. Thus, each HIO board can have up to eight SCSI-2 controllers allowing maximum of 160 MBps storage throughput.

The ID, IA chips shown in Fig. 10–16 act as bus adapters and provide interface to the POWERPATH bus. They perform virtual address mapping for DMA operations—maintain cache coherency between system bus and I/O systems.

The SGI server runs a UNIX-like operating system called IRIX with file system extensions. Specifically, it supports a data layout method called **logical volume striping** that treats multiple independent storage devices such as disk arrays to be treated as a single logical device or volume. Another level of striping called **Application Level Striping** allows an application to decide it's own striping scheme for distributing data over multiple logical volume. Both these extensions are aimed at increasing the number of concurrent accesses to the

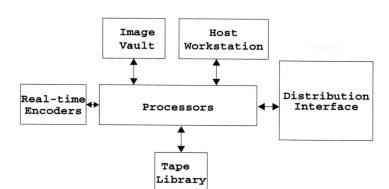

Figure 10–15   Silicon Graphics symmetric shared memory MIMD multiprocessor machine.

same document and parallelism in data accesses. Detailed performance measurements on a fully configured 20-processor system with 512-Mbs memory and 32 RAID 3 disk arrays have been reported in [19].

Massively Parallel SIMD Multiprocessor Based Servers

Another approach to developing large-scale storage servers is to employ massively parallel SIMD multiprocessor machines which traditionally have been used for performing high-performance signal processing and numerical computations. The Sarnoff Real-time Systems **MAGIC** media server, and the NCube/Oracle-M10 MediaNet server are two examples of this approach. Here we will take a brief look at the MAGIC media server [5].

The MAGIC architecture consists of five main components: input boards, output boards, a processor array of SIMD processors, a special purpose disk array called *ImageVault*, and the host computer. The processor array uses a special purpose 144-bit VLIW video signal processor VSP developed at David Sarnoff Research Center. Each processor is capable of a specialized video processing function, thus equipping the MAGIC server with a formidable real-time data processing power. The array is constructed out of boards of 128 processors and uses a proprietary Inter Processor Connection (IPC) network operating at 1.3 Gbps for communication between the processors. Each processor in the array has a a 160 Mbps data path to a SCSI-2 disk controller in the *ImageVault* disk array. Each disk controller controls one disk in the disk array. In the full scale configuration, the server has a maximum of eight such boards or a total of 8196 processors and a total of 8196 disks in the disk array. The multimedia data is

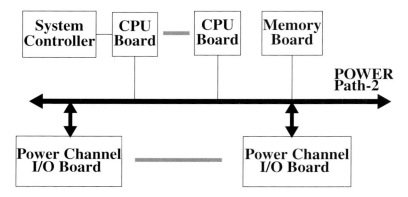

Figure 10-16   Silicon Graphics symmetric shared memory MIMD multiprocessor machine.

striped over all disks in the image vault allowing extensive concurrency and high throughput. The aggregate output bandwidth of the processor array is approximately 10.8 Gbps, which is connected to the variety of external interfaces for data rates of OC3, STS-3, DS-3, OC12. The input boards provide seamless interfaces between the processor array's input bandwidth of 5.4 Gbps and external data sources such as networks and real-time video encoders. Both these boards can handle in hardware incoming data in ATM formats. The host computer block in this architecture is implemented by a Silicon Graphics SGI Indy machine running a UNIX-like operating system. It communicates and controls the processor array through a GIO32 interface operating at 672 Mbps. It also communicates control messages from the clients to the processor array and also, implements billing and meta-database searches.

An example configuration of the MAGIC server with 1024 processors rated at aggregate 44,000 MIPS and an I/O BW of 2016 MB/sec (≈ 1000 SCSI-2s!) sports close to a terabyte of ImageVault storage (with 1024 1-Gb SCSI disks!). It supports a true-MOD DV service for as many as 6000 MPEG-1 connections and supports a stream operation latency of approximately 1.2 seconds [5].

Comparison of the Three Architectures

The MARS architecture has the advantage that it uses off-the-shelf commodity components such as Pentium PCs, ATM chips or switch-based interconnects, and RAID-based high-performance reliable storage systems. The storage nodes constructed out of Pentium PCs provide excellent performance and have the advantage of low cost due to high volume market. Also, the MARS architecture provides a zero-copy direct path between the storage devices and the network and is truly scalable. However, a distributed storage architecture such as the

MARS architecture may pose difficulties in an environment that requires media edits with very stringent QOS guarantees.

The primary drawback of the MIMD architecture-based storage servers is that providing zero-copy data path from the storage devices to the external network is difficult. The data moves twice over the high-speed bus: once from the storage devices to the main memory and from memory to the external network, reducing the available throughput by a factor of two. Also, the bus-based architecture of the server does not scale well and is prohibitively expensive.

Similarly, the SIMD architecture-based storage servers represent a very expensive solution that employs a lot of proprietary components such as the VSP processors, the interconnection network for the processor array, and the Image-Vault.

10.4   Data Layout and Access

The purpose of this section is to discuss the layout of data in storage servers. We will follow a hierarchical approach: we will first describe data layouts in servers that store multiple video streams on a single disk system. We will highlight advantages and disadvantages of this approach. In the end, we will describe distributed data layouts in large-scale storage servers. These data layouts can potentially use disk level and disk array level layouts and support high concurrency and parallelism.

Data Layouts on Disks

In this subsection, we describe mechanisms for managing the storage of real-time digital media such as motion video and audio. We call a sequence of continuously recorded video frames or audio samples a *Strand*. Each strand is organized on the disk in terms of media blocks separated by gaps of free space. The storage pattern for a strand consists of a *media block size, M,* and a *gap size, G*, both in terms of sectors on the disk. We develop a model that generates a *storage pattern* for a given strand. The model relates disk and device characteristics (such as disk read/write latency, and video capture/display times) to the media recording rate, and derives the block and gap sizes that result in continuous retrieval.

Given multiple strands each with its own storage pattern, we develop mechanisms for merging their storage so as to utilize disk space efficiently. In the merging of strands, gaps between media blocks of one strand are filled with media blocks of other strands. Hence, the storage pattern and hence the continuity of the second strand may not be maintained strictly for each media block. However, it must be possible to introduce read-ahead and buffering of a finite number of blocks so as to preserve the storage pattern and continuity properties

Symbol	Explanation	Unit
s_{mu}	Size of media unit	bytes
s_{ds}	Size of a disk sector	bytes
M_i	Media block size in storage pattern of strand s_i	sectors
G_i	Gap size in storage pattern of strand s_i	sectors
B_i	Buffer size for retrieval of strand s_i	bytes
R_i	Size of read-ahead for retrieval of strand s_i	bytes
r_{dt}	Rate of data transfer to or from disk	sectors/sec
T_{tt}	Track-to-track seek time of the disk	sec
T_{rot}	Rotation time of the disk	sec
T_{dis}	Display time of a media block	sec
L	$LCM(M_1 + G_1, M_2 + G_2)$	sectors

Table 10–2 Symbols.

on an average over those finite number of blocks. Otherwise, merging of real-time media strands (without violation of their continuity requirements) is impossible.

Preliminary Definitions

Frame   is the basic unit of video.

Sample   is the basic unit of audio

Strand   is a sequence of continuously recorded audio samples or video frames.

Sector   is the basic unit of disk storage.

Media block is a sequence of consecutive sectors storing media units (frames or samples). The size of a media block of a strand s_i is denoted by M_i.

Media Gap   is the separation between successive blocks of a strand. The size of a media gap of a strand s_i is denoted by G_i.

Media blocks are assumed to be homogeneous, i.e., each block contains exactly one medium. This permits the file system to exploit the properties of each medium to independently optimize its storage. Heterogeneous blocks on the other hand may entail additional processing for combining media during storage and separating them during retrieval.

Each media block M_i and gap G_i is assumed to span an integral number of sectors. The tuple (M_i, G_i) is referred to as the storage pattern of strand s_i. A strand consists of repetitions of this pattern.

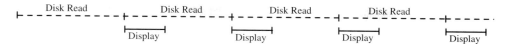

Figure 10-17   Continuous retrieval of media blocks of a strand.

Storage Pattern of a Media Strand

The guiding factor in determining the storage pattern of a strand is the requirement of continuous retrieval. Continuity in retrieval can be guaranteed if each media block is available at the display device at or before the scheduled time of its playback. If blocks of a strand are located in a random fashion on a disk, separations between successive blocks of the strand may not be constrained enough to support continuous retrieval of media strands. At the other end of the spectrum, employing a contiguous allocation of blocks can guarantee continuous retrieval, but entails enormous copying overheads during insertions and deletions. Both of these drawbacks can be overcome if blocks are allocated such that (1) the block size is bounded from below, and (2) the gap size is bounded from above, with both of these bounds determined from the requirement of continuity.

Equation (1) below formulates the continuity requirement. The continuity requirement is met if the time to skip over a gap and read the next media block (left hand side of the equation) does not exceed the duration of its playback (right-hand side of the equation) (see Fig. 10–17).

$$\frac{M_i + G_i}{r_{dt}} \leq T_{dis} \tag{1}$$

The storage pattern (M_i, G_i) for a strand must satisfy the above equation. However, since there are two variables and one equation, the storage pattern is not unique for a strand. The exact storage pattern may be determined by fixing one of the variables (for instance, the block size may be made equal to the memory page size in the system), and substituting its value in Equation (1) to compute the other.

If the disk is always sufficiently empty, then each strand may be stored on the disk exactly in accordance with its storage pattern. However, this may not be possible in reality. Typically, a disk would contain a large number of strands. Hence, blocks of a new strand have to be stored in the gaps of already existing strands on the disk. As a result, it is not guaranteed that the blocks of the new strand can be laid out on disk in accordance with its storage pattern. In order to utilize disk space efficiently, it is desirable to fill the gaps between media blocks of existing strands with media blocks of the new strand. In doing so, the continuity of the new strand may not be maintained strictly for each media block. However, it must be possible to introduce read-ahead and buffering of a finite number of blocks so as to satisfy its continuity requirements on an average over those

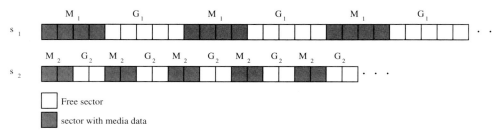

Figure 10-18 Media strands as repetitions of storage patterns.

finite number of blocks. We will now derive the conditions for merging, and obtain the read-ahead and buffering requirements that guarantee continuous retrieval of media strands.

Merging the Storage of Two Strands

Consider two media strands s_1 and s_2 with storage patterns (M_1, G_1) and (M_2, G_2), respectively (see Fig. 10–18). Let the blocks of strand s_1 be laid out on the disk in accordance with its storage pattern (thus, guaranteeing continuous retrieval of s_1). To efficiently utilize the storage space, the file system must store the blocks of s_2 in the gaps of the pattern for s_1. The constraint in this process of merging is that the continuity requirement of s_2 must not be violated.

Real disks are organized in tracks, and a non-negligible track-to-track seek time, T_{tt}, is incurred in changing between tracks. However, if the storage pattern of strand s_1 is chosen such that $T_{rot} \times r_{dt}$ is a multiple of $M_1 + G_1$, and $M_1 \geq T_{tt} \times r_{dt}$ (see Fig. 10–19), the track-to-track seek time incurred during the retrieval of a merged strand s_2 is "hidden" in the time to jump over M_1 of s_1. Hence, in the analysis that follows, we will not separately consider track-to-track seek times.

Merging of s_2 into s_1 is straight-forward if $G_1 = M_2$ and $M_1 = G_2$. In such a case, each media block of s_2 will exactly fit into a gap of s_1. However, in general, this can be very restrictive. If we introduce a buffer between the file system and the display (for temporary storage of media blocks during the retrieval of a strand), and read-ahead a sufficient number of media blocks before initiating the display of a strand (prefetch and store media blocks in the buffer), the continuity requirement may need to be satisfied only on an average. This is because, buffering can nullify the effects of jitter in the pattern, and result in the relaxation of the condition for merging multiple strands. We will now derive the exact condition for the merging of two strands to be possible. We assume that the lengths of media strands may not be bounded at the time of the start of its recording, but the read-ahead and the buffer sizes are required to be bounded.

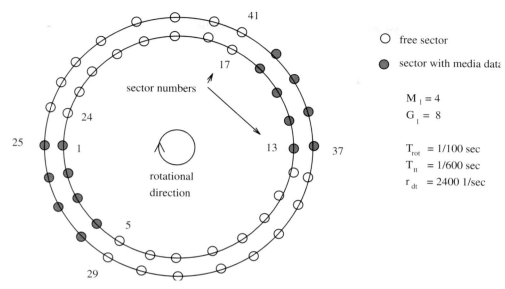

Figure 10–19   Availability of gaps of s_1 to store s_2.

Intuitively, a strand s_2 can be merged into s_1 if the fraction of space occupied by media in s_2's pattern does not exceed the fraction of empty space available in strand s_1. That is,

$$\frac{M_2}{M_2 + G_2} \leq \frac{G_1}{M_1 + G_1} \qquad (2)$$

Simplification of the above equation yields the following proposition that formally derives the condition for merging:

Proposition 1 (Merge Condition)   Let s_1 and s_2 be two strands with associated storage patterns (M_1, G_1) and (M_2, G_2) respectively. We can merge strand s_2 into strand s_1 if and only if

$$\frac{G_1}{M_2} \geq \frac{M_1}{G_2} \qquad (3)$$

The proof of this proposition can be found in the papers [31], [32].

Layout of Media Blocks

If the merge condition is satisfied, the simplest way to lay out s_2's media blocks is to fill them into s_1's gaps continuously starting from the very first gap. After storing the blocks belonging to one cycle, the remaining gaps would be left free. However, if s_2's pattern is sparse compared to the empty space available in s_1, a large

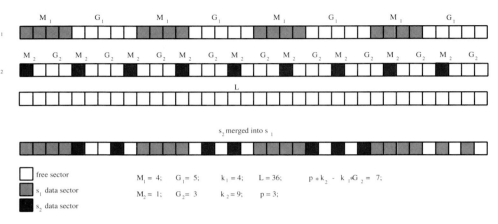

Figure 10-20   Layout of strand s_1 merged into strand s_1.

number of media blocks of s_2 are read earlier than their time of display leading to peaks in buffering requirements. The buffering requirements can be reduced by distributing the media blocks uniformly over all the gaps of s_1. Formally, let k_1 patterns of strand s_1 and k_2 patterns of strand s_2 span over a merge cycle L. We define the pseudo block size of s_2 with respect to s_1 as the smallest integer M_2' such that

$$k_2 \times M_2' \geq k_1 \times G_1 \qquad (4)$$

The merge condition guarantees that $M_2' \geq M_2$. If $M_2' = M_2$, then the merge condition is exactly satisfied, and the media blocks of s_2 occupy all the gaps of s_1. If $M_2' > M_2$, in each cycle L of the merge pattern, we can distribute the k_2 blocks of s_2 such that there are either $M_2' - 1 - M_2$ or $M_2' - M_2$ free sectors between consecutive media blocks of s_2. (To be exact, in each cycle of k_2 blocks, $k_2 \times M_2' - k_1 \times G_1$ blocks will have a separation of $M_2' - 1 - M_2$ sectors, and the remaining will have a separation of $M_2' - M_2$ sectors.) The $(k_2+1)^{\text{th}}$ block of s_2 will be stored exactly L sectors away from the first media block of s_2, resulting in a pattern of filled and free sectors that repeats after every L sectors, which is the length of one merge cycle (see Fig. 10–20). Such a distribution is almost uniform in the sense that the number of free sectors between successive blocks of s_2 can differ only by one.

An important consequence of merging s_2's pattern into that of s_1 is that the continuity requirements, which hold for each block in s_2's pattern, are now guaranteed to hold only over an average of k_2 blocks in the merged pattern for s_2. Thus, a read ahead of at most k_2 blocks of s_2 may be necessary. We will now compute the exact read-ahead requirements of the merged strand.

Determining the Read-Ahead

Let us consider the playback of strand s_2 after merger. If $\mathcal{R}$ is the number of blocks that are read ahead, the process of displaying s_2 at the media output device starts immediately after $\mathcal{R}$ blocks have been transferred. In order to satisfy the continuity requirements, the total time to access and transfer any n blocks of s_2 *after the read ahead*, should not exceed the playback duration of $\mathcal{R}$ blocks that have been read ahead plus the $n-1$ subsequent blocks that have been transferred thereafter. Formulation of this condition yields:

$$\forall n: \sum_{i=1}^{n} T_{access}^{i} \leq (n-1) \times T_{dis} + R \times T_{dis} \tag{5}$$

where T_{access}^{i} is the time needed to access the ith media block, and T_{dis} is the playback duration of a media block.

$$R \geq \max_{n} \left(\left(\frac{\sum_{i=1}^{n} T_{access}^{i}}{T_{dis}} \right) - (n-1) \right) \tag{6}$$

However, since (1) s_2's merged pattern repeats after k_2 blocks and (2) the pattern of s_2 before merger meets the continuity requirement (Equation (1)), satisfying Equation (6) for values of $n \leq k_2$ automatically implies that it is satisfied for all the media blocks of s_2.

The total time to access n media blocks of merged strand s_2 is the sum of the times to (1) read n blocks, (2) skip over media blocks of strand s_1, denoted by ϕ_1 (colored grey in Fig. 10–20), that are present in the separations between the n blocks of s_2, and (3) skip over free sectors, denoted by ϕ_2 (colored white in Fig. 10–20), that are present in the separations between the n blocks of s_2. That is,

$$\sum_{i=1}^{n} T_{access}^{i} = \frac{n \times M_2}{r_{dt}} + \frac{\phi_1(n)}{r_{dt}} + \frac{\phi_2(n)}{r_{dt}} \tag{7}$$

where r_{dt} is the disk rotation rate in sectors per second (which is assumed to determine the speed at which blocks can be read or skipped).

The value of read-ahead $\mathcal{R}$ can be computed using following equation derived in [31].

$$R \geq \max_{1 \leq n \leq k_2} \left(\frac{\left(n \times \left(M_2' \times \left(\frac{M_1}{G_1} + 1 \right) \right) \right)}{M_2 + G_2} - \frac{n}{M_2 + G_2} + n \times \left(\frac{M_1}{M_2 + G_2} + 1 \right) \right) \tag{8}$$

The read-ahead reaches a maximum when the term containing n in the above equation takes the maximum value. This term reaches a maximum when n is 1 or k_2 depending on whether its coefficient is positive or negative. It can be shown that the coefficient is positive [31]. Therefore, the read-ahead required to guarantee continuity of strand s_2 after merger can be derived as follows [31].

$$R \geq \frac{k_2 \times \left(M_2'\left(\frac{M_1}{G_1} + 1\right) - M_2 - G_2\right)}{M_2 + G_2} + \frac{M_1}{M_2 + G_2} + 1 \tag{9}$$

This condition can be used to determine the read-ahead when the patterns of s_1 and s_2 are given. However, if the continuity requirements are oversatisfied and T_{dis} is known, the read-ahead can be calculated more accurately using Equation (10).

$$R \geq \max_{1 \leq n \leq k_2}\left(n \times \left(\frac{M_2' \times \left(\frac{M_1}{G_1} + 1\right)}{T_{dis} \times r_{dt}}\right)\right) - n + \left(\frac{M_1}{T_{dis} \times r_{dt}} + 1\right) \tag{10}$$

Determining Buffer Sizes

The blocks that are retrieved during a read-ahead need to be stored in an intermediate buffer between the file system and the media output device. When the display of the retrieved media blocks starts, media blocks are both (1) continuously removed from the buffer by the output device, and (2) continuously retrieved from the disk and added to the buffer by the file system. The size of the buffer grows and diminishes during the retrieval. Continuity of playback requires that the buffer should never be empty when the output device is ready to remove a block from the buffer. If s_2 were to be stored as an unmerged pattern (M_2, G_2) and continuity requirements were satisfied exactly, each block would be transferred to the buffer and then played back immediately. However, after the merge, continuity requirements are satisfied only over a merge cycle (i.e., k_2 media blocks), and the buffer size starts with being equal to the read ahead, and grows and diminishes over a period of the merge cycle at the end of which it is equal to the read ahead again. The maximum value of buffers assuming that the continuity requirements are satisfied exactly can be computed by following equation [31],

$$B = R + \left\lceil \frac{q \times G_1 + \min(r \times (M_1 + G_1), G_1)}{\left\lfloor \frac{k_1 \times G_1}{k_2} \right\rfloor} \right\rceil - (n - 1) \tag{11}$$

where $\mathcal{R}$ is the read-ahead given by Equation (9) or (10). Generally additional buffering requirements will result from oversatisfied continuity requirements.

These can be caused by variations in the rate of playback (e.g., in slow motion), where the retrieval of media blocks proceeds faster than their display. Moreover the storage pattern of a strand can be determined in a way that continuity requirements are oversatisfied even during the playback with the fastest rate. File systems designed to satisfy several requests simultaneously have to compute those kind of storage patterns. In order to prevent unbounded accumulation of media blocks in buffers, the disk can switch to some other task after all the buffers allocated to the retrieval of a media strand are filled, and switch back when sufficient buffers become empty. However, after the disk switches to some other task, the disk head may have moved to a random location. Hence, besides the time used for other tasks T_{ot} the disk head may have to incur maximum seek (and latency) time, l_{seek}^{max} before being able to resume the transfer of blocks of the earlier media strand. Thus, in order to guarantee that the display does not run out of media blocks during a switch to another task, the disk must read ahead additional blocks into buffers before the switch, given by:

$$(T_{ot} + l_{seek}^{max}) \times \frac{r_{dt}}{M_2 + G_2}$$

Merging More than Two Strands

The above binary merging techniques can be easily extended to interspersed storage of three or more strands. Let us suppose that we have to merge m strands, $s_1, s_2, s_3, \ldots, s_m$. When the first two strands s_1 and s_2 are merged, the resulting storage pattern can be viewed as that of a *composite strand* s_{12}, whose media block size M_{12} and gap size G_{12} are given by:

$$M_{12} = k_1 \times M_1 + k_2 \times M_2$$

$$G_{12} = k_1 \times G_1 - k_2 \times M_2$$

$$= k_2 \times G_2 - k_1 \times M_1$$

where $L_{12} = LCM(M_1+G_1, M_2+G_2)$ is the length of the pattern, $k_1 = \dfrac{L}{M_1 + G_1}$, and

$k_2 = \dfrac{L}{M_2 + G_2}$. The merger of s_3 with s_{12} can now be carried out using the binary merging techniques to yield strand s_{123}. Continuing the merge operation in this fashion, the m strands can be merged using a sequence of m-1 binary merge operations to result in a final composite strand, $s_{1,2,3,\ldots m}$. The derivations for read-ahead and buffer sizes of binary merging can also be extended to *M-ary merging* in a similar fashion.

Deletion of a strand s_s from a composite strand s_c can be slightly tricky: the sectors occupied by the media blocks of strand s_s are released back to the pool of gaps of the composite strand s_c. Assume (M_s, G_s) is the pattern of s_s, and (M_c, G_c) of s_c. After deletion, the resulting strand s_c' will have a pattern given by (M_c',

G_c'), where $M_c' = M_c - M_s$, and $G_c' = G_c + M_s$. Generally the pattern cycle length $(M_c + G_c)$ of the composite strand remains unchanged.

However, when the strand to be deleted was the last one to be merged, deletion restores the pattern to that before the last merge. For example, if strand s_m is deleted from a composite strand $s_{1,2,...,m}$, the parameters $L_{1,2,...,m}$, $G_{1,2,...,m}$, and $M_{1,2,...,m}$ are restored back to $L_{1,2,...,m-1}$, $G_{1,2,...,m-1}$, and $M_{1,2,...,m-1}$, respectively, which are the values prior to the merging of strand s_m into $s_{1,2,...,m-1}$.

Data Layouts in Scalable MOD Servers

A data layout scheme in a multimedia server should possess the following properties: 1) it should support maximal parallelism in the use of storage nodes and be scalable in terms of the number of clients concurrently accessing the same or different document, 2) facilitate interactive control and random access, and 3) allow simple scheduling schemes that can ensure periodic retrieval and transmission of data from unsynchronized storage nodes.

We use the fact that the multimedia data is amenable to spatial striping to distribute it hierarchically over several autonomous storage nodes within the server. One of the possible layout schemes, called *Distributed Cyclic Layout* (DCCL), is shown in Fig. 10–21. The layout uses a basic unit called *"chunk"* consisting of k consecutive frames. All the chunks in a document are of the same size and thus, have a constant time length in terms of playout duration. In case of a Variable Bit Rate (VBR) video, a chunk therefore represents a Constant Time Length (CTL) but a variable data length unit. In case of a Constant Bit Rate (CBR) source, it also has constant size [6], [7], [22]. Different documents may have different chunk sizes, ranging from $k=1$ to $k=F_{max}$, where F_{max} is the maximum number of frames in a multimedia document. In case of MPEG compressed streams, the group-of-pictures (GOP) is one possible choice of chunk size. A chunk is always confined to one storage node. The successive chunks are distributed over storage nodes using a logical layout topology. For example, in Fig. 10–21 the chunks have been laid out using a ring topology. Note that in this scheme, the two consecutive chunks at the same node are separated in time by kDT_f time units, D being the number of storage nodes and T_f the frame period for the stream. Thus, if the chunk size is one frame (DCL layout), the stream is slowed down by a factor of D from the perspective of each storage node or the throughput required per stream from each storage node is reduced by a factor of D. This in turn helps in masking the large prefetch latencies introduced by very slow storage devices at each node.

Note that each storage node stores the chunks assigned to it using a local storage policy. For example, if the node uses ordinary disk storage, the *storage pattern* based methods described above can be employed. On the other hand, if the node uses a disk array, the way each chunk is stored or striped on the array may depend on the type of the disk array. For example, a RAID-3 disk array will

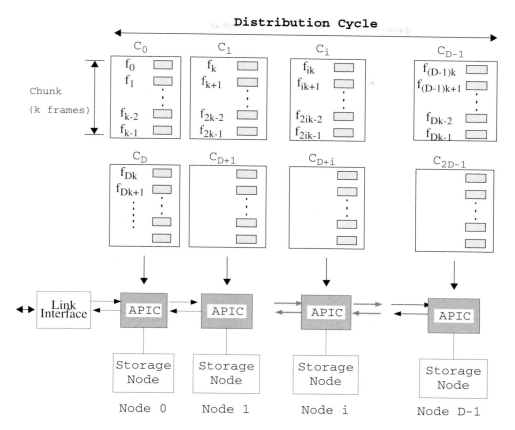

Figure 10–21 Distributed chunked layout.

use byte striping, whereas a RAID-5 will use block striping. Other striping techniques such as [9] are also possible. Clearly, our data layout is hierarchical and consists of two levels: Level-1 which decides the distribution of data over storage nodes, and Level-2 which defines how the data assigned to each node by Level-1 layout will be stored on the local storage devices.

Performance Metrics

We will evaluate Level-1 distributed layouts using two performance metrics. The first one called *parallelism* (P_f), is defined as the **number of storage nodes participating concurrently in supplying the data for a document *f*.** The second metric called *concurrency* (C_f) defines the **number of active clients that can simultaneously access the same document *f*.**

The value of P_f ranges from 1 to D, where D represents the number of storage nodes. P_f is D, when the data is distributed over all nodes, whereas, it is one when the entire document is confined to a single storage node. A higher value of P_f implies larger number of nodes are involved in transfer of data for each connection/request, which in turn improves node utilization and proportionately increases concurrency. The P_f metric also has implications on reliability. If a document is completely confined to a storage node ($P_f = 1$), in the event of a failure of that node, it is entirely unavailable. However, with loss-tolerant media, such as video, animation, and graphics, a higher P_f will still keep the document partially available.

If each storage node n ($n \in [1 \dots D]$) has an available sustained throughput of B_n, and the average storage/network throughput required for accessing the document f is R_f, then the concurrency supported by a layout with parallelism P_f is

$$C_f = \min_n\left(\frac{B_n P_f}{R_f}\right)$$

The maximum value of the concurrency metric is a function of the total interconnect bandwidth I_{bw} and is defined as

$$C_{f,\,\max} = \frac{I_{bw}}{R_f}$$

Clearly, maximum concurrency is achieved if $I_{bw} = B_n D$. From above expressions, we can see that the concurrency is a function of the parallelism supported by the data layout. Higher concurrency is desirable as it allows larger number of clients to simultaneously access the same document and thus minimizes the need for replicating the document to increase concurrent accesses.

The parallelism $P_f(n)$ supported by the Level-2 layout at a node n decides for each active connection, how many of the local storage devices are accessed in parallel to retrieve the data assigned by Level-1 layouts. For example, in case of a RAID-3, all disks participate in transfer of every data access, whereas in case of a RAID-5 only a subset of all the disks may be accessed. Clearly, a Level-2 layout should support high parallelism, even distribution of load, and high disk utilization, and thus, in turn support good statistical multiplexing of large number of retrievals of VBR streams.

10.5 Admission Control

A multimedia server may be required to service multiple subscriber requests simultaneously. In the best scenario, all the subscribers request the retrieval of the same media stream and the multimedia server only needs to retrieve the media stream once from the disk and then multicast it to all the subscribers. However, more often than not, different subscribers may request retrieval of different media streams; even when the same media stream is being requested by multiple subscribers, there may be phase differences among their requests (such as each subscriber retrieving a different portion of the stream at the same time). A simple scheme for guaranteeing real-time retrieval of each of the requests is to dedicate a disk head per request. However, this limits the total number of requests that can be serviced simultaneously to the number of disk heads, which may be orders of magnitude smaller than the number of subscribers needed to make the multimedia on-demand server economically viable.

Admission Control for Disk-System Based Storage Servers

In this section, we develop algorithms for maximizing the number of subscriber requests that can be serviced simultaneously, under the constraint that the retrieval of all of the requested media streams must proceed at their respective playback rates. In order to precisely formulate this requirement, let us suppose that a multimedia server has admitted τ subscribers, each of whom is retrieving a media stream. The multimedia server multiplexes among all the τ subscriber requests, retrieving a finite number of blocks k_i of each request $i \in [1,\tau]$, before switching to the next request. Each sequence of k_1, k_2, ..., k_τ retrievals constitutes a *service round*, and the multimedia server repeatedly executes service rounds until the completion of all the requests. Whereas the granularity and scattering parameters govern the rate of retrieval of successive media blocks of a media stream, switching from one media stream to another may entail an overhead of up to the maximum seek time to move the disk head from a block in one stream to a block of another stream (since the layout does not constrain the relative positions of different streams). Thus, the total time spent retrieving k_i blocks of ith request in a service round consists of: (1) α: the overhead of switching from the $(i\text{-}1)$th request to the ith request, and then transferring the first block of the ith request, and (2) β: the time to transfer remaining $(k_i - 1)$ blocks of the ith request in this service round. If η_{ms}^1, η_{ms}^2, ..., η_{ms}^τ denote the granularities, l_{ds}^1, l_{ds}^2, ..., l_{ds}^τ denote the scattering parameters, and R_{pl}^1, R_{pl}^2, ..., R_{pl}^τ denote the playback rates of the τ streams being retrieved simultaneously, then the continuous retrieval of each of the requests can be guaranteed if and only if the total service time per round does not exceed the minimum of the playback durations of all the requests. That is,

$$\sum_{i=1}^{\tau} \underbrace{\left(l_{seek}^{max} \frac{\eta_{ms}^i \times s_{mu}^i}{R_{dr}} \right)}_{\alpha} + \underbrace{(k_i - 1) \times \left(l_{ds}^i + \frac{\eta_{ms}^i \times s_{mu}^i}{R_{dr}} \right)}_{\beta} \leq \min_{i \in [1, \tau]} \left(k_i \times \frac{\eta_{ms}^i}{R_{pl}^i} \right)$$

$$(12)$$

The multimedia server can service all the τ requests simultaneously if and only if k_1, k_2, ..., k_τ can be determined such that above equation is satisfied. Since this formulation contains τ variables and only one equation, determination of the values of k_1, k_2, ..., k_τ requires additional policies.

The simplest policy is to assign equal values to k_1, k_2, ..., and k_τ, yielding what is generally referred to as a round robin servicing algorithm. Formally, if $k_1 = k_2 = ... = k_\tau = k$, Equation (12) yields the maximum number of subscriber requests that can be serviced in a round robin algorithm to be:

$$\tau_{max}^c = \frac{\eta_{ms}^{avg}}{R_{pl}^{max} \times \left(l_{ds}^{avg} + \dfrac{\eta_{ms}^{avg} \times s_{mu}^{avg}}{R_{dr}}\right)} \tag{13}$$

Clearly, the number of subscriber requests that can be serviced by the round robin algorithm is limited by the request with maximum playback rate. Furthermore, the request with the maximum playback rate will have retrieved exactly the number of data blocks it needs for the duration of a service round, whereas other requests whose playback rates are smaller will have retrieved more data blocks than they need in each service round. Consequently, by reducing the number of data blocks retrieved per service round for such subscriber requests, it may be possible to accommodate larger number of subscribers.

At the other extreme is an *exhaustive* algorithm, which initially assigns the minimum value to each k_i, i.e., $k_1 = k_2 = ... = k_\tau = 1$, and then selectively increments the values of each k_i until the continuous retrieval equation (Equation (12)) is satisfied. The values of k_1, k_2, ..., k_τ thus obtained can be shown to be minimal, thereby guaranteeing that minimal time is spent on each subscriber and maximum number of subscribers are serviced during a service round. However, the computational overhead of such an algorithm can be prohibitive.

Clearly, a Quality Proportional Multi-subscriber Servicing (QPMS) algorithm, in which the number of blocks retrieved during each service round for each subscriber request is proportional to its playback rate would be a better choice. Thus, if k is the proportionality constant, we get, $k_1 = k \times R_{pl}^1$, $k_2 = k \times R_{pl}^2$, ..., $k_\tau = k \times R_{pl}^\tau$. Substituting the values of k_i in Equation (12) yields:

$$\sum_{i=1}^{\tau} \left(\left(l_{seek}^{max} + \frac{\eta_{ms}^i \times s_{mu}^i}{R_{dr}} \right) + (k \times R_{pl}^i - 1) \times \left(l_{ds}^i + \frac{\eta_{ms}^i \times s_{mu}^i}{R_{dr}} \right) \right) \leq k \times \min_{i \in [1, \tau]}(\eta_{ms}^i)$$

$$\tag{14}$$

Furthermore, we can derive the maximum number of requests r^p_{max} that can be serviced simultaneously from Equation (14), and is given by:

$$\tau^p_{max} \leq \left\lfloor \frac{\eta^{avg}_{ms}}{R^{avg}_{pl} \times \left(l^{avg}_{ds} + \frac{\eta^{avg}_{ms} \times s^{avg}_{mu}}{R_{dr}} \right)} \right\rfloor \tag{15}$$

Given the number of subscriber requests $r \leq r^p_{max}$, Equation (4) can also be used to determine k, from which we can obtain the values of k_1, k_2, ..., k_τ. However, the values of k_i so obtained may not be integral. Since playback of media streams proceed in terms of quanta such as video frames, if each block is assumed to contain a quantum, then retrieval of a fraction of a block cannot be used for playback, causing the playback to starve until the remaining fraction arrives, possibly in the next service round. To avert such situations, the number of blocks retrieved in each service round must be integral for all the requests, to accomplish which we have proposed a staggered toggling technique in [18]. In this technique, the number of blocks retrieved for each subscriber request i during each round toggles between $\lfloor k_i \rfloor$ and $\lceil k_i \rceil$, so that on an average, the retrieval rate is k_i blocks per service round. Furthermore, the toggling for various subscriber requests is staggered: the toggling up for one subscriber is matched by the toggling down for another subscriber, so that, over all, there is no net increase in the service time of any round and hence, no violation of continuity requirements. The subscribers for whom the number of blocks toggles up are exactly those who may face an impending starvation owing to an earlier toggling down in a preceding service round. This technique is shown to be provably correct, i.e., it satisfies the continuity requirements of each media stream in each service round [18].

It can be seen from Equation (15) that the QPMS algorithm can admit a much larger number of subscriber requests compared to the round robin algorithm, if there is a large variation in the playback rates of media streams requested by subscribers. In fact, it can be shown that the QPMS algorithm is provably optimal, that is, given any set of τ subscriber requests a priori, if there is a set of k'_1, k'_2, ..., k'_τ satisfying the continuous retrieval equation (Equation (12)), then the QPMS algorithm is guaranteed to yield non-negative integers k_1, k_2, ..., k_τ that also satisfy Equation (12).

If the total number of subscriber requests that need to be admitted are not known a priori, but may change dynamically, then continuity should not only be maintained during steady state, but also during transitions accompanying dynamic admission of new subscribers. To see why, suppose that a multimedia server receives a new request while servicing a set of r requests. If $\tau + 1 \leq \tau^p_{max}$, then the multimedia server can compute the new value of k, namely k^{new}, necessary for satisfying $(\tau+1)$ requests. If $k^{new} = k^{old}$ (where, k^{old} is the value of k using which the multimedia server has been servicing the existing τ requests), then the multimedia server can immediately admit the $(\tau+1)^{\text{th}}$ subscriber request. However, if $k^{new} \neq k^{old}$, then $k^{new} > k^{old}$, and the multimedia server computes the new values of k_i, namely $k_i^{new} = k^{new} \times R_{pl}^i$, for all $i \in [1,\tau+1]$, and begins transferring k_i^{new} blocks for each $i \in [1, \tau+1]$. However, during the first service round after admitting the $(\tau+1)^{th}$ subscriber, the number of blocks available to the ith subscriber for playback are those of the previous service round, namely k_i^{old}, the time for which may fall short of the time spent to transfer k_i^{new} blocks for each $i \in [1, \tau+1]$, leading to a violation of continuity requirement during this transitional service round. In order to avoid such a transitional discontinuity, the QPMS algorithm can be modified such that the time to transfer (k_i+1) blocks (i.e., $k \times R_{pl}^i$ instead of $k \times R_{pl}^i - 1$) is used in the left hand side of Equation (4), but the time to playback k_i blocks is used on its right hand side (i.e., no change in the right hand side). In such a case, it can be shown that $\forall \ \tau < \tau_{max}^p$, the difference between right hand side and the left hand side of Equation (4) increases with increase in k, as a consequence of which a smooth transition from k^{old} to k^{new} can be guaranteed in steps of 1, yielding a QPMS admission control algorithm that supports both transient and steady state continuity of media playback for subscribers.

Admission Control in Large-Scale Storage Servers

The large scale storage servers that consist of multiple cooperating storage nodes providing data for a multimedia document need to employ hierarchical admission control. Each storage node in such an architecture has finite resources in the form of buffer of capacity B and the storage bandwidth R_N. A fraction of these resources must be reserved for each active periodic real-time connection to provide guaranteed accesses. Such resource reservation requires an admission control procedure that must be consulted before any new reservations are made. Since, compressed data is typically VBR in nature, providing deterministic guarantees requires the wasteful approach of peak BW reservation. Also, multimedia data is tolerant of occasional errors and missed deadlines. Given this, statistical or probabilistic guarantees, an approach in which guarantees can be occasionally violated, if the "bursts" for different connections collide, is more useful. For this approach to work successfully, multiple VBR streams must be statistically multiplexed together. In a cycle-based scheduling scheme such as one described above, the lack of sufficient BW due to burst collisions translates to total retrieval time exceeding the cycle length required to meet the periodic requirements of all clients. We characterize such multiplexing overloads in two steps: the buffer overflow and the cycle overflow. Some of this characterization is similar to the one in [6], [7].

Due to the VBR nature of streams, the amount of data fetched at each node for each connection varies from cycle to cycle, or stated formally, it is a random variable (RV) D_i, $i \in [1 \ldots C_a]$, whose distribution depends on the statistical properties of the MPEG compressed document being accessed. If such distribution is known for each RV D_i, the probability that the sum of D_i's exceeds the total buffer capacity B can be computed. If the tolerable buffer overflow probability is $P_{buffover}$, and if the Equation (16) is true for $n = C_a$, then upon admitting $(C_a+1)^{th}$ client, it should still be valid.

$$Pr\left[\sum_{i=1}^{n} D_i \geq B\right] \leq P_{buffover} \tag{16}$$

Similarly, the probability of cycle overflow can be estimated using the knowledge of node level layout and node throughput characteristics, such as disk transfer rate, minimum/maximum disk seek and rotation times. The various node level prefetch schemes and transmit options will have different cycle overflow performance. Specifically, if for a given setup, $T_r(D_i)$ represents time to fetch data of size D_i, and if Equation (17) is true for $n=C_a$, then upon admitting $(C_a + 1)^{th}$ client, Equation (17) should still hold true.

$$Pr\left[\sum_{i=1}^{n} T_r(D_i) \geq T_{cycle}\right] \leq P_{cycleover} \tag{17}$$

Note that Equation (16) and Equation (17) need to be satisfied at each node in our architecture. Thus, the admission control policy uses a computation procedure at each node which, given a pair of values $[P_{buffover}, P_{cycleover}]$, verifies if the aforementioned two equations are satisfied in the event of admission of a new request. This formulation is versatile: for example, an aggressive admission control can be realized by using higher buffer and cycle overload probabilities. Alternatively, a conservative admission control policy can be realized using smaller overload probabilities. We can also construct a service with multiple levels of QoS. Specifically, we can consider different values for 2-tuples $[P_{buffover}, P_{cycleover}]$ to represent different classes of clients. We order such classes in increasing order of overflow probabilities. Thus, a client belonging to class C_1 can tolerate smaller overflow probabilities than the client belonging to the class C_5. In other words, $P_{buffover,1} < P_{buffover,5}$ and $P_{cycleover,1} < P_{cycleover,5}$. In the event of overloads, the service is discontinued for clients from higher classes. Thus, the server can overbook its resources and on an average admit larger number of customers.

In the above formulation of performance of statistical multiplexing, Equation (16) depends on the chunk size used by the layout over the nodes, whereas Equation (17) depends on how the chunks are stored at each node, that is on the node level data layout. The node level data layout depends on the local storage devices at the node. If the storage node has a disk array, it can be of two types: one, an ordinary disk array in which all disks are used to store the data and the second, called Redundant Array of Inexpensive Disks (RAID) [28], in which some of the disks are used to store redundant information to improve reliability and data availability in the event of disk failures. When using commercial RAID devices, the node level striping scheme is fixed to the one enforced by the RAID device. Given this, the chunk size happens to be the only design parameter that affects the efficiency of statistical multiplexing. The larger the chunk size, the smaller is the variability of the chunk size and offered load. Also, large chunk sizes amortize seek and rotational latency overhead at the disks in a disk array over large data transfers and thus, improve disk utilization. On the other hand, for good subjective quality of ff by chunk skipping, a small chunk size is desirable. In the presence of a large number of concurrent clients, small chunk size minimizes per connection buffer requirements. Also, a smaller chunk size allows quick response time for interactive playout control operations.

10.6 Multimedia Information Caching—Technique for Realizing TVOD

On-demand movie viewership patterns are highly dependent on the time of the day. Drawing a parallel to the telephone network, there are peak hours during which the traffic is maximum and the majority of the titles demanded is a small subset of the most recent set of hit movies. As a result, there is significant confusion as to whether True Video-on-Demand is more lucrative than Near Video-on-Demand. Caution has been expressed about the success of True Video-on-Demand because it is felt that cable and telephone companies pushing Video-on-Demand are investing heavily to create massive storage providers to deliver thousands of programs when all that consumers want are the eight or ten hit movies every month.

Information Caching has the potential not only to smoothen out the peak, but also to amortize storage costs and maximize network utilization. In the system configuration proposed at the UCSD Multimedia Laboratory, a synergy between several enterprises occurs: *Storage Providers* that manage information storage at multimedia servers (a role akin to that of video rental stores and libraries in today's context), *Network Providers*, that are responsible for media transport over integrated networks (a role akin to that of cable and telephone and cable companies of today), and *Content Providers* such as entertainment houses, new producers etc., that offer a multitude of services to subscriber homes using multimedia servers and broadband networks. In the proposed

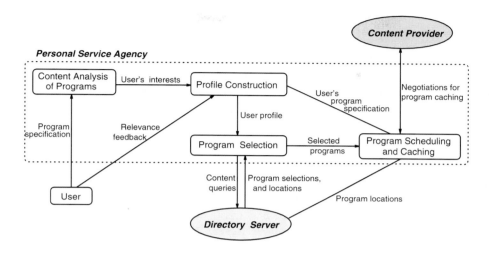

Figure 10–22   Functions of a Personal Service Agent (PSA).

architecture, multimedia servers of suitable capacities are installed at the different hierarchical levels and function as temporary caches for information delivered from metropolitan repositories. The locations of switching equipment in the network are obvious choices for locating the multimedia servers. For managing distribution of the selected multimedia programs to each subscriber's home, we propose *Distribution Agents* that negotiate the storage and retrieval times of programs with storage and network providers, and program authorizations with the content providers. The distribution agents judiciously determine locations of programs and their distribution times depending upon the anticipated demand for the future, the costs of storage and the utilization of bandwidth.

To facilitate the process of program selection, we propose *Personal Service Agents* (PSAs) that search and locate programs that match each subscriber's needs, and customize the content providers' offerings to deliver personalized services. The main functions of a PSA are: (i) It monitors each subscriber and constructs a behavioral profile for the subscriber. (ii) Based on this profile, the PSA queries the network directory service to identify content providers offering relevant programs. (iii) Then, the PSA contacts each of the content providers, navigates through their content bases, and constructs a list of programs relevant to the subscriber. (iv) Once the subscriber makes a selection of programs to view, the PSA continuously interacts with the content bases and chooses portions of programs and even their levels of detail to display to the subscriber. (v) The PSA also solicits explicit *relevance feedback* from the subscriber for its selections, so as to tailor its selections in the future to better suit the subscriber's needs [30].

Program Retrieval and Caching

The different programs requested by a user on a personal channel could be offered by different content providers. The PSA can judiciously schedule retrieval (from storage providers) and subsequent transmission (via network providers) of the programs so as to minimize costs borne by the user. For instance, a PSA can retrieve programs a priori and cache them either at the user's site or at a neighborhood server, during a period when the network and server are relatively underutilized. In practice, however, the storage capacities necessary for caching all the programs that a user views daily on a personal channel are prohibitively large: For instance, assuming that a user views up to five, one-hour long video programs daily, and that the videos are MPEG-2 encoded (requiring storage of 4 megabits/second for each program), storage of 18 gigabytes is necessary. Even assuming that in future, storage prices drop down to a half of the current list price of 25 cents per megabyte, the investment necessary for providing 18 gigabytes of storage at a user's site is $2,250, which is about seven times the price of a high-quality VCR. Therefore, based on the above computations, we infer that caching all of the programs on a personal channel well in advance of their viewing times at a user's site itself is not likely to be economically viable.

Resource optimizations are most likely when several users indicate similar preferences for programs (e.g., popular movies). In the best case, all the users may choose to view the same programs, at the same times. For such users, PSAs can arrange with the content providers to simulcast programs of the users' common choice, thereby amortizing network transmission costs amongst all those users. More often than not, however, users' preferred viewing times do not match. In such cases, multiple independent transmissions of the requested program may have to be incurred, all the way from a storage server located at one end of a network to users' sites located at another end. As an example, consider the metropolitan-area network shown in Fig. 10–23(a). Suppose that a program P, created by a content provider at 1PM and stored at server S_1, is requested by users U_1, U_2, and U_3 for viewing at 1PM, 2PM, and 11PM, respectively. Further, suppose that (i) the storage cost for program P at the server increases with duration of storage (the rate of increase depending upon program P's storage space requirement), (ii) the cost of each transmission of P over the network links is fixed (depending upon the bandwidth required for transmission of program P), and (iii) the delay between the transmission of program P from the servers and its reception at the users' sites is negligible compared to the total duration of program P. For servicing users U_1, U_2, and U_3, program P must be transmitted thrice over the network, at 1PM, 2PM, and 11PM, respectively, incurring a cost of $18 each time.

With a view to reducing service costs, we propose that metropolitan-area networks be configured with multimedia servers of suitable capacities installed at various strategic locations, such as basements of residential complexes, recreational areas in townships, and libraries of universities. The neighborhood

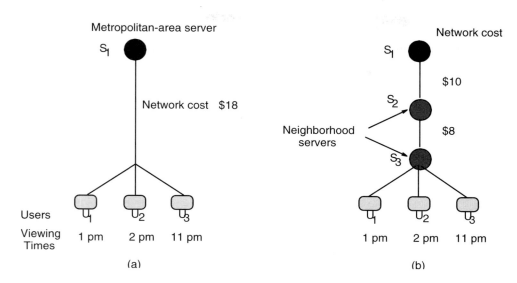

Figure 10–23   (a) A metropolitan-area network with a central server S_1, which transmits program $\mathcal{P}$ to users U_1, U_2, and U_3; in this case, since users' viewing times do not match, three independent transmissions of program $\mathcal{P}$ are necessary. (b) A more efficient network configuration, with intermediate servers S_2 and S_3 functioning as neighborhood caches. In this case, program $\mathcal{P}$ can be cached at server S_3 while it is transmitted down the network, to service user U_1, thereby reducing the overall transmission cost by 66%.

servers can function as *temporary caches* for frequently accessed video programs, thereby avoiding the cost of repeated transmissions of the same programs all the way from a remote metropolitan server. In order to facilitate information caching, we propose that the storage servers should be co-located with the network switches to constitute "multimedia hubs" that support both storage and transmission of programs. In such a configuration, it is possible for neighborhood servers to cache the video programs *as and when they are transmitted* via their respective switches (possibly for servicing users in other neighborhoods), thereby avoiding even the cost of program transmissions to the neighborhood servers explicitly for the purpose of caching.

Fig. 10–23(b) illustrates a possible configuration for the metropolitan-area network of Fig. 10–23(a). Intermediate servers S_2 and S_3 function as neighborhood stores for programs requested by the users U_1, U_2, and U_3. By caching programs at servers S_2 and S_3, PSAs can avoid the costs of retransmissions from the distant metropolitan-area server S_1. For instance, caching program P at server S_3 when the program is transmitted to user U_1 reduces the overall transmission cost by $36.

In practice, there are interesting trade-offs between the cost of renting storage space at neighborhood servers and the cost of repeated transmissions from a metropolitan server, which must be evaluated by PSAs and content providers before deciding to cache programs. In the following section, we elaborate on these trade-offs and devise simple, yet effective strategies for information caching in metropolitan area networks.

Information Caching

At the time of caching, PSAs, or the content providers must evaluate the various storage and network alternatives. The storage costs may differ from server to server, depending upon the capacities of the servers, their data transfer rates, and current demands. Likewise, transmission costs of programs may also differ from one network link to another, depending upon the available link bandwidth, and the desired real-time performance: end-to-end delay, delay jitter, and reliability of transmission.

In order to illustrate the storage-network trade-offs, as before, consider the simple, tandem configuration of storage servers shown in Fig. 10–24(a). Suppose that users U_1, U_2, and U_3, all belonging to the same neighborhood (and hence, connected to the same neighborhood server S_3) request for a program P that is created and stored at the metropolitan server, by a content provider at 1PM (see Fig. 10–24(a)). Clearly, no optimizations are possible for servicing the first user U_1 at 1PM: the program must be transmitted all the way from server S_1 to user U_1. However, during this transmission, any of the servers S_2 and S_3 can cache the program for future usage. Whereas caching at S_3 only entails a storage cost, caching at S_2 entails an additional network cost, but a lower storage cost. Considering such trade-offs, for the period [1PM, 11PM], it is cheaper to cache program $\mathcal{P}$ at server S_2, entailing a total cost of $54, as compared to a cost of $68 if the program $\mathcal{P}$ were cached at server S_3. The *Caching Schedule* thus derived (see Fig. 10–24(b)), although it amortizes storage costs between U_2 and U_3, does not constitute the overall optimum. For instance, a schedule that besides caching program P at server S_2 for the period [1PM, 11PM], also caches program $\mathcal{P}$ at server S_3 for the period [1PM, 2PM] (see Fig. 10–24(c)) entails a lower overall service cost, amounting to $51.

In general, the storage-network optimization is carried out at the time of scheduling programs on users' personal channels. PSAs, together with the content providers, must determine *when, where*, and for *how long* programs must be cached, so as to minimize the costs borne by users. [27], [26] outline an efficient dynamic programming technique that can be used by a PSA to derive an optimal caching schedule for a program $\mathcal{P}$ that is requested for viewing by several users located in the same neighborhood of a metropolis.

Surprisingly, even in the worst-case, this heuristic performs *no worse than twice the optimal*; this is analytically provable [26]. Preliminary performance

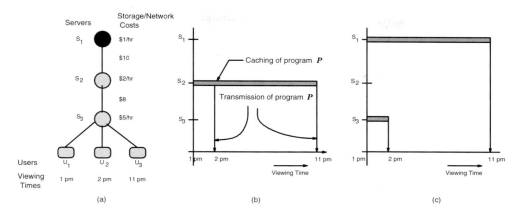

Figure 10-24 Illustration of storage-network trade-offs.
(a) depicts the network configuration: S1 is the metropolitan-area server, S2 and S3 are the neighborhood caches. Program $\mathcal{P}$, created and stored at S1 at 1PM is requested by users U1, U2, and U3 for viewing at 1PM, 2PM, and 11PM, respectively. The storage and transmission costs for $\mathcal{P}$ are indicated in the figure.
(b) illustrates a caching schedule that amortizes program storage between users U2 and U3. The total cost of this schedule is $54;
(c) represents the overall optimal schedule, the total cost of which is $51.

simulations indicate that in practice, this caching strategy performs even better. Several thousand configurations of storage servers, together with several combinations of users' viewing schedules were generated and the performance of the heuristic caching strategy was compared with that of the optimal. These simulations reveal that the heuristic caching strategy performs within 1 percent of the optimum on an average, with the worst-case deviation being at most 10 percent.

Discussion

There are some realistic generalizations of the above caching problem. Until now, we have assumed that entire programs are cached between storage servers. In many a case, users' interests pertain only to selected portions of programs offered by content providers. Moreover, the storage-network trade-offs may differ for the different media components of a program. For example, due to the larger bandwidth and storage requirements of the video component, it may be profitable to cache the video component at a neighborhood server. The audio component, on the other hand, requires much smaller bandwidth and storage space, and hence, repeated transmissions of the audio component of programs from a metropolitan server may be preferred.

At the time of caching, PSAs must not only consider heterogeneity in storage costs and transmission costs, but they must also adapt to any changes that may occur in these costs. For instance, as in today's telephone networks, there may be "peak hours" (e.g., 8AM to 8PM) when the networks are in greater demand (this holds for storage servers too), and hence, more expensive to use. Cost changes may occur even on-the-fly; for example, a storage provider, upon anticipating an overcommitment of server resources, may increase the storage cost so as to discourage further demand. The caching strategies we propose adapt easily to dynamic changes in storage and network costs. Consequently, these cost change times must be incorporated into the dynamic programming technique described in [27], [26]. The complexity of determining caching schedules is now a function of both the number of distinct viewing times of users and the number of cost-change times (and of course, the number of servers).

10.7   Concluding Remarks

In this chapter, we have explored and expanded on each of the aspects of video servers and have given performance evaluations of various architectures ranging from those that are in the market to those that are in prototype form in research labs. We envision that personalized multimedia on demand services will trigger a radical change in the role of many enterprises of today: For instance, video rentals will be reduced to the role of storage providers; cable companies and telephone carriers will be reduced to the role of network providers. Libraries too are expected to take on a different role: Rather than being a central storehouse for information, libraries will function more as rapid access mechanisms to geographically distributed multimedia databases.

The practical realization of personalized multimedia services poses a number of interesting and challenging problems in the areas of multimedia content-extraction, database organization, information retrieval, and caching. Research in these areas is, relatively speaking, in the preliminary stage.

Work is in progress to develop information analysis and feature-extraction methods for content-based multimedia retrieval, that will form the basis of personalized service agents. Efforts are also underway to integrate these content-based retrieval techniques with adaptive, connectionist approaches that have been developed for retrieval of text information from a corpus in which various documents have little structure in common. In conjunction with researchers in library science, visual arts, music, medicine, and psychophysics, researchers are investigating expanded applications of personalized multimedia services in a broad range of areas.

In short, rapid advances in the practical realization of multimedia on demand heralds the arrival of an unprecedented information epoch.

References

[1] Buddhikot, M., Parulkar, G., and Cox, J.R. Jr., "Design of a large scale multimedia storage server," in *Proceedings of the INET'94/JENC5*, Conference of the Internet Society and the Joint European Networking Conference, Prague, June 1994.

[2] Buddhikot, M., Parulkar, G., and Cox, J.R., Jr., "Design of a large scale multimedia storage server," *Journal of Computer Networks and ISDN Systems*, Dec 1994, pp. 504–517.

[3] Buddhikot, M., Parulkar, G.M., and Cox, J.R., Jr., "Distributed layout, scheduling, and playout control in a multimedia storage server," in *Proceedings of the Sixth International Workshop on Packet Video*, Portland, Oregon, Sep 26–27, 1994, pp. C1.1–C1.4.

[4] Buddhikot, M., and Parulkar, G.M., "Distributed scheduling, data layout and playout control in a large scale multimedia storage server," Technical Report WUCS94-33, Department of Computer Science, Washington University in St. Louis, Sep 1994.

[5] Cable Labs Inc. "Request for Information (RFI) on Digital Media Servers," June 1994.

[6] Chang, Ed, and Zakhor, A., "Admissions control and data placement for VBR video servers," in *Proceedings of the First International Conference on Image Processing*, Nov 1994.

[7] Chang, Ed, and Zakhor, A., "Variable bit rate MPEG video storage on parallel disk arrays," presented at First International Workshop on Community Networking, San Francisco, July 1994.

[8] Chen, P., *et al.*, "RAID: High-performance, reliable secondary storage," submitted to ACM Computing Surveys.

[9] Chen, M., Kandlur, D., and Yu, S.P., "Support for fully interactive playout in a disk-array-based video server," in *Proceedings of Second International Conference on Multimedia, ACM Multimedia '94*, 1994.

[10] Chervenak, A, "Tertiary storage: An evaluation of new applications," PhD dissertation, Department of Computer Science, University of California, Berkeley, 1995.

[11] Cranor, C. and Parulkar, G., "Universal continuous media I/O: Design and implementation," Washington University Department of Computer Science, Technical Report 94-34, Dec 1994.

[12] Cranor, C. and Parulkar, G., "Design of universal continuous media I/O," in *Proceedings of the 5th International Workshop on Network and Operating Systems Support for Digital Audio and Video (NOSSDAV '95)*, pp 83–86, Apr 1995.

[13] Dittia, Z., Cox., J., and Parulkar, G., "Catching up with the networks: Host I/O at gigabit rates," Technical Report WUCS-94-11, Department of Computer Science, Washington University in St. Louis, Apr 1994.

[14] Dittia, Z., Parulkar, G., and Cox, J., "The APIC approach to high performance network interface design: Protected DMA and other techniques," Technical Report WUCS-96-12, Department of Computer Science, Washington University in St. Louis, Feb 1996.

[15] Gopalakrishnan, R. and Parulkar, G.M., "A framework for QoS guarantees for multimedia applications within an end-system," presented at Swiss German Computer Science Society Conf., 1995.

[16] Gopalakrishnan, R. and Parulkar, G.M., "A real-time upcall facility for protocol processing with QOS guarantees," (Poster) *ACM Symposium on Operating Systems Principles (SOSP)*, Copper Mountain, Colorado, Dec 1995.

[17] Gopalakrishnan, R.,and Parulkar, G.M., "Real time upcalls," Tech. Rep. WUCS-95-06, Washington Univ., Mar 95.

[18] Guttag, K., Gove, R., and Aken, V., "A single-chip multiprocessor for multimedia: The MVP," *IEEE Computer Graphics and Applications*, Nov 1992, pp. 53–64.

[19] Hsieh, J. *et al.*, "Performance of a mass storage system for video-on-demand," in *Proceedings of IEEE INFOCOM'95*, pp. 771–778, Apr 1995.

[20] Hylton, T., Coffey., K., Parker, A., and Kent, H., "AdStaR scientists detect giant magnetoresistance in small magnetic fields, using easy to make sensor," *SCIENCE*, Aug 1993.

[21] Jessel, A.H., "Cable ready: The high appeal for interactive services," *Broadcasting & Cable*, May 23, 1994.

[22] Keeton, K. and Katz, R., "The evaluation of video layout strategies on a high bandwidth file server," in *Proceedings of International Workshop on Network and Operating Support for Digital Audio and Video (NOSSDAV'93)*, Lancaster, U.K., Nov 1993.

[23] Little, T.D., *et al.*, "A digital on-demand video service supporting content-based queries," in *Proceedings of ACM Multimedia'93*, Anaheim, CA, Aug 1993, pp. 427–436.

[24] Nussbaumer, J., Patel, B., Schaffa, F., and Sterbenz, J.P.G., "Networking requirements for interactive video on demand," *IEEE Transactions of Selected Areas in Communication*, Jan 95.

[25] Papadimitriou, C. and Steiglitz, K., *Combinatorial Optimization: Algorithms and Complexity*, Englewood Cliffs, NJ: Prentice Hall, 1982.

[26] Papadimitriou, C.H., Ramanathan., S., and Rangan, P.V., "Information caching for delivery of personalized video programs on home entertainments channels," in *Proceedings of IEEE International Conference on Multimedia Computing and Systems*, Boston, May 1994.

[27] Papadimitriou, C. and Rangan, V., U.S. Patent Pending.

[28] Patteson, D. *et al.*, "A case for redundant arrays of inexpensive disks (RAID)," in *Proceedings of the 1988 ACM Conference on Management of Data (SIGMOD)*, Chicago IL, pp. 109–116, June 1988.

[29] Pugh, W. and Boyer, G., "Broadband access: Comparing alternatives," *IEEE Communications Magazine*, Aug 1995, pp. 34–46.

[30] Ramanathan, S. and Rangan, V., "System architectures for personalized multimedia services," *IEEE Multimedia*, Vol. 1, No. 1, Feb 1994, pp. 37–46.

[31] Rangan, V. and Vin, H., "Designing file systems for digital video and audio," in *Proceedings of the 13th Symposium on Operating System Principles, Operating Systems Review*, Oct 1991, pp. 81–94.

[32] Rangan, V. and Vin, H., "Efficient storage techniques for digital continuous media," *IEEE Transactions on Knowledge and Data Engineering*, Aug 1993.

[33] Sarnoff Real Time Corporation, *MAGIC™ Media Server: A Scalable and Cost Effective Video Server*, Princeton, NJ 08543.

[34] Silicon Graphics Computer Systems, "Symmetric Multiprocessing Systems," Technical Report, Mountain View, California.

[35] Storage Concepts, Inc., "Storage Concepts, Concept 810-SW real-time RAID," Product Description, Irvine, CA

[36] Turner, J. "An optimal nonblocking multicast virtual circuit switch," in *Proceedings of IEEE INFOCOM94*, Vol. 1, June 1994, pp. 298–305.

[37] Turner, J., "A gigabit multicast switch: System architecture document," Applied Research Laboratory, Washington University in St. Louis, Feb 1994.

[38] U.S. Bureau of Census, *Statistical Abstract of the United States*, 113th ed., 1993.

[39] Venkatramani, C. and Chiueh, T., "Survey of near-line storage technologies: Devices and systems," Experimental Computer Systems Laboratory, Technical Report #2, Department of Computer Science, SUNY Stony Brook, NY, Oct 1993.

Multimedia Communications

Multimedia Communications— Synchronization

Shahab Baqai, M. Farrukh Khan, and Arif Ghafoor

Distributed Multimedia Systems Laboratory
School of Electrical & Computer Engineering
Purdue University
West Lafayette, Indiana 47907
ghafoor@ecn.purdue.edu

11.1   Introduction

*T*he development of multimedia applications over broadband networks have introduced new challenges for storage and communication of diverse multimedia objects like video, audio, images, etc. Typically, a multimedia document contains media objects which need to be presented to the end user according to some temporal as well as spatial constraints. Multimedia applications may require live data being generated in real time at remote locations, and/or some form of pre-orchestrated information stored at various servers interconnected over broadband networks [1]–[20]. Retrieval and

335

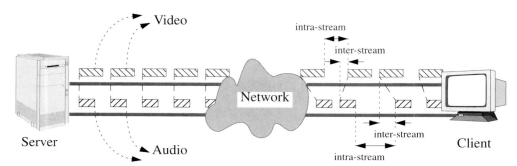

Figure 11-1   Inter-stream and intra-stream synchronization requirements.

communication of multimedia data impose strict performance and reliability requirements on the underlying communication infrastructure. For example, while transmitting video and audio data streams, network delays must be bounded to maintain inter-stream and intra-stream temporal synchronization requirements [1]. Inter-stream synchronization deals with the synchronized play-out of related streams, such as the lip-sync requirements of concurrent audio and video streams. Intra-stream synchronization is required for a smooth and continuous presentation of each stream. Fig. 11–1 illustrates the two types of synchronization.

Multimedia information generally has a highly time-varying bandwidth requirement. To achieve proper synchronization without excessive pre-fetching of multimedia data at the client site, advance reservation of network resources can be made in order to ensure that the peak throughput requirements of multimedia data are met. Various static resource reservation schemes can be employed for this. Static schemes are simple to implement, but with large variations in the bandwidth requirements, such schemes can usually result in considerable wastage of network resources. This can be avoided by using dynamic schemes where allocation of resources can be made on an on-demand basis consistent with the changing throughput requirements of the multimedia data. Although the dynamic schemes can help in efficient resource utilization, they may require complex control and management protocols for the network and thus introduce excessive connection setup latencies.

Network resources include *channel capacity* and *buffers*. Allocation of such resources can be effective if the temporal characteristics and inter-relationship of multimedia objects are available prior to their transmission [13]. By identifying the temporal inter-relationships and the desired presentation quality of the multimedia information, the overall resource requirements can be established precisely. In this chapter, we elaborate on these issues and focus our discussion on synchronization and resource management schemes in broadband networks. In particular, we focus our discussion on a set of Quality of Presentation (*QOP*) parameters to specify the desired quality of presentation of multimedia information and assume that the users provide them as part of their multimedia consumer profiles. We then discuss the role of *QOP* parameters in designing various network management schemes for resource allocation.

This chapter is organized as follows: In Section 11.2 the quality of presentation for synchronization and scheduling issues of multimedia data are introduced. Section 11.3 describes the models and data abstractions commonly used to specify the temporal relationships, along with the presentation quality, of multimedia objects. In Section 11.4 various synchronization mechanisms for multimedia information are discussed. Finally, Section 11.5 concludes the issues related to multimedia communication synchronization.

11.2   Quality Requirements of Multimedia Information

The Quality of Presentation (*QOP*) parameters constitute a set of user-specified tolerable degradations of multimedia presentations that may occur due to resource limitations. These parameters can be used to quantify the presentation process from the user's point of view and establish network resource requirements to ensure the delivery of multimedia information with the desired quality. In the following subsections we elaborate on some of the user's perceivable presentation parameters which influence the play-out quality of multimedia information from a synchronization perspective.

Skew

Strict presentation requirements demand that multimedia objects be played out with zero slippage [14]. This can be achieved through inter-stream synchronization which requires that all objects must be delivered prior to their deadlines [1]. Concurrent objects may be transmitted over independent virtual channels which may have different delay characteristics. Therefore these objects can experience different jitter delays, causing some of them to miss their temporal deadlines. Objects with missed deadlines start lagging while the data on other streams is continuously used up during presentation [15]. Such synchronization failure is defined as *deadline miss*. The acceptable delay or slippage of a media object (video clip, an image, audio segment, etc.) with respect to its deadline, depends on object type and the multimedia application. For example, the acceptable delay values for video and audio objects in various applications are shown in Table 11–1 [16]. The relative skew between two concurrent media objects can lead to inter-stream synchronization failure. We can express acceptable level of presentation degradation due to such skew in terms of the maximum percentage of deadline misses that are tolerable. In a probabilistic sense, the quality parameter can be expressed as the maximum tolerable probability, with which each presentation

Object		Mode, Application	Delay α_i
video	animation	correlated	±120 ms
	audio	lip synchronization	±80 ms
	image	overlay	±240 ms
		non-overlay	±500 ms
	text	overlay	±240 ms
		non-overlay	±500 ms
audio	animation	event correlation	±80 ms
	audio	tightly coupled (stereo)	±11 ms
		loosely coupled (dialog)	±120 ms
		loosely coupled (background)	±500 ms
	image	tightly coupled (music with notes)	±5 ms
		loosely coupled (slide show)	±500 ms
	text	text annotation	±240 ms
	pointer	related audio	−500 ms
			+750 ms

Table 11–1 Acceptable delay α_i for various applications [16].

unit of media object can miss its deadline by more than some allowable slippage. In other words, the probability of deadline miss expresses the user-acceptable level of presentation degradation in terms of *maximum tolerable percentage of deadline misses.*

Presentation Rate and Resolution

Isochronous objects such as video and audio can tolerate some information loss due to limited capacity and buffer availability without affecting their play-out degradation perceivable by the users. These tolerance levels depend on the application and the media type used in that application, and hence can be chosen as a *QOP* parameter. From a user's perspective, the rate and resolution can also describe the bound for acceptable quality of a multimedia object. In a certain time interval the overall capacity of the network may not be sufficient to accommodate all the users' throughput requirements. An option to overcome this limitation is to pre-fetch enough data for every user to compensate for the limited capacity. However, due to the limited buffer availability, this option may not be feasible. Also, in case of live multimedia data, pre-fetching may result in delaying the presentation process at the user site. Another factor which can effect reliability is early arrival of data at destination. This data which must be buffered to ensure synchronization, can lead to buffer overflow. Such loss of data cannot be

Reliability	Voice	Video	Image	Text
(ω_i)	0.98	0.90	1.0	1.0

Table 11–2   Reliability of multimedia information type.

recovered and retransmission strategies can result in synchronization failure and generally are not feasible for multimedia applications [17]. One way to operate within a limited buffering capability and restricted capacity is to deliver objects partially. The acceptable bound on data loss can be obtained from the required presentation rate and resolution of a multimedia object for a given application. Such loss of data can occur either due to destination buffer overflow or forced dropping of data as a result of channel capacity limitations. Depending on the required quality, a user can quantify the acceptable data loss for each object, in terms of some *maximum allowable percentage data loss*. For applications which require lower resolution and/or presentation rate, we can afford to drop some fraction of the object at the source. The required resolution and presentation rate of a multimedia object can be used to determine the nature and the amount to be dropped at the source in case of capacity constraints. For example if the user can tolerate a presentation rate of 20 frames per second for a video object (instead of 30 frames per second for NTSC quality video), every third frame can be dropped without degrading the required play-out quality beyond the acceptable level. This data drop can be specified by the user in the form of a ratio called *presentation rate ratio* for an object. Alternatively if the data is coded using multi-band coding schemes [18], [19], appropriate band in the network can be dropped. For isochronous objects (video and audio) it is the ratio of the required rate of presentation to the nominal one. In case of an-isochronous objects like text and images, this ratio is expressed in terms of resolution. Typical values of the presentation ratio, for various types of data objects, are given in Table 11–2 [17].

11.3   Synchronization Models

Presentation of multimedia information requires synchronous play-out of time-dependent multimedia data according to some specified temporal relations and *QOP* requirements, as discussed in Section 11.2. At the time of creation of multimedia information, a user needs to model temporal interrelationships among various media objects and the possible options for the quality requirements which must be observed at the time of playback for each object. Coordinating the real-time presentation of information and maintaining the temporal relationships among component media is known as temporal synchronization [20]. In this section we discuss the problem of temporal synchronization in detail and highlight various temporal models that have been proposed in the literature.

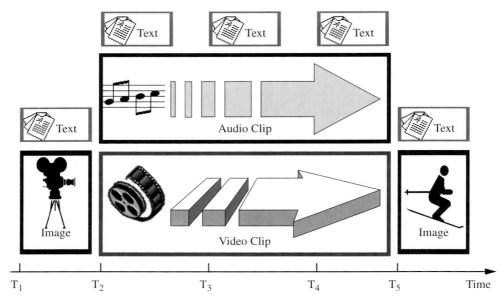

Figure 11-2   Time-ordered multimedia data.

The Temporal Synchronization Problem

The concept of temporal synchronization is illustrated in Fig. 11–2, where a sequence of text, images, audio, and video clips are presented in time to compose a multimedia document. One may notice from this figure that the system must observe some timing relationships among various data objects in order to present the information to the user in a meaningful way. These relationships can be *natural* or *synthetically created* [14]. Simultaneous recording of voice and video through a VCR is an example of a natural relationship between audio and video information. A voice-annotated slide show, on the other hand, is an example of a synthetically created relationship between audio and image information. In this case, change of an image and the end of its verbal annotation represent a synchronization point in time.

A user may access various objects randomly, while browsing through a multimedia information system. In addition to simple forward play-out of time-dependent data sequences, other modes of data presentation are also viable, and should be supported by a multimedia information management system. These include user interactions like reverse play-out, fast-forward/fast-backward play-out, and random access of arbitrarily chosen segments of the presentation. These operations are quite common in TV technology, (e.g., VCRs), but their implementation in distributed multimedia systems is a challenging task. The reasons include the non-sequential storage of multimedia objects, the diversity in the

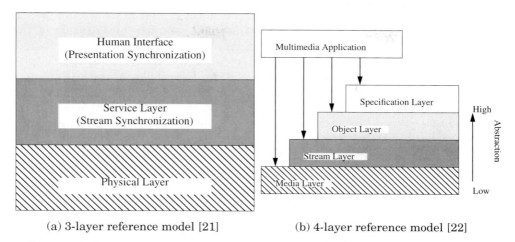

(a) 3-layer reference model [21]   (b) 4-layer reference model [22]

Figure 11-3   Levels of synchronization of multimedia data.

features of hardware used for data compression, and random communication delays introduced by the network. Such factors make the provision of these capabilities infeasible with the current technologies.

Synchronization of multimedia information may be classified into three categories, depending upon the "granularity of information," requiring synchronization. These are the physical level, the service level, and the human interface level [21], as shown in Fig. 11–3(a). At the physical level, data from different media are multiplexed over a single physical connection or is arranged in physical storage. This form of synchronization can be viewed as "fine-grain." The service level synchronization is "more coarse grain," since it is concerned with the interactions between the multimedia application and the various elements/media of the application. This level deals primarily with inter-media synchronization necessary for presentation or play-out. The human interface level synchronization is rather "coarse grain" since it is used to specify the random user interaction to a multimedia information system such as viewing a succession of multimedia objects.

Another synchronization reference model classifies multimedia synchronization into four layers [22] as shown in Fig. 11–3(b). Each layer can be accessed directly by the application or indirectly through higher layers. The media and stream layer are similar to the physical and service layer of the model of Fig. 11–3(a), as they deal with intra-stream and inter-stream synchronization of multimedia objects. The object layer operates on all types of media (continuous and discrete). This layer ensures the correct scheduling of the overall presentation. The specification layer provides the synchronization requirements and could incorporate the *QOP* parameters related to the objects being scheduled.

In addition to time-dependent relational classification (i.e., synthetic/natural), data objects can also be classified in terms of their presentation and application lifetimes. A persistent object is one that can exist for the duration of the application. A non-persistent object is created dynamically and discarded when obsolete. For presentation, a transient object is defined as an object that is presented for a short duration without manipulation. The display of a series of audio or video frames represents transient presentation of objects, whether captured live or retrieved from a database. The terms static and transient are used to describe presentation lifetimes of objects, while persistence expresses their storage life.

In another classification, multimedia data have been characterized as either continuous or discrete [23]. This distinction, however, is vague since time ordering can be assigned to discrete media, and continuous media are time-ordered sequences of discrete ones after digitization. According to the definition in [23], continuous media can be represented as sequences of discrete data elements that are played out contiguously in time. However, the term continuous is most often used to describe the fine-grain synchronization required for audio or video.

Modeling Time

The problem of multimedia synchronizing at presentation, user interaction, and physical layers reduces to the satisfaction of temporal precedence relationships among various data objects under real-time constraints. Models to represent time are needed for this purpose. Temporal intervals and instants provide a means for indicating exact temporal specification. In this section, we discuss these models and then describe various conceptual data models to specify temporal information necessary to represent multimedia synchronization.

To be applicable to multimedia synchronization, time models must allow synchronization of components having precedence and real-time constraints, and provide representations of relaxation in meeting deadlines. The primary requirements for such a specification methodology include the representation of real-time semantics, concurrency, and a hierarchical modeling ability. The nature of presentation of multimedia data also implies that a multimedia system has various additional capabilities, like handling reverse presentation, allowing random access (at an arbitrary start point), permitting an incomplete specification of inter-media timing, handling sharing of synchronized components among applications, and to provide data storage for control information. In light of these additional requirements, it is, therefore, imperative that a specification methodology must be well suited for unusual temporal semantics. An instant-based temporal reference scheme has been extensively applied in the motion picture industry, as standardized by the Society of Motion Picture and Television Engineers (SMPTE). This scheme associates a virtually unique sequential code to each frame in a motion picture. By assigning these codes to both an audio track and a motion picture track, inter-media synchronization between streams is achieved. This absolute, instant-based scheme presents two difficulties when applied to a multimedia applications. Since unique absolute time references are assumed, when segments are edited or produced in duplicate, the relative timing between the edited segments becomes lost in terms of play-out. Furthermore, if one medium while synchronized to another becomes decoupled, then the timing information of the dependent medium becomes lost. This instant-based scheme has been applied using Musical Instrument Digital Interface (MIDI) time instant specification [24]. The scheme has also been used to couple each time code to a common time reference [25].

In another approach, temporal intervals are used to specify relative timing constraints between two processes. This model is able to represent simple parallel and sequential relationships. In this approach, synchronization can be accomplished by explicitly capturing each of the thirteen possible temporal relations [14] that can occur between the processes. Additional operations can be incorporated in this approach to facilitate incomplete timing specification [23].

The above approaches can be used to develop conceptual models for multimedia objects. We discuss the pros and cons of these models and compare them in terms of their effectiveness to represent objects and user's data manipulation functions.

Temporal Models

A number of attempts have been made to develop conceptual models for representing multimedia presentations and documents. These models may be classified into three categories: language-based models, Petri-net-based models, and temporal abstraction models. Some models are primarily aimed at synchronization aspects of the multimedia data while others are more concerned with the browsing aspects of the objects. The former models can easily render themselves to an ultimate specification of a multimedia database schema [26]. Some models, especially those based on graphs and Petri-Nets have the additional advantage of pictorially illustrating synchronization semantics, and are suitable for visual orchestration of multimedia presentations.

Language-Based Models

Concurrent languages have been extensively used to specify parallel and distributed process structures. These languages have the power to specify multimedia synchronization requirements. One such scheme which is an extension to the language called *Communicating Sequential Processing* (CSP) was proposed [20]. This extension supports multimedia process synchronization, including semantics for real-time synchronization of multimedia data. The extension is based on a proposed concept, called *restricted blocking* which provides a resolution mechanism for the synchronization problem encountered while handling continuous media. In the restricted blocking mode, an object may be forced to wait for an other object, to perform synchronization if the later does not arrive in time. For this purpose, the extension to CSP includes various constructs such as SYNCHRONIZE_WITH *object-name*, AT *end*, MODE *type-of-blocking*, or WHILE_WAITING *do-something*. In this command, an object is forced to wait for the other object to arrive for synchronization. For this purpose, the parameter for the MODE (type-of-blocking) primitive can be set as *restricted_blocking*. The waiting object can be replayed or slowed down during the wait state. These constructs are initiated by the system. Also, various time operands can be specified in this command to adjust the relative display time of two objects.

Various other language-based approaches have also been proposed. Two such examples include the specification using LOTOS (Language Of Temporal Ordering Specification) [27] and process-oriented synchronization in CCWS [28]. The major advantage of language-based models is that they can directly lead to an implementation. However, their drawback is that, unlike graphical models, they are hard to conceptually visualize and are difficult to verify.

Petri-Net Models

Several researchers have proposed the use of Petri-nets to develop conceptual models for synchronization of multimedia objects [29], [14], [30]. The basic idea in these models is to represent various components of multimedia objects as places and describe their inter-relations in the form of transitions. These models have been shown to be quite effective for specifying multimedia synchronization requirements. For example, one such model is used to specify high level (object level) synchronization requirements which is both a graphical and mathematical modeling tool capable of representing concurrency. In this approach Timed Petri Net has been extended to develop a model that is known as Object Composition Petri Nets (OCPNs) [14]. The particularly interesting features of this model are the ability to explicitly capture all the necessary temporal relations, and to provide simulation of presentation in both the forward and reverse directions. Each place in this Petri-Net derivative represents the play-out of a multimedia object while transitions represent synchronization points.

Thirteen temporal relationships between two objects are presented in [14]. These are sufficient to specify temporal composition of any complex multimedia object. An OCPN model can represent all these relations. It has been shown in the paper that an arbitrarily complex process model of temporal relations can be constructed with an OCPN. Fig. 11–4 shows an example of an OCPN that describes a slide show. As can be noticed, in this model the duration of each object is also specified. The OCPN model specifies exact presentation time play-out semantics, useful in real-time scheduling.

OCPN models lack capabilities to specify communication requirements and control functions for distributed composition of multimedia documents. An attempt has been made in [29] where another Petri-Net-based hierarchical model, called G-Net, has been proposed. This model does allow specifications of communication primitives and types of connections that can be established

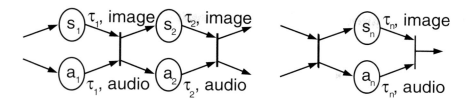

Figure 11-4   An OCPN model for a slide show.

among communicating sites. However, the model is rather over simplified since, unlike OCPN, it does not facilitate generation of the multimedia document. One major advantage of the OCPN model is that QOP parameters can be specified as attributes of the places representing media objects. Quality attributes associated with an object can include its type (continuous/discrete media), size s_i, duration of its presentation τ_i, allowable skew α_i, probability of deadline miss, probability of buffer overflow, and presentation rate ratio r_i, etc. as depicted in Fig. 11–5. These attributes are given by the user at the time of creation of the multimedia document and incorporated in the OCPN model. A transition in the OCPN represents a synchronization point as it marks the play-out start time or deadline of new concurrent objects. At the time of presentation, OCPN structure is evaluated and objects associated with places are retrieved and communicated to the end user [2]. Due to multiplicity of concurrent objects (e.g. video and audio) not only intra-stream but inter-stream synchronization is necessary.

User Interaction Models

Some of the requirements for multimedia presentation are not fully captured by either of the above mentioned models. For example, to reduce (slow motion) or increase (fast-forward) the speed of a multimedia presentation, the temporal models are deficient. These requirements can be addressed by temporal abstractions, which are the means to manipulate or control the presentation of a temporal specification via time reference modification. Various virtual time abstractions have been described in the literature [23], [31]. These describe the maintenance of a time reference that can be scaled to real-time and adjusted to appropriate play-out speeds. If real time is defined as nominal clock time as we perceive it, then virtual time is any other time reference system suitable for translation to real time. For example, a unit-less reference can be converted, or projected to a real-time system by any scaling or offsetting operations. In this manner, the output rate and direction for a sequence of data elements can be changed by simply modifying this translation, i.e., an entire temporal specification, either language- or graph-based, can track a specific time reference or translation process.

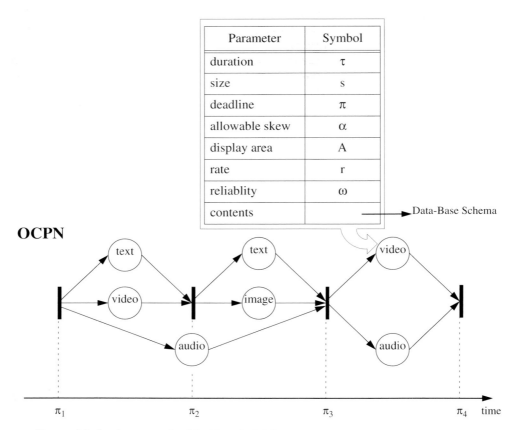

Parameter	Symbol
duration	τ
size	s
deadline	π
allowable skew	α
display area	A
rate	r
reliablity	ω
contents	

Data-Base Schema

OCPN

Figure 11-5   An example OCPN with QOP parameters.

11.4   Synchronization Mechanisms over Broadband Networks

In distributed multimedia systems, users access multimedia information stored at various servers connected over the network. These servers act as repositories for multimedia information orchestrated according to user-specified models. On a user's request the appropriate server retrieves the required data from its databases and ultimately communicates it to the user through the network. A number of different users can simultaneously request multimedia data from one or more multimedia servers on the network. Each multimedia server is capable of catering to multiple data requests from multiple users, simultaneously. In addition to this scenario, where pre-orchestrated or stored information is retrieved, users may also exchange or share live multimedia data. Presentation of pre-orchestrated and/or live multimedia information requires synchronous play-out of time-dependent multimedia data according to some specified temporal relations. At the time of creation of multimedia information, the temporal constraints among various data, which must be observed at the time of playback, are expressed in terms of a model (as discussed in Section 11.3). An-isochronous data (e.g., text and images) needs to be available to the play-out device at the destination before their play-out deadlines. On the other hand isochronous objects, such as video and audio, can be transmitted at the same rate as the play-out rate [17]. To minimize destination buffer requirements and provide continuity in playback, the rate of communication and presentation of an isochronous object need to be equal. Furthermore network transmission schedules require transmission time specifications for individual units of information that are used for transmission. For this purpose we introduce a fine-grained data unit of an object. Objects can be divided into smaller user perceivable units of information for maintaining synchronization. We refer to the smallest unit as a *Synchronization Interval Unit* (SIU) [2]. For example, the smallest interval for a video object can be taken as $\frac{1}{30}$th of a second, which corresponds to the play-out duration of a single video frame. Thus an SIU for a video object could be a video frame. For audio data, the smallest unit can be an audio sample. In case of discrete media objects (images and text), the entire object can be viewed as an SIU. A complete data object is transmitted as a stream of SIUs. Since SIU is the basic unit for a play-out device, its delayed arrival may make it obsolete in the play-out process. Therefore, it is important that the presentation deadlines of SIUs should be known. The deadline of the jth SIU of ith object can be easily derived from the ith object deadline in an OCPN.

All SIUs associated with the same temporal interval must be played out simultaneously within their common temporal interval. For this, it is required that the source delivers SIUs for all objects at a constant rate. Also an SIU can be further packetized by the network. The transmission time for the individual packets within an SIU can be determined using the constant rate assumption. The number of packets may not be same for all the SIUs of an object because of some compression/coding scheme employed to reduce the transmission bandwidth requirement. However, rate assumption at the packet level within an SIU can still be used because of the fairly short duration of an SIU as compared to the duration of the object. To support synchronized delivery of diverse multimedia objects with different *QOP* requirements, the networks of today face the following challenges;

- Allocation of resources for optimum utilization.

- Transport of each multimedia stream within the specified *QOP* parameters.

- Simple inter-switch signaling for low connection setup latency.

In the following sections a framework for network resource management for synchronized presentation of multimedia information is given.

Deadline-Based Scheduling for Synchronization

To preserve the continuity in the presentation of a multimedia stream (intra-stream synchronization) the SIUs of that stream need to be available at the destination before their respective play-out deadlines. The SIUs generated at the source experience random delays over the network before reaching the destination. Therefore the SIUs need to be pre-scheduled, by a factor greater than their respective deadlines, to account for the random delays. This pre-scheduling time is referred to as *control time* [1]. Since the delays are random, some SIUs may in fact arrive earlier than their deadlines, and would need to be buffered. The amount of buffering required depends on the control time, which in turn is dependent on the network delay distributions. In case of multiple streams, inter-stream synchronization along with intra-stream is also required. Concurrent streams may have to be played out at the same time instance, although they may be carried on channels with different delay characteristics. Also different media streams' SIUs, representing the same temporal interval, can have different sizes. Thus data streams possessing the same schedule, in terms of play-out times, may not necessarily produce identical control times, or require the same buffering. To maintain inter-stream synchronization each stream must experience the same overall delay. This can be achieved by accommodating the control time so that each stream is delayed as long as the largest control time. In [1], various algorithms to determine the deadlines of data retrieval and the required buffer space are discussed. A play-out schedule can be decomposed into sub-schedules for each traffic or resource class. These derived schedules can be used by the data source to determine the time instances at which objects need to be scheduled on the network. The receiver can then buffer the incoming objects until their deadlines occur. In another approach, these schedules can be used to determine the worst-case skew between any two objects. Each object may then be delayed by that factor so that synchronization can be achieved at the destination. The first method minimizes both buffer utilization (which may vary depending on the buffer usage profile) and delay, since the schedule is derived based on minimizing these criteria. The second method allocates fixed buffering for objects well ahead of their deadlines, all of which may not even be required. The advantage of the latter is that it provides a simpler implementation mechanism. For live data the destination has no control over SIU generation times, and sufficient capacity must be present to preserve real-time characteristics of the streams. In such cases control time is based on the size, delay, and channel capacity requirements of a representative data object. In case capacity is not adequate for all the multimedia traffic then either the connection is denied altogether, or a reduced quality service is offered. The partial dropping of data according to some quality constraints (given by the *QOP* parameters) as discussed in the section Network Resource-Controlled Synchronization Mechanisms on page 352.

In a resource-constrained environment, the network may not be able to meet the multiple channel demands of each multimedia connection. To overcome the network limitations and minimize the delay in connection establishment, server-based scheduling procedures can be used for synchronized presentation of multimedia data at the destination. It is assumed that the network uses a static reservation scheme, and provides multiple channels with guaranteed bandwidth and delay bounds. Each channel may have different delay bounds and bandwidth. If the capacity of each channel and their number may not be sufficient for transferring multimedia data within the given *QOP* requirements, the connection request may be denied, or as mentioned earlier some amount of multimedia data can be pre-fetched at the user station, for presentation later at the play-out deadline. This results in some initial delay which increases the system response time. The objective of the resource management scheme is to reserve resources to minimize the system response time and destination buffer requirements, while ensuring synchronized play-out of multimedia data. Since the presentation process has to be delayed because of the resource constraints, this scheduling scheme is more suited for application requiring pre-orchestrated or stored multimedia data rather than live data.

Suppose there are n SIUs in a multimedia document that have to be transmitted over the network and the network can provide a set of m channels. Each channel has a guaranteed effective bandwidth rate c_j and a bound on the transit delay δ_j, but their aggregate capacity is not sufficient to provide inter-stream and intra-stream synchronization without pre-fetching. If the ith SIU (having size s_i and play-out deadline π_i) is scheduled for transmission on the jth channel at time γ_j, according to some scheduling policy, then its arrival time, a_i, at the user site becomes

$$a_i = \gamma_j + \frac{s_i}{c_j} + \delta_j$$

The *tardiness* of SIU_i with respect to its play-out deadline is defined as $T_i = \max[0, a_i - \pi_i]$. When $T_i > 0$, SIU_i misses its play-out deadline, resulting in intra-stream as well as inter-stream asynchrony. To ensure synchronization and avoid missing play-out deadlines of SIUs, the start of presentation may need to be delayed until the tardy SIUs become available. Thus, the play-out of each SIU has to be delayed by the maximum tardiness $T_{\max} = \max\limits_{1 \leq i \leq n} [T_i]$. This suggests that the *induced play-out deadlines* $(\pi_i + T_{\max})$, for $1 \leq i \leq n$, are the earliest play-out deadlines that can be met to get synchronized presentation. The time $T_{\max}$ is required to the pre-fetch data and represents the end-to-end delay in the network caused by insufficient channel bandwidth.

This scheduling of n SIUs on m channels to minimize maximum tardiness has been shown to be equivalent to the NP-hard problem of assigning n independent tasks to m uniform parallel processors with different processing speeds and no transit delays [34], [32]. Thus polynomial time algorithms for optimal solutions are unlikely to exist. However, to service user requests the server needs to schedule the multimedia documents in real-time. Various heuristic greedy algorithms for scheduling multimedia data over a resource constrained network have been proposed in [33], [34].

Feedback Techniques for Synchronization

In distributed multimedia applications, a multimedia server may service multiple remote users which need to have synchronized play-out of multimedia data streams not only at their respective stations but they also need to maintain data synchronization with respect to each other. The network may have jitter delays and the multimedia data streams may have non-deterministic variations in recording and playback. The minimum buffer size required to maintain intra-stream synchronization in the presence of bounded network delays is the sum of buffering needed to compensate for network jitter that is independent of the stream size, and buffer required to counteract the variations in play-out rates which is dependent on the size of the media stream. The dependence of buffer required for intra-stream synchronization on the stream size is undesirable. To ensure continuous and synchronized play-out of multimedia data across the remote user stations, in the absence of globally synchronized clocks, a feedback technique, suggested by Ramanathan *et al.*[37] can be used.

In the feedback technique, the responsibility of performing intra-stream synchronization to ensure play-out continuity at the remote stations rests on the server. Light-weight feedback messages, referred to as *feedback units*, are transmitted periodically by the remote clients sites back to the multimedia server. These are used by the server to estimate the play-out instants of media streams at the respective remote station. The server uses these estimates to detect impending buffer overflow or underflow at the remote client sites. Based on the feedback information the server can readjust the transmission rate of the multimedia data streams so as to avoid the loss of data and synchronization at the remote station. Knowing the size of buffer at the remote stations, the minimum rate at which feedback units must be transmitted for maintaining play-out continuity is determined. Upon receiving a feedback unit, the multimedia server estimates the earliest and latest playback times of the SIUs which are yet to be transmitted to the remote users. These estimates provide the earliest and latest possible transmission times. The transmission of SIUs at the earliest transmission times results in a high destination buffer occupancy, while transmission at the latest transmission times keep the destination buffer usage at a minimum. Frequent transmission of feedback units, i.e., a high feedback ratio, enables the server to make more precise estimates of transmission times for a better approximation to the actual playback rate. However this puts additional load on the remote stations, network, and multimedia server which have to generate, carry, and compute the feedback units and transmission times.

In wide-area networks, where end-to-end delays are large, a higher level of destination buffering may be required. In these conditions the buffering can be distributed among the intermediate nodes in the source-to-destination paths. For inter-stream synchronization the temporal characteristics among all the concurrent or overlapping streams must be known in advance. To maintain inter-stream synchronization the multimedia server may either have to speed up some streams or slow down others, causing breaks in their presentations. The playback of at least one stream, referred to as *master* [38], can be maintained continuously. The other "slave streams" may be subject to discontinuities in their play-outs. The master stream play-out continuity is maintained in the same fashion as described above while for inter-stream synchronization the slave SIUs with the time stamps corresponding to the master SIU being transmitted are sent. Thus if a slave is leading the master, media units may arrive at the slave later than their deadlines, causing underflow of the slave destination buffer. This automatically forces the slave to wait until the master stream catches up. Conversely if a slave stream is lagging, media units will arrive at the slave earlier than their deadlines and so would be kept in the buffer until that is filled. Any more early arrivals, before any previously buffered SIUs can be consumed, can result in buffer overflow, making the slave skip SIUs. This would force the lagging slave stream to catch up with the master stream. Although this inter stream synchronization scheme is easy to implement, and does not burden the system with additional network or computational overheads, it does suffer from some disadvantages. The maximum possible lag or lead of the slave stream with respect to the master stream can be as high as the buffering capacity allocated to the slave or master stream. To overcome these drawbacks, each of the slave streams also generate feedback units. The server estimates the earliest and latest possible play-out times of the slave SIUs corresponding to feedback units from the respective slave streams. From the estimates of the play-out deadlines of master and slave SIUs, the server determines the skew among the set of concurrent SIUs. The server then increases or decreases the transmission rate of the slave SIUs by the extent it lags or leads, respectively.

By using re-synchronization strategies based on the most recent estimates of the time to asynchrony of each stream, a multimedia server can adaptively control the feedback transmission rate from a remote play-out device [37]. The control is exercised to minimize the associated overheads without allowing the asynchrony to exceed the tolerance limits specified by the *QOP* parameter α. The re-synchronization policies are

- **conservative:** This scheme reacts only when play-out of different streams is guaranteed to be asynchronous

- **aggressive:** In this approach the server reacts as soon as there is even a slight chance that playback is asynchronous

- **probabilistic:** The server reacts on the average (assuming the network delay distributions and play-out rate variations are known).

By applying these re-synchronization strategies to video and audio play-back, it has been shown [37] that the conservative policy performs well at lower levels of asynchrony, but its effectiveness reduces at higher levels of asynchrony. On the other hand, the performance of aggressive policy fluctuates at lower asynchrony levels, but outperforms the conservative strategy at higher levels. Both the policies become ineffective in a high network jitter environment. In this case the probabilistic policy continues to perform uniformly well.

Synchronization in MPEG

In the multimedia encoding standard *Motion Picture Experts Group* (MPEG) [35] audio and video streams are multiplexed onto a single stream for transmission over a channel. The MPEG stream is organized into packs which constitute a common system layer wrapped around a media-specific compression layer. In the encoder, audio and video data is compressed and packetized independently. Each audio and video packet is time stamped and then multiple audio and video packet streams are interleaved to generate a pack. The pack headers specify the multiplexing rate, audio and video bounds, correlation between audio and video, required buffer sizes at the decoder for continuous play-out, etc. In each packet the compressed audio/video data is preceded by a packet header which contains time decoding and presentation time stamps, packet length, etc. Intra-stream synchronization is handled at the pack layer, while inter-stream synchronization is done at the packet level. The effect of random network delays on playback continuity and inter-stream synchronization for MPEG streams have been discussed in [36].

Network Resource-Controlled Synchronization Mechanisms

Management of network resources is fundamental to the overall operation of distributed multimedia systems. Recently new concepts of resource-controlled synchronization of multimedia services have emerged. In this section we elaborate on these approaches with special emphasis on broadband land-based packet switching and mobile networks.

Land-Based Broadband Networks

Packet switching networks, in which data follows a fixed path from source to destination over a virtual path for the life of the connection, are expected to play a major role in broadband communication networks supporting multimedia services. To ensure synchronized delivery and maximum utilization of the limited resources of the network (capacity and buffer), efficient network resource management scheme can be designed. In this section we discuss resource allocation mechanisms and their role in providing synchronization of multimedia data over broadband networks. Typically in these networks users and multimedia servers are connected via switching nodes. Each switch, in turn, is connected to one or more other switches. An example of such a system is depicted in Fig. 11–6, where users 1 and 2 are being serviced by multimedia servers 2 and 1, respectively. Data transfer between the source-destination host pair is in the form of packets over a virtual path (VP) which is established by some routing strategy through one or more switches. In the figure, VP1 and VP2 represent two possible virtual paths for data transmission from multimedia server 1 to user 2. The VP over which data transfer finally takes place for a connection is determined at the time of connection setup from one or more candidate VPs, depending on shortest distance, least delay, traffic load at each intermediate switch, available switch capacity, etc.

The emerging broadband ATM technology [39], [40] fits well for the definition of such a network. The ATM environment is ideally suited for the transport of heterogeneous streams of multimedia data, with different reliability and tolerance characteristics, to the same destination through the use of virtual channel (VC) and virtual path (VP) identifiers [41]. The VC and VP are used by the routing protocols to determine the path and channel a data packet would follow. When a connection is established between two or more hosts on the network a virtual path having one or more ATM switches is defined. To determine the amount of bandwidth allocated to a connection, ATM requires connection admission control (CAC) and usage parameter control (UPC) protocols at each switch along the VP [5]. These protocols are used to manage the ATM resources for connection requirements.

In a network, traffic load at each switch can change dynamically due to various factors, such as the number of users concurrently served by that switch, the changing level of concurrency of multimedia data streams, and the initiation of new requests. In the network shown in Figure 11–6, if VP1 and VP3 are used by multimedia server 1 and 2 for transmitting data to user 2 and 1 respectively, then the switch Sw_2 has to manage multimedia data streams for both users. The bandwidth requirement profile of users 1 and 2 at switch Sw_2 is shown in Figure 11–7 where the time instances—T_1, T_2, ..., T_8—indicated on the time axis, correspond to the transitions in traffic characteristics of the users' multimedia data.

Static resource assignment schemes to support synchronized multimedia services, although simple, can be very inefficient and wasteful for managing mul-

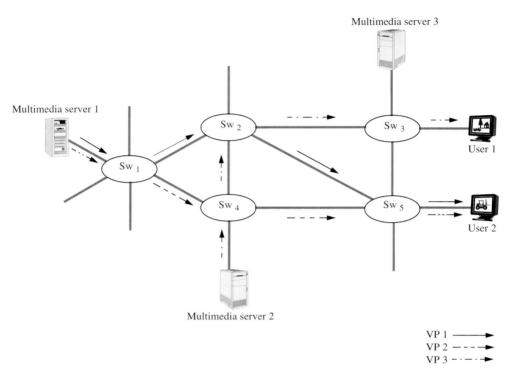

Figure 11-6   An example of distributed multimedia communication architecture.

timedia connections when bandwidth requirements may vary significantly for the duration of a connection. On the other hand dynamic resource allocation schemes, while being able to allocate capacity/buffer efficiently, may require elaborate inter-switch signaling. This may result in longer connection setup delays. Furthermore, the network may not allow dynamic management or each switch may not be capable of dynamically assigning resources for each channel at any arbitrary instant of time. The development of high-speed broadband networks have however increased the bandwidth and processing capability available at each switch in a network. Also, the usual duration of multimedia connections is considerably larger than the initial connection establishment delay. Thus dynamic resource allocation schemes can be used for optimum network resource utilization.

In packet-switched networks a connection request can only be serviced on a candidate VP if all the intermediate switches along it are able to allocate sufficient resources to satisfy the *QOP* demands of the multimedia streams in consideration. The resource allocation in such a scenario needs to be performed at each switch, in coordination with the other switches which constitute the VP, to satisfy the *QOP* requirements of the multimedia data. In other words, each switch

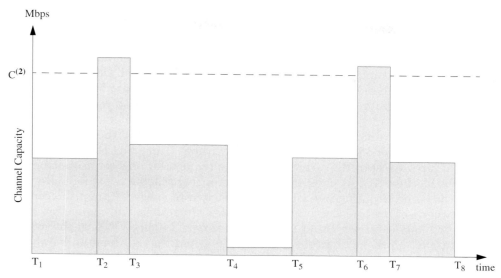

Figure 11-7   Capacity requirement profile at switch Sw_2.

is responsible for assigning appropriate channel capacity for the duration of every multimedia object being handled. For efficient allocation of resources, it is necessary that the throughput and inter-stream synchronization requirements of each connection are available to the switches at the time of connection establishment. Note that in a certain time interval the overall capacity of the switch may not be sufficient to accommodate all the users' *QOP* requirements, especially those pertaining to the throughput. An example of cumulative throughput requirement profile of User 1 and 2 at switch Sw_2 is given in Fig. 11–7. The total capacity requirement exceeds the total available of the switch in the time intervals $[T_2, T_3)$ and $[T_6, T_7)$. In this case, reassignment of channel capacity must be carried out at time instances T_2 and T_3.

One option to overcome the limitations of a switch's capacity is to pre-fetch enough multimedia data to compensate for the slower transfer rate. However, this may not be possible for live data and providing a large buffer at every switch may not always be practical. For real time applications and to operate within a limited buffering capability and capacity at switches, one possible approach is to deliver objects partially and drop some SIUs at the previous switch or the server. For concurrent data streams, determining the number of SIUs to be dropped for each stream is equivalent to distributing some penalty among the streams. Criteria for such decisions can be based on the user's specified *QOP* parameters. These parameters can establish the bounds for the acceptable delivery of data to the user. From a user's point of view, data dropping represents a measure on the network's limitation of not meeting the desired throughput rate of each object over the VP.

Another factor that determines capacity reassignment requirements, at each switch, is the request for a new connection. Newly originated requests are less sensitive to initial set-up delay. Therefore they should be handled in such a way that other ongoing multimedia sessions are not disturbed. Depending on the availability of the bandwidth at each switch in the VP, the possibility of denying the new requests cannot be ruled out. When a switch receives a request for a new connection from its local server or another switch, it first determines if there is enough capacity available to accommodate the new request. If the capacity is not sufficient to accommodate the new request, without degrading the presentation quality of already established connections, the request for new connection on this VP can be blocked. At this point it's up to the routing scheme to explore alternate VPs. If the same situation persists at some switch in every VP then the connection between source and destination is denied altogether. For connection to be established between user 1 and multimedia server 2 along VP 3, in the system configuration shown in Figure 11–6, Sw_4, Sw_2, and Sw_3 all have to be able to allocate the required resources.

A fair capacity allocation policy at a switch requires that if transmission of streams need to be degraded, then degradation should be evenly spread across all the streams that are being transmitted concurrently. Under such a policy, the problem of finding dropping ratios for all concurrent objects, in an interval, to conform to the limited switch capacity, can be formulated as an optimization problem with constraints specified by the QOP parameters [42]. Such optimization can be integrated as a part of the overall resource reservation and allocation protocol, as depicted in Fig. 11–8. The connection request at the kth switch contains the synchronization, throughput, and reliability requirements for the request. If the switch can serve the requested connection while satisfying the specified reliabilities of existing ones for the duration of the connections, the new connection is accepted and resources assigned accordingly. On the other hand, if an optimization solution is not feasible, then the request for new connection is blocked and a "request denied" signal is sent to the previous switch on the VP. The switch, $Sw_{(k-1)}$, checks if it also is on the next VP, i.e. $VP_{(j+1)}$. If yes, then it modifies the OCPN for the new delays (if they are different) and repeats the allocation procedure. In case the switch is not on the $(j+1)^{th}$ VP, then the switch sends the request denied to the previous switch, i.e $Sw_{(k-2)}$.

The dynamic resource allocation scheme generates a throughput profile for each switch. Existing resource reservation protocols like ReSerVation Protocol (RSVP) [43] and Session Reservation Protocol (SRP) [44] can be used to accommodate the generic protocol of Fig. 11–8.

Multimedia Synchronization for Mobile Networking

Recent advances in digital cellular radio technology and high-performance portable computers with networking capability have brought in a new concept of

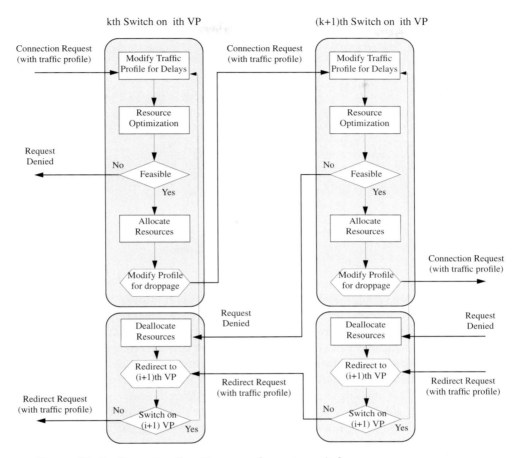

Figure 11-8   Capacity allocation procedure at a switch.

ubiquitous accessibility for mobile users. Such access can allow users to develop and share novel multimedia applications over networks without any geographical restrictions. As radio frequency (RF) channel capacity is a valuable resource in a mobile environment, the resource assignment problem has been given a great importance in the literature. For achieving improved channel utilization, both fixed and dynamic schemes with various variations have been proposed [45]–[50]. As channel capacity for each connection has been standardized to the fixed value such as 48.6 Kbps per channel in the North American standard (IS-54) or 270.833 Kbps per channel in the European standard (GSM[1]) [51], most of the emphasis has been on fixed channel capacity assignment. The future

---

[1] Global System for Mobile telecommunication.

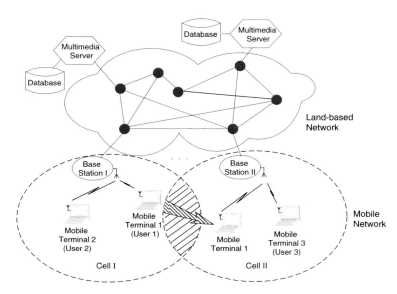

Figure 11-9 An example mobile networked system configuration.

mobile communication environment will allow users to access multimedia information stored at various network-based servers. A multimedia server retrieves the requested data from its databases and communicates it on multiple channels to the base station that has the connection to the requesting mobile user. Ultimately the base station transmits data on the RF channel connection to the user. The overall configuration of such a system is depicted in Figure 11–9. In such systems, a base station serves as an interface between the land-based and the mobile networks and it needs to perform an important internetworking function. Interfacing with the land-based network requires buffering at the base station for carrying out some necessary functions such as rate adaptation, clocking adjustment, bit alignment across the boundary between the heterogeneous networks, etc.

Figure 11–10 shows the flow of multimedia data in the overall system. Multimedia data is first transmitted from the multimedia server to the base station, where it is buffered temporarily, if necessary, prior to its transmission to the mobile user through the assigned out-bound RF channel. The buffers at the base station provide temporary storage for some fraction of the data objects, in order to perform intra-stream synchronization and smooth inter-packet jitter delay which occurs inside the land-based network. These buffers can also be used to provide compensation for the rate difference between the land-based and the mobile networks. As a result, they also ensure inter-stream synchronization among multiple data streams.

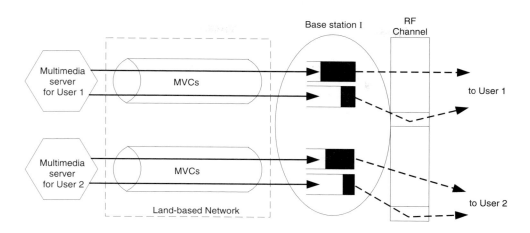

Figure 11-10   Flow of multimedia data.

The main function of a base station is to manage its out-bound RF channel for supporting multimedia connections to a large population of mobile users. Since channel capacity is a precious resource in a mobile environment, it needs to be managed intelligently. Therefore, the base station needs to allocate sub-channel to multiple mobile users. Since we assume that users access pre-orchestrated multimedia information, at the time of connection establishment, a priori knowledge of the traffic profile of multimedia information, e.g., in the form of OCPN, can be readily available to the base station from the servers. However, the traffic load at the base station can change dynamically due to various factors such as the number of users concurrently served by the base station, the changing level of concurrency of media structure for a user, the arrival of new calls, and migration of calls from/to other cells. For example, when a user migrates, it is not possible to maintain an ongoing connection with the current base station. Consequently, the current base station needs to transfer its ongoing connection and appropriate state information of a user (for example, the part of the OCPN that still needs to be transmitted) to the next base station prior to the termination of connection. If the new base station has enough channel bandwidth to allocate, the transfer of such information and ultimately the connection can provide a transparent environment for the user. Handling migrating multimedia traffic requires real-time hand-off procedures and protocols in order to maintain continuity of sessions. In this chapter, however, we do not consider any protocol issue.

Newly originated calls are less sensitive to initial call set-up delay. Therefore they should be handled in such a way that other ongoing sessions are not disturbed by them. Depending on the availability of the RF channel, the possibility of denying the new call cannot be ruled out. When a base station receives a request for a new call, it can take different actions according to the availability of its RF channel capacity. First, it determines whether or not there is enough channel capacity available to accommodate the new call. The new call can be blocked if there is not enough channel capacity available to accommodate it without degrading the presentation quality of already established calls. In view of these requirements the management of RF channel capacity allocation can be treated as an optimization problem, when the objective is to satisfy quality of connection as best as possible [52]. Other important issues include a time-constrained hand-off procedure to satisfy the real-time requirement of multimedia data and statistical modeling of multimedia traffic, which are expected to provide new impact on the resource allocation problem.

11.5   Conclusion

In this chapter we have discussed issues related to synchronization of multimedia information over broadband networks. Various aspects of presentation quality and their impact on system resources form the basis of designing multimedia synchronization protocols for supporting distributed multimedia services. For a multimedia document, the temporal relationships among multimedia objects and their quality characteristics need to be specified. Various specification models used for defining the characteristics of the multimedia objects, specifically for transport over communication networks, are introduced in Section 11.2. Presentation of time-dependent multimedia information involves intra-stream and inter-stream synchronization. Random delays in a communication network may result in loss of intra-stream synchronization failures. Multiple streams may be transported over different channels, having different delay characteristics, resulting in inter-stream synchronization failure. Different schemes and techniques to recover from intra-stream and inter-stream asynchrony are outlined in Section 11.4. In addition, allocation and management of constrained network resources for synchronized delivery of multimedia information over land-based and mobile networks, within the quality constraints specified in the model, are also described. Depending on the type of multimedia service and application, each technique has certain advantages and disadvantages. Currently synchronization of multimedia information, over broadband land-based and mobile networks is an active area of research with continuing innovations. With all this activity it is expected that new and improved synchronization techniques will revolutionize the area of distributed multimedia systems.

References

[1]   Little, T. and Ghafoor, A., "Multimedia synchronization protocols for broadband integrated services," *IEEE Journal on Selected Areas in Communications*, Vol. 9, Dec

1991, pp. 1368–1382.

[2] Woo, M., Qazi, N.U., and Ghafoor, A., "A synchronization framework for communication of pre-orchestrated multimedia information," *IEEE Network Magazine*, Vol. 8, No. 1, Jan/ Feb 1994, pp. 52–61.

[3] Furht, B., "Multimedia systems: An overview," *IEEE Multimedia*, Vol. 1, Spring 1994, pp. 47–59.

[4] Karmouch, A., Orozco-Barbosa, L., Georganas, N., and Goldberg, M., "A multimedia medical communications system," *IEEE Journal on Selected Areas in Communications*, Vol. 8, Apr 1990, pp. 325–339.

[5] Kim, B.G. and P. Wang, "ATM network: Goals and challenges," *Communications of the ACM*, Vol. 38, Feb 1995, pp. 39–44.

[6] Barbosa, L.O., Karmouch, A., Georganas, N.D., and Goldberg, M., "Multimedia inter-hospital communications system for medical consultations," *IEEE Journal on Selected Areas in Communications*, Vol. 10, No. 7, 1992, pp. 1145–1157.

[7] Naffah, N., "Multimedia applications," *Computer Communications*, Vol. 13, May 1990, pp. 243–249.

[8] Dupuy, S., Tawbi, W., and Horlait, E., "Protocols for high-speed multimedia communications networks," *Computer Communications*, Vol. 15, Jul/Aug 1992, pp. 349–358.

[9] Rangan, P.V., Vin, H.K., and Ramanathan, S., "Designing an on-demand multimedia service," *IEEE Communication Magazine*, Vol. 30, No. 7, July 1992, pp. 56–64.

[10] Fox, E.A., "Advances in interactive digital multimedia systems," *IEEE Computer*, Vol. 24, No. 10, Oct 1991, pp. 9–21.

[11] Rosenberg, J., Cruz, G., and Judd, T., "Presenting multimedia documents over a digital network," *Computer Communication*, Vol. 15, No. 6, July/ Aug 1992, pp. 374–380.

[12] Sheng, S., Chandrakasan, A., and Brodersen, R., "A portable multimedia terminal," *IEEE Communications Magazine*, Vol. 30, Dec 1992, pp. 64–75.

[13] Little, T. and Ghafoor, A., "network considerations for distributed multimedia object composition and communication," *IEEE Network Magazine*, Vol. 15, Nov 1990, pp. 32–49.

[14] Little, T. and Ghafoor, A., "Synchronization and storage models for multimedia objects," *IEEE Journal on Selected Areas in Communications*, Vol. 8, Apr 1990, pp. 413–427.

[15] Ravindran, K. and Bansal, V., "Delay compensation protocols for synchronization of multimedia data streams," *IEEE Transactions on Knowledge and Data Engineering*, Vol. 5, No. 4, Aug 1993, pp. 574–589.

[16] Steinmetz, R., "Human perception of jitter and media synchronization," *IEEE Journal on Selected Areas in Communications*, Vol. 14, Jan 1996, pp. 61–72.

[17] Ferrari, D., "Client requirements for real-time communication services," *IEEE Communication Magazine*, Vol. 28, No. 11, 1990, pp. 65–72.

[18] Lam, S., Chow, S., and Yau, D., "An algorithm for lossless smoothing of MPEG video," in *ACM SIGCOMM '94*, Aug 1994, pp. 281–292.

[19] International Standards Organization, JTC 1 SC 29/WG10, Digital Compression and Coding of Continuous-Tone Still Images, Jan 1992.

[20] Steinmetz, R., "Synchronization properties in multimedia systems," *IEEE Journal on Selected Areas in Communications*, Vol. 8, Apr 1990, pp. 401–412.

[21] Sventek, J., "An architecture for supporting multi-media integration" in *Proceedings of IEEE Computer Society Office Automation Symposium*, IEEE Computer Society, Apr 1987, pp. 46–56.

[22] Blakowski, G. and Steinmetz, R., "A media synchronization survey: Reference model, specification, and case studies," *IEEE Journal on Selected Areas in Communications*, Vol. 14, Jan 1996, pp. 5–35.

[23] Herrtwich, R., "Time capsules: An abstraction for access to continuous-media data," in *Proc. 11th Real-Time Systems Symposium*, Dec 1990, pp. 11–20.

[24] Moore, D., "Multimedia presentation development using the audio visual connection," *IBM Systems Journal*, Vol. 29, No. 4, 1990, pp. 494–508.

[25] Hodges, M., Sasnett, R., and Ackerman, M., "A construction set for multimedia applications," *IEEE Software*, Jan 1989, pp. 37–43.

[26] Little, T. and Ghafoor, A., "Interval-based conceptual models for time-dependent multimedia data," *IEEE Transactions on Knowledge and Data Engineering*, Vol. 5, No. 4, Aug 1993, pp. 551–563.

[27] Weiss, K., "Formal specification and continuous media," in *Proc. 1st International Workshop on Network and Operating System Support for Digital Audio and Video*, Berkeley, CA, Nov 1990.

[28] Poggio, A., Garcia-Luna-Aceves, J., Craighill, E., Moran, D., Aguilar, L., Worthington, D., and Hight, J., "CCWS: A computer-based multimedia information system," *Computer*, Vol. 18, Oct 1985, pp. 92–103.

[29] Deng, Y. and Chang, S.-K., "A framework for the modeling and prototyping of distributed information systems," *International Journal of Software Engineering and Knowledge Engineering*, Vol. 1, No. 3, 1991, pp. 203–226.

[30] Stotts, P.D. and Furuta, R., "Petri-net-based hypertext: Document structure with browsing semantics," *ACM Trans. on Office Automation Systems*, Vol. 7, Jan 1989, pp. 3–29.

[31] Anderson, D., Tzou, S., Wahbe, R., Govindan, R., and Andrews. M., "Support for continuous media in the DASH system," in *Proc. 10th Intl. Conference on Distributed Computing Systems*, Paris, May 1990, pp. 54–61.

[32] Blazewicz, J., Ecker, K., Schmidt, G., and J. Weglarz, *Scheduling in Computer and Manufacturing Systems*.Berlin/Heidelberg: Springer-Verlag, 1993.

[33] Woo, M., "A synchronization framework for networked multimedia services, PhD thesis, Purdue University, Dec 1995.

[34] Baqai, S., Shinkai, S., Woo, M., and Ghafoor, A., "Performance evaluation of multimedia synchronization protocols using server-based scheduling mechanisms," *IEEE Journal on Selected Areas in Communications*, to appear in 1996.

[35] International Standards Organization, JTC 1/SC 29/WG11, MPEG I: Coded Representation of Picture, Audio and Multimedia/Hypermedia Information, Nov 1991.

[36] Rangan, P., Kumar, S.S., and Rajan, S., "Continuity and synchronization in MPEG," *IEEE Journal on Selected Areas in Communications*, Vol. 14, Jan 1996, pp. 52–60.

[37] Ramanathan, S.and Rangan, P.V., "Adaptive feedback techniques for synchronized multimedia retrieval over integrated networks," *IEEE/ACM Transactions on Networking*, Vol. 1, No. 2, Apr 1993, pp. 246–259.

[38] Ramanathan, S.and Rangan, P., "Feedback techniques for intra-media continuity and inter-media synchronization in distributed multimedia systems," *The Computer Journal*, Mar 1993.

[39] Partridge, C., Gigabit Networking.Reading, MA: Addison-Wesley, 1994.

[40] Minzer, S.E., "Broadband ISDN and Asynchronous Transfer Mode (ATM)," *IEEE Communications Magazine*, Vol. 27, No. 9, Sep 1989, pp. 17–57.

[41] Vetter, R., "ATM concepts, architectures, and protocols," *Communications of the ACM*, vol. 38, Feb 1995, pp. 30–38.

[42] Baqai, S., Woo, M., and Ghafoor, A., "Network resource management for enterprise-wide multimedia services," *IEEE Communications*, Vol. 34, Jan 1996, pp. 78–83.

[43] Zhang, L., Deering, S., Estrin, D., Shenker, S., and Zappala, D., "RSVP: A new resource ReSerVation Protocol," *IEEE Network*, Vol. 7, Sep 1993, pp. 8–18.

[44] Anderson, D.P. and Herrtwich, R.G., "SRP: A resource reservation protocol for guaranteed-performance communication in the Internet," Tech. Rep. TR-90-006, Berkeley, CA, Feb 1990.

[45] MacDonald, V., "Advanced mobile phone service: The cellular concept," *Bell System Technical Journal*, vol. 58, Jan 1979, pp. 15–41.

[46] Cox, D. and Reudink, D., "Increasing channel occupancy in large-scale mobile radio systems: Dynamic channel reassignment," *IEEE Transactions on Vehicular Technology*, vol. 22, Nov 1973, pp. 218–222.

[47] Tajima, J. and Imamura, K., "Strategy for flexible channel assignment in mobile communication systems," *IEEE Transactions on Vehicular Technology*, Vol. 37, May 1988, pp. 92–103.

[48] Zhang, M. and Yum, T., "Comparisons of channel-assignment strategies in cellular mobile telephone systems," *IEEE Transactions on Vehicular Technology*, Vol. 38, Nov 1989, pp. 211–215.

[49] Oh, S. and Tcha, D., "Prioritized channel assignment in a cellular radio network," *IEEE Transactions on Communications*, Vol. 40, July 1992, pp. 1259–1269.

[50] Chuang, J., Sollenberger, N., and Cox, D., "Pilot-based dynamic channel assignment scheme for wireless access TDMA/FDMA systems," *International Journal of Wireless Information Networks*, Vol. 1, Jan 1994, pp. 37–47.

[51] Cox, D., "Wireless network access for personal communications," *IEEE Communications Magazine*, Vol. 30, Dec 1992, pp. 96–115.

[52] Woo, M., Prabhu, N., and Ghafoor, A., "Dynamic resource allocation for multimedia services in mobile communication environments," *IEEE Journal on Selected Areas in Communications*, Vol. 13, June 1995, pp. 172–181.

Prototype Systems

C H A P T E R 12

Image Database Prototypes

Carole Goble

Department of Computer Science
University of Manchester
Manchester, M13 9PL, UK
cgoble@cs.man.ac.uk

*I*mage databases, otherwise known as pictorial or visual databases, are not new—they have been an area of active research since the 1970s, developing from simple libraries to support image interpretation to sophisticated prototypes with elaborate data models, content-based retrieval, and visually driven user interfaces. Many prototypes have been developed within the context of image-oriented applications such as remote sensing, geographic information systems, medicine, security surveillance, CAD, document archiving, and digital libraries. In this chapter we discuss the preoccupations of such prototypes and present a detailed discussion of four: MMIS, QBIC, ART MUSEUM, and VIMSYS. We also refer to others, including PICQUERY+, AMOS, CORE, MORE, and PICTION.

12.1   A Brief History of Image Database Prototypes

Image databases arose in the 1970s and early 1980s from the image interpretation/analysis and pattern recognition community. Early systems were tailored for specific application domains and the associated databases were frequently nothing more than libraries of test-bed images indexed and retrieved on alphanumeric header file information. Favored applications include medical imaging [23], including hospital Picture Archiving and Communication Systems, and remote sensing satellite data—many early prototypes, e.g., [46], were LANDSAT image databases for image analysts. These systems are characterized by their (perceived) archival nature, relatively primitive descriptions of the images (BLOBs (Binary Large Objects) labeled with conventional scalar types), their management of high volumes of data, high bandwidth multimedia communications, and their sophisticated image manipulation. Little emphasis was placed on database issues such as query languages and concurrency, and the database community largely ignored the whole application area; the unsophisticated nature of the relational DBMSs has been cited as a limiting factor.

Throughout the 1980s, Geographic Information Systems pioneered the representation of spatial modeling—features and their spatial positions are identified semiautomatically or by users, and related to other data (population sizes, rainfall, etc.). One of the best known early prototypes is PROBE [37]. Important contributions of these systems are effective spatial indexing techniques, e.g., R* trees, GRID files and k-d-trees, efficient support for spatial operations and their segment or polygon-based models.

From the mid 1980s office automation provided the impetus for large multimedia document systems—documents that were primarily text but also included images and graphics. Well known examples are MINOS [10] and MULTOS [33]. Both of these had a limited form of retrieval, known as Content-Based Retrieval (CBR), that used images directly. Today this work has been recast in the form of Digital Libraries, fuelled by the rise of CD-ROMS and the World Wide Web [2].

The late 1980s saw new interest in *multimedia* databases from the database community. The development of new data models, notably the extensible relational and object-oriented models, meant that non-standard data applications requiring structurally richer representation (such as multimedia) could be addressed. Consequently, image database management systems experienced a major revival of interest fueled by the declining cost of image storage, the rise of powerful workstations, and the renewed emphasis on CBR. Unlike the early prototypes, attention is now paid to conventional database issues such as data modeling, metadata, concurrency, storage management, security, reliability, versioning, and index management. Although multimedia databases imply the support of other media (text, video, audio), in reality all require image management and many are heavily biased towards images (frequently only implementing image retrieval and storage capabilities with some text or keyword management). Reflecting the requirements of the image processing community, many prototype systems still form a "framework" into which a variety of image processing and indexing techniques can be slotted and applied depending on their appropriateness for particular images or application domains.

One area that has had only passing influence on the prototypes is hypermedia which is mainly of interest as a means of browsing. Most hypermedia systems do little in the way of image management or retrieval, an exception being [30].

The rest of this chapter is organized in the following way: Section 12.2 discusses the general requirements of a prototype, emphasizing data modeling and retrieval aspects. Sections 12.3–7 discuss a number of prototype systems in turn. We conclude with a brief summary.

12.2   Issues for Image Database Prototypes

Images and graphics have a number of characteristics that distinguish them from more conventional data types: data is typically static, variably sized and large (1K for a graphic up to 100M for an uncompressed raster image), and requires different I/O devices that may have to be reserved. Most are archival so updating is infrequent, and an insertion /deletion model will often suffice.

What really makes an image database different from a conventional one is the *atomicity of the base* data. Images are not unstructured—they are highly structured data in their own right with shape, texture, or color features which can be combined into image objects. All image and conventional alphanumeric data should be treated equally and in a *uniform* way, hiding the differences of internal formats at a media-independent conceptual level. The identification of image objects and features will not be precise and depends on the application, the image analysis, and image interpretation algorithms, and the state of any models or domain knowledge known at input and retrieval time. Should the raw image data be reused for different applications, or be the subject of more than one interpretation algorithm, the image database will have different, possibly contradictory, interpretations of the same object.

Imprecise descriptions of image content will naturally mean imprecise and inexact matching of queries. Thus the user interface is more interactive than in conventional databases, requiring special interfaces for the input of queries by visual means. Query by example, "retrieve all images whose content is similar to this one," requires the identification of the necessary attributes for content, the choice of the range bounds, and the specification of some distance measure that quantifies similarity [25].

Data Models and Meta Image Representation

The identification of image features and their representation is a pre-occupation of all prototypes. Upon this rests the possible retrieval strategies, indexing strategies, etc. Naturally, the data model mutually reflects retrieval requirements. Most commercial systems describe and retrieve images based on keywords or text associated with the image, using SQL as the query language. This is generally considered to be an inflexible approach as keywords cannot always be pre-assigned; there is often no common vocabulary and describing texture or shape with words is hard [35].

For many applications, images are selected because they are "similar to" another image. This means that the image must be converted into some sort of "meta-image" representation so that spatial reasoning, image information retrieval and image interpretation can be supported. The images must be assigned some sense of "meaning," the sophistication of which depends on the application. The representation progressively bridges the gap between the uninterpreted raw image and the application's semantic domain of "world" objects. A multi-abstraction approach appears in a number of prototypes [16], [21], [44] and has been formalized by [20] into three broad dimensions, given below with some elaborations: world-only data, image-only data, and annotation data:

1. World-only data: media independent, domain specific   Also known as "symbolic" or semantic data. These objects and their relationships model conventional non-multimedia application domain concepts, acting as a focus for "fusing" different media related to the same world object. e.g., politicians are kinds of people; people have names.

2. Image-only data: media-specific, domain independent The images are themselves complex (and usually hierarchical) information sources with their own representations. However, these are self-contained and not explicitly related to the semantic "world objects" the database is modeling. Such information can be an application-neutral general resource, shared by any number of applications, which is essential if we are to avoid redundancy and duplication with large and expensive media resources. Image-only data includes:

Uninterpreted raw image, e.g., the Binary Large OBject;

Registration information e.g., compression method, digitization method, date of capture;

Interpreted contents, also known as image meta-data [1], e.g., image features, such as shape, texture and color signatures, identified by automatic, semi-automatic or user-directed processing. Contents can be classified into the following major information types that must be interrelated and operationally supported:

- structural: spatial and temporal;

- whole image features: encoding of the whole image, e.g., color histograms and texture signatures;

- image object[1] features: encoding and identification of regions, e.g. color, shape, texture.

Such information can be used for both semantic interpretation and similarity matching, and can be represented by static structural relationships or by dynamic processes, particularly in an encapsulated object-oriented paradigm. It may not be related to world objects, in which case it is described as "content-based non-information bearing" [20]. It can still, however, be used for content-based retrieval as it still represents a description of the content of the object;

Transformation relationships, usually implemented as functions of the media data type, e.g., a raster image can be transformed to a graphic (but not vice versa). Automatic translation is not always possible, hence it can be necessary to store both representations, each *substitutable* for the other depending on context [34].

3. Annotation data: media-specific, domain specific   These are the relationships that link the world application objects with the images and their features. Such information facilitates semantic-based content retrieval of media objects, described as "content-based information-bearing" [20], e.g., John Doe appears in this image; this image shape object is a house, this image texture feature represents "haziness." Image databases use a variety of methods to form these relationships and to classify and describe an image and its contents. The three major categories of descriptive mechanism are:

Textual descriptions (captions or labels)—using keywords to describe the whole image or image objects, e.g. a textual label "tree" is linked to an image or possibly an image object.

Semantic descriptions—using higher level semantic representations (e.g. semantic networks or object models) to represent the image contents, e.g., the object representing a tree, an instance of class plant, is directly associated with the image object.

Content based—using the actual content or the high-level representations of the content (features indexes, signatures etc.) to classify the image objects. If the feature is the combination of a green canopy above a brown trunk, it is a tree. This might also describe a beach umbrella.

Textual attribution requires complete user input, whereas automatic or semi-automatic feature extraction can be used as a basis for semantic descriptions. Feature recognition can be classified into two types:

---

[1] Image objects are also known as sub-images, image subparts, image fragments, regions, segments, blots, elements, etc.

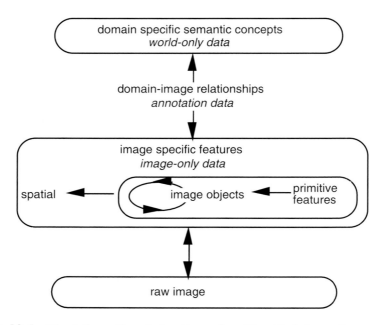

Figure 12-1   The information abstractions of multimedia information.

> **User-assisted outline generation** with automatic spatial, temporal, shape, texture, color, movement analysis, e.g., [35].

> **Automatic content-indexing** [16], [44] using model or feature-based techniques.

A database of image-only data that does not model any semantic data is simply an image resource or repository for use by any application. It can still be used for retrieval, but retrieval based purely on the data model of the image itself and not on any world semantics.

Fig. 12–1 illustrates the information abstractions for the multimedia information. The mapping between domain and image is many-to-many. The same objects can be viewed in any number of different ways depending on the conceptual model, the user or the application domain. The image-specific information is separated (logically if not physically) from the domain-specific information in order to reuse expensive general media resources, and in order to exploit media-appropriate serving mechanisms.

The image metadata, as shown in Fig. 12–1 is recursive and compositional. Inter-media relationships are those that associate different media, usually centered around some real world concept, e.g. collections of images associated with John Doe, a document, or a hypermedia web [32]. Intra-media relationships are those that associate different components of an image object itself and are encapsulated within it, e.g., image fragments such as shape features or regions and their spatial and temporal relationships. The image fragments are themselves composite objects[2] perhaps made up of other fragments, or form the component of a number of identifiable image objects. Rich composition techniques are required to deal with object clusters, references between objects and the separation of objects from their components. Early pictorial databases dealt with image data organized as vectors or grids, with semantic information held as keywords in relations linking back to the picture [9].

A sequence of images representing overlaid annotations is a form of composition. The components of these compositional objects can themselves be composed objects, so a *recursive data model* is essential. We must also distinguish between components that are *properties* of a compositional object and hence are dependent for their existence on the parent object, and those that are independent, e.g., an image feature is a property of its parent image and must be deleted upon deletion of the image. An image aggregated together with some text in a document is independent of that composition—upon its removal the image and text still exist.

Operations as first class objects   Many types of knowledge are held in the procedures of feature extraction and image processing. They can be expressed as methods encapsulated in data objects but we may wish to:

- have libraries of such methods that are alternatives and are simultaneously applied to image and image objects, especially if media instances are used by many different applications with different interpretation requirements;

- access the internal details of the process so that we can see if it is appropriate;

- store and retrieve intermediate results in the database;

- use operations in queries by specifying the operation to use to match or recognize the required data items.

Searching, Retrieval, and Browsing of Images and Image Objects

An essential function of any database management system is support for unanticipated data access. Specifically we must deal with five query aspects: expressivity, formulation, optimization, presentation of results, and reformulation. Selections should be expressible on spatial data, temporal data and image features (together with conventional data types) in the same query expressions. Images should be retrievable by:

---

[2] Composite objects are sometimes called part-whole objects, complex objects, component objects or aggregations.

data type e.g., "retrieve all the JPEG images";

structure e.g., "retrieve all documents that have an image in them";

association e.g., "retrieve all the objects that are linked to the Gettysburg address"—an image of Abraham Lincoln, the recording of a reading of it, etc. The *navigation* of hypermedia webs falls under this category;

browsing e.g., "browse through the collection of images of churches." Browsing can be through an extension in the database or a query result;

content e.g., "retrieve an image (or set of ranked images) which looks like X," "retrieve an image that has a shape like x in the top-right-hand corner(ish)," "retrieve all the images containing a car," "retrieve an image fragment containing a car, or this image object."

Content-Based Retrieval and Similarity Matching

Content-based retrieval is addressed in some way by all prototypes. Text has a long tradition of retrieval based on statistical distance measures of word positions, layout vs. logical structures, etc. Graphic types have a well-defined alphabet of features and spatial/compositional relationships and a number of prototype query systems exist. Images are more problematic. The key issue is *similarity*. What does it mean to match two images or to match two image objects? Traditional query processing methods accept precisely-specified queries and provide only exact answers, thus requiring users to understand the problem domain and database schema. They return limited or null information if exact answers are not available. Images do not have well-defined symbolic alphabets, so this is not appropriate—we need to be able to cater for imprecision, uncertainty, incompleteness, and multiple interpretations and emphasis. We also have the added dimensions of time and space which can rarely be expressed exactly, only in intervals, ranges, or permitted margins of error.

Content-based retrieval is only as good as the description of content and the indexing mechanisms. Conversely, the index required depends on the queries that the application is likely to present. Therefore retrieval is tied-up with feature extraction and the linking of features with "world" objects. Many commentators have classified selection mechanisms based on the type of search specification and what the selection criteria are:

Exact feature match, only possible with user-generated textual descriptions and multi-levels of keywords, or some sort of Picture Description Language [5].

Inexact feature match, a range query given an arbitrary specified range, and the best possible with automatic or imprecise feature extraction. Inexact retrieval can use *semantic descriptions* when image features have been mapped to semantic domain objects, and *image-content-based* descriptions when retrieval is based upon image content encodings. Matches can be partial (find k objects that are closest, or within or beyond some distance X), best, or most distant. Similarity retrieval will almost never result in one object being retrieved. Queries are more likely to result in a best-fit candidate-set, some of which may be wide of the mark. Thus all queries are fuzzy and many systems have made use of fuzzy logic in their query models [44].

Structural match. Visual information means spatial reasoning and queries on layout, proximity, containment, etc. of image objects and regions. Queries can be location based, ("What is at or near location x?") and feature based ("Does y occur in region x"?). Spatial relationships are frequently stored implicitly in a spatial data structure such as an R* tree. The same index should be capable of supporting both relative and absolute locations.

Query formulation and presentation   For text-based descriptions, or data type retrieval, an SQL or SQL-like query language is a common choice. The database community regards a declarative ad hoc query language as essential. The select, project, and join operations that the SQL community are familiar with must be redefined to include spatial notions such as overlay.

For content-based retrieval that isn't keyword-based, the presentation of queries depends on being able to express the image features that have been extracted. In the conventional database field the Query-By-Example paradigm is popular and it seems not only desirable but essential to retrieve an image by example; Query-by-Pictorial-Example [7] was an early attempt applied to graphics. Image formulation using other images frequently requires on-line image processing and extraction when processing an exemplar query image of the kind performed when populating the database. Fig. 12–2 illustrates the usual tasks within query processing, where the image is part of the query.

Expression of similarity distance. As similarity queries are imprecise, each expression must be accompanied by some indication of acceptable distance from the target object for ranking results.

Weightings and preferences. The imprecision of queries coupled with multi-clause queries makes it desirable to express the relative importance of clauses. This raises a number of open questions, such as how weightings should be combined and how candidate images should be ranked. E.g. "Retrieve images containing 'John Major' [priority 1] and containing (two [priority 4] people [priority 3]) and image texture is like sample X [priority 2]." The intention

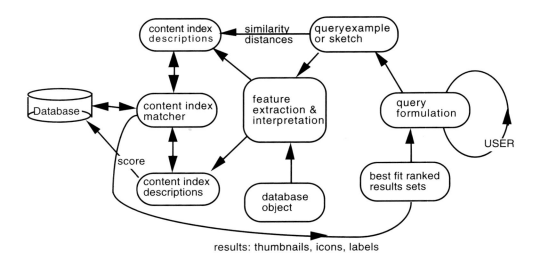

Figure 12-2   Inexact similarity based query by example.

is that an image with John Major with a certain image texture but without people in it will still be retrieved, and if there is only one person in the picture it will be included.

Compositional queries. Media composition leads to the requirement to retrieve based on such compositions, e.g., "Retrieve all image sequences where image X is part of the sequence."

Query optimization   Querying may require complex and time-consuming transformations on image types in order to test for matches, so an optimizer that considers the query along with the database and system characteristics to plan the most efficient search approach is an important component of an image query system. A term referring to a keyword will cost less than a similarity transformation matching process on an image. A major difficulty is how to optimize a selection containing user-defined operations.

Query results and search reformulation   Many users have vaguely defined information needs, and often will need to recognize what they are looking for rather than describe it. The query process must be "cooperative" [12]: interactive and iterative, with feedback, selective browsing of result sets, search-reformulation or changes to link-following behavior. Refinement requires the maintenance of search histories (both the query and the result set), refinement of the query, refinement of the target database set, and caches of results that can be application or user specific. The results of queries lead to other, new, data manipulation tasks including visualization, integration with knowledge-based systems and data analysis etc. Other issues include:

Ranking results. Based on similarity distance measures or user/ application preferences.

Statistical queries. Queries such as "How many images are in this database" result in statistics, not image instances, possibly collected at media capture and interpretation time.

Presentation of results. Composite objects may need synchronization or restructured presentation. Expensive objects may be displayed as textual descriptions, icons, or summaries in the form of miniatures (thumbnail low-resolution or monochrome versions of images) in order to avoid fetching the full versions of large objects where storage, transmission, and transformation/rendering costs may be high.

Transactions

Although little work has been done in this area, the perceived wisdom is that a multimedia database transaction is *long duration, non-atomic* with *high data volumes* [31], [43]. Supervisory applications, such as command and control situations, have real-time constraints. Transactions involving continuous or composite media additionally have synchronization constraints. The majority of scenarios strongly suggest that multimedia systems foster or require cooperation among many people, and hence transaction control will need to reflect the *cooperative* and distributed nature of those applications. However, the majority of multimedia applications are read-only—capturing base media data is relatively high cost, and most users will use the database as a read-only repository. Objects are interpreted relatively infrequently and in a controlled way. Updates are infrequent and usually the whole object is checked out and replaced. This seems to indicate that base objects have a minimum concurrency requirement. Content-based indexes and descriptions are derived from the base media object, so any changes to the base object must be propagated via referential integrity constraints. New or updated content-based recognition techniques may mean deriving or re-deriving content descriptions and content-indexes.

Summary

In this section we have presented the overriding preoccupations of most prototypes. We now take four prototypes and examine them in more detail. Each has a slightly different emphasis, but they can be broadly differentiated by their support for semantic metadata, the richness of their data models, their support for content based retrieval and object interpretation, and their user interfaces.

12.3 The Manchester Multimedia Information System

The Manchester Multimedia Information System resulted in two proto-types, MMIS-1 and MMIS-2, between 1988 and 1993 [36], [16], [17]. Work continues in the use of description logics for describing and annotating image data [19].

The chief purpose of MMIS was to experiment with image retrieval by using automatic image object identification—referred to as *automatic content retrieval*. Manual annotation is time consuming and expensive, and is an inhibitor to more widespread use of content-based queries. Fully automatic methods eliminate this effort but cannot match the precision of matching on user-defined objects. MMIS *classified* image objects by their feature sets into hierarchical and indistinct classes that could characterize some domain concept. Direct and exempler-based retrieval was by means of the object class, spatial location and some other simple attributes. A domain knowledge base was used to annotate image objects automatically with world semantics based on the image object classes. This is only possible when working in a closed application domain: MMIS was prototyped using botanical images and fossils. The images were complex enough to provide useful query data but offered tractable automatic interpretation without being too noisy.

MMIS's second aim was the development of an expressive data model that would represent multiple abstractions of image data to support content address-ability, and to demonstrate the applicability of the model to text, documents (as structured, composite types) and other media types. The model chosen was that of a multi-level semantic net.

Thirdly, MMIS developed a general "plug-and-play" modular architecture for different image analysis and interpretation techniques, applicable to different kinds of images and different application domains. The architecture was generic, including interpreters and editors for monochrome images, text and documents and Basic Logical ObjecTs or "blots" (image objects forming distinct regions that could be held separately from their enclosing images).

Architecture

Fig. 12–3 gives the principle modules of MMIS-2—note that this a multimedia prototype and didn't just cater to images. Image and text instances are generated by users externally to the system and then dispatched for interpretation. Instances become available for retrieval almost immediately and interpretation results become available a short time later. The chief components were:

- **Text and Image Editors** for creating interpretable items. Text items can be generated by any available editor which produces ASCII output or from within the system using hypermedia facilities. Images require special device support for input and output—different users may have different facilities which requires the image I/O subsystems to adapt to the resources

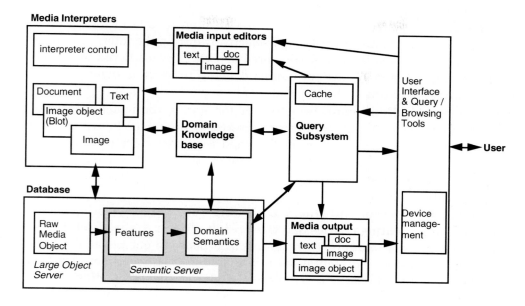

Figure 12-3 General architecture of MMIS-2.

that are available. For example, if a user's device cannot handle 24-bit color then any 24-bit color images will have to be transformed before they are displayed. If a transformation is impossible, then the user must be informed of the existence of the instance as a result of a query even if it cannot be rendered (by displaying an icon or a data type label, for example).

- **Media Interpreters** which support "plug-and-play" for processing batches of each type of item undergoing interpretation. The same images may be interpreted in different ways, which implies that raw image data may have a number of semantic interpretations, driven by domain-specific information. Once an image object, or blot, is identified, it is held separately and has its own domain-independent interpreter.

Image interpretation has two levels:

  low-level blots are segmented from the image and their base attributes extracted using pluggable image analysis algorithms, often dependent on the application domain;

  high-level declarative derivation for more abstract attributes and structural relationships, driven by rules in a domain knowledge base.

- **An Interpretation Controller** for organizing the assignment of items being interpreted to the interpreters themselves.
- **Large Object Server** for raw storage of interpretable instances (image, blot, text). Instances are retrieved selectively during the interpretation and querying phases. Instances are stored as byte streams keyed by a unique identifier—the same instance entered many times is assigned the same identifier each time.
- **A Semantic Representation Server** for storing the image meta-data—the image objects and features interpreted by the image interpreter—and semantic domain data. Intermediate and complete query results are also stored here for further processing during the querying phase. The semantic server representation is a multi-level semantic net described in the section Data Model on page 378.
- **Query Subsystem and Query Browsing Tools** for formulating, processing and presenting queries and their results. There is a trade-off between the time taken to interpret instances in response to queries and the space required to store representations of the results of interpretation. Automatic interpretation of images was considered to be too time consuming to be performed on demand. MMIS catered for both approaches—most interpretation is performed off-line pre-query, so that users query the results of that interpretation, but further processing can be performed post-query or by the use of lazy evaluation. Any prototype images or sketches represented as the query must, of course, be interpreted at query time using the media input editors and media interpreters.

All system modules are separate processes, major modules acting as clients and/or servers on separate machines in the network.

MMIS-2 was prototyped on Sun workstations in SunView and implemented in a mixture of C++ and Prolog. Prolog was used as the implementation vehicle for the Query Subsystem Prolog tightly coupled to a Binary Relationship Model engine, a bulk tuple store specifically aimed at the storage and fast retrieval of knowledge representation structures such as semantic nets. The Large Object Server was implemented using a relational database, INGRES, which was later replaced with a simple B-tree indexing system.

Data Model

MMIS took the view that it is difficult or impossible to describe the contents of an image at one time or to pre-define the attributes of an image. Descriptions for semantically meaningful scenes or new features now discernible in an image by new image feature recognition techniques, a change of domain, or a different user, should be added incrementally. Image attributes depend on the application,

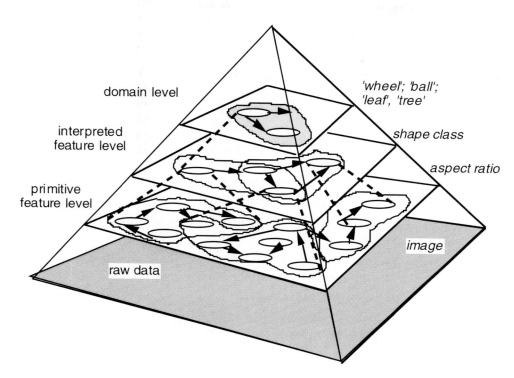

domain level

interpreted
feature level

primitive
feature level

raw data

'wheel'; 'ball';
'leaf', 'tree'

shape class

aspect ratio

image

Figure 12-4   Four levels of abstraction in the MMIS data model.

interpretation algorithms, queries, users, and the evolving knowledge base. The
schema must be descriptive, or permit instance level additions to the attribute
set [29] rather than entirely prescriptive as in the early prototypes. MMIS used a
multi-layered, semantic net, shown schematically in Fig. 12–4 to cater for the
incremental addition of descriptions of images.

The aim was to progressively refine low-level feature data to provide more
user-oriented semantic data. Low-level data should never be discarded because it
is impossible to predict at which levels users will wish to query and because low-
level data may be used to infer other data in the light of future knowledge or
image interpretation algorithms. Low-level primitives are clustered together to
represent higher-level concepts; the same primitives may appear in many clusters and contribute to many more abstract concepts. The four layer "pyramid" of
abstractions is similar to that proposed by Grosky [20].

Because of the dynamic nature of the schema, new attributes need to be
made known to users in order to ask queries and browse the database.

Sophisticated schema evolution and meta-data retrieval is required in such dynamic systems. The question is "What can I ask?"

Relationships are spatial, compositional or semantic. The relationships between the layers could be mapped manually but textual attribution requires complete user input, whereas automatic or semi-automatic feature extraction (notably in text and images) can be used as a basis for semantic descriptions. MMIS used domain knowledge to automatically relate image objects to domain objects, and to derive image objects from image fragments. Its chief approach was by classifying image objects. This approach can be used on media-specific but domain-independent information sources where no link has been made to any application domain semantics.

Each image is characterized by:

- raw image with an assigned unique identifier;
- registration attributes such as scan date, interpretation date, compression technique, etc.;
- a set of <feature attribute-similarity score> pairs for the whole image. Features include: height, width, blot count, and image class;
- a set of blots derived from the image;
- a set of relative structural and spatial relationships between the blots, represented as 4-tuple {<$blot_i$, relationship, $blot_j$, $score_i$>, ..};
- a set of relative structural, spatial relationships between a blot and the image represented as 3-tuple {<$blot_i$, relationship, $score_i$>, ..}.

Each blot is characterized by:

- a unique identifier;
- a set of <feature attribute-similarity score> pairs for the blot. The main primitive features are: area and perimeter length, circularity, upright bounding box, longest chord, true bounding box, length, width, aspect ratio, convex hull and hull area, transparency and irregularity [24]. Other features are inferred, e.g., "bounding box overlaps";
- shape, texture and color classifications.[3] Each classification is a set of <class-score > pairs where the score represents the degree of certainty of membership of the class.

Confidence level *scores* for image and blot attributes are used as part of the similarity measure for retrieval. Every image attribute has an associated score in the range [0..1] where 1 represents absolutely certainty. Relative spatial and image/blot classification are derived and imprecise, and hence can have a degree

---

[3] Only shape classification was implemented in MMIS-2.

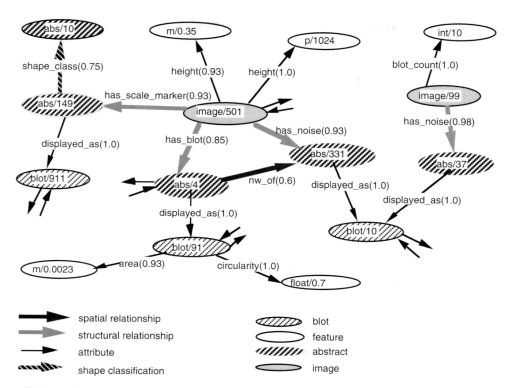

Figure 12–5   Part of an image's semantic net. The net shows two images, the first with at least one blot (leaf) and a piece of noise. Images and blots have spatial relationships ("nw_of"), structural relationships ("has_blot") and attributes ("circularity").

of fuzziness reflected by the score; all other attributes have a value 1. The similarity between attribute-score pairs for a set of f features describing blots, images and spatial characteristics is calculated as:

$$dis(q, t) = weight|(tattrvalue \times qscore) - (tattrvalue \times tscore)|$$

$$sim(Q, T) = 1 - \sum_{i=1}^{f} dis(q_f, t_f)$$

The above model is represented as a multi-layered semantic net; an example fragment of the semantic network is shown in Fig. 12–5.

Nodes represent features, blots and images, as well as an "abstract node" which allows interpreted instances to be shared by different contexts. For example, an image could appear in two documents—we would then have two abstract nodes referring to the image, one to represent its occurrence in the first docu-ment and the other to represent its occurrence in the second; we could then gather two separate bodies of data about the image, specific to each context. At a higher semantic level nodes represent semantic concepts. Arcs represent struc-tural and spatial relationships and attributes. Feature value nodes are not allowed to have further attributes or structural relationships to abstract nodes.

Nodes are typed as interpreted items (e.g. "image" or "text") or values (e.g., "pixels" or "integer"). Values have a notion of units (in SI notation) allowing an attribute to have several representations in different units. All arcs are labeled with an atom (a simple name), with interpreted items or with values.

Content Similarity Retrieval

The similarity measures used by MMIS are the classification of the object or its sub-parts and the structural relationships of the image's objects—i.e. the objects in the image have a similar shape/texture/color and/or are positioned with simi-lar spatial relationships.

Image Object Classifications

The image interpretation in MMIS was straightforward; the most interesting aspect is the automatic classification of image blots. This provides users with a powerful notion of "similarity" and can be used as a key for sketch-based and example-based retrieval. Each blot can be assigned to one or more shape, tex-ture, or color classes—the assignment is made according to the values of any of its attributes which in some way contribute to the notion of the class type. Shape class had indicator attributes: area, transparency, aspect ratio, irregularity, length of perimeter, circularity, and number of maxima and minima. Indicator attributes are partially domain-specific. Classes are hierarchical, branching on discriminating attribute-values. So, for instance, class 1 might be a general class containing all blots; class 1 includes all blots in classes 2, 3, and 4; class 2 is pop-ulated mainly by blots which have sub-blots and contains classes 5, 6, 7, and 8; class 3 represents highly convex blots, and so on. Fig. 12–6 gives a simple exam-ple of a shape class of leaf shapes:

The mechanisms used for extracting classes automatically are described in detail in [24]. As a simplification, consider the graph shown in Fig. 12–7.

Blots are plotted in a two-dimensional space described by the attributes "transparency" and "circularity." A large number of blots are selected to use as training data, and each is plotted in this manner. The classification tool then searches the training data for "clusters" of blots in the attribute space, assigning an arbitrary unique number to each. Once the classes have been selected, the average position—or "centroid"—is calculated for each one. When a new blot is presented to the system, it can be assigned to a class (or more than one for over-lapping or hierarchical classes). This idea is extended to an n-dimensional attribute space (5 attributes are used to classify the notion of shape). Classes can

Figure 12-6   A simple shape class.

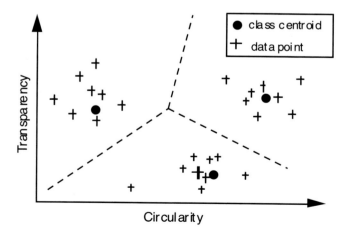

Figure 12-7   A simple class graph.

be annotated with a semantic "real-world" object, so that the class characterizes that world object, so we can ask for "blots that are like oak leaves."

Classification Scores

Each blot's classification is given a *score,* or *confidence level*, based on the Euclidean distance of the blot from the class centroid, and normalized to be in the range [0..1], calculated in the manner described in the section Data Model on page 378. MMIS uses this score as a class similarity. This allows us to specify that some value or relationship is based on an estimate—1.0 stands for "this fact is certain" and 0.0 stands for "certainly not the case." Classes have *fuzzy boundaries* so that each blot has a degree of membership of several classes and queries. Similarity between the set of n classifications of one blot Q with another, T, can be calculated by using a classical vector similarity coefficient:

$$\frac{\displaystyle\sum_{i=1}^{n} (qscore_i \times tscore_i)}{\sqrt{\sum (qscore)^2 \times \sum (tscore)^2}}$$

Classes and classification scores provide a means of retrieving blots and their associated images. Queries such as:

"retrieve blots that fall in class X, score >= 0.25 and class Y, score >= 0.75"

are possible. Informally, this means "retrieve blots that are somewhat similar to blots in X and very similar to blots in Y." The scores are also used for ranking the results of queries—an image with a blot in class Y with a score 0.9 ranks higher than one with a score 0.85.

Classification scores are used as similarity measures between two blots:

- **directly**, as the score is a distance measure representing an average and standard deviation from an shape centroid, e.g., "Find all the other blots that are in the same shape class as blot X."
- **by coupling with a threshold range** so the blots are within the same shape class given a margin, e.g. "Find all the other blots that are in the same shape class as blot X with the same score given a ±0.1 interval." This means that if blot X is on the edge of the shape class, get other blots on the edge, not the ones that are closest to the centroid in the shape class.

An image presented as an example is processed, the blots shape classified and the database searched for blots that fall within the same classification.

Spatial Relationship Scores

Compass sectors can be used to describe positional relationships, for example, on the basis of hard boundaries between sectors. Such a scheme means that if the bearing, b, between two blots (B1, B2) = 22.5 degrees then B1 is considered to be south west of B2, but if b = 22.499999 degrees then B1 is south of B2 when there is clearly little difference. Instead inexact (or fuzzy) relationships are used. An alternative model is the degree of overlap of true bounding boxes: "Blot X's true bounding box overlaps 11 percent of the true bounding box of blot Y."

Query Languages and User Interface

Queries can be formulated by expressions on data types, structure and content. In addition queries can be expressed upon the instance of an image or blot: "what do we know about this image." Because the contents are held as an evolving semantic net the images' meta-data attributes themselves can be queried and need to be. For example "what image attributes are stored" and "what characterizes this class." The user interface supports:

Direct use of attributes   The user specifies the desired attributes of the image/blot by:

- Prolog expressions of the actual values; this is not user-friendly but accurate;
- Shape classes from a palette of prototypes for visual query construction, an interface on top of the Prolog expressions.

The query specifies the interpreted blots and attribute values to be retrieved along with details of how to rank the results. A ranking score is created using classification and spatial scores and the weighted Euclidean distance from the query values or a class centroid. All features, not just shape classification or spatial relationships, can be directly referenced by the user in a query, and can have distance functions ascribed to them by the user. The distance functions were really only investigated for shape and relative spatial relationships—they usually need to be a function of an average and a standard deviation, or some sort of probability function. Query sub-clauses can be weighted and composite query expressions are catered for.

Query by example   By choosing an image or a blot object (held separately from the image) from a cached library, the blots classified and the database can be searched for blots that fall within the same shape classification or spatial relationship within a threshold range for the confidence scores provided by the user.

Results and Query Refinement

Results are returned as ranked lists of items. The ranking represents the closeness of the whole result to the query and is calculated by combining the various clause weightings, similarity measures and distances as a user- or application-specific function. Results are not necessarily images, they can be structured ranked lists of: images, blot shape outlines, image fragments, instance identifiers and type, texts, statistics, and lists of any of the above. Any part of this ranked list which represents an interpreted item can be retrieved on demand, postponing full image presentation and greatly increasing system performance. The retrieved lists can be structured and contain other lists so that arbitrary networks of items can be built by the query—any item in a list which is also a list can be expanded. Results are presented as domain specific icons, labels or thumbnail sketches. Query results can be named, cached for the session or stored in the database and reused in further queries. The query expression, session and user are stored with the result list. Caches are session-specific though shared caches were contemplated. Arbitrary hypermedia-style links between items in the system are supported, including annotation labels on links, held separately from the links relating the deduced results of interpretation.

12.4   QBIC: Query by Image Content

IBM's QBIC (Query By Image Content) project [3], [14], [15] is perhaps the most fully developed prototype for images. The emphasis is on querying large image databases using image content for the queries. The prototype is written in X/ Motif and C running on RS/6000s, with an initial test database of over 1000 images and 2000 objects populated from commercially available photo clip-art images. The QBIC project team have taken many ideas from other prototypes and made them practical and robust. QBIC is now part of IBM's Ultimedia Manager [41], which combines image-feature retrieval with traditional database structured data stored in a DB2 relational database with all the attendant database services. It is also part of IBM's Digital Library.

QBIC's first major characteristic is its recognition of the partnership between the human and the machine, and its intention to be an interactive tool working in a dialogue with the user. The emphasis is on semiautomated tools, though recent work has developed some more fully automated object recognition tools. The developers believe that machines are good at quantitative feature detection and that people are good at identifying objects and attaching semantic meaning to those objects or images. QBIC aims to act as an "information filter" to reduce the search space, with the user interactively discarding false hits and refining queries. Searches are expected to be approximate without exact matches.

Secondly, there is no characteristic application domain. Images are general and arbitrary, with scenes of people, landscapes, buildings, animals etc. Semantics are added by the user in the object recognition stage of image population— there is no attempt to automatically assign semantic characteristics.

QBIC emphasizes the retrieval of images on a number of image content descriptors, not just one. The descriptors currently are color, texture, shape, and relative location of image objects and regions, as well as their spatial layout.

Data Model

The data model is simple. Still images and associated descriptive text are catered for and objects are not represented compositionally. QBIC has two main data types (color) images (or "scenes"), and objects, which are part of a scene, e.g. a person, an apple, etc. Objects do not have to relate to world "objects", for example a piece of outlined texture is an object. A scene can have an arbitrary number of objects, determined by an outline that is generated manually or semi-automatically (see below). Global features are attributed to the whole image and image objects have local features.

Architecture

The QBIC architecture is a modular framework. The extensible relational database Starburst holds image registration details, object/image identifiers and the textual semantic descriptors, while features are stored in flat files. Within QBIC itself no attention has been paid to conventional database services, as it is presumed that QBIC will form part of a larger information management product. QBIC splits its operations into 3 major processes:

>   **Database population**. An image, a thumbnail and registration data are input. An arbitrary number of image objects (or elements) are identified by the user using semiautomatic tools for assistance. Textual descriptions or keywords can be added to the image object or the whole image: this is the only connection of the image/objects to any application semantics.

>   **Feature calculation** A compute-intensive one-off batch process that computes the local features for the objects identified in the previous stage, and global features for the full image. The features, stored for later use by queries, include color, texture, shape, location, and sketch.

>   **Image query** Queries are created by visual example of features, objects, images, sketches, and painting. The process is interactive; the user navigates and refines the queries until satisfied with the results. All queries on features are approximate similarity queries.

Content Similarity Retrieval

Image objects are not classified automatically using hardcoded procedures. The QBIC team believe that automatic object identification methods are not sufficiently advanced or robust enough, so generally opt for semiautomatic methods.

Figure 12-8   Interactive outlining with the snake tool.[*]

[*] With permission of the International Society for Optical Engineering (1995), Fig.5 in [3].

The user identifies areas and significant edges, and each object becomes a binary mask. Objects can overlap and be multiple disconnected components (e.g., the polka dots on a dress).

Semi-Automatic Object Identification

An interesting aspect of QBIC is the semi-automatic object identification called interactive outlining. The user provides some starting information, a point for example, and guides image analysis techniques that compute the outline by taking this cue and others. Two techniques used are:

> **Snakes**. The user enters an approximate outline using conventional drawing tools, and the method interactively adjusts the outline using the outline curvature and total image edge strength along the outline. The effect is that the approximate outline, perhaps created by a conventional polygon drawing tool, is "shrink wrapped" around the object. Fig. 12–8 gives an example.

> **Floodfill**. Given an initial point specified by the user, all the adjacent pixels with a specified color distance are included. The perimeter of points becomes the object boundary. This is a quick and effective object identification technique for uniform objects against shape backgrounds. Plates 8 and 9 give an example.[4]

There are tuning panels for floodfill, snake and zoom control, as well as conventional drawing tools.

---

[4] With permission of the Institute of Electrical Engineers (1995), Figs 3, 8, & 9 in [15].

Automatic Object Identification

Automatic techniques attempted by QBIC are confined to partition-based and region-based "Query-by-painting" for color. Painting is provided using two methods:

Partition-based The image is partitioned into a fixed grid superimposed on the image. The score for each image against the query image is computed by averaging scores for each grid element.

Region-based Instead of using a grid, images are approximately segmented into a hierarchical set of colored rectangles, and matching is based on these sets. This proves to be the more robust technique.

All object extraction is feature based, not model based, and there is no attempt to infer world objects. Variations include "halos" around each drawn query object so that the search includes a term to score the area surrounding each object, looking for contrasting colors (e.g. a blue rectangle matches a blue rectangle on a non-blue background rather than a solid blue image), and "floating objects" in which objects are specified by their color but not localized by their absolute or relative position in the query drawing.

Image Features

Features are computed globally for the whole image and locally for objects. The images are heterogeneous, so techniques that assume image homogeneity, particularly in texture extraction, are inapplicable. Features and algorithms are described in detail in [3], [14], [13], [35].

Colors The average (R,G,B) and Munsell coordinates, plus a k element histogram. Colors are quantized to a space of k levels. The result is a normalized color histogram for both images and objects.

Texture A three-dimensional space of coarseness (scale of texture), contrast (vividness of pattern), and directionality (favored, e.g., grass, or isotropic, e.g., smooth).

Shape All shapes are assumed to be non-occluded and planar so that each can be represented as a binary image. Shape is the hardest feature to extract and characterize; currently heuristics such as area, circularity, eccentricity, major axis, and a set of algebraic moments are used. Unlike MMIS, shapes are not classified.

Scene Sketch QBIC uses the rough sketch techniques of ART MUSEUM [28] described in Section 12.5. A reduced resolution edge-map of each image forms an "image abstraction" on which a retrieval by rough sketch can be performed.

Location: normalized (x,y) coordinates of an object centroid within its image. The location distance measure is a two-dimensional

Euclidean distance (so the position is relative to the overall image).

Similarity Measures Similarity measures (also called "scores") are (user-adjustable) weighted Euclidean distances, usually weighted by inverse variances across samples in the database. As in MMIS, "scores" range from 0 to 1, where 0 represents no similarity and 1 represents perfect similarity. Distance functions are inverse scores, which vary with different applications. Recent work has dealt with non-Euclidean distance measures [14].

> **Color** The distance between a query object and a database object for average color and a distribution histogram of colors (red and blue objects matches other red and blue objects better than to purple objects). Normalized color histograms are matched so that differences in amounts of any color (e.g., a shade of red) and difference between different similar colors (e.g., red and orange) are accounted for.
>
> **Texture** Weighted Euclidean distance in 3-D texture space for each feature.
>
> **Shape** Weighted Euclidean distance in n-d space for each feature. Any subset of features can be selected which are sensitive/insensitive to size and orientation. Moments turn out to be poor differentiators of shape, so experiments in curvature and turning angles are being made.
>
> **Scene Sketch** The query object is a rough set of dominant edges sketched by the user, which is compared to the automatically extracted "image abstraction." Scores are computed by block partitioning the image abstractions and the target sketch and correlating each block, summing the block scores. The technique is resilient to some spatial warping.

Queries and User Interface

QBIC has a sophisticated and comprehensive interactive query interface and supports the following interchangeable modes:

Query by example Choose an image or object already displayed (as the result of a query or from a libraries of useful images) and ask for images/objects similar to the selected one.

Direct query The user specifies the desired color/shape/texture/sketch directly by combining:

> **Feature palettes or pickers** for the full image or image objects. Features can be picked and used individually or in weighted com-

binations. Color uses sliders and color patches, textures are synthetically generated, and shapes use either a blackboard or a set of pre-defined shapes. Plates 10 and 11 give an example of a query by shape that also shows a histogram color palette. Requests such as x percent of color A and y percent of color B are supported by the color picker and have been found to be useful, for example 50 percent blue and 20 percent yellow returns beach scenes.

Query by sketch for the full image. The user roughly sketches the shapes they wish to retrieve (see Plates 10–13).

Query-by-painting for the full image. The user paints a simplified color image which is used as the query specification. Images with similar colors in the same spatial arrangement are retrieved. This is the counterpart to query-by-sketch for shapes.

Results and Query Refinement   Results are sets of ranked thumbnail images that may be browsed, the maximum number of returns is set by the user (Plates 10 to 13). Whole images are returned rather than partial images or encoded data representing objects (as in MMIS). Returned hits are used in subsequent "queries-by-example," and may: be displayed full scale; have image operations performed on them; form the basis for future queries; be pasted into documents; etc. To help the query refinement process, a similarity curve which plots similarity values against order of retrieval is produced. The user is able to see the turning point where similarity falls off and can use this to refine the queries.

12.5   Art Museum

The ART MUSEUM project is an experimental database system for an electronic gallery dating from 1989 [28], [22]. Along with an associated project TRADEMARK, its major contribution to image databases is in visual interaction and intelligent content based retrieval for the whole image by sketch and example through Query by Visual Example (QVE). In addition ART MUSEUM attempts to link the user-subjective descriptions of images with image features through Query By subjective Descriptions (QBD). The chosen domain is of color landscape and portrait paintings. Around 200 images form the initial test set. This work has been incorporated into QBIC.

Data Model

ART MUSEUM caters for still color images. It does not seem to cater to image objects, only the whole image. The system is implemented using a conventional relational database to hold the image name and ID, feature spaces, and presumably could also hold textual descriptions, registration, and world data. The image data model is simple in that image objects are not identified.

Content-Based Similarity Retrieval

The strength of ART MUSEUM's contribution lies in its retrieval by sketch and visual example. The Query by Visual Example is composed of two stages:

1. Adaptive Image Abstraction   A reduced resolution edge map of each image automatically creates an image abstraction. This abstraction forms a pictorial index of the global features of the image describing the outline composition. The chief feature used for edge detection is color. Gradations of color may cause a noisy pattern on the refined edge image, so thinning and shrinking procedures are used to sharpen up the abstraction. The abstract images need to be normalized, small enough for storage/computation purposes but expressive enough for effective differentiation.

2. Flexible Pattern Matching   The presentation of a rough sketch by the user is considered to be good enough to retrieve image instances. The query templates presented can either be:

- **Sketches**: both well drawn and rough, including partial, shifted, or deformed.;
- **Examples**: a monochrome photo, a xerox copy or a color fair copy;
- **Compositions**: a domain specific form as the general composition for a painting is one of the major factors in the viewer's visual impression, for example, a horizontal line gives a stable feeling to the painting [22].

The similarity between sketch and images is evaluated by producing a reduced resolution edge map of each sketch using line segments to produce a linear sketch. Matching sketches requires compensation for deformities, shifted positioning, and white space (where white space can mean "nothing there" or "don't care"). To compensate, local correlations, as well as global, are part of the matching process between the image abstraction and the linear sketch.

Similarity Measures and Ranking   To evaluate the QVE results and rank the candidates in order the system uses:

> **global correlation**: the sum of all the local correlations between the abstract image and a linear sketch; this is used to rank the abstract images into descending order;

> **deviation**: the relative matching score between individual full color images and the visual example in the normalized scale. Each image deviation is calculated against the average global correlation and average deviation. The higher the deviation value the closer the similarity.

Plates 12 and 13 in QBIC give an example of sketch retrieval by rough sketch. Kato [28] suggests that similarity retrieval can be used for clustering paintings based on their composition and hence classify them and partition the database. Browsing through navigation could be guided by similarity measures on the image composition, so that similar paintings are linked automatically rather than prescribed by manually defined links.

Query by Subjective Descriptions (QBD)

QBD goes a stage further than QVE in that it attempts to capture user-specific subjective descriptions ascribed to images. Whereas QVE operates on graphic features, QBD attempts to relate subjective keywords with the pictorial features, capturing the user's impressions. As visual impressions differ, similarity must be evaluated on the user's criterion of similarity and must be learned for each user. Hence the QBD system has two related models: an image model and a user model. In order to make this approach viable we need to avoid the laborious task of associating keywords with each image. We also need to address the fact that the keyword thesaurus would have no direct relationship with the pictorial data. ART MUSEUM deals with this by attempting to characterize a keyword by image features (the pictorial index of QVE) in a training set and thereby auto-matically attribute the keyword with the feature vector. For each image in the learning set two feature spaces are extracted: the graphic feature (GF) space and the subjective feature (SF) space which is a weighted vector of predefined adjec-tives. The user classifies the images into several discrete clusters. These two spaces are combined into the Unified Feature space which relates the keywords to the characterizing graphics. Hence the user can ask for "soft" images. The approach works in reverse, as words can be suggested based on the feature val-ues. In the TRADEMARK system there were no keywords, instead there is an attempt to capture by training and discriminate analysis a user-classified subjec-tive feature space as well as a GF for a library of graphical trademarks. The results of GF similarity and SF similarity showed some variations. The tech-nique of associating features with a semantic concept or keyword is similar to the classification approach used in MMIS.

12.6   VIMSYS

The major contribution of VIMSYS (Visual Information Management System) [21] is in data modeling for images, and incremental, model-directed query for-mulation. The goal of the project is to create an information management system for retrieving images and image parts by similarity-based queries but with an emphasis on the semantics of the information in the image rather than image interpretation. Images have headers in a prescribed format and a textual descriptor field. VIMSYS, part of the InfoScope project, has been used by Xenomania [4] for face management and retrieval. The emphasis on semantics means that VIMSYS has been developed within the context of applications, including SAR images of Arctic ice floes.

Data Model

VIMSYS establishes relationships between semantic (non-computable) attributes of images and computable features of those attributes, treating image features as independent entities organized in the rich compositional hierarchy suggested in the section Data Models and Meta Image Representation on page 368. The meta-image model is held in an Object-Attribute-Relationship (OAR) representation, similar to MMIS's semantic net. All objects have attributes and methods, relations may be spatial, functional or semantic, and the model includes declarative constraints. Four layers, one more than MMIS, represent different levels of semantic interpretation:

- *Image Representations and relations* (IR), representing the actual image data and upon which all the objects are constructed. The representation is an abstract data type or "multivalued function" for each image object, which can have more than one representation. Representations are compositional.

- *Image Objects and relations* (IO), are images, image features (e.g., texture, color, line, region) and feature organization extracted from the image, organized through collection, generalization and attribution relationships, e.g., `image_set`. Set and sequence-like operations, and others, are possible on both the whole image and their decompositions (e.g., regions). Two existing features can create a third composite feature. Relationship networks include arrangement and containment, with defined necessary conditions, e.g., adjacency. Features are divided into three categories: manually user-specified, automatically derived, and not calculated (hence lazily evaluated on demand). Approximate locations of objects with respect to the overall image and relative locations of image objects with respect to one another are represented using R+ trees, although other techniques are under investigation.

- *Domain Objects and relations* (DO), representing the semantic interpretation of the image objects. Any object may be a subclass of one or more objects in the Image Object plane, `ice_image_set` is a subclass of `image_set`; `open_water` (a semantic feature) inherits from `surface_roughness` and `color` [21].

- *Domain events and relations* (DE) associating domain objects with each other to capture semantic spatial and temporal relationships. An event is an ensemble of features, constraints, and methods collected over a sequence of images. This is an extra layer to the MMIS one.

The relationships between the layers are mapped by the users. Each image instance has multiplane, multithreaded access to each image instance through any related object instance. Transformational and computable functions are catered to, so not all relationships need to be pre-computed. A consequence of this rich model is that high-level semantic concepts are translatable to content-based queries using the corresponding image data, so queries on object similarity can be expressed at a semantic level rather than an image feature level.

Architecture

The architecture is a fairly conventional one, similar to that of MMIS, with a heavy reliance on domain knowledge. The major system components are:

Insertion module: for inserting and evaluating images, computing features and manually (mostly) or automatically relating to domain objects.

Image Database: for storing the information about instances of objects, features, attributes and statistics in a relational, and later an object-relational, DBMS. A *representation scheme library* maintains the available image representations and transformations to translate image objects to their corresponding representation: different applications can use the same objects and change the characteristics that are important to them by altering the internal representation without altering any other part of the system.

Query module: the emphasis is on interactivity, and queries may be presented as user-specified or based on the results of previous queries.

Knowledge Module: maintains the domain-specific and metadata information in the OAR data model, and similarity functions. It is used at every step of the system, driving feature recognition, relating features to domain objects, driving query specification, determining the access path for a query and controlling the navigation of image objects.

Content Similarity Matching

Similarity-based queries are based on exemplar image instances with incompletely specified feature attributes. For single-valued attributes, threshold ranges are set by user-manipulated palettes; for set-values (e.g., ice-class regions) sets have to be created by some domain-specific classification or simple

enumeration, where each member of the set is weighted by the user. The similarity measure is the threshold plus a distance from norm, which can be a weighted
averaged, a Euclidean norm, or a city block distance.

A user confidence value is used when assigning values to features: more
certain less tolerance; less certain more tolerance—this is similar to the weight-
ing of clauses used in MMIS. Xenomania used a static rating of importance for
the feature, a users confidence level, an initial tolerance value, a final tolerance
value, and a delta function representing the deviation of two images with respect
to the feature. Similarity is the normalized difference.

The user chooses the attributes that are to be used for indexing and
retrieval, or composes a new one; feature extraction methods are invoked on the
scanned input image and a query class of feature and attribute clusters is created. Retrieved images are cached in a query history, containing the pre-computed entities on all four planes so they can be used as examples later in the
session. The user can specify feature values in terms of data retrieved previously
using relative terms such as "wider" or "darker" thus systematically refining feature descriptions.

Querying and User Interface

VIMSYS places great emphasis on the knowledge of the interactive user in addition to the pre-specified domain knowledge, actively supporting the imprecision
prevalent in formulating the query. The user does not explicitly specify a complete selection operation in one statement, but develops the query incrementally.
The task is to direct the user to formulate the selection as precisely as possible,
using a graphical (forms-based) user interface, the knowledge module (KM) to
direct the user's refinements, and the data dictionary (DD) of database statistics.
Queries can be specified in two ways:

1. The user is recursively guided down a decision tree by the KM, selecting first
   the domain of interest (e.g., ice floes), then an aspect of interest in the domain
   (e.g. motion) and then features of interest and their attributes (e.g., regions >
   200 sq km). The result is rewritten in terms of objects in the image object
   plane. Descriptive values such as "wide" and "dark" can be mapped to actual
   feature values. Features can be specified with respect to examples held in the
   query history.

2. The OAR diagram is available for query formulation, so objects, relations and
   access paths can be selected. The result is a well-formed path expression to
   reduce the effort to create an efficient access pathway from an ill-specified
   query.

The user can also specify an attribute not defined within the database by
composing the attribute using lower level features such as text or icons. Icons are
feature or image based—miniaturized bitmaps of an image retrieved for brows-

ing. Parts of the icon are marked with the location of features used to retrieve it. Attributes are prioritized by a domain expert to direct the query manager.

The benefits of a tight coupling with the user are the support of feedback from users on unsuccessful matches thereby altering feature-values that cause incorrect results, and enabling query modification to retrieve correct results and the assignment of confidence levels to adjust the weightings in the query clauses. Additional semantic data only known to the user can be used to narrow the search space, such as sex or age. The disadvantage is that the system is not autonomous.

12.7   Remarks and Other Prototypes

The four prototypes illustrate a number of aspects. MMIS and VIMSYS have sophisticated data models that include semantic annotation of images and world semantics, represented by semantic nets or variants, and image objects composed of primitive features. They differ in that MMIS attempts similarity-based content addressability via object classification and the automatic annotation of classes with world concepts, whereas VIMSYS leaves this to the user. In both, considerable reliance is made on the knowledge base which is domain driven and hence domain specific.

At the other extreme, QBIC does not have a sophisticated data model and clearly arises from the image processing community rather than the database community. QBIC does not attempt to represent semantic world or annotation data; instead it concentrates on the comprehensive coverage of image modeling and image object features and the use of similarity measures and indexing techniques. Its emphasis is on retrieval methods based on similarity matching, high-dimensional indexing, query-by-image example, or user-drawn image and automatic and semiautomatic database population. By concentrating on image-only data QBIC is domain independent.

ART MUSEUM sits between the extremes by linking images to domain objects in its attempt to characterize global image features with subjective labels. ART MUSEUM's chief strengths are in its innovative image abstraction and similarity retrieval for query-by-example and sketch, adopted by QBIC and others; however it lacks a principled data model and only deals with whole images. None of the prototypes convincingly support the notion of operations as first class objects.

All the prototypes cover the searching and retrieval of images and image objects to some degree, most concentrating on CBR. All support the ranking of results. The user interface tools and query language in MMIS are appropriate for experts and testing but are not appropriate for end-users, whereas QBIC has a comprehensive user interface, with a collection of query formulation and result presentation tools. VIMSYS uses its elaborate model to guide the querying process in partnership with the user. VIMSYS and MMIS support the expression of similarity measure thresholds in queries and only MMIS appears to attempt multi-clause weightings.

Architecturally, both MMIS and VIMSYS have generic module architectures for a multimedia database, with an emphasis on a "framework" into which a variety of image processing and indexing techniques can be slotted or co-exist, depending on their effectiveness and appropriateness for particular images or domains. QBIC also has this framework approach, but is proposed as part of a larger system rather than being a full multimedia information system itself.

None of these prototypes address issues of distribution, storage, performance, transaction management or resilience. QBIC technology is incorporated in a commercial database Ultimedia where DB2 supports the conventional aspects of data management. Both VIMSYS and QBIC have recently been extended to cater for video [26], [15]. A couple of other interesting image prototypes are discussed below.

PICQUERY+, PICDMS, and KMeD

The PICQUERY+ language and underlying PICDMS (Pictorial Data Management System) have been developed by UCLA primarily for a medical multimedia distributed database system called KMeD [11], [6]. KMeD places a layer on top of a federated collection of multimedia databases. Each database is maintained separately and their heterogeneity is hidden by an unifying PICQUERY+ language interface. KMeD is implemented using Smalltalk for the user interface, Gemstone and Sybase for data storage and C++ for the visualization and image processing routines.

The overall data model appears to link images and features with domain objects and events, though how is unclear. The data model has two interesting aspects:

- A temporal "evolutionary" object-oriented model to support conventional association and inheritance relationships and queries involving the life-span, fusion, and fission of objects and/or events, which is a particularly requirement for medical applications. This caters for world-only and annotation data, and is quite elaborate.
- A hierarchical stacked-image model for image attributes where the stack consists of two-dimensional variables registered to the same gridded coordinate system. Multiple stacks of images can provide additional temporal, spectural and spatial information: each layer of the stack stores different image information. A new image is added as a new attribute in the data record, not a new instance so the schema can evolve dynamically. The image stack caters to the images-only data.

The query process is interactive and iterative. Chu [12] calls this "co-operative query answering." Query refinement and reformulation provides approximate, summary and conceptual answers to queries within a certain "semantic distance" (domain-specific and user-defined). Information conceptually related to but not explicitly asked for is provided as part of the solution. Domain knowledge is represented in abstract type hierarchies; if no answer is available to a query, key concepts are relaxed using the generalization and association relations.

PICQUERY+ encourages the use of application-specific menu-icon interfaces, and expects heavy tailoring to the application domain for its operators, fuzzy values, and interface. The strengths of the project overall are in the user interface and language and in the evolutionary and temporal data model. There is comparatively little information on the similarity retrieval measures and the content retrieval algorithms, and much of the power of PICQUERY+ depends on its tailorability to an application domain, so that modeling world data and annotation data is important and well catered to. The image stack models images-only data.

Active Media Object Stores (AMOS)

The Active Media Object Stores (AMOS) project [39] extends the VODAK OODBMS and its modeling language VML with distributed multimedia capabilities and built-in data types with extensions to support timing, synchronization, real time continuous data transport, and reactive adaptive play-out management [42]. AMOS is capable of modeling a sophisticated level of metainformation and multimedia presentations through the VODAK object model. The prototype has a strong architectural approach, emphasizing quality of service, playback, and continuous storage management. In keeping with a "document" emphasis in the data model, AMOS has been integrated with an information retrieval system INQUERY. AMOS is viewed as an application-independent MMDBMS platform, so the authors claim that the metamodeling capabilities and the incorporation of behavior in the object model should support content-based retrieval, but the project itself does not develop this aspect. The prototype has been used in a number of sample applications including MuSE, a hypermedia system engineering application.

Other Image Database Prototypes

Woelk *et al.* [43] used the OODBMS ORION to develop a multimedia DBMS with a composite data model, presentation and storage but without any attention to synchronization, presentation control or content-based retrieval. PICTION [40] uses the interaction of linguistic and photographic information in an integrated text/image database. Speech and text descriptions of pictures (e.g., captions for newspapers pictures) are used to drive the image interpretation and image retrieval processes: objects and regions mentioned in the text are hunted for in the image, and annotated. Images matching natural language queries are ranked for presentation to the user. Content-based retrieval uses four sources of similarity: text-based (using natural language processing), word-based, image-based semantic knowledge (derived by image interpretation), and image similarity (image-only methods). CORE [44] and MORE [45] are prototypes with a similar approach to domain knowledge representation, classification and architecture as MMIS and VIMSYS.

From an historical perspective, a couple of image prototypes have been influential. REDI/IMAID [8] was a relational database system interfaced with an image analysis system, manipulating satellite images of cities. It was one of the first to use Query by Pictorial Example as a retrieval language based upon QBE. The image extraction concerned points and segments, representing roads and cities, which were stored as predefined attributes in relations, and annotated with names by the users; the images themselves were stored as pixel matrices outside the database. Only metadata in the relations was queryable by a combination of conventional relational operations with image-based operations. The data model was simple and quite domain specific but some similarity retrieval was possible by direct bounded comparisons of values in relations derived from a sketch. Reference [8] gives a useful summary of picture query languages of the late 1970s, all of which were based on the relational model. Others include GRIM-DBMS [38], which included a graphically based Query By Visual Example for CAD with a well defined grammar.

12.8   Summary

In this chapter we hope to have given a taste of the many image database prototypes that have been, and continue to be, developed. We are able to make some general observations. Work has tended to concentrate on image feature extraction and low level visual representation and similarity measures; more work is needed to link image-only features with world semantics, including automatic and semi-automatic object extraction. However, domain experts are often the best annotation device, and should be supported by sophisticated "keyword" or concept annotation environments [19]. Systems should support multiple subjective interpretations and similarity judgements, particularly when the same images will be shared and reinterpreted for different applications by different users in different time frames—ART MUSEUM can be seen as an early attempt in this direction. The image prototypes discussed here pay attention to image metadata to varying degrees but have tended to be media and application specific. In the future we hope to see more general techniques to support the integration and sharing of multimedia data [27]. Reuse should not be restricted to the images themselves but should extend to the methods and tools so that we move to general matching functions—none of the prototypes convincingly support the notion of operations as first-class objects.

Although relational DBMS have been the common platform for image prototypes, OODBMS are expected to feature more prominently in the future, in particular the hybrid object-relational systems. Most prototypes have paid scant attention to conventional database and presentation services such as transaction management, integrity, and integration with multiple search modes such as content-based retrieval with SQL and keywords—in general the content-based retrieval needs to be considered as only part of a toolkit for image information management. This will become more common as prototype work is incorporated in commercial software such as QBIC in Ultimedia. Further work is required on efficient indexing and search techniques for multidimensional data, and performance and scalability in a distributed environment. A chief area of neglect is the user; systems have concentrated on low-level technical or architectural developments rather than user interaction and support with regard to annotation acquisition, querying, browsing and authoring, though VIMSYS has made progress in this area. These observations and others are discussed further in [18], [27].

Finally, most of the image prototypes outlined above are moving into the area of video, e.g., [15], [26]. This does not mean that image databases are a "closed" topic, rather that still images are considered to be a simpler form of the moving image or image sequence problem. It is hoped, however, that in the rush to jump on the video bandwagon that basic work on still image is not neglected.

Acknowledgments

The author would like to acknowledge all those who worked on the MMIS prototypes, in particular Michael O'Docherty for his invaluable help in Section 12.3 of this chapter, and Andreas Marr, Norman Paton, Ian Cottam, Phran Ryder, and Sean Bechhofer for their helpful and constructive comments. Thanks also to Myron Flickner and Wayne Niblack of IBM for their help with the QBIC images.

References

[1] *ACM SIGMOD Record,* Special Issue on Metadata for Digital Media, Vol. 23, No. 4, Dec 1994.

[2] *Communications of ACM,* Special Issue on Digital Libraries, Vol 38, No 4, Apr 1995.

[3] Ashley, J., Barber, R., Flickner, M., Hafner, J., Lee, D., Niblack, W., and Petkovic, D., "Automatic and semi-automatic methods for image annotation and retrieval in QBIC" in *Proceedings of Storage and Retrieval for Image and Video Databases III,* SPIE, Vol. 2420, pp. 24-35, Feb 1995.

[4] Bach, J., Paul, S., and Jain, R., "An interactive image management system for face information retrieval," *IEEE Trans. on Knowledge and Data Engineering,* Vol. 5, No. 4, Aug 1993.

[5] Besser, H., "Visual access to visual images: The UC Berkeley image database project," *Library Trends,* Vol. 38, No. 4, 1990, pp. 787–798.

[6] Cardenas, A.F., Ieong, I.T., Taira, R.K., Barker, R., and Breant, C.M., "The knowledge-based object-oriented PICQUERY+ language," *IEEE Trans. on Knowledge and Data Engineering,* Vol. 5, No. 4, Aug 1993, pp. 644–656.

[7] Chang, N.S. and Fu, K.S., "Query-by-Pictorial-Example," *IEEE Trans. on Software Engineering,* Vol. 6, No. 6, pp. 519–524, June 1980.

[8] Chang, N.S. and Fu, K.S., "Picture query languages for pictorial databases," *IEEE Computer,* Vol. 14, No. 11, Nov 1981, pp. 23–33.

[9] Chock, M., Cardenas, A.F., and Klinger, A., "Manipulating data structures in pictorial information systems," *IEEE Computer,* Vol. 14, No. 11,Nov 81, pp. 43-50.

[10] Christodoulakis, S., Theodoridou, M., Ho, F., Papa, M., and Pathria, A., "Multimedia document presentation, information extraction and document formation in MINOS: A model and a system," *ACM Trans. on Office Information Systems,* Vol. 4, No. 4, Oct 1986, pp. 345–383.

[11] Chu, W.W., Ieong, I.T., Taira, R.K., and Breant, C.M., "A temporal evolutionary object-oriented data model and its query language for medical image management," in *Proc. 18th VLDB Conference,* 1992, pp. 53–64.

[12] Chu, W.W. and Chen, Q., "Neighbourhood and associative query answering," *Journal of Intelligent Information Systems: Integrating Artificial Intelligence and Database Technologies,* Dec 1992.

[13] Equitz, W. and Niblack, W., "Retrieving images from a database using texture-algorithms from the QBIC system," *IBM RJ,* Vol. 9805, 1994.

[14] Faloutsos, C., Barber, R., Flickner, M., Hafner, J., Niblack, W., Petkovic, D., and Equitz, W., "Efficient and effective querying by image content" *Journal of Intelligent Information Systems,* Vol. 3, No. 3/4, July 1994, pp. 231–262; also *IBM RJ,* Vol. 9453.

[15] Flickner, M., Sawhney, H., Niblack, W., Ashley, J., Huang, Q., Dom, B., Gorkani, M., Hafner, J., Lee, D., Petkovic, D., Steele, D. and Yanker, P., "Query by image and video content: The QBIC System," *IEEE Computer,* Vol. 28, No. 9, Sep 1995, pp. 23–32.

[16] Goble, C.A., O'Docherty, M.H., Crowther, P.J., Ireton, M.A., Oakley, J., and Xydeas, C.S., "The Manchester Multimedia Information System," in *Advances in Database Technology EDBT'92,* Third International Conference on Extending Database Technology, Vienna, Mar 1992, Springer-Verlag, pp. 39–55.

[17] Goble, C.A., O'Docherty, M.H., Crowther, P.J., Ireton, M.A., Daskalakis, C.N., Oakley, J., Kay, S., and Xydeas, C.S., "The Manchester Multimedia Information System" in *Multimedia Systems, Interaction and Applications,* 1st Eurographics Workshop, Stockholm, Mar 1991, Springer-Verlag, 1992, pp. 269–282.

[18] Goble, C.A., "Multimedia databases: Status, challenges and issues," Technical Report, University of Southampton, UK, CSTR-94-03.

[19] Goble, C.A., Haul, C., and Bechhofer, S., "Describing and classifying multimedia using the description logic GRAIL," *Proceedings of Storage and Retrieval for Image and Video Databases IV,* SPIE, Vol. 2670, Feb 1996.

[20] Grosky, W.I., "Multimedia information systems," *IEEE Multimedia,* Vol. 1, No. 1, Spring 1994, pp. 12–24.

[21] Gupta, A., Weymouth, T., and Jain, R., "Semantic queries with pictures: The VIMSYS model," in *Proc. 17th VLDB,* Barcelona, 1991, pp. 69–79.

[22] Hirata, K. and Kato, T., "Query by visual example" in *Advances in Database Technology EDBT'92*, Third International Conference on Extending Database Technology, Vienna, Mar 1992, Springer-Verlag, pp. 56–71.

[23] Hohne, K.H., "Perspectives of computer assisted medical imaging," in *Proc. MIE 1991*, Lecture Notes in Medical Informatics 45, Springer-Verlag, pp. 10–18.

[24] Ireton, M.A., Oakley, J.P., and Xydeas, C.S. "A hierarchical classification method and its application in shape representation," in *SPIE*, Vol. 1662, 1992.

[25] Jain, R., ed., "Workshop report: NSF workshop on visual information management systems," in *Proceedings SPIE-Image Storage and Retrieval Systems*, San Jose, CA, Feb 1993, pp. 198–218.

[26] Jain, R. and Hampapur, A., "Metadata in video databases" in *SIGMOD Record*, Vol. 23, No. 4, Dec 1994, pp. 27–33.

[27] Jain, R., Pentland, A.P., and Petkovic, D., "Workshop report: NSF-ARPA Workshop on Visual Information Management Systems," available from Electrical and Computer Engineering, UCSD, 1995.

[28] Kato, T., "Database architecture for content-based image retrieval" in *SPIE*, Vol. 1662, 1992, pp. 112–123.

[29] Klas, W., Neuhold, E.J., and Schrefel, M., "Visual databases need data models for multimedia data," in *Visual Database Systems*, Kunii, T.L., ed., Proceedings IFIP TC2/WG2.6 Working Conference on Visual Database Systems, Tokyo, Apr 1989, North Holland, pp. 433–462.

[30] Lewis, P.H., Davis, H.C., Griffiths, S.R., Hall, W., and Wilkins, R.J., "Content-based retrieval and navigation with images in the Microcosm model," in *International Conference on Multimedia Communications*, 1995, pp. 86–90.

[31] Lockemann, P.C., "Multimedia databases: Paradigm, architecture, survey and issues," Interner Bericht Nr. 15/88, Fakultat für Informatik, Universitat Karlsruhe, 1988.

[32] Marmann, M. and Schlageter, G., "Towards a better support for hypermedia structuring: The HYDESIGN model," in *Proceedings of the ACM Conference on Hypertext*, Milan, 1992, pp. 232–241.

[33] Meghini, C., Rabitti, F., and Thanos, C., "Conceptual modeling of multimedia documents," *IEEE Computer*, Vol. 24, No. 10, Oct 1991, pp. 23–30.

[34] Meyer-Wegener, K., "Database management for multimedia applications, multimedia: System architectures and applications," in *Proc. Dagstuhl Workshop*, Encarnacao, J. and Foley, J., eds., Germany, Nov 1992.

[35] Niblack, W., Barber, R., Equitz, W., Flickner, M., Glasman, E., Petkovic, D., and Yanker, P., "The QBIC project: Querying images by content using color, texture and shape" in *Proceedings of Storage and Retrieval for Image and Video Databases I*, Vol. 1908, SPIE, Feb 1993, pp. 173–187.

[36] O'Docherty, M.H., Daskalakis, C.N., Crowther, P.J., Goble, C.A., Ireton, M.A., Oakley, J., and Xydeas, C.S., "The design and implementation of a multimedia information system with automatic content retrieval" in *Information Services & Use*, Vol. 11, 1991, pp. 345–385.

[37] Orenstein, J.A. and Manola, F.A., "PROBE: Spatial data modeling and query processing in an image database application," *IEEE Transactions on Software Engineering*, Vol. 14, No. 5, May 1988, pp. 611–629.

[38] Rabitti, F. and Stanchev, P., "GRIM_DBMS: A GRaphical IMage DataBase Management System," in *Visual Database*, Proceedings IFIP TC2/WG2.6 Working Conference on Visual Database Systems, Kunii, ed., 1989, pp. 415–430.

[39] Rakow, T., Lohr, M., and Neuhold, E.J., "Multimedia databases—The notions and issues," GI-Fachtagung Datenbanksysteme in Buro, Technik und Wissenschaft BTW 95, Dresden, March 1995, Springer, pp. 1–29.

[40] Srihari, R.K., "Use of multimedia input in automated image annotation and content-based retrieval," in *SPIE,* Vol. 2420, 1995, pp. 249-260.

[41] Treat, H., Ort, E., Ho, J., Vo, M., Jang, J-S., Hall, L., Tung, F., and Petkovic, D., "Searching images using Ultimedia Manager," in *Proceedings of Storage and Retrieval for Image and Video Databases III*, Vol. 2420, SPIE, pp. 204–215, Feb 1995.

[42] Thimm, H. and Klas, W., "Playout management—An integrated service of a multimedia database management system," in *First International Workshop on Multimedia Database Management Systems*, Blue Mountain Lake, Aug 28–30, IEEE Computer Society Press, 1995.

[43] Woelk, D. and Kim, W., "Multimedia information management in an object-oriented database system," in *Proceedings 13th International Conference on VLDB*, Brighton, 1987, pp. 319–329.

[44] Wu, J.K., Narasimhalu, A.D., Mehtre, B.M., Lam, C.P., and Gao, Y.P., "CORE: A content-based retrieval engine for multimedia information systems," *ACM Multimedia Systems*, Vol. 3, No. 1, Feb 95, pp. 25–41.

[45] Yoshitaka, A., Kishida, S., Hirakawa, M., and Ichikawa, T., "Knowledge-assisted content-based retrieval for multimedia databases," *IEEE Multimedia,* Vol. 1, No. 4, Winter 1994, pp. 12–21.

[46] Zobrist, A.L. and Nagy, G., "Pictorial information processing of LANDSAT data for geographic analysis," *IEEE Computer,* Vol. 14, No. 11, Nov 1981, pp. 34–41.

Video Database Systems—Recent Trends in Research and Development Activities

Eitetsu Oomoto and Katsumi Tanaka

Dept. of Information
    & Communication Sciences
Kyoto Sangyo University
Kamigamo-Motoyama, Kita-Ku,
Kyoto 603, Japan
(oomoto@ics.kyoto-su.ac.jp)

Dept. of Computer & Systems Engineering
Kobe University Rokkoda
Nada-Ku
Kobe 603, Japan
(tanaka@in4wolf.in.kobe-u.ac.jp)

13.1 Introduction

*R*ecently, a great deal of attention has been focused on multimedia information systems. The Object-Oriented Database Management Systems (OODBMS) [9] are considered as a candidate for constructing such systems for several reasons, including their modeling power and encapsulation capability. Many object-oriented data models, prototype systems based on their own object models, and a variety of commercial OODBMS systems have been developed. Also, workstations and high-performance personal computers have evolved to possess hardware for handling multimedia data, for example, image compression hardware and digital signal processors for handling voices. Multimedia information systems are used to store, retrieve, and manage still images, video, and voices and other forms of data (*multimedia data*). For describing the structure and semantics of multimedia data, in general, the object-oriented concept is regarded as suitable for a data modeling framework.

With this background, several multimedia (database) systems [27] for handling video data have been developed, and several video server systems have appeared. This chapter describes the technical background, basic problems, and research activities involved in realizing video databases, a data model called *Video Object Data Model* for modeling and retrieving video data, and the design and implementation of the video database prototype system, **OVID** (**O**bject-oriented **V**ideo **I**nformation **D**atabase) [26].

In Section 13.2 we discuss the fundamental types of technology applied in realizing video databases. Several basic problems involving video databases are described in Section 13.3. We survey several current areas of research activity concerning video information/database systems in Section 13.4. As an example of one area of research, we describe a prototype video database system, *OVID*, which we have been developing for several years, in Section 13.5 and Section 13.6. In Section 13.5, we describe our video object data model together with illustrative examples. The features of the OVID system are described in Section 13.6. Section 13.7 consists of concluding remarks.

13.2   Fundamental Technologies for Video Databases

In this section, the fundamental technology required to produce a multimedia database, in particular a video database, as a realistic system are described.

Hardware Technology

- **High-Performance Microprocessor**   Because of the dramatic evolution undergone by VLSI technology, such as RISC chips, the performance of microprocessors has improved drastically. For example, a standard chip has a processing speed of more than 100 MIPS, and it is forecasted that a 1000-MIPS chip will be realized in the near future. Furthermore, the utilization of parallel processing techniques will boost this speed to a higher level. With these powerful computation capabilities, it will gradually become possible to process sound and video data with sufficiently high speed at a reasonable cost.

- **Image Compression Technique**   In general, visual data sets are very large. Therefore, considering the bandwidth necessary for storing, transferring and other forms of processing these data sets, compression technology to reduce their size is indispensable. Considering factors of portability, cost and convenience, standard, commonly accessible technology should be employed in this application. Recently, several standards for image compression, for example JPEG, MPEG, and DVI, have been defined, and several types of hardware based on these standards, DSP chipsets and custom LSIs, are being developed. In the case of the Macintosh from Apple Computer, the video support facility QuickTime [7] is embedded in the operating system.

- **Very Large Storage Devices** Compared to conventional numeric and string data handling, video and image data requires a very large amount of memory. In order to directly manipulate video data on computers, corresponding main memory space should be provided. Fortunately, memory chips are being produced with steadily increasing capacity and lower cost.

    On the other hand, if we use current video compression techniques and can achieve maximum compression, a one-hour video stream will consume about 600 Mb to 1 Gb storage space. To actually realize a video database system, a much larger storage system is required. To satisfy this requirement, a variety of very large storage systems, such as optical disks, are under development. Furthermore, parallel disk access methods (e.g., RAID systems) will be introduced to insure high fetch and transfer speed from storage media to main memory.

- **High-Speed Networks** With the present distributed computing environment, video data will be transferred over the network to be shared by and delivered among workstations. Ethernet (10 Mbps) do not have a wide enough bandwidth to transfer video data. However, FDDI (100 Mbps) and ATM (155 ~ 600 Mbps) have now become available. These are both sufficient for video. Furthermore, network media over 1 Gbps will be available in near future. Several protocols for multimedia communications to transfer very large sets of multimedia data, voices, and video are currently being developed, as well as high-speed communication media.

Software Technology

The following software technology is useful for video databases:

- **Graphical User Interfaces** As the basic background of active usage of multimedia information, it is very essential that we became familiar with graphical user interfaces (GUIs) [2] such as window systems, pointing devices, icons, and menus. The character-oriented display is sufficiently powerful when computers are used for numerical computations and simple string-represented information processing. However, in the GUI environment with window systems, visual representations of information are easily realized, and are considered to be very important. The visualization of information with GUIs makes using computers intuitive. As a typical example, the usage of image data is very effective with the World Wide Web (a GUI). It is natural that the next step will be from the use of still images to moving images.

- **Object Database Management Systems** In the case that images are stored in a database system, treating their complex structure and the procedures required to process them elegantly is a difficult problem. Relational database systems, which are common in commercial business use, are generally said to have insufficient facilities for multimedia data. Contrastingly, Object Database Management Systems (ODBMSs) [11] are experimentally and commercially maturing, and are said, generally, to be suitable for such multimedia data. ODBMSs support the notion of complex objects, which directly represent complex data structure with the recursive use of tuple-type and set-type constructors, and possess the facility of encapsulation. Using encapsulation, we can combine data and their procedures and can store them in an integrated manner in a database. Because of the above features, ODBMSs are considered to be the basis of integrated management of multimedia data.

13.3 Major Problems for Realizing Video Database Systems

Research activity involving video databases is currently increasing and many problems have arisen. In particular, the following are important points:

1. **Framework for Data Modeling** What data model is suitable for the construction of a video database? Unfortunately, the ultimate answer, we believe, does not currently exist. The object-oriented approach is generally considered to be suitable for the framework of data modeling of video databases. However, this approach does not have the capability for modeling in the following situation: In general, the semantic viewpoints of users regarding multimedia data, including video, vary widely. For instance, consider a scene of a basketball game at a university. This can be impressed as a scene of "playing sports," "students," or "campus life." What is the most suitable? This will depend on the viewpoint of each user. In the conventional framework of object orientation, these situations cannot be well represented. That is, different interpretations exist for each different viewpoint of a given object.

Furthermore, the semantic description for each video scene should be given in order to search for the derived scene and retrieve it from video databases. If all these descriptions are described by users manually, the task will be very tedious and very difficult. Some mechanism decreasing the degree of description necessary for scenes must be prepared in data models for video databases.

2. **Query Language and Retrieval System** In the video retrieval system, the following issues are important: What type of languages are needed to retrieve the suitable video scenes from the database? With what facilities should the video retrieval systems be equipped? Since database query languages in general have a strong relationship with their data models, issues regarding the facilities of query languages should not be discussed independently of the data models. However, the expressive power of query languages, which are the ways for users to represent the video scenes desired, will determine the capabilities and possibilities of the system. Furthermore, in video databases, facilities acting to specify the presentation for retrievals are necessary. That is, if a retrieved scene is too long to replay in the given time interval, the user must determine whether the replay should be interrupted or quick-played in the permitted interval. On the other hand, video indexing using image processing techniques will enrich the retrieval facilities of video databases.

3. **Storage Management System** The size of video data sets is very large in general, and if the minimum data access rate is not guaranteed, the replay image will not be fluent. This, of course, is very undesirable for applications of video data. Since the video objects are very large, conventional caching techniques are not sufficient. Furthermore, the file structure of UNIX in its present form is apparently not suitable for video storage. Similarly, storage structures for traditional DBMSs, such as B-tree and hash tables, are not sufficient because they are indexing techniques for attribute values. A new storage system architecture is required to guarantee a minimum data transfer rate however large the accessed video and however large the number of users.

4. **Delivery System for Video** In most computer environments, it is impossible to store very large video data sets on each local machine. Therefore, it is necessary for the server to possess very large storage devices for video images and for the clients to access these images through high speed networks. With such an architecture, using a network with sufficient bandwidth for video image transfer is fundamental. In addition, the communication protocol is also important. In the case of video image transfer, the minimum constant transfer rate to display smoothly must be guaranteed. If this rate cannot be attained, the delivery system should drop the quality of the images, that is, the frame rate, resolution, number of colors, etc. Using caching techniques whereby frequently accessed video images are transferred to the client machines in advance may be an effective manner.

5. **Transaction Management** The update operation for video may consist mainly of additions to the database. Deletion and modification may be rare operations. In such systems, a transaction management method different from conventional methods should be needed.

6. **Copyright Issues** Copyright issues for video images on video databases/ servers are very important in actual applications. Although this is not a technical problem, some provisions to protect the copyrights may be provided by the video databases themselves. Currently, multimedia data is largely limited to personal use. However, when the situation that anyone can access the video on video databases at any time from any place on the network is realized in the near future, many problems involving illegal copies may arise. Copyright protection should be provided not only from the side of lawyers but also from the engineers for video databases.

13.4 Current Activities Involving Video Database Systems

Currently, the research activity for video database systems is in its early stages, and therefore there is little to report. In this section, several related areas of research are described.

Multimedia Information Systems with Video Images

Computer-Aided Instruction System

Parkes [27] introduced a mechanism for handling descriptive data for video information in his video-based CAI system. He introduced the notions of *events* and *settings*. An *"event"* is a hierarchical description of a video scene based on PART-OF relationships. Suppose a video scene A shows how to use a micrometer. The event "USING THE MICRO METER" is assigned to A. This is the root of the description. The event "USING THE MICRO METER" consists of four sub-events, that is, "REMOVE MICRO FROM CASE," "CLEAN MICRO," "MEASURE METAL" and "RECORD MEASURE." Each event corresponds to some portion of video A. The event "CLEAN MICRO" consists of four events, "HOLD MICRO," "LIFT CLOTH," "WIPE ROD" and "REPLACE CLOTH," and so on. The other notion, "settings," corresponds to different representations of the same object in the real world. Binary relations, for instance, zoom in, zoom out, etc., are defined between these settings. In summary, his model consists of PART-OF relationships among descriptional data and binary relationships between settings. This model offers an interesting method for organizing a large amount of descriptional data of video information. Parkes, however, did not address the issue of inheritance of descriptional data.

Muse in Project Athena

Hodges, Sasnett, and Ackerman [17], [18], [21] developed the *Athena Muse* system, which is a multimedia environment for education. In these papers, they introduced the notion of *multidimensional information*. As an example of one dimensional data, they discussed video data which is annotated by several text segments that switch with video images synchronously. Muse is a useful system to compose multimedia applications, but these authors did not address the aspect of database facilities. That is, neither data model issues nor the associated mechanism for handling descriptional data of video information was mentioned.

EVA

EVA [21], [22] is a video annotator system developed by MIT. It provides software researchers with the annotation facility for video. Although EVA is a useful tool with which to analyze video data, its capability to share descriptional information among annotated video scenes is relatively weak.

Harmony

Harmony [28] is a multimedia presentation system. It adopts the *hyper-object model,* which is the integration of the object-oriented model and the hypertext model. Harmony can manipulate temporal media, video, sound, animation, etc., in an integrated way. Due to the modified model of the *timed Petri net,* synchronization among different media can be described.

Data Models for Video Databases

Time-Interval-Based Model

The composition of multimedia data was addressed by Little and Ghafoor [20]. They classified methods to compose multimedia data into two categories: *spatial composition* is the notion of spatial arrangement of data, and *temporal composition* is concerned with how to maintain the synchronization of data in a process of data presentation. They introduced a *timed Petri net model* to synchronize the data presentation. Their model focuses on the description of *synchronization,*[1] and they did not discuss the mechanism for handling descriptional data of video information.

Temporal Logic for Time Intervals

Allen [4] introduced interval-based temporal logic as a framework to represent knowledge and inference concerned with time. He addressed the notion of constraint propagation. Intuitively, if a condition P holds during a time interval T, then P holds during any subinterval t of T. His notions of *temporal logic* will be useful in the discussion of video composition operations.

---

[1] We recognize the importance of synchronization issues of multimedia data, but in this chapter, we focus only on the treatment of descriptional data of video information.

Virtual Museum

Gibbs introduced the notion of the multimedia framework [15], [16] in the *Virtual Museum,* a multimedia information system. In this sense, he provided a data model which resembles the E-R data model. Video and sound data are considered as *media objects* in this model, and several operations such as clipping, filtering, and concatenation are defined. The *multimedia objects* are the composition of each media object using these operations.

Video Document Model: VDM

Hara *et al.* introduced the video document model, VDM, and a prototype system based on this model is currently being developed [31]. This model is basically a hypertext model. That is, the arbitrary scenes and objects in each scene are defined as *nodes*. Each node can have its own attributes and values. Additionally, several types of links among these nodes are also introduced, enabling to the inheritance of attributes/attribute values among nodes in order to share common semantic descriptions.

Video Retrieval Systems

Video Indexing

Tanaka *et al.* [24] developed a full video search system which automatically detects the flipping point of cuts in a given video stream and searches for a similar object in each scene.

Automatic Video Database Building

The challenge presented by the automatic video database building using television news video is currently being addressed by Ariki *et al.* [8]. They have employed the following automatic video processing techniques: 1) detection of scene flipping, 2) extraction of camera work such as paning or zooming, 3) keyword extraction from narration and 4) keyword extraction from superimposed text.

Storage and Delivery System

Digital TV Studio

A storage system for video and, as its application, a news video database system are under construction by Maier *et al.* [23]. Two notable points with regard to this system are:

- Constrained-Latency Storage Access (CLSA) is a method by which the system can control the delivery and display of video images in multimedia object (video) retrieval. In this method, delivery of multimedia objects is restricted by DBMS.
- It is difficult to always deliver video data via networks with the best quality. Therefore, they introduced scripts to describe the quality of the data. In

each script, the quality of services (QOS) for each object is described. DBMS schedule the fetch and delivery of media objects based on these scripts.

Video Server

In [14], Ghandeharizadeh *et al.* propose several techniques for video servers. In particular, the notion of *object declustering* is introduced as a way to replay video continuously and to improve the response for multi-user access. With this technique, each video is not compressed, but rather stored in distribution on several servers mutually connected via a high speed network. These authors also introduce the replication method used to repeatedly store video fragments. This improves the response of simultaneous multi-user access. At USC, a multimedia information system is under construction based on these approaches.

In a related work, Anderson [5] discussed the algorithm and architecture for continuous media such as video images and sounds in order to guarantee a minimum transfer rate from disks.

13.5   Video Object Data Model

In this section, we first discuss motivating problems to describe the contents of video data (for example, a video disc) when using conventional ODBMSs. Next, we describe our *Video Object Data Model*, with which we have designed and implemented our prototype video-object database system, OVID.

Problems

Difficulties in Defining Attributes

If we wish to describe the contents of a video disc, and also wish to define a database schema using conventional ODBMSs, first, we should decide what the basic *objects* are. A video disc consists of a sequence of video frames, and so, each video frame (a still image) can be regarded as a single object. However, usually a (semantically) meaningful scene is a sequence of (not always continuous) video frames. Thus it seems natural to define an object corresponding to each semantically meaningful sequence of video frames. This is possible when using conventional ODBMSs. That is, the description for a semantically meaningful scene is represented as a tuple:

(starting frame#, ending frame#, other attributes to describe the scene).

However, we should note the following problems concerned with the difficulties in defining attributes in advance:

- Depending on the describers' viewpoints, a given scene (a given sequence of video frames) may be given different descriptions. That is, it may have multiple different sets of attribute definitions.

- Since it is difficult to describe the entire contents of a video disc at one time, descriptions for semantically meaningful scenes should be incrementally added. This also results in a difficulty in defining all attributes in advance.

- A semantically meaningful scene s_1 may contain another semantically meaningful scene s_2 as its subinterval. Suppose that the description of s_2 contains the same information as that of s_1. In this situation, the user must describe the same information twice, once for each object. If there were some mechanism by which common descriptive information could be shared among scenes based on time-interval inclusion relationships, it would be useful for decreasing the work required to describe video scenes. However, conventional ODBMSs do not provide such an inheritance mechanism. They provide a mechanism only for the inheritance of attribute structures and methods among classes.

Difficulties in Querying

In conventional database systems, in general, a query is formulated by knowing database schemata such as table definitions and class hierarchy. Users must know the attribute structures or class structures in order to retrieve desired objects. If we allow each object to have a different attribute structure, then the following problems should be considered:

- Since each data object has its own structure, users must inspect the attribute definition of each object in order to know what attributes are defined for the objects. This is very inconvenient, and so, some mechanism able to cope with this problem is necessary.

- All the complete definitions of attributes and their values for objects must be described by users if there is no database schema. It may be a very difficult task for users to describe many attribute definitions for objects. A mechanism to decrease the required number of descriptions of attribute definitions for objects is necessary.

Treatment of Composed Objects

Video data stored in video databases may be used for several editorial works. That is, video data are often cut and/or concatenated for preparing multimedia presentations. In order to do this using video database systems, these systems should possess the facility to retrieve video data and compose the resulting data into a new video object, as well as the facility for carrying out several editing operations. Also, these newly composed video objects may need to be stored in the database. Conventional ODBMSs, however, do not have the capability to store the retrieved and/or composed objects into their object databases. This is because a class for storing the retrieved and/or composed objects is needed, but most conventional ODBMSs do not have sufficient facility to generate new classes dynamically. Also, after composing a new video object from retrieved objects, it is desirable for the new video object to inherit some attribute information from the original objects. However, conventional ODBMSs do not support the inheritance of attributes and their values among instance objects.

Basic Ideas

We consider every portion of a video frame sequence to be an independent entity, and so, we wish to make it possible to define an object which has its own attributes and attribute values for arbitrary video frame sequences. We call this a *video object*. More generally, a video object corresponds to a certain set of video frame sequences, and it has its own attributes and attribute values to represent the content (meaning) of the corresponding video scene. The following are the features of our video object model:

- **Schemaless Description of Database**
- **Interval Inclusion Inheritance**
- **Composition of Video-Objects Based on is-a Hierarchy**

In the *schemaless description,* we do not take an approach of assuming a specific database schema such as classes and class hierarchy, hence users can define any attribute structure for each video object. For example, broadcast stations such as the ABC Network have many varieties of video tape libraries. These may be news reports such as an airplane accident, movies, documentaries, and so on. We believe that it is very difficult to offer a common attribute structure for these. Also, users have different viewpoints to describe and/or retrieve video scenes and many various requirements for retrieving from their various standpoints. Therefore, it is difficult to decide rigidly the attribute structures which denote the meanings of the video scenes. Also, they should be freely and incrementally extensible by users.

As new objects are defined in a database, new attributes to represent the contents of video objects may become needed. In our model, arbitrary attributes can be attached to each video object whenever they are necessary. For instance, when a user defines a video object over the video scene concerned with *John*, the user may want to describe his name, "John," as the attribute value of the *name* attribute. If the *name* attribute does not exist in the database, we can add it to this video object at any time.

We also introduce the notion of inheritance based on the *interval inclusion relationship.* By means of this notion, some descriptional data of video objects can be inherited by other video objects. For instance, consider a night scene to be defined as a video-object A and another object B to be defined over some portion of object A. The object B is also a night scene. If object A has the attribute *situation* and its value "night," then object B has the same attribute and value by the *interval inclusion relationship.*

In addition we will also define several operations, *interval projection, merge*, and *overlap*, for video-objects to compose new video objects. For example, in broadcast stations, video scenes are edited from source video. They are chopped in order to remove redundant scenes and/or concatenated with each other to make TV programs. Our operations for video objects correspond to this kind of video editing. They do not only synthesize a new video object, but also derive, based on the *is-a* hierarchy, the attributes and attribute values of the synthesized object from the original video objects.

In the following, we describe our video object data model in detail.

Video Objects

Intuitively, our notion of *video object* is descriptional data of a meaningful scene (motion picture), and it consists of (1) its *object identifier* (*oid* for short), (2) an *interval*, and (3) a collection of attribute/value pairs. Each video-object has a unique object identifier. Each video object corresponds to a video frame sequence, and the contents of the video frame sequence are described by a collection of attribute/value pairs. An *interval* is represented by the pair of starting frame# and ending frame# and denotes a continuous sequence of video frames. In this chapter, since we define a video object that corresponds to more than one video frame sequence, a set of *intervals* is associated with the corresponding video object. Thus, note that a video object does not necessarily correspond to a single continuous sequence of video frames. This is because a meaningful scene does not always correspond to a single continuous sequence of video frames.

In this chapter, we assume the following mutually disjoint (countably infinite) sets: A set $\mathcal{D}$ of atomic values (numbers, strings, and special symbols $\top$ and $\bot$), a set $\mathcal{ID}$ of *object identifiers*, a set $\mathcal{I}$ of intervals, and a set $\mathcal{A}$ of attribute names.

Definition 13.1   *Video-Object*
   A *video-object* is a triple (oid, I, v), where

1. *oid* is an object identifier which is an element of $\mathcal{ID}$.

2. I is a finite subset of $\mathcal{I}$.

3. v is an n-tuple $[\ a_1 : v_1, \ ..., \ a_n : v_n\ ]$, where each a_i $(1 \le i \le n)$ is an attribute name in $\mathcal{A}$, and v_i is a value defined recursively in the following manner:

   - Each element $x \in \mathcal{D}$ is a value.
   - Each interval $i \in \mathcal{I}$ is a value.
   - For values $v_1, \ ..., \ v_n$ $(0 \le n)$, $\{\ v_1, \ ..., \ v_n\ \}$ is a value called a *set value*.
   - Each video-object is also a value.

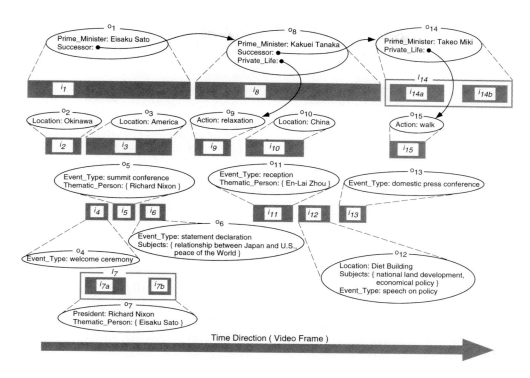

Figure 13-1   Example video object database.

For a given video-object, $o = (oid, I, v)$ with its value $v = [a_1 : v_1, ..., a_n : v_n]$, $attr(o)$ or $attr(v)$ denotes the set of all the attributes in v, and $value(o)$ denotes the value v, i.e., $v = value(o)$. The value v_i is denoted by $o.a_i$ and/or $v.a_i$.

Hereafter, as a realistic example, we will use a documentary video disc [25] about `Prime Ministers of Japan`. Fig. 13–1 summarizes the whole example database.[2]

Generalization Hierarchy for Values and Objects

A *generalization (is-a) hierarchy* [29] for atomic values is assumed to constitute a lattice $G = (A, \succeq, \top, \bot)$, where A is a set of atomic values, $\succeq$ is an *is-a* relationship (a reflexive, transitive, and anti-symmetric binary relation) among atomic values, $\top$ denotes *unknown*, and $\bot$ denotes *undefined*. The binary relation $\succeq$ denotes *more informative*. That is, $a_1 \succeq a_2$ means that a_1 is-a a_2 and that the atomic value a_1 is more informative than the atomic value a_2. Fig. 13–2 shows an

---

[2] Figures are from [26], © 1993 IEEE, reprinted by permission.

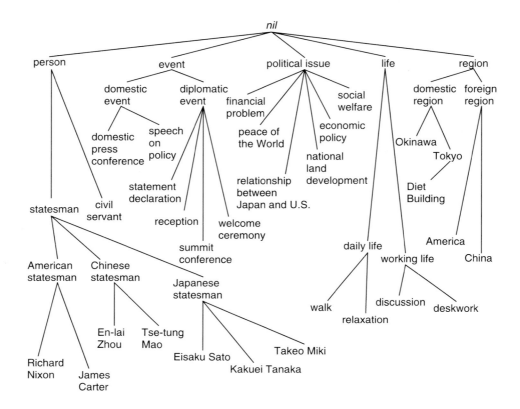

Figure 13-2   Example generalization hierarchy of atomic values.[*]

[*]© 1993 IEEE

example generalization hierarchy of atomic values of our example database. In this figure, the symbol top is denoted by *nil*, and the symbol ⊥ is omitted. In this example, the following holds:

- Japanese statesman ⪰ statesman.
- Eisaku Sato ⪰ Japanese statesman.
- Eisaku Sato ⪰ statesman.

We assume that a generalization hierarchy for atomic values is given in advance by users.

The above *is-a* relationship can be extended to general values (including atomic values) and also to video-objects in the following manner: Suppose that we have two video-objects $o_1 = (oid_1, I_1, v_1)$ and $o_2 = (oid_2, I_2, v_2)$. First, given these two values v_1 and v_2, two video-objects o_1 and o_2, and a generalization hierarchy G, we extend the is-a relationship[3] in the following recursive manner:

- If both v_1 and v_2 are set-type values, then v_1 is-a v_2 if for each element y in v_2, there exists an element x in v_1 such that x is-a y.
- Let v_1 and v_2 be two tuple-type values. Then v_1 is-a v_2 if $v_1.a$ is-a $v_2.a$ for each attribute a of v_2.
- For video-objects[4] $o_1 = (oid_1, I_1, v_1)$ and $o_2 = (oid_2, I_2, v_2)$, if v_1 is-a v_2, then o_1 is-a o_2.

Definition 13.2   *Least Upper Bound of Values*
For two values v_1 and v_2, $v = v_1 \vee v_2$ is the *least upper bound* of v_1 and v_2 if the following conditions hold.

1. v_1 is-a v.

2. v_2 is-a v.

3. There exists no v' satisfying all of the following: $v' \neq v$, v' is-a v, v_1 is-a v', and v_2 is-a v'.

For example, suppose that we have the following values:

v_1 = [**Prime_Minister**: Kakuei Tanaka, **Location**: Tokyo, **Action**: relaxation],

v_2 = [**Year**: 1974, **Location**: Tokyo, **Action**: walk].

Also, assume the following is-a relationships:

relaxation is-a *daily life* and *walk* is-a *daily life*.

The least upper bound of v_1 and v_2 is given as follows:

$v_1 \vee v_2$ = [**Location**: Tokyo, **Action**: daily life]

Intuitively, the obtained value $v_1 \vee v_2$ represents the *maximum* information that is common to both of the values v_1 and v_2. This notion will be used to define our composition operations for video-objects later.

Definition 13.3   *Greatest Lower Bound of Values*
For two values v_1 and v_2, $v = v_1 \wedge v_2$ is the *greatest lower bound* of v_1 and v_2 if the following conditions hold.

1. v is-a v_1.

2. v is-a v_2.

3. There exists no v' satisfying all of the following: $v' = v$, v is-a v', v' is-a v_1, and v' is-a v_2.

---

[3] This extension follows the work by Khoshafian *et al.*[10].

[4] In this chapter, we assume that the *is-a* relationship between video-objects is independent of their object identifiers and intervals.

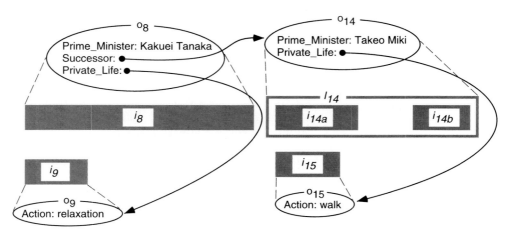

Figure 13-3 An example of video objects.[*]

Suppose that

$v_1 = [$ **Location**: Tokyo, **Year**: 1972,

   Subjects: { national land development, financial problem }],

$v_2 = [$ **Year**: 1972, **Subjects**: { financial problem, social welfare }].

The greatest lower bound of v_1 and v_2 is:

$v_1 \wedge v_2 = [$ **Location**: Tokyo, **Year**: 1972,

   Subjects: { national land development, financial problem, social
welfare }]

Intuitively, the obtained value $v_1 \wedge v_2$ represents the *minimum* information contained in at least one of the values v_1 or v_2. This notion will be also used to define our composition operations for video-objects later.

Example 13.1   In Fig. 13–3, we assume that the interval i_8 of a video-object o_8 corresponds to the scene of the Prime Minister Kakuei Tanaka, and that the interval set I_{14} of o_{14} corresponds to the scene concerned with Mr. Takeo Miki, who was the next prime minister, that is, the *successor* of Kakuei Tanaka. Also, suppose that the scene i_{15} shows that Mr. Takeo Miki is taking a walk around his house in his private time. We can define the following video-objects:

$o_8 = (d_8, \{i_8\}, v_8)$

$v_8 = [$ **Prime_Minister**: Kakuei Tanaka, **Successor**: o_{14},

   Private_Life: o_9],

$o_9 = (d_9, \{i_9\}, v_9), v_9 = [$ **Action**: relaxation],

$o_{14} = (d_{14}, I_{14} = \{i_{14a}, i_{14b}\}, v_{14}),$
$v_{14} = [\,\textbf{Prime\_Minister}\colon \text{Takeo Miki}, \textbf{Private\_Life}\colon o_{15}\,],$
$o_{15} = (d_{15}, \{i_{15}\}, v_{15}), v_{15} = [\,\textbf{Action}\colon \text{walk}\,].$

When describing the contents of a video scene, it is sometimes difficult to determine the value of an attribute in textual form. For instance, `private life` can be described better by the video image itself than by text. Note that in our model, a video-object is allowed to be used as an attribute value (for example, the **Private_Life** value of o_8 is another video-object, o_9).

Inheritance Based on Interval Inclusion Relationship

In this subsection, we will introduce a new inheritance mechanism, by which some attribute/value pairs of a video-object are inherited by another video-object if the former video-object's interval contains the latter video-object's interval. It should be noted that this type of inheritance is between *instances*, not between traditional classes and subclasses in OODB systems.

Since our video-object may contain more than one interval as its component, we first define the inclusion relationship between two sets of intervals. For two given interval sets I_1 and I_2, the *inclusion relationship* between them is defined as:

- For each $i \in I_1$, if there exists $i' \in I_2$ such that $i \subseteq i'$, then I_1 is said to be *included* by the interval set I_2. This is denoted by $I_1 \sqsubseteq I_2$.

Suppose that we have video-objects $o_1 = (oid_1, I_1, v_1)$ and $o_2 = (oid_2, I_2, v_2)$ such that $I_1 \sqsubseteq I_2$ holds. Then, some of the attribute/value pairs of v_2 are inherited by the video-object o_1. As will be discussed later, not all attribute/value pairs should be inherited. The *inheritable attributes* should be defined in advance by users.

Definition 13.4 *Evaluation of Interval Inclusion Inheritance by a Single Object*

Suppose that we have video-objects $o_1 = (oid_1, I_1, v_1)$ and $o_2 = (oid_2, I_2, v_2)$ such that $I_1 \sqsubseteq I_2$, and a set A of inheritable attributes. The result of applying the interval inclusion inheritance is called an *evaluation*. The *evaluation* of o_1 by o_2 and A, denoted by $eval(o_1, o_2, A)$, is a video-object $o_1' = (oid_1, I_1, v_1')$, where the following are satisfied:

- $attr(v_1') = attr(v_1) \cup (\,attr(v_2) \cap A\,)$.

- $v_1'.a = v_1.a$ if a is in $attr(v_1)$.

- $v_1'.a = v_2.a$ if a is in $attr(v_2) \cap A$, but not in $attr(v_1)$.

It should be noted that the object identifiers and the interval sets of o_1 and o_1' are identical. This implies that the *evaluation* is not physically stored in the database and is dynamically calculated.

Definition 13.5   *Evaluation of Interval Inclusion Inheritance by Multiple Objects*

Suppose that we have a video-object $o_1 = (oid_1, I_1, v_1)$. Let $O = \{ o_{21}, ..., o_{2m} \}$ be the set of all video-objects in the database such that $I_1 \subseteq I_{2i}$ for each $o_{2i} = (oid_{2i}, I_{2i}, v_{2i})$. The *evaluation* of o_1 by $O - \{o_1\}$ and a set A of inheritable attributes, denoted by $eval(o_1, O, A)$, is a video-object $o_1' = (oid_1, I_1, v_1')$ such that the following hold:

- $attr(v_1') = attr(v_1) \cup (attr(v_{21}) \cap A) \cup ... \cup (attr(v_{2m}) \cap A)$.

- $v_1'.a = v_1.a$ if a is in $attr(v_1)$.

- For each a in A, let $V_a = \{ v_{2i}.a \mid a \in attr(v_{2i}), a \notin attr(v_1), \text{ and } 1 \leq i \leq m\}$. For each non-empty set V_a, $v_1'.a = \text{glb}(V_a)$, where $\text{glb}(V_a)$ denotes the greatest lower bound of all the elements in V_a.[5]

Example 13.2   Let us consider another example. Suppose that we have the following video-object:

$$o_{12} = (oid_{12}, \{i_{12}\}, v_{12}),$$

where

$v_{12} = [$ **Event_Type**: speech on policy,

Location: Diet Building,

Subjects: { national land development, economic policy }].

We do not consider the attribute **Subjects** as *inheritable* for the following reason. The attribute **Event_Type** denotes the kind of an event which occurred in the interval i_{12}, **Location** denotes the place where the event occurred, and **Subjects** denotes the contents of a prime minister's speech, for example, {national land development, economic policy}. Assume that another object, o', is defined over the interval i', which is a subinterval of i_{12}, and that o' does not have any attributes in $attr(v_{12})$. The set-type value { national land development, economic policy } represents the entire content of the speech. Since i' is a subportion of i_{12}, the Prime Minister might not refer to some of these subjects. Therefore, it is not suitable, we believe, for the attribute **Subjects** and its value of o_{12} to be inherited by o'. On the other hand, it seems reasonable for the **Event_Type** and **Location** attributes and their values of o_{12} to be inherited by o', since i' is also a video scene of the speech in the Diet Building. Therefore, the attributes **Event_Type** and **Location** can be declared as inheritable attributes.

---

[5] Intuitively, V_a denotes a set of candidate values of attribute a, one of which is actually inherited by o_1'. In our definition, the greatest lower bound among V_a, that is, the most informative value is inherited by o_1'. In the OVID system described in Section 13.6, the evaluation is done according to this definition.

Inheritable Attributes	Event_Type, Location, President, Prime_Minister, Thematic_Person, Year
Non-Inheritable Attributes	Action, Private_Life, Subjects

Table 13–1 Inheritable attributes in the example video database.

Intuitively, an inheritable attribute of a video-object o_i is an attribute whose value is valid at an arbitrary time point in the interval (set) of o_i. We assume the inheritable attributes shown in Table 13–1 in our example video database.

Composition Operations for Video-Objects

In this subsection, we introduce basic operations to compose new video-objects from existing video-objects. First, we define the *interval projection* operation.

Definition 13.6   *Interval Projection Operation*
Let $o = (oid, I, v)$ and I' be a given video-object and an interval set, respectively, such that $I' \sqsubseteq I$ holds. Also, let A be a set of inheritable attributes. The *interval projection* of o onto I' is a video-object $o' = (oid', I', v')$ for which oid' is a new object identifier, and the value v' satisfies the following:

- $attr(v') = attr(v) \cap A$.
- $v'.a = v.a$ for each attribute a in $attr(v')$.

The interval projection operation is useful when defining a new video-object for a certain portion of a scene corresponding to an already existing video-object, since the descriptional data of the existing video-object is automatically inherited, and the required degree of description can be decreased.

Next, we will define two important composition operations on video-objects called *merge* and *overlap*. In order to make these definitions, we first need the notion of the *merge* and the *overlap* of two *interval sets,* which are defined as follows.

Definition 13.7   *Merge and Overlap of Interval Sets*
For two interval sets, I_1 and I_2, the *merge* and the *overlap* of I_1 and I_2, denoted by $I_1 \sqcup I_2$ and $I_1 \sqcap I_2$, respectively, are defined as:

- $I_1 \sqcup I_2$ is the minimal set of intervals such that

    1. There exists an interval i' in $I_1 \sqcup I_2$ such that $i' \supseteq i$ for each interval i in I_1.[6]

---

[6] $i_1 \subseteq i_2$ for given two intervals i_1 and i_2 means that the interval i_1 is completely included in or is equal to the interval i_2.

2. There exists an interval i' in $I_1 \sqcup I_2$ such that $i' \supseteq i$ for each interval i in I_2.

3. For every interval i_1 and i_2 in $I_1 \sqcup I_2$ such that $i_1 \neq i_2$, the relations i_2 is not a subset of i_1 and i_1 is not a subset of i_2 hold.

- $I_1 \sqcap I_2$ is the maximal subset of $\{i_1 \cap i_2 \mid i_1 \in I_1 \text{ and } i_2 \in I_2\}$ such that i_2' is not a subset of i_1' and $i_2' \supseteq i_1'$ for arbitrary intervals i_1' and i_2' in $I_1 \sqcap I_2$.

Intuitively, the *merge* operation creates a new video-object o from existing video-objects o_1 and o_2 such that some descriptional data common to both o_1 and o_2 is inherited by o, and that o's interval (set) is the union (merge) of the intervals (interval sets) of o_1 and o_2. In other words, the *merge* operation abstracts two existing video-objects into a new video-object. The *overlap* extracts the scene described by both of two existing video-objects to form a new video-object.

Definition 13.8   *Merge of Video-Objects*
The *merge* of two video-objects $o_1 = (oid_1, I_1, v_1)$ and $o_2 = (oid_2, I_2, v_2)$, denoted by $o_1 \sqcup o_2$, is the video-object $o = (oid, I_1 \sqcup I_2, v)$ for which $v = [\, a_1 : v_1, \ldots, a_i : v_i, \ldots, a_n : v_n \,]$, where each $a_i \,(1 \leq i \leq n)$ is in $attr(v_1) \cap attr(v_2)$, and for each a_i, we have:

- If both of $o_1.a_i$ and $o_2.a_i$ are values, then $v_i = o_1.a_i \vee o_2.a_i$.
- If both of $o_1.a_i$ and $o_2.a_i$ are video-objects, then $v_i = o_1.a_i \sqcup o_2.a_i$.

Example 13.3
In our example database, we have:

$o_8 = (\, oid_8, \{i_8\}, [\textbf{Prime\_Minister}: \text{Kakuei Tanaka},$

$\qquad\qquad \textbf{Successor}: o_{14},$

$\qquad\qquad \textbf{Private\_Life}: o_9 \,] \,),$

$o_9 = (\, oid_9, \{i_9\}, [\,\textbf{Action}: \text{relaxation}\,]\,),$

$o_{14} = (\, oid_{14}, \{i_{14a}, i_{14b}\}, [\textbf{Prime\_Minister}: \text{Takeo Miki}, \textbf{Private\_Life}: o_{15}\,]\,),$

$o_{15} = (\, oid_{15}, \{i_{15}\}, [\,\textbf{Action}: \text{walk}\,]\,).$

Further, assume the following *is-a* relationships:

`relaxation` *is-a* `daily life` and `walk` *is-a* `daily life`.

The merge of o_8 and o_{14} is given as:

$o_8 \sqcup o_{14} = (\, oid', \{i_8, i_{14a}, i_{14b}\}, [\,\textbf{Prime\_Minister}: \text{Japanese statesman},$
$\textbf{Private\_Life}: o_9 \sqcup o_{15}\,]\,),$

where

$o_9 \sqcup o_{15} = (\, oi'', \{i_9, i_{15}\}, [\,\textbf{Action}: \text{daily life}\,]\,)$

(see Fig. 13–4).

It should be noted that the *merge* operation is recursively applied to **Private_Life** attributes, since they have video-objects as their values. Intuitively, this example's *merge* operation extracts the common information of

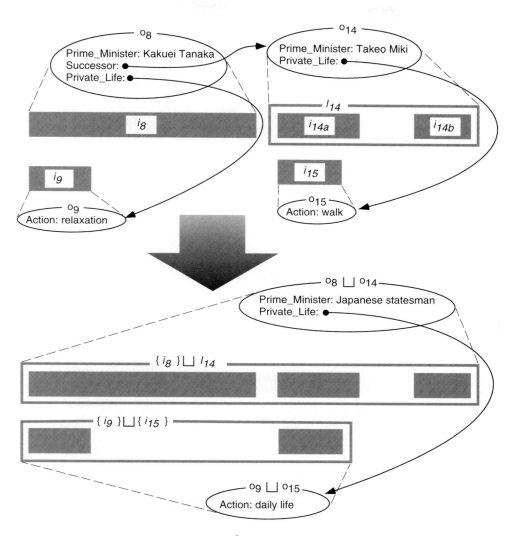

Figure 13-4 Merging video-objects.[*]

two video-objects o_8 and o_{14} and assigns this information to a newly created composition video-object. This operation corresponds to *editing* of films together with their descriptional data done by movie companies and broadcast stations.

The final composition operation is *overlap*, which is intuitively understood as taking an intersection of two video-objects. From two existing video-objects o_1 and o_2, this operation creates a new video-object o such that o's interval (set) is the intersection (overlap) of intervals (interval sets) of o_1 and o_2, and that o's descriptional data is roughly equal to the greatest lower bound of the descriptional data of o_1 and o_2.

Definition 13.9   *Overlap of Video-Objects*
For two video-objects $o_1 = (oid_1, I_1, v_1)$ and $o_2 = (oid_2, I_2, v_2)$ such that $I_1 \sqcap I_2$ is non-empty, the *overlap* of o_1 and o_2, denoted by $o_1 \sqcap o_2$, is the new video-object $o = (oid, I_1 \sqcap I_2, v)$ for which *oid* is a new object identifier and $v = [\, a_1{:}v_1, ..., a_n{:} v_n\,]$, where we have:

- Each attribute a_i is in $attr(v_1) \cup attr(v_2)$.
- If both $v_1.a_i$ and $v_2.a_i$ are values,[7] then $v.a_i = v_1.a_i \wedge v_2.a_i$.
- If both $v_1.a_i$ and $v_2.a_i$ are video-objects, then $v_i = v_1.a_i \sqcap v_2.a_i$.

Example 13.4
As shown in Fig. 13–5, suppose we have:

$o_5 = (\, oid_5, \{i_5\}, [\, \textbf{Event\_Type}: \text{summit conference},$

$\qquad\qquad \textbf{Thematic\_Person}: \{\text{ Richard Nixon }\}\,]\,),$

$o_7 = (\, oid_7, \{\, i_{7a}, i_{7b}\,\}, [\, \textbf{President}: \text{Richard Nixon},$

$\qquad\qquad \textbf{Thematic\_Person}: \{\text{ Eisaku Sato }\}\,]\,).$

The overlap of o_5 and o_7 is:

$o_5 \sqcap o_7 = (\, oid', \{\, i_5 \cap i_{7a}\,\}, [\, \textbf{Event\_Type}: \text{summit conference},$

$\qquad\qquad \textbf{President}: \text{Richard Nixon},$

$\qquad\qquad \textbf{Thematic\_Person}: \{\text{ Richard Nixon, Eisaku}$
$\qquad\qquad\qquad \text{Sato }\}\,]\,).$

Note that in this example, the greatest lower bound of the `Thematic_Person` values of o_5 and o_7 corresponds to the set union of `Thematic_Person` values of o_5 and o_7.

13.6   OVID: A Video-Object Database System

In this section, we describe the overall configuration and the functionalities of our video-object database system OVID, which was developed based on our video object data model and is currently running.

Features of OVID

The following is a list of notable features of our OVID system.

---

[7] If either $v_1 \times a_i$ or $v_2 \times a_i$ is not given in v_1 or v_2, then top is automatically assigned to $v_1 \times a_i$ or $v_2 \times a_i$.

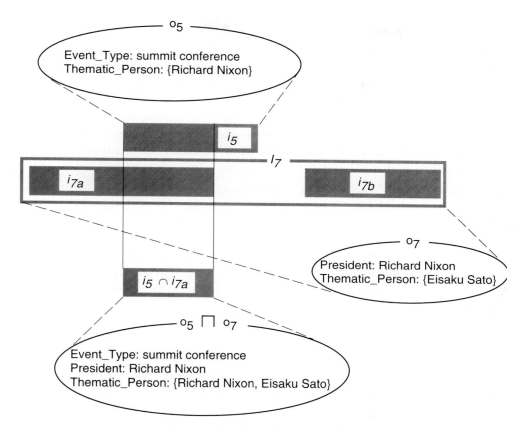

Figure 13-5 Overlapping video-objects.[*]

[*]© 1993 IEEE

- **Video Objects as Central Units** The *video-objects* described in Section 13.5 are the central units of the OVID system. Described in intuitive terms, each video-object consists of (1) the *oid* of the video-object, (2) a set of pairs of starting video frame numbers and an ending video frame numbers of the video scene, (3) a set of attribute/value pairs which describe the contents of the corresponding video frame sequence, and (4) basic operations such as play, inspect, and disaggregate.[8] Note that users can define different video-objects for the same sequence of video frames since their *oids* can differ. Each video-object is represented as a bar chart in our OVID user

---

[8] In Section 13.5, we did not discuss methods of video-objects. In the OVID, the methods are encapsulated into each video-object.

interface called VideoChart. Through the VideoChart interface, users can play/inspect/decompose a video-object, and define/compose new video-objects.

- **Dynamic and Incremental Object Identification and Definition**
  Since our video object data model does not assume the existence of a database schema, users should be able to identify a meaningful scene at any time and define the meaningful scene with its descriptional data as a video-object. Thus, the system should allow users to add necessary attributes as well as to use attributes of predefined video-objects. Currently, the attributes and attribute values are given to each object interactively in a manual fashion.

- **Video Object Composition**   A meaningful scene does not always correspond to a single consecutive sequence of video frames. Therefore, the system should facilitate the definition of a video-object which corresponds to more than one consecutive sequence of video frames. This operation corresponds to the *merge* operation described in Section 13.5. In the case of merging two video-objects into a new composite video-object, some descriptional data for these two video-objects may also be employable as descriptional data of the newly merged object. This kind of inheritance of descriptional data is achieved in our video object data model. Furthermore, OVID supports the creation of a video-object by applying the *overlap* operation to predefined video-objects. Some descriptional data for the predefined video objects are also inherited by the *overlapped* video-object.

- **Browsing by Video Object Disaggregation**   In order to browse a large[9] video-object, OVID generates a decomposition of a video-object into smaller video-objects. This decomposition corresponds to the *interval projection* operation described in Section 13.5. In OVID, the operation is called *disaggregation,* and the result of the disaggregation operation is a collection of smaller video-objects, each of which inherits some descriptional data from the original video-object. The disaggregation operation can be repeatedly applied, and so, this operation is useful in finding a desired scene contained in a large video-object in a navigational manner.

- **Generalization Hierarchy for Atomic Values**   OVID supports the use of a generalization (is-a) hierarchy which consists of atomic values that are used as attribute values of video-objects in both the phases of video-object creation and retrieval of video-objects.

- **Video Objects as Attribute Values**   As described in the video object model in Section 13.5, our model allows a video-object itself to be an

---

[9] Here, the term *large* refers to a video-object corresponding to a long sequence of video frames.

attribute value of another video-object. This is very useful in situations where it is difficult to describe a meaningful scene using text.

- **Ad Hoc Query Facility for Video Objects**   OVID has an ad hoc query facility, called *VideoSQL*. This facility allows for the retrieval of a collection of video-objects that satisfy a given condition. The inheritance based on the *interval inclusion relationships* is supported, and hence, users can formulate their queries as if the stored video-objects had already inherited necessary descriptional data from larger video-objects. Also, VideoSQL supports queries to retrieve video-objects that contain a specified video-object as their attribute value. Furthermore, we extend VideoSQL to audio/video object databases. That is, spatial and temporal compositions of audio and video objects can be treated.

The OVID system consists of the following components:

- VideoChart: A bar-chart type visual interface for manipulating video-objects.
- VideoSQL: An ad hoc query facility to retrieve video-objects.
- Video Object Definition Tool: A facility for object definition.

Each of these components will be described in the following subsections.

VideoChart

VideoChart has the following facilities:

1. Browsing video-objects in bar-chart form.
2. Playing video-objects as live video.
3. Inspecting and updating video-objects.
4. Composing (merge and overlap) video-objects.
5. Decomposing (disaggregating) video-objects.
6. Moving to the video object definition tool and VideoSQL.

Browsing of a Video Database
Using VideoChart, we can view the contents of a video database[10] in a visual form. The abscissa represents the sequence of video frame ID's (time-axis), and the numbers located at the top left and right corners denote the current range of the frame ID#. A collection of video-objects appearing in the specified range are displayed in bar-chart form. Each line denotes a single video-object. Fig. 13–6 shows that the currently displayed range is from frame #26830 to frame #31140.

---

[10] Currently, OVID can handle one video database at a time. The name of the video database for the current session should be specified at system start-up time.

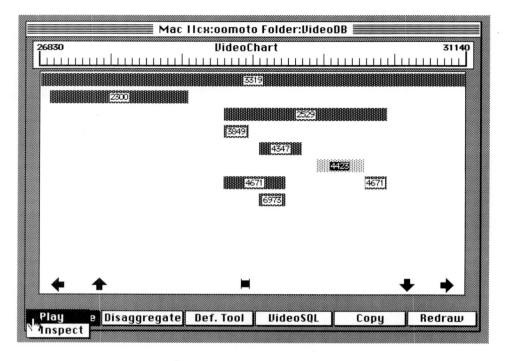

Figure 13–6   VideoChart.*

*© 1993 IEEE

The frame range can be scrolled with the arrow button, and its scale can be changed to an arbitrary range.

The number located in the center of each bar denotes the object identifier of the video-object. If a video-object consists of more than one frame sequence (for instance the object ID:4671), then those component video sequences are drawn in the same line.

Users can select an arbitrary video-object among these objects by clicking with the pointing device. After a video-object is selected, several operations can be applied by clicking the buttons below the chart. If a user clicks the Copy button, then the selected video-object is copied into a buffer in order to form Video-SQL queries later or to define another video-object. VideoChart offers play, inspect, and disaggregate operations, as the applicable operations (methods) for video-objects. Fig. 13–9 shows an example of the play operation for a certain video-object. The play operation simply replays the selected video-object on the monitor screen as live video.

Figure 13-7 *Play* operation for a video-object.*

*© NHK Service Center

The inspect operation first *evaluates* the specified video-object based on *interval inclusion inheritance,* and displays the attributes and the attribute values (including the inherited ones) of the video-object. For example, as shown in Fig. 13–7, the video-object with ID:4423 is defined for the range from frame #29635 to frame #30110. The window entitled Evaluated Value shows a list of attribute/value pairs. Each line in this window consists of an attribute name followed by its value. In this example, the evaluation of this video-object has three attributes, Prime_Minister, Location and Event_Type. Fig. 13–8 shows the original attribute/value pair which was defined for this video-object. Originally, this video-object had one attribute Event_Type and its value statement declaration. The interval of this video-object is included in video-objects with ID:2529 and ID:3319. The contents of the video-objects with ID:2529 and ID:3319 are shown in Fig. 13–10 and Fig. 13–11, respectively. The object with ID:2529 has the attribute Location, which is defined as *inheritable.*[11] The

---

[11] A collection of inheritable attributes is declared by our object definition tool, which will be described later.

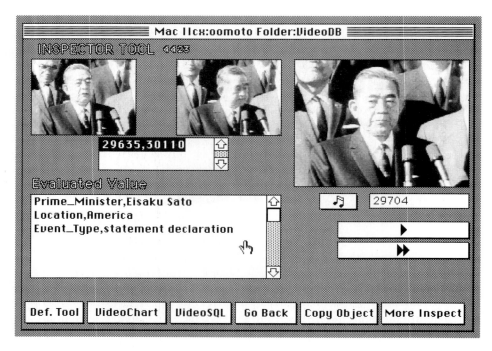

Figure 13-8   Inspection of a video-object.[*]

[*]© NHK Service Center

object with ID:3319 has the attributes `Prime_Minister` and `Successor`, where `Prime_Minister` is *inheritable,* and `Successor` is *non-inheritable.* Hence, the attribute/value pairs of `Location` and `Prime_Minister` are inherited by the video-object with ID:4423. This is an actual example of *interval inclusion inheritance* discussed in Section 13.5.

Merge and Overlap Operations in VideoChart

After a user selects two arbitrary video-objects, he or she can apply the operations *merge* and *overlap* to those video-objects. Suppose that a user selects the two video-objects with ID:6501 and ID:6762, and applies the `merge` operation to them. Then, as a result of merging these two video-objects, a new video-object, in this case, with ID:7757, is created. This situation corresponds to Example 13.3 in Section 13.5.

The video-objects with ID:6762 (concerned with Mr. Kakuei Tanaka) and with ID:6501 (concerned with Mr. Takeo Miki) are shown in Fig. 13–12 and Fig. 13–13, respectively. The former video-object (ID:6762) has three attributes,

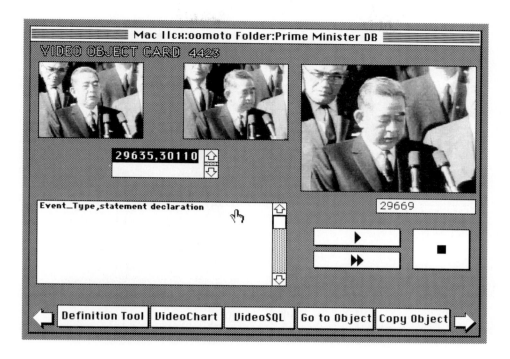

Figure 13-9 The original definition of the object with ID:4423.[*]

[*]© NHK Service Center

Prime_Minister, Successor, and Private_Life. Its Successor value is another video-object (ID:6501), and it is denoted by a string expression, video(6501). Also, its Private_Life value is the video-object with ID:5042. The latter video-object (ID:6501) has the attributes Prime_Minister and Private_Life. Its Private_Life value is also the video-object with ID:6240. The video-object (with ID:7757) resulting from the *merging* the objects with ID:6762 and ID:6501 is shown in Fig. 13–14. Note that the Prime_Minister value of this video-object becomes Japanese statesman based on the generalization hierarchy mentioned in Section 13.5, since the Prime_Minister values of the original video-objects are Kakuei Tanaka and Takeo Miki. Since the merge operation is applied to attribute values recursively, the objects with ID:5042 and ID:6240 are also merged, and a new video-object, in this case with ID:7653, is automatically created. Intuitively speaking, the video-object with ID:7757 is a video scene concerned with two Japanese prime ministers, and the video-object with ID:7653 concerns their private lives.

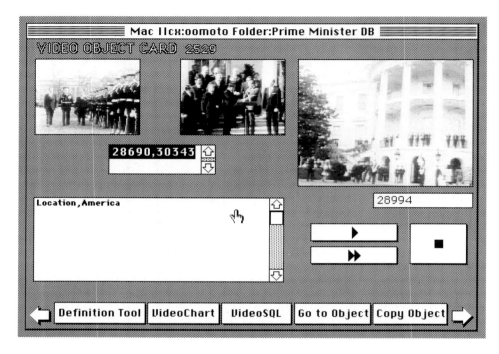

Figure 13–10   The definition of the object with ID:2529.*

*© NHK Service Center

Users can also apply the *overlap* operation to objects in a similar manner.

Disaggregation of a Video-Object

In OVID, an arbitrary video-object is automatically divided into ten sub-video-objects when the operation `disaggregate` is applied to it. Fig. 13–15 shows that Video Disaggregation System has just launched. In this example, a video-object defined over the frame interval from frame#:28690 to frame#:30343 is disaggregated into ten sub-video-objects. The system displays the ten sub-video-object icons, each of which represents a resultant of the *interval projection* of the original video-object onto ten overlapping intervals. (Here, the frame interval of the original video-object is simply (mechanically) divided.) Since these sub-video-objects can be treated as ordinary video-objects, the user can apply several further operations to them. When a user selects an arbitrary icon and applies the `play` operation to it with the menu selection, the corresponding live video is replayed in the region of the icon. If the `disaggregate` operation is applied to the sub-video-object, it is divided into smaller sub-sub-objects on the lower part

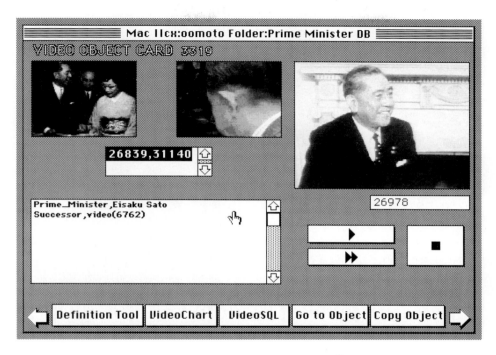

Figure 13-11 The definition of the object with ID:3319.*

*© NHK Service Center

of the screen. Further operations can be applied to these sub-sub-video-objects in a similar manner.

These sub-video-objects are treated as ordinary video-objects. That is, they have no attribute/value pairs, but are *evaluated* based on the *interval inclusion inheritance*.

VideoChart can also select and manipulate an arbitrary portion of the video frame sequence as a video-object. In such cases, the specified portion is considered to have no attribute/value pairs. Users can manipulate it as if it were an ordinary video-object. Therefore, the `play`, `inspect` and `disaggregate` operations can be applied to it. If `disaggregate` is applied, then the disaggregation system divides it into sub-video sequences in a similar manner.

We consider the proposed *disaggregation* facility to be suitable for the following situation: Suppose that we are going to define a new video-object over some portion of a large video sequence or to take out some appropriate video sequence for another purpose, for example, editing multimedia documents or desktop presentations. It may be complicated to search the entire sequence of the source video in order to pick up a desired scene, especially, in the case that the

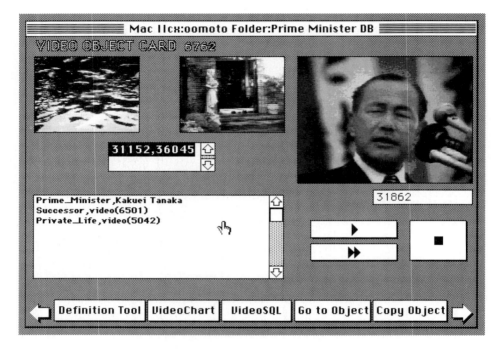

Figure 13-12   Definition of the object with ID:6762.*

*© NHK Service Center

source is very large, such as a two-hour movie. Even if users have an opportunity to see all the contents of the source video, it is not easy to remember the exact position of the target scene by its frame ID or by absolute time. It is usually only possible to remember the approximate order of several scenes. Disaggregation enables us to browse the whole video sequence from a view on an abstract level, approach the detailed scene gradually, and finally select the desirable sequence by this disaggregation facility.

VideoSQL

VideoSQL is a query language of OVID for retrieving video-objects. Fig. 13–16 shows an example query formulated by VideoSQL. Users can formulate Video-SQL queries in a fill-in-the-blank manner. The result of a VideoSQL query is a collection of video-objects that satisfy the specified condition. Before evaluating queries, the target video-objects are first *evaluated* based on the mechanism of

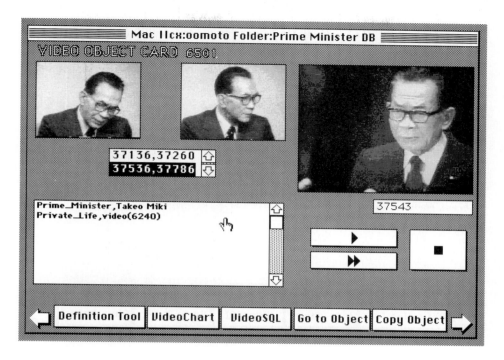

Figure 13-13   Definition of the object with ID:6501.[*]

[*]© NHK Service Center

the interval inclusion inheritance. Then, for each *evaluated* video-object, the specified condition of the query is examined. A VideoSQL query consists of the following clauses:

- **SELECT** clause:
  This clause is quite different from ordinary SQL. It specifies only the category of the resulting video-objects, i.e., `Continuous`, `Incontinuous`, or `anyObject`.

  - `Continuous` implies that only the video-objects, consisting of a single continuous video frame sequence, are retrieved.

  - `Incontinuous` implies that video-objects, consisting of more than one continuous video frame sequence, are retrieved.

  - `anyObject` implies that the system retrieves all types of video objects, whether they are continuous or not.

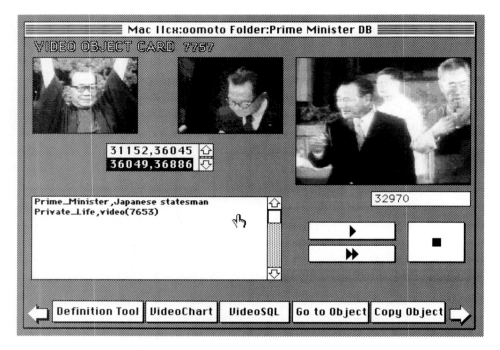

Figure 13-14 Definition of the *merge* of two objects.[*]

[*]© NHK Service Center

For instance, assume that a video-object o_1 consists of more than one video frame sequence, $\{i_1, i_2, i_3\}$, and o_2 consists of $\{i_4\}$. If Continuous is specified in the **SELECT** clause, then o_2 may be retrieved, but o_1 is not contained in the retrieval result. On the other hand, o_2 is not retrieved if Incontinuous is specified.

- **FROM** clause:
  This clause is used to specify the name of the video database.

- **WHERE** clause: This clause is used to specify the condition, consisting of attribute/value pairs and comparison operators. The video frame# also can be used in the qualification condition. The user can select the necessary attribute names by means of a pop-up menu. Currently, the user can specify the following conditions:

  1. [attribute] is [value | video object]

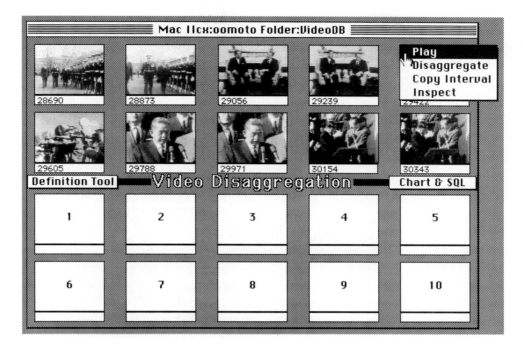

Figure 13–15   *Disaggregation* of a video-object.[*]

[*]© NHK Service Center

This condition results in the return of video-objects which have the specified attribute value or video-object. For instance, Fig. 13–16 is an example of retrieving video-objects, each of which has a certain video-object as the value of the `Successor` attribute. Users can paste the video-object into the `WHERE` clause,[12] which was already copied by the VideoChart `Copy` command. The pasted object is expressed in the string expression `video`(*object id*).

The atomic values used in OVID form a generalization hierarchy as a rooted tree (see Fig. 13–2). A user can specify an arbitrary node in the `WHERE` clause of his or her query. By means of this facility, we can formulate a query at a more abstract level. For instance, the following is a usage example of an abstract value. The *is-a* relationships, "walk *is-a* daily life" and "relaxation *is-a* daily life," are predefined. The query,

---

[12] In order to confirm the contents of the scene, the pasted object can be replayed in the query field by clicking the "Replay" button.

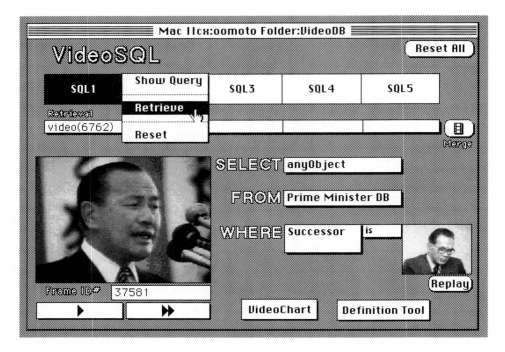

Figure 13-16 VideoSQL.*

*© NHK Service Center

Action is daily life

retrieves the video-objects for which the attribute value of Action in the evaluation is any of walk, relaxation, or daily life.

2. [attribute] contains [value | video object]
This condition is concerned with set-type attributes. It stipulates to return video-objects which contain the specified value or the specified video-object in the set value of the specified attribute.

3. definedOver [video sequence | video frame]
This condition orders the return of video-objects that are defined over the specified video frame sequence or frame. For example,

definedOver frame(15000)

causes the retrieval of the video-objects which include the video frame with frame#:15000 in their defined video sequence.

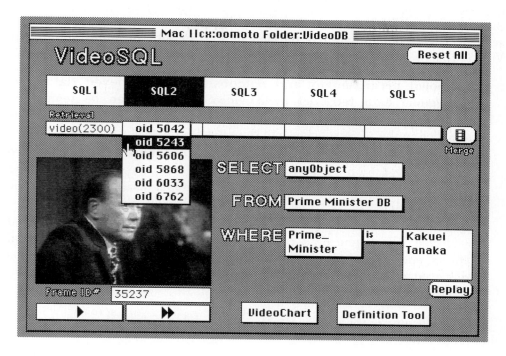

Figure 13-17   The selection of one of the retrievals.[*]

[*]© NHK Service Center

VideoSQL can formulate more than one query and save their retrieval results at the same time. The retrieved video-objects are able not only to be replayed, but also to become operands of the `Merge` operation. The display for each query is switched when a `SQL-X` button is clicked, where X denotes a query number. The oid's of the retrieved video-objects for each query are listed under the corresponding `SQL-X` button, and users can select the desired video-object from the list (see Fig. 13–17). The selected video-object for each query is entered into the `Retrieval` field. Clicking the arrow button on the lower left corner, the highlighted video-object is replayed in the window.

VideoSQL offers the facility to `Merge` the retrieved video-objects for multiple queries. After executing several queries and selecting one video-object from the answer list for each query, these video-objects can be merged into a new video-object by means of clicking the `Merge` button.

As an extension of the above facilities, we recently modified our VideoSQL to support both audio and video objects. In most cases, data manipulation languages (DML) are used mainly for retrieving and updating data, and not so much for arranging and displaying retrieved data, which forces every client application program to have a code for arranging and displaying retrieved data. Since every data set retrieved from our OVID system is a collection of time-sequenced video/audio data, we decided to add the following functions to our VideoSQL:

- **Temporal arrangement and composition of retrieved data** The video/audio data retrieved by a VideoSQL query can be temporally arranged and composed. The temporal arrangement of video/audio data is specified in the `time` subclause in the `select` clause of a VideoSQL query.
- **Spatial arrangement and composition of retrieved data** The video data retrieved by a VideoSQL query can also be spatially arranged and composed. The spatial arrangement of video/audio data is specified in the `space` subclause in the `select` clause of a VideoSQL query.
- **Special effect for retrieved data** Temporally- and spatially- arranged retrieved video/audio data can be displayed with several special visual effects, such as mosaic, fade-in/out, etc. The special effects to display the retrieved objects are specified in the `option` subclause in the `select` clause of a VideoSQL query.

The following is the outline syntax of a modified VideoSQL query with the above functions:

```
select window1 { time{ -- }
                 space{ -- }
                 option{ -- }}
from Video v1, v2
     Audio a1, a2
where < condition >
```

The `window` subclause in the `select` clause specifies the unit of window to display the series of retrieved video data. The `time` subclause in the `select` clause specifies temporal arrangement and composition, such as "A and B start at the same time" or "A starts first, and B starts t seconds later" using `start(A,B)` and `startstart(A,B,t)`. The `space` subclause in the `select` clause specifies the spatial arrangement and composition, such as screen size and location. The `option` subclause in the `select` clause specifies visual effects, mosaic, fade-in/out, etc. The `from` clause specifies video/audio object variables in the given query. The `where` clause specifies conditions for attribute values, using object variables to retrieve video/audio objects from the given database.

By realizing the above functions at the DML level (in our system, at the level of VideoSQL), we are provided with the following advantages:

Spatial Arrangement of windows   Temporal Arrangement of audio/video objects

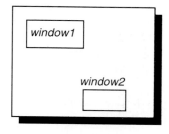

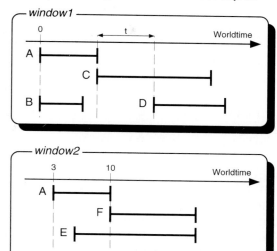

Figure 13-18   An example spatial and temporal arrangement of audio and video objects.[*]

- Application programs are simplified, since DMLs, as our VideoSQL, are responsible for arranging, composing and displaying a collection of retrieved video/audio data.
- DBMSs can be responsible for optimizing database access and delivering retrieved data.

The following is an example query using the above facilities. This example is illustrated in Fig. 13–18.

```
select window1{ time{ start(A,B);
                      follow(A,C);
                      startstart(C,D(t));
                      Worldtime(A:0,*) }
               space{ +50+50@200x100 }
               option{ A:fast } }
       window2{ time{ Worldtime(A:3,10);
                      follow(A,F);
                      end(E,F) }
```

```
                        space{ +300+300@150x60 }
                        option{ F:fade-in } }
        from    Video A,C,F;
                Audio B,D,E;
        where   A.car = 'skyline' and C.car = 'corona' and
                B.title = 'yesterday' and D.title = 'freedom' and
                E.creature = 'dog' and F.title = 'thriller'
```

In this example, the `window1` subclause specifies the following: The temporal arrangement of the audio/video objects is that the video A and the audio B start at the same time, the video C follows A, the audio D starts t seconds later than C, and the duration of video A is from the origin of the replay standard time (absolute time) to the end of A. The spatial arrangement of `window1` is that the top-left of the video window is located at (50,50), and the window size is 200 by 100. Additionally, the video A is replayed quickly. The `window2` subclause specifies the following: The replay A takes place from 3 to 10 seconds of the replay standard time, and the video F follows this 7 second duration. The audio E is replayed so that E will finish at the same time as video F. In the `option` subclause, video F should start with a *fade-in* style. In this example, the video objects are A, C, and E, and the audio objects are B, D, and F. Futhermore, the attribute values which these objects should have are specified in the `where` clause.

An example retrieval by this modified VideoSQL is shown in Fig. 13–19.

Video Object Definition Tool

The video object definition tool, shown in Fig. 13–20, is used to define or to update video-objects. There are several functions to control the video replay and facilities to search an arbitrary video frame with the frame ID in the left part of the tool. In the right part of the definition tool, the facilities for video object definition are arranged, and the object definition is accomplished by filling-in-the-blanks with attribute values with a pointing device. Attribute names are selected by a pull-down menu. Atomic values can be specified by selecting an appropriate value from the scroll window of the `Generalization Browser` in the lower right part. Fig. 13–20 indicates that "Richard Nixon *is-a* American statesman," "James Carter *is-a* American statesman," and the current selected node in the hierarchy is "American Statesman."

To maintain the dictionary of the generalization hierarchy, a visual tool is provided. With this tool, users can browse and navigate in the generalization hierarchy and add arbitrary nodes. The maintenance of attribute names is also supported by this tool. The *inheritability* of attributes is globally effective over the entire database.

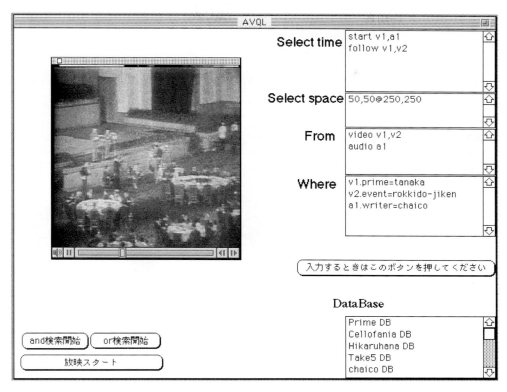

Figure 13-19 An example retrieval for both audio and video objects.[*]

[*]© NHK Service Center

Implementation

Our current OVID system was implemented on a Macintosh with HyperCard [6]. We chose the platform of prototyping for the OVID for the following reason: HyperCard provides rich facilities to construct the interactive and graphical user interface, and decreases the amount of the effort required for implementation of the user interface. It also has the capability to build simple databases in its native facilities.

Each video-object is represented by a "card" of HyperCard, and a database, which is the set of video-objects, is represented by a set of cards, a "stack." Currently, a single database can be specified in each session. The card id of each card is used as the object identifier because it is unique in given stack. The process procedures for deriving the attribute value on the merge and overlap operations are provided in the system as the program codes of HyperTalk, which is the pro-

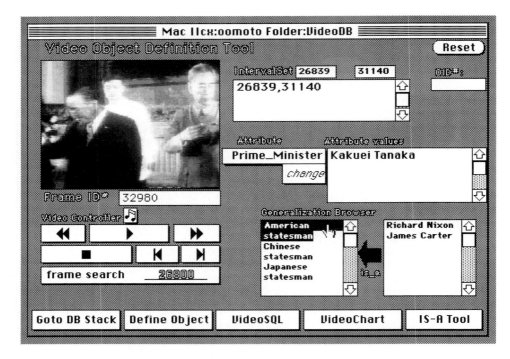

Figure 13-20   Video-object definition tool.*

*© NHK Service Center

gramming language for HyperCard. The video images are stored on a hard disk whose format is QuickTime. A video image is displayed on the monitor screen by an XCMD of HyperCard. Therefore, the video images and descriptional data for each video object are stored separately.

13.7   Conclusion

In this chapter, the technical background, basic problems, and current research activity involved with video databases were described. Concerning our prototype video database system, OVID, the basic concepts were described and the system overview of OVID was illustrated. Currently OVID-II is under development for further performance improvement.

Research concerning video technology and video databases is beginning to make progress, and further research is needed to realize practically useful video database systems. Since video data is a very intuitive representation of information, its use in computer systems will lead to great progress. We must provide the necessary concepts and technology for video databases with which we can freely manipulate video data without being restricted by the type of computer systems being used.

References

[1] Fox, E.A., Special Issue on Digital Multimedia Systems, *Communications of the ACM*, Vol. 34, No. 4, Apr 1991.

[2] Mandalkern, D., Special Section on Graphical User Interfaces: The Next Generation, *Communications of the ACM*, Vol. 36, No. 4, Apr 1993.

[3] Adiba, M. and Quang, N.B., "Historical multi-media databases," in *Proc. of the 12th International Conference on Very Large Data Bases*, Kyoto, Aug 1986, pp. 63–70.

[4] Allen, J.F., "Maintaining knowledge about temporal intervals," *Communications of the ACM*, Vol.26, No.11, Nov 1983, pp. 832–843.

[5] Anderson, D.P. and Osawa, Y., "A file system for continuous media," *ACM Trans. on Computer Systems*, Vol. 10, No. 4, Nov 1992, pp. 311–337.

[6] Apple Computer Inc., *HyperCard Script Language Guide: The HyperTalk Language*. Cupertino, CA: Addison-Wesley, 1988.

[7] Apple Computer Inc., *QuickTime 2.0 Developers Guide for Macintosh*, 1994.

[8] Ariki, Y., Iwanari, E., and Motegi, Y., "Detection and description of TV news article," in *47th International Federation for Information and Documentation*, Saitama, Japan, 1994, pp.198–202.

[9] Atkinson, M., Bancilhon, F., DeWitt, D., Dittrich, K., Maier, D., and Zdonic, S., "The object-oriented database system manifesto," in *Deductive and Object-Oriented Databases*. New York: North-Holland, 1990, pp. 223–240.

[10] Bancilhon, F. and Khoshafian, S., "A calculus for complex objects," in *Proc. of ACM PODS*, Cambridge, MA, Mar 1986, pp. 53–59.

[11] Cattell,R.G.G, *Object Data Management*. Reading, MA: Addison-Wesley, 1991.

[12] Chorafas,D.N., *Intelligent Multimedia Databases*. Englewood Cliffs, NJ: Prentice-Hall, 1994.

[13] Christodoulakis, S., Ho, F., and Theodoridou, M., "The multimedia object presentation manager of MINOS: A systematic approach," in *Proc. of the ACM SIGMOD International Conference*, Washington, DC, May 1986, pp. 295–310.

[14] Ghandeharizadeh, S. and Ramos, L., "Continuous retrieval of multimedia data using parallelism," *IEEE Trans. on Knowledge and Data Engineering*, Vol.5, No.4, Aug 1993, pp. 658–669.

[15] Gibbs, S., Breiteneder, C., and Tsichritzis, D., "Audio/video databases," in *Proc. of the 9th International. Conference on Data Engineering*, 1993, pp. 381–390.

[16] Gibbs, S.J. and Tsichritzis, D.C., *Multimedia Programming*. New York: ACM Press, 1994.

[17] Hodges, M.E., Sasnett, R.M., and Ackerman, M.S., "A Construction set for multimedia applications," *IEEE Software*, Vol.6, No.1, Jan 1989, pp. 37-43.

[18] Hodges, M.E. and Sasnett, R.M., "Plastic editors for multimedia documents," in *Proc. of USENIX Summer '91*, Nashville, TN, June 1991, pp. 463–471.

[19] Little, T.D.C. and Ghafoor, A., "Interval-based conceptual models for time-dependent multimedia data," *IEEE Trans. on Knowledge and Data Engineering*, Vol. 5, No. 4, Aug 1993, pp. 551–563.

[20] Little, T.D.C. and Ghafoor, A., "Multimedia object models for synchronization and databases," in *Proc. of Sixth International Conference on Data Engineering*, Los Angeles, Feb 1990, pp. 20–27.

[21] Mackay, W.E., "EVA: An experimental video annotator for symbolic analysis of video data," *SIGCHI Bulletin*, Vol.21, No.2, Oct1989, pp. 68-71.

[22] Mackay, W.E. and Davenport, G., "Virtual video editing in interactive multimedia applications," *Communications of the ACM*, Vol.32, No.7, July 1989, pp. 802–810.

[23] Maier, D., Jonathan, W., and Staehli, R., "Storage system architectures for continuous media data," in *Proc. of 4th International Conference on Data Organization and Algorithms (FODO '93)*, Lecture Notes in Computer Science 730, Berlin: Springer-Verlag, Oct 1993, pp. 1–18.

[24] Nagasaka, A. and Tanaka, Y., "Automatic video indexing and full-video search for object appearances," in *Visual Database Systems, II*, (Knuth, E. and Wegner, L.M. Eds.), Amsterdam: North-Holland, 1992, pp. 113–127.

[25] NHK Service Center., *Showashi 9 Saisho Retsuden (The Showa Era: The History of Prime Ministers)*. PIONEER LDC Corp., Japan, 1987.

[26] Oomoto, E. and Tanaka, K., "OVID: Design and implementation of a video-object database system," *IEEE Trans. on Knowledge and Data Engineering*, Vol. 5, No. 4, Aug 1993, pp. 629–643.

[27] Parkes, A.P., "CLORIS: A prototype video-based intelligent computer-assisted instruction system," in *Proc. of R.I.A.O. '88 Conference*, Cambridge, MA, Oct 1987, pp. 24–50.

[28] Shimojo, S., Matsuura, T., Fujikawa, K., Nishio, S., and Miyahara, H., "Harmony: Its design and implementation," in *Proc. of International Conference on Multimedia Information Systems*, Singapore, June 1991, McGraw-Hill, pp. 243–257.

[29] Smith, J. and Smith, D.C.P., "Database abstractions: Aggregation and generalization," *ACM Trans. of Database Systems*, Vol.2, No.2, 1977, 105–133.

[30] Smith, K.E. and Zdonic, S.B., "Intermedia: A case study of difference between relational and object-oriented database systems," in *Proc. of OOPSLA '87*, Orlando, FL, Oct 1987, pp. 452–465.

[31] Takano, H., Matoba, H., and Hara, Y., "VDM: A video data model for handling video data in a hypermedia system," in *Proceedings of the 46th Annual Convention IPS Japan*, 7G-4, 1993, pp. 4-221–4-222.

[32] Tanaka, K. and Yoshikawa, M., "Towards abstracting complex database objects: generalization, reduction and unification of set-type objects (extended abstract)," in *Proc. of the 2nd International Conference on Database Theory*, Bruges, Belgium, Aug 1988, *Lecture Notes in Computer Science* 326, Springer-Verlag, pp. 252–266.

[33] Woelk, D., Kim, W., and Luther, W., "An object-oriented approach to multimedia databases," in *Proc. of the ACM SIGMOD '86*, Washington,DC, May 1986, pp. 311–325.

[34] Woelk, D., and Kim, W., "Multimedia information management in an object-oriented database system," in *Proc. of the 13th International Conference on Very Large Data Bases*, Brighton, England, Sep 1987, pp. 319–329.

Third-Generation Distributed Hypermedia Systems

John F. Buford and Lloyd Rutledge

Distributed Multimedia Systems Lab
Department of Computer Science
University of Massachusetts Lowell
Lowell, MA 01854
{buford,lrutledg}@cs.uml.edu

What is a distributed hypermedia system? Many different hypermedia systems have been described as distributed systems. Some use a distributed storage model for the hyperdocument database. Others provide a shared hypermedia system to a group of users distributed on a LAN. Still others provide hypermedia access to information repositories that are distributed over a wide-area network.

We use the following informal definition for a distributed hypermedia system: A distributed hypermedia system provides a group of users logically transparent access to heterogeneous hypermedia information repositories that are distributed across local- and wide-area networks. The minimal access mode is browsing via associative addressing and authoring; searching, annotating, and collaborative access are examples of others modes that may be supported. An important aspect in the design of distributed hypermedia systems is scalability to large amounts of multimedia information, large numbers of users, and large numbers of repositories.

This chapter examines the design of third-generation distributed hypermedia systems. The identification of generations of hypermedia systems is borrowed from Halasz [25] who put existing contemporary systems in the category of second generation, and identified seven areas of functionality which third-generation hypermedia systems should address (Table 14–1). Halasz' issues

Issue	Description
Integration of Search and Query Functionality	Integration of information retrieval and DBMS facilities; pattern matching languages for hypergraph manipulation
Composite Node Types	In addition to content nodes, need container or collection nodes
Virtual Structures over Node Collections	Computationally defined hypergraphs, analogous to database views
Computation over Hypermedia Networks	Integrated computational engines available to the application
Versioning of Nodes and Subgraphs	Maintaining change history at both node and graph level; version identification as an attribute in search and query
Support for Collaborative Work	Support for shared access to hypertext, and group protocols
Extensibility and Tailorability	Easier customization of hypermedia system by end user

Table 14–1 Halasz' Seven Issues for third-generation hypermedia systems [25].

involve enriching the hypertext paradigm, but do not address its use in a network of distributed heterogeneous hypermedia systems. Consequently we add to his list the following issues (Table 14–2):

> Open hyperdocument and hyperlinking architecture
>
> Mobile and distributed objects
>
> Multimedia document models and coupling of the hypermedia system with distributed multimedia system services
>
> Security, which includes transaction security and safety of mobile objects

Second-generation hypertext and hypermedia systems have been reviewed by a number of authors [16], [42]. Many of the key ideas of these systems have been incorporated into the Dexter Hypertext Model [26] and the HyTime standard [33]. An overview of HyTime is provided in Section 14.3.

Third-generation distributed hypermedia systems are not yet available. The most widely used *distributed* hypermedia system today is the World Wide Web (WWW). Although it is widely used, the WWW lacks features that have been part of earlier second-generation hypertext systems. However, it is evolving rapidly and a number of improvements are being pursued which are discussed in the next section.

Issue	Description
Open hyperdocument and open hyperlinking architecture	Support the delivery of any document type Supporting linking between any application mediated content or content type Use of content-based addressing Integration with hyperapplications
Mobile and distributed objects	The ability to deliver active behavior integrated with or in addition to static documents Allow objects to be dynamically deployed anywhere in the system
Interactive time-based multimedia document models	The ability to represent and deliver hypermedia documents which include rich interactive time-based multimedia presentation Integration with continuous media system services
Security	Transaction security; safety of mobile objects

Table 14–2 Issues for third-generation distributed hypermedia systems.

Later in this chapter we summarize the key features of several other distributed hypermedia systems including Hyper-G [36], [41], Microcosm [29], [30], [27], and HyOctane [8], [14]. These systems support interoperation with WWW, but provide additional features. Hyper-G and Microcosm are commercially available and deployed systems.

Third-generation distributed hypermedia systems permit interoperability between servers providing *heterogeneous* document types. These systems are open not only to a specific category or type of document model, but provide an *open hyperdocument* architecture. Using distributed object management facilities and an *open hyperlinking* mechanism, hypermedia documents will link to or include embedded *hyperapplication* content as well as arbitrary stored media. Powerful mobile object virtual machines permit a range of dynamic behavior to be delivered, from simple interaction to agents to full applications. Content addressing and search capabilities include *content-based retrieval* for multimedia data types. Hypermedia document services are integrated with multimedia system services for *real-time scalable delivery* of temporally composed multimedia content. The system provides security services for access control and authentication to support transactions, safe mobile objects, protection of intellectual property, and privacy, in addition to the collaboration support described by Halasz.

The next section provides a brief review of the WWW, including various enhancements that are being developed. Section 14.4 discusses the four issues for third-generation distributed hypermedia systems in detail. The next three sections present Hyper-G, Microcosm, and HyOctane.

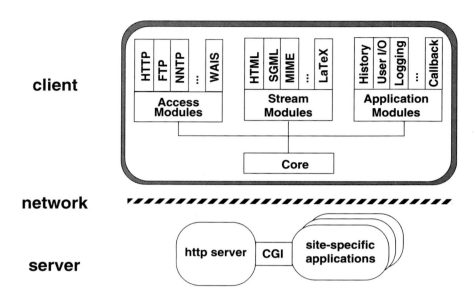

Figure 14-1 Client and server components of the WWW architecture. The client architecture follows the W3C reference model.

14.1   World Wide Web

Basic Features

The World Wide Web (WWW) was developed by Tim Berners-Lee at CERN in the 1989–1991 period as an information system for collaborating physicists. By 1992 there were about fifty sites connected throughout the Internet. After the NCSA Mosaic client was released it grew rapidly. Today there are many thousands of sites and a significant percentage of traffic on the Internet backbone is estimated to be WWW-related [50].

The key features of the WWW have become well known. Because of its pervasive deployment it has become the reference point by which other systems are differentiated. Further, its universality on the Internet has led to the notion of the HTML browser as a new application delivery platform, one that transcends hardware and operating system dependencies faced by conventional applications.

The WWW architecture (Fig. 14–1) is based on client-server transfer of hypertext documents which are encoded using a document markup language called HTML (hypertext markup language) [3]. Clients and servers communicate using a light-weight protocol called Hypertext Transfer Protocol (http) [6]. Content addressing uses the URL (Uniform Resource Locator) notation[4].

Simple request ::

    GET <URL I URN> CR LF

Full request ::

    <Method> UR HTTP/<version #> CR LF [<HTRQ Header>] [CR LF <data>]

    <Method> ::

        GET I HEAD I CHECKOUT I SHOW METHOD I PUT I DELETE I POST

        I LINK I UNLINK I CHECKIN I TEXT SEARCH I SEARCH

Figure 14-2   Summary of http 1.0 used in the WWW.

Version	Major Features
HTML 1.0	Basic document structure, anchors, links
HTML 2.0	Forms
HTML 3.0	Tables, mathematical equations

Table 14–2 Evolution of HTML

The http protocol is a simplified file transfer protocol with extensions for hypertext operations (Fig. 14–2). Clients connect directly to the http server specified in a given URL document address. The required document is transferred in its entirety to the client's system for viewing. The text of the document is contained in the HTML file. Non-text media such as image files, audio, and video may be referenced in an HTML file, which are retrieved in bulk after the client has downloaded the HTML file.

A novel aspect of http is its format negotiation algorithm. When making a request, a client can specify several acceptable alternative formats for a given object. These formats can be ranked by the client, which can also specify a maximum transfer time and a maximum object size. The server then selects the best format given these constraints.

HTML as a relatively simple markup language contributed to the rapid use of the WWW. New features have been added to increase the functionality of HTML (Table 14–2). The current server design is independent of document type. The World Wide Web Consortium (W3C) has defined a reference architecture for clients and servers (Fig. 14–1). This illustrates the open-protocol, open-content model direction of the WWW.

Application Interface and Integration

The server can be extended in arbitrary ways by using the Common Gateway Interface (CGI) (Fig. 14–1). This method is widely used to provide interfaces to databases, text search engines, and input forms support. However CGI is a primitive integration method compared to other client-server technologies. Integration of the WWW with the OMG Common Object Request Broker Architecture (CORBA) [44] and Microsoft Component Object Model (COM) is currently underway and will accelerate the integration of applications with the WWW.

Perhaps the most significant development for the WWW in 1995 was the introduction of Sun's Java programming language [23] and its virtual machine for platform-independent delivery of applets. Java is similar to the C++ programming language, but with some restrictions that are intended to make its scripts safe to download, simplify programming, and minimize the chances of programming error. Java is compiled to a virtual machine, the Java VM, which is a 32-bit stack machine. Each Java-aware browser provides an implementation of the Java VM. An HTML document includes a Java applet by reference; the applet is then automatically transferred to the browser for execution when the document is loaded.

In addition to being an elegant programming language, Java introduced a number of important ideas for extending the WWW, including:

A model for secure application delivery

Incremental delivery of applets

Platform-independent delivery of applications

It is likely that other virtual machines will be introduced which could support other programming languages or provide better performance. For example, Omniware [40] is a virtual machine that could be used to deliver other general purpose programming languages and which has reported smaller code size and faster execution time compared to Java VM code.

Information Retrieval and Search

The absence of integrated search and retrieval facilities in the WWW server design has not yet prevented convenient access to its wide-ranging information. Many sites provide search interfaces that are designed for searching the contents of that site. Some web sites are maintained as search interfaces over much of the web. Such sites continuously index other sites by retrieving documents automatically from each site on a periodic basis. To maintain up-to-date search indices today requires regularly moving large amounts of data around the Internet; more efficient techniques are currently being considered [7], [52].

Similarly the absence of a predefined link hierarchy or global Web server directory has not precluded organization of web resources by category, topic, or interest. Instead, various sites have developed specialized index structures for a community of users, such as musicians, investors, sports enthusiasts, etc.

Evolution of the WWW

The WWW architecture is flexible enough to support many different improvements and evolutionary scenarios. Many proposals for enhancements and tools can be found in the WWW conference proceedings [54], [55], [56]. An industry consortium, W3C, has been formed to specify standards for Web practice.

Current directions for W3C activities include:

Document style sheets

Support for virtual reality based on the Virtual Reality Modeling Language (VRML)

Collaboration

Secure transactions

Mobile code and distributed objects

The Web is at the early stages of becoming a platform-independent application delivery vehicle. With the plugable client architecture, third-party content types can be delivered via the Web. The Java programming environment permits access to other services on the network. This open architecture makes it possible for sophisticated applications to be delivered via the Web.

14.2   Issues for Distributed Hypermedia Systems

Overview

In this section we describe the four issues for distributed hypermedia systems presented in Section 14.1. In addition to presenting some of the background research done in the hypertext community, we present motivations as to why these issues are important functionally. The overall concept is that distributed hypermedia systems are a key facility in building global networked information and collaboration systems.

Open Hyperdocument and Hyperlinking Architecture

The concept of hyperlinking is strikingly simple: the ability to create and traverse associations between any arbitrary information elements. Despite the generality of this paradigm, few if any hypermedia systems have been developed which can claim a universal link service—the ability to support hyperlinking between any two objects, no matter what the content model, application interface, or computing environment. The ability of a hypermedia system to be inclusive of arbitrary information sources is a powerful feature for users. With this ability, associative access becomes an intrinsic facility of the user's desktop. Without it, the user must consider and maintain separate spaces. of information access.

The hypertext community has been concerned with the design of open hypermedia systems for some time. Sun's link service [48] and Englebart's open hyperdocument model [20] were some of the first articulations of this. A summary of research in open hypermedia systems is available [53]. The Flag taxonomy [43], building on concepts from the Dexter model, can be used to analyze specific hypermedia systems with regard to openness.

System services for distributed objects such as Distributed COM [47] and CORBA [44] provide a substrate by which the extent of open hypermedia systems can be enlarged. Distributed object systems combine a general object model with location transparent access to any object. Any application or service can be integrated into a distributed computing environment by defining language-independent interfaces. For example, the linking in OLE used to place embedded objects from one application in container objects in another application is an example of hyperapplication functionality.

Surprisingly, the object services included in these systems do not include specific hyperlink-style link services. For example, the relationship service in CORBAservices [45] is not designed for hyperlink traversal.

Little has been done so far to take advantage of distributed object systems in the design of distributed hypermedia systems [49].

The ability to support linking to any type of information requires content-based addressing, for example, a link to an instrument in a musical score or an object in an image. The development of such addressing forms is related to research in content-based retrieval [24].

Mobile Code and Distributed Objects

A distributed hypermedia system forms an information structure over which useful computation can be performed for users, including search, dynamic document creation, event generation, generalization, and discovery. The efficient performance of these activities depends on the available computing and network resources throughout the system. Integration of the hypermedia system with distributed computing environments such as those described in the previous section provides a flexible foundation from which such computation can be performed.

Mobile code refers to the ability to relocate applications or applets for execution at any server or client in a distributed system, possibly for the purpose of performing computation locally or for managing resources. The ability of HTML documents to embed Java applets is a special case of mobile code. Allowing applets to be downloaded to servers and to be dynamically distributed offers additional benefits.

Mobile object systems appear technically feasible and could be implemented using distributed object systems. For some purposes, they offer advantages over conventional client-server techniques. For example, an object might be resident at a particular server in order to trigger a message to a user when some set of conditions occurs. Further, mobile code might lead to better performance by moving computation to the server side.

There are a number of interesting issues related to the design of these systems [51]. These include:

1. Scalability: How much local resource is needed per mobile object? How many mobile objects can be expected? What is the lifetime of a mobile object at a given site?

2. Security: How can mobile objects be authenticated? How are mobile objects authorized? How can service access be controlled to specific subsets of services? Give that access to a service interface is authorized, what external information flows should be allowed?

3. Management: How can mobile objects be metered for resource usage? What classes of mobile objects should be defined (e.g., transient vs. persistent; mono vs. group)? Should management be done on collections of objects rather than individual ones?

4. Services: Should there be standard service interfaces at each server, or is an interface repository sufficient?

5. Computation flow: What is the best way to structure mobile objects for a particular task? What should be done client-side and what should be done server-side?

The integration of mobile code and distributed objects with the WWW is attracting interest. Table 14–3 summarizes some of the topics to be discussed at an upcoming workshop sponsored by OMG and W3C. Recent work in mobile code systems has been described [39], [40], [51].

Topic	Description
Web object types	How can the Web architecture and content model be modeled as a set of distributed objects
Applets and agents	Use of mobile code at the client and the server Agent services
Digital Libraries, Databases, & Object File Systems	Use of persistence stores in document delivery Large-scale distributed hypermedia systems
Wire Protocols & Binding	http vs. CORBA 2.0 IIOP (Internet Interoperability Protocol)
Future of CGI	CGI vs. CORBA vs. Distributed OLE
Directory Services & Trading	Document address versus service locating

Table 14–3 Joint W3C/OMG Workshop on Distributed Objects and Mobile Code

Multimedia Document Models

Integrating a multimedia document model with a hypermedia system increases the representational power of the system and the generality of the system design. Examples of multimedia document models include the Amsterdam Hypermedia Model (AHM) [28] and HyTime [33], [19]. We first give an overview of HyTime's modeling concepts since the HyOctane system discussed later in this chapter uses the HyTime model. Subsequently we consider HyTime's features for time, content addressing, scriptware, and interaction. In earlier work we have provided a detailed assessment of HyTime [13].

HyTime is an SGML-based metalanguage for designing multimedia document models. The main modeling abstractions provided by HyTime include hyperlinks, location addressing (anchoring), N-dimensional spaces called finite coordinate spaces, transformations between spaces (projection and rendering), and time/space composition. HyTime has a document query language called HyQ, and facilities for tracking document access. HyQ can be used to form dynamic links and to define the contents of a document by a search for document property or attribute. The HyQ query language coupled with the underlying structured document model available through SGML makes it possible for a HyTime system to immediately address several of Halasz' issues for third-generation systems—search and query functionality, virtual structures over node collections, and computation over hypermedia networks.

HyTime provides many different addressing techniques that can be used to form an anchor (Table 14–4). These forms can be directly applied to any text content. An application can also define its own content specific notations and create HyTime anchors which use these notations. A set of different addresses can be aggregated (aggloc) in various ways, and a set of addresses can define the span of an anchor (spanloc).

Address Attribute	Brief Description
Name space	Position based on unique name associated with document node
Data	Position based on treating content as ordered units of quanta
Node	Position in document structure, including locating by position in: 1) document tree, 2) one or more paths in a tree; 3) position in a list of nodes of a document; 4) relative position with respect to some other node
Property	Position based on property attributes associated with nodes
Bibliographic	A bibliographic reference to off-line material

Table 14–4 Summary of HyTime addressing forms

HyTime introduces the notion of a location ladder which generalizes the concept of an anchor. Any location reference can refer to an already existing location, and an arbitrary series of location references can be chained together. This allows a newer anchor, perhaps created in a different document owned by another user, to build upon existing anchors.

As discussed in previous work [13], HyTime is an extensive yet incomplete model for multimedia documents since it intentionally excludes representing interaction and presentation features. It provides no framework for integrating scriptware [10]. Media content addressing can be accommodated by defining new location address notations, but no forms are defined in the standard.

Putting multimedia modeling semantics in the hypermedia system allows many hypermedia applications to leverage this functionality and adds generality to the system design. We next discuss some of the challenges in integrating the hypermedia system with system services for continuous media.

Today's distributed hypermedia systems have simplistic use of multimedia data types both because of the limited semantics of document models and because of lack of underlying system support for delivery of multimedia information. Consequently today's document transfer protocols such as http are bulk transfer oriented. Once suitable multimedia system services are available, it will be possible to support real-time scalable delivery of hypermedia content in addition to the current bulk transfer model. This should lead to more efficient and responsive delivery, at the cost of greater management overhead.

Most approaches for resource management in distributed multimedia systems involve resource reservation based on the application's required quality of service [9]. The system provides an orchestration service which manages the resource allocation and monitoring in a distributed environment. The unit of system resource allocation is called a session. Sessions are typically created on a per-media basis.

In a hypermedia system, resource requirements depend on the characteristics of the document being presented. Additionally, the user's navigation through a collection of documents may cause frequent changes to the resource

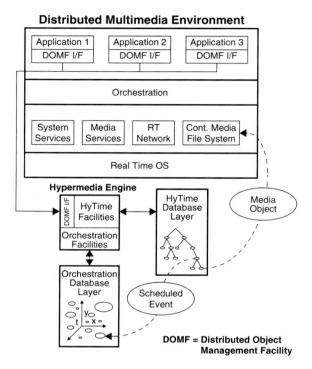

Figure 14-3 Hypermedia document and meta-information databases used to specify HM session parameters for orchestration layer [12].

requirements. Consequently, we have suggested [12] the concept of a hypermedia session (HM) which extends the concept of a continuous media (CM) session used in various models of CM schedulers. A hypermedia session is an aggregation of a number of continuous (CM) and discrete (DM) media sessions for a given hyperdocument. The hypermedia session can be used by an application to describe the presentation and delivery requirements of a hypermedia document.

A hypermedia application constructs the description of the hypermedia session which it wants the orchestration layer to perform resource management for. The orchestration layer in turn uses this session description to request initial allocation of session resources from the disk server and other resource managers. This sequence is shown in Fig. 14–3. The hypermedia structure stored in the hypermedia document database is processed to extract the meta-information needed for the orchestration of resources associated with the document. This meta-information is available in the orchestration database. The application consults the orchestration database and generates a HM session request to the orchestration layer, which internally performs the resource allocation associated with the HM session.

As the application's requirements change during a session, the application and the orchestration layer interact to negotiate these changes in terms of resource allocation. This may require further access to the hypermedia meta-information.

Security

The requirements for security in distributed hypermedia systems are varied because of the wide range of activities for which the system might be used. Consider the following examples.

1. (Confidentiality) Private information is delivered over insecure networks only to those who are authorized to access it.

2. (Intellectual property rights) Publishers wish to deliver licensed material and desire a technical solution to preventing unauthorized redistribution.

3. (Authentication) To enforce access rights, systems wish to verify the identity of the user.

4. (Privacy) Users wish to access information without disclosing their identity, or may wish that information about their browsing history, search, and information access is restricted.

5. (Access rights) Groups of users may use the system for collaboration, requiring synchronized shared access and different modalities of access, such as read, write, update, annotate, create, and delete.

6. (Access rights) Search and browsing of documents by users might be limited to only publicly accessible files, or those that have the proper access level.

7. (Transaction integrity) The hypermedia system is integrated with a database system which uses transactions when performing updates to guarantee atomic, consistent, isolated, and durable results.

8. (Authentication, secure communication) The hypermedia system is used to carry financial transactions which require secure data entry, secure transmission, secure authentication of all parties, etc.

9. (Non-repudiation) A user cancels a financial transaction and requires verification that the cancellation request was received.

10. (Safety) Applets or agents can be downloaded to servers to perform computation on behalf of users and extend the functionality of the hypermedia system. Mobile objects (viruses) might intentionally or inadvertently lead to denial of service for other users.

11.(Management) The system's security policies must be unambiguously specified. The policies must be applied consistently as new users, information, and
services are added to the system.

The distributed hypermedia system should base its security facilities on the
security services provided by the operating system software wherever possible.
For example, OMG's CORBAServices [46] defines a security model for both intra-
ORB and inter-ORB environments. This specification includes a security reference model, a security architecture, and security interfaces for applications and
system designers.

14.3   Hyper-G[1]

Hyper-G [36], [1], [41] is a distributed hypermedia system developed at the
Institute for Computer-Supported New Media at the Graz University of
Technology. Hyper-G has become a popular distributed hypermedia system
because of its more robust support for the hypertext paradigm and server management tools than WWW servers. The designers of Hyper-G describe it as a second-generation distributed hypermedia system.

Each Hyper-G server maintains a hierarchical organization of its documents. This hierarchy, based on a hyperdocument node type called a collection,
provides a fixed structure for users to locate information. The collection node is
not a visible document type, but is hardwired into the server, protocol, and clients. Dynamic views of sets of documents can also be created.

Each Hyper-G server has a document server, a link server, and a full-text
server (Fig. 14–4). The document server provides Hyper-G documents to the presentation clients. The link server stores and processes links separately from
their documents, facilitating the use of link overlays and enabling the storage of
links in a database so that documents processed by Hyper-G can show the links
that lead to them as well as from them.

The full-text server (Fig. 14–4) is a text search engine that permits full-text
search of Hyper-G collections both within a single server and across server
boundaries. The user is able to select sections of the document hierarchy to focus
the search. Hyper-G supports a document format called HTF (hypertext format)
as well as HTML; support for full SGML is anticipated.

Hyper-G uses a client-server protocol that is similar to http. However,
Hyper-G clients connect to only one home server. The home server acts as the
gateway to all remote repositories including non-Hyper-G servers such as
gopher, WWW, and wais. Each server is separately administered, and has consistent facilities for node level access control. Access control is based on the Unix
file system access control.

---

[1] Hyper-G is being distributed commercially under the name HyperWave™.

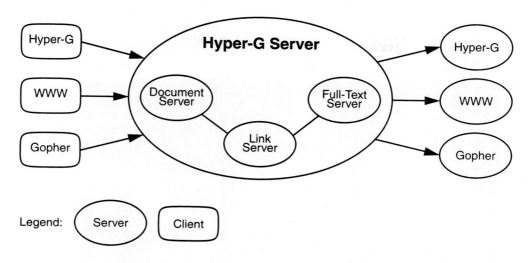

Figure 14-4   Hyper-G server architecture diagram [2].

The Hyper-G server architecture includes a link database and support for object-access management. Hyper-G maintains a database of links separate from the documents. This makes it possible to provide bidirectional links, so that a user can navigate both in-coming and out-going links. It also makes possible the display of a link map which shows adjacent documents in the Web. Bidirectional links are maintained for links which point to remote as well as local documents.

Fig. 14–5 shows the Harmony viewer in a browsing session for a collection of documents created by the first author for a course on hypermedia. Users were able to create both private and shared document collections for project work in teams. The Harmony browser provides maps of the hypergraph, an image viewer with sub-area anchors, and a 3D navigator with hyperlinks to objects in the 3D world.

14.4   Microcosm

Microcosm is an open and extensible hypermedia architecture developed at the University of Southampton[30]. It allows users to browse and query large multimedia collections. Microcosm is distinguished from many other hypermedia systems by storing links separately from their documents. It is also distinguished by its ability to store and process links connecting to information provided by third-party applications as well as connecting to information stored in documents.

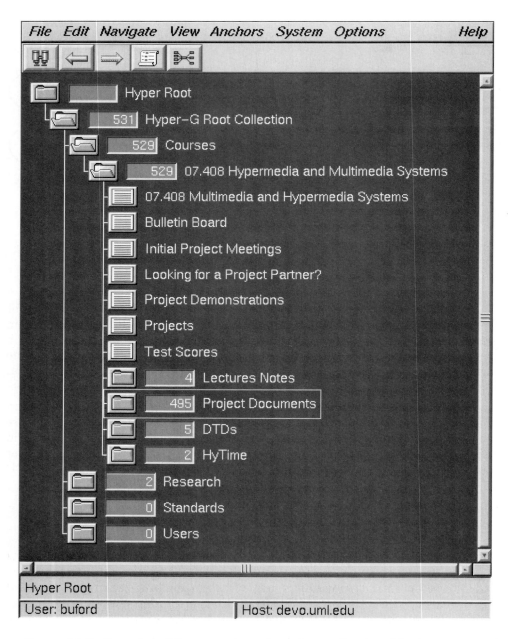

Figure 14-5 Snapshot of Harmony viewer browsing a collection of documents created for a hypermedia class. Numbers by each collection node indicate the number of documents contained within the collection.

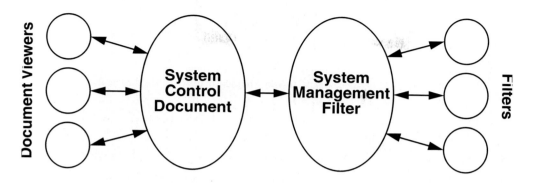

Figure 14-6   Microcosm distributed model [29].

Microcosm orchestrates multiple document viewers for a single presentation. In preparation for a document's presentation, Microcosm also coordinates multiple filters, each of which is a source for information and external processing that makes up part of the document (Fig. 14–6). A filter can be, for example, a database that provides hypertext links for use with a particular collection of documents. A filter may also simply provide access to a particular document. The Filter Management System (FMS) receives messages from the running filters and coordinates their processing. The FMS communicates with the Document Control System (DCS) about the message received so the DCS can provide the proper instructions to the document, or node content, viewers. It is with this model that Microcosm's separation of links from document storage and presentation is achieved.

This division between presentation and link processing requires cooperation between the mechanisms that handle each. The activation of a link consists of selecting an object within the presentation and then selecting a link involving that object. With Microcosm, multiple-node content viewers are coordinated for a single seamless presentation. However, the selection of a single object within that presentation involves only one node content viewer, the one responsible for that object. With one of its object selected, a node content viewer can display an *action menu* for the user showing the possibilities for link activity involving that object. When a link activity is chosen, the node content viewer then communicates with the appropriate link filter to request the link activity. Table shows the action menu options, the type of link filter each option involves, and the activity performed.

Many different applications can be document, or node content, viewers in a presentation orchestrated by the DCS. Applications can be coded so that they communicate with the DCS using Microcosm's message protocol. This communication provides the DCS with much control over the viewers, and thus over the presentation as a whole. However, many applications that can act as viewers

Action Menu Option	Link Filter Involved	Action Performed
Follow Link	Linkbase Filter	Accesses a link database to determine the end of the link starting at selected object. Asks Microcosm to active node content viewer for displaying link end.
Compute Link	Computed Linker	Computes a link that has not been manually created, such as a run-time query.
Start Link	Linker	Stores the selected object in a link database as the start of a link.
End Link	Linker	Stores the selected object in a link database as the end of a link.

Table 14–5 Microcosm Action Menu Options [18].

have been coded without awareness of this protocol. Microcosm controls such applications through its Universal Viewer (UV).

The UV provides a wrapper around the application's interface. This interface wrapper provides the action menu shared by other Microcosm node content viewers. When an action is chosen, the UV communicates with the application to determine what object has been selected as a component of the link. The UV then sends the appropriate message to a filter for processing the link. In order for the UV to interface as such with an application, it must be coded with an understanding of how that application communicates. This interface must provide the ability for the UV to determine the current object selected using the application.

Fig. 14–7 and Fig. 14–8 show examples of authoring and following Microcosm links with image and video data, respectively.

14.5 HyOctane™

Overview

HyOctane™ is a hypermedia engine for HyTime [33], [19] hypermedia documents previously developed by the authors [8]. The HyOctane system has three fundamental features:

1. The document model is open to any HyTime or SGML DTD, including HTML.

2. The hypermedia semantics of HyTime related to links, time and space, and anchoring are available.

Figure 14-7   Microcosm link authoring process with images [38]. © 1996 Association for Computing Machinery, Inc. Reprinted by permission.

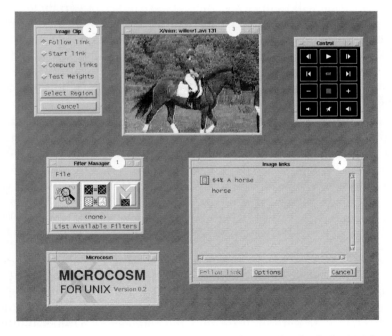

Figure 14-8   Microcosm link following process from video [38]. © 1996 Association for Computing Machinery, Inc. Reprinted by permission.

3. The server stores a parsed compact version of the document, simplifying the design of the client, allowing incremental document access, and leading to reduced network overhead.

System Description

A HyTime engine takes as input the parse tree produced by the SGML parser. It performs HyTime-specific validation of the parse tree, and may create special index structures to make navigation of the HyTime constructs in the document more efficient. It provides a HyTime-specific application programmer interface so that an application can transverse the document tree and locate the HyTime structures of interest. The HyTime standard does not specify the design of HyTime engines, nor does it define an API. A natural way to organize this API, as we describe in the development of the HyOctane™ HyTime engine [8], is to provide classes which are associated with each functional area such as linking, locating, scheduling, etc.

A HyTime application accesses the HyTime document structure stored in the engine and presents this to the user. User interaction may lead to presentation state change, and ultimately to navigation within the document. All presentation and interaction decisions are handled by the application. Any non-trivial HyTime application will require specific software or scriptware in order to implement the presentation and interaction semantics. This is an impediment to the development of HyTime application development and delivery. On the development side it means that an application developer faces both a DTD design task and a programming task. On the delivery side, while the HyTime document instance is portable, the application software or scriptware that interfaces with the engine is generally not.

Our solution to this problem is to integrate the HyTime engine with a standard script player, such as the virtual machine player specified in MHEG-3 [35]. This addresses the portability issue of the presentation/interaction software and also makes the delivery model open to arbitrary scripting languages. In this model, an application designer creates a HyTime DTD and writes a presentation script for this DTD. The presentation script is interchanged with the DTD and document instance whenever the document is to be delivered to the end user. We refer to the resulting delivery architecture as an open hyperdocument model.

The initial client-server model of our engine used a server-side OODBMS to store the parse tree directly as a tree of objects. This mapping turned out to be inefficient for storage of large numbers of documents. Subsequently we have revised the internal organization to create a compact representation of the document which is still convenient for indexing substructure within the document. Our measurements to date indicate that the compact OODBMS storage format that we have designed is compressed from the native text files by a ratio of 3.5:1. These measurements on based on a HyTime application we have designed called HMP (Hypermedia Presentation DTD). We have done similar measurements on storing parsed HTML 2.0 documents in the database. For small documents (1K to 3K bytes) we obtained compression ratios in the range of 1.5: 1 to 2.0:1. For a large document (about 300K bytes) we obtain a compression ratio of 3:1.

We obtain more compression for HyTime documents than HTML documents due to two factors. First, a HyTime DTD like HMP has many levels of nesting due to the structural requirements in the HyTime meta-DTD. For example, to associate a location with an image in a HMP document, the HyTime meta-DTD requires it to be three levels down from the root element of the document. This high degree of nesting results in many repetitions of an element's begin and end tags. Second, HMP documents also use a large number of attributes. Most elements in a HMP document have no data, but contain several attributes. This is due to HyTime element type forms which make extensive use of attributes. HMP is a representative HyTime DTD. Its extensive used of attributes and the high degree of element nesting are a direct result of the requirements placed on it by the HyTime meta-DTD. Our server-side preprocessing and storage technique takes advantage of these two features, leading to more efficient storage and delivery of HyTime, HTML, and SGML documents compared to existing systems.

The HyOctane engine uses a OODBMS to store parsed documents as objects. It also implements the HyQ document query language. HyQ queries are translated to queries in the query language of the OODBMS in which the document structure is stored. In previous work [13] we present sample HyQ queries for the following cases:

Obtaining the anchors of a link

Obtaining the links attached to a given anchor

Finding the anchors for a given anchor role for the hyperlink

Finding the depth one Web from current document

Halasz' issue-position query [25]

Guided tour via keyword attribute or keyword in content of node

The HyOctane engine is interfaced to an http server which passes the preparsed, compact HTML and HyTime documents to the client for direct presentation. Compared to the current httpd server design, the HyOctane approach: 1) saves significant storage space at the server; 2) eliminates the need for client side parsing; 3) reduces the amount of information being transmitted over the network; 4) is the basis for incremental delivery of SGML-encoded documents; 5) facilitates server-side document structure queries.

14.6   Conclusions

Existing distributed hypermedia systems, while powerful information access tools, should be extended in the direction of third generation hypermedia functionality. The requirements for third generation systems have been described by previous researchers.

In this chapter we have extended the ideas of third-generation hypermedia systems to address issues that are important to distributed hypermedia systems. The four issues presented here are complementary to advances in distributed systems, including research in system services for continuous media and the specification of distributed object services and frameworks. The integration of distributed hypermedia system design with the infrastructure being developed by systems vendors and researchers will accelerate the delivery of new distributed hypermedia applications. The interplay between the hypermedia system design and the system services will influence the scalability of these future information systems, an important issue mentioned in the introduction.

By virtue of its large-scale deployment, the WWW has become a reference model for what minimal facilities a distributed hypermedia system should provide. The other systems described here—Hyper-G, Microcosm, and HyOctane—provide further capabilities in different dimensions that are important for the realization of third generation distributed hypermedia systems.

References

[1] Andrews, K., and Kappe, F. "Soaring through hyperspace: A snapshot of Hyper-G and its Harmony client," in *Proc. Eurographics Multimedia 1994.*

[2] Andrews, K., Kappe, F., and Maurer, H. "Serving information to the Web with Hyper-G," in *Proc. Third International World-Wide Web Conference*, Darmstadt, Germany, Apr 1995.

[3] Berners-Lee, T., and Connolly, D., *Hypertext Markup Language—2.0*, RFC 1866, Nov 1995.

[4] Berners-Lee, T. *Universal Resource Identifiers in WWW: A Unifying Syntax for the Expression of Names and Addresses of Objects on the Network as used in the World-Wide Web*, RFC 1630, June 1994.

[5] Berners-Lee, T., Masinter, L., and McCahill, M. *Uniform Resource Locators*, RFC 1738, Dec 1994.

[6] Berners-Lee, T., Fielding, R., and Frystyk, H. *Hypertext Transfer Protocol—HTTP 1.0*, Internet Draft, Feb 1996.

[7] Bowman, C.M., Schwartz, M.F., McBowman, C., Danzin, P.B., Hardy, D.R., and Manber, U. "The Harvest information discovery and access system" in *Proc. Second Intl. World-Wide Web Conference*, Chicago, Oct 1994. pp. 763-771.

[8] Buford, J. F., Rutledge, L., Rutledge, J. L., and Keskin, C. "HyOctane: A HyTime engine for an MMIS," *Multimedia Systems*, Vol. 1, No. 4, Feb 1994, pp. 173-185.

[9] Buford, J. F. K. (contr. ed.). *Multimedia Systems*. ACM Press and Addison-Wesley, 1994.

[10] Buford, J.F., Rutledge, L., and Rutledge, J. "Integrating object-oriented scripting languages with HyTime," in *1994 Intl. IEEE Conf. on Multimedia Computing and Systems*, Boston, May 1994.

[11] Buford, J. F., Rutledge, L., and Rutledge, J. "Toward automatic generation of HyTime applications," in *Proc. Eurographics Multimedia 1994*, Graz, Austria, June 1994.

[12] Buford, J. F., Rutledge, L., and Gopal, C. "Storage server requirements for delivery of hypermedia documents," in *Proc. Multimedia Computing and Networking 95*, San Jose, CA, Feb 1995

[13] Buford, J. F. "Evaluation of a query language for hypermedia documents," in *Proc. DAGS 95 Electronic Publishing and the Information Superhighway,* Boston, May 1995.

[14] Buford, J. F. "A transfer protocol for an open hyperdocument model server," in *Proc. ED-MEDIA 95*, Graz, Austria, June 1995.

[15] Buford, J. F. "Distributed multimedia information systems," in *Standards for Electronic Imaging Technologies, Devices, and Systems* (M. Nier, ed.) SPIE, Vol. CR61, Feb 1996.

[16] Conklin, J. "Hypertext: An introduction and survey." *Computer*, Sep 1987, Vol. 20, No. 9.

[17] Davis, H. C., Hall, W., Heath, I., Hill, G., and Wilkins, R. "Towards an integrated information environment with open hypermedia systems," in *Proc. ECHT '92*, ACM Press, Milan, Italy, 1992, pp. 181-190.

[18] Davis, H.C., Knight, S., and Hall, W. "Light hypermedia link services: A study of the third party application integration," in *Proc. ECHT '94*, Edinburgh, Scotland, pp. 41-50.

[19] DeRose, S. and Durand, D. *HyTime: Making Hypermedia Work*. Kluwer Press, 1994.

[20] Englebart, D. "Knowledge-domain interoperability and an open hyperdocument system," in *Proc. CSCW-90*, Boston, Oct 1990.

[21] Goldfarb, C. *SGML Handbook*. Oxford: Oxford University Press, 1991.

[22] Gopal, C., and Buford, J. "Delivering hypermedia sessions from a continuous media server" in *Multimedia Information Storage and Management* (S. Chung, ed.) Kluwer Press, to appear.

[23] Gosling, J., and McGilton, H. "The Java Language Environment. A White Paper." Sun Microsystems, Oct 1995.

[24] Gudivada, V., and Raghavan, V. (eds.). Special Issue on Content-Based Retrieval. *Computer,* Vol. 28, No. 9, Sep 1995.

[25] Halasz, F. "Reflections on notecards: Seven issues for next generation systems." *CACM,* Vol. 31. No. 7, July 1988, pp. 836-855.

[26] Halasz, F., and Schwartz, M., "The Dexter hypertext reference model," *Communications of the ACM*, Vol. 37, No. 2, Feb 1994, pp. 30-39. (Also in *Proc. NIST Hypertext Standardization Workshop*, Jan 1990.)

[27] Hall, W., Davis, H., and Hutchings, G. *Rethinking Hypermedia: The Microcosm Approach*. Norwell, MA: Kluwer Press, 1996.

[28] Hardman, L. Bulterman, D.C.A., and Rossum, G.V. "The Amsterdam hypermedia model: Extending hypertext to support real multimedia," *Hypermedia,* Vol. 5, No. 1, 1993, pp. 47-69.

[29] Hill, G., Wilkins, R., and Hall, W. "Open and reconfigurable hypermedia systems: A filter-based model," *Hypermedia,* Vol. 5, No. 2., 1993, pp. 103-118.

[30] Hill, G., and Hall, W. "Extending the microcosm model to a distributed environment," in *Proc. ECHT '94*, Edinburgh, Scotland, Sep 1994, pp. 32-40.

[31] Hill, G., Hall, W., De Roure, D., and Carr, L. "Applying open hypertext principles to the WWW," in *Intl. Workshop on Hypermedia Design 95*, Montpelier, France, 1995.

[32] Interactive Multimedia Association. *Multimedia System Services Specification Version 1.0.* June 1993.

[33] ISO/IEC IS 10744. Hypermedia/Time-based Document Structuring Language (HyTime) (August 1992).

[34] ISO/IEC IS 13522-1 MHEG Part 1 (Nov. 1995).

[35] ISO/IEC DIS 13522-3 MHEG Part 3 (Feb. 1996)

[36] Kappe, F., Andrews, K., Fasuhingbauer, J., Gaisbauer, M., Maurer, H., Pilcher, M., and Schipflinger, J. "Hyper-G: A new tool for distributed hypermedia." in *Proc. Distributed Multimedia Systems and Applications 1994,* Honolulu, Aug 1994. pp. 209-214.

[37] Kappe, F., Pani, G., Schnable, F. "The architecture of a massively distributed hypermedia system," *Internet Research: Electronic Networks Applications and Policy,* Spring 1993, Vol. 3, No. 1, pp. 10-24.

[38] Lewis, P., Davis, H., Griffiths, S., Wilkins, R., and Hall, W. "Media-based navigation with generic links," in *Proc. ACM Hypertext 96*, pp. 215-223

[39] Lingnau, A., Drobnik, O. and Dömel, P. "An HTTP-based infrastructure for mobile agents," in *Proceedings of the Fourth International World Wide Web Conference*, Boston, Dec 1995.

[40] Lucco, S., Sharp, O. and Wahbe, R. "Omniware: A universal substrate for Web programming," in *Proceedings of the Fourth International World Wide Web Conference*, Boston, Dec 1995.

[41] Maurer, H. "Advancing the ideas of World Wide Web," in *Proc. Distributed Multimedia Systems and Applications 1994*, Honolulu, Aug 1994. pp. 201-203.

[42] Nielsen, J. *Hypertext and Hypermedia*, Academic Press, 1990.

[43] Østerbye, K., and Will, U. K. "The flag taxonomy of open hypermedia systems," in *Proc. ACM Hypertext 96*, Washington, DC, 1996, pp. 129-139.

[44] Object Management Group. *The Common Object Request Broker: Architecture and Specification*, Rev. 2.0, July 1995.

[45] Object Management Group. *CORBAservices: Common Object Services Specification.* Mar 31, 1995.

[46] Object Management Group. *CORBASecurity.* Dec 1995.

[47] Orfali, R., Harkey, D., and Edwards, J. *The Essential Distributed Objects Survival Guide.* New York: John Wiley, 1996.

[48] Pearl, A. "Sun's link service: A protocol for open linking," in *Proc. Hypertext 89*, Pittsburgh, 1989, pp 137-146.

[49] Pinto, J.S., Martins, J.A., Pauwels, W.H.J.B., and Santos, B.S. "Hypermedia authoring tools based on OLE technology," *J. Multimedia Tools and Applications,* Vol. 1, 1995, pp. 245-262.

[50] Schulzrinne, H. "World Wide Web: Whence, whither, what next?" *IEEE Network,* Mar/Apr 1996, Vol. 10, No. 2, pp. 10-17.

[51] Rutledge, L., Buford, J., and Price, R. "Mobile objects and the HyTime hyperdocument server," in *Proc. IMC 96*, Rostock, Germany, Feb 1996.

[52] Weiss, R., Vélez, B., Sheldon, M.A., Manprempre, C., Szilagye, P., Duda, A., and Gifford, D.K. "HyPursuit: A hierarchical network search engine that exploits content-

link hypertext clustering," in *Proc. ACM Hypertext 96*, Washington, DC, 1996, pp. 180-193.

[53] Will, U.K., and Osterbye, K. (eds.) *Proc. of the ECHT '94 Workshop on Open Hypermedia Systems*. Edinburgh, Scotland, Sep 1994.

[54] Selected Papers of the First World-Wide Web Conference (R. Cailliau, ed.). *Computer Networks and ISDN Systems*, Vol. 27, No. 2, Nov 1994.

[55] Proceedings of the Third International World-Wide Web Conference (D. Kroemker, ed.) *Computer Networks and ISDN Systems*, Vol. 27, No. 6, Apr 1995.

[56] Proceedings of the Fourth World-Wide Web Conference. *World-Wide Web Journal*, Vol. 1, No 1. Nov 1995.

About the Contributors

A. Atarashi

Atsushi Atarashi was born in Japan in 1960. He received his M.S. degree in computer science from the Tokyo Institute of Technology in 1985. He joined NEC Corporation in 1985 and is currently an assistant manager at C&C Research Laboratories. From 1994 to 1995, he was a visiting industrial fellow at the Berkeley Multimedia Research Center at the University of California, Berkeley. His primary research interest lies in multimedia communication architectures based on object-oriented technology.

Shahab Baqai

Shahab Baqai received his B.S. degree in Aeronautical Engineering in 1985 from the College of Aeronautical Engineering (CAE), NED Engineering University, Pakistan. He obtained his M.S. degree in Electrical Engineering in 1994 from the University of Southern California, Los Angeles. Currently, he is working toward a PhD degree in the School of Electrical and Computer Engineering (ECE) at Purdue University, West Lafayette, Indiana.

From 1985 to 1988, he worked for the Pakistan Air Force. In 1988, he joined the faculty of CAE, where he taught undergraduate courses until 1991. He is currently a graduate research assistant in the department of ECE at Purdue University. His research interests include distributed multimedia systems, high-speed networking, and image and video representation formats. He is also a member of Eta Kappa Nu.

Christian Breiteneder

Christian Breiteneder received his PhD in 1991 from the University of Technology in Vienna, Austria. Currently he is a research scientist with the Institute of Communication at GMD, where he is working in the Digital Media Lab.

Milind M. Buddhikot

Milind Buddhikot received the Bachelor of Engineering (B.E.) degree in electrical engineering, with Distinction, from the University of Bombay, India, in August, 1987, and the Master of Technology (M.Tech) degree in communications engineering from the Indian Institute of Technology, Bombay, in December 1988. He is presently a D.Sc candidate in the Department of Computer Science at Washington University in St. Louis. His research interests are in the areas of high-speed networking and multimedia computing. He has served on the program committee of IEEE Local Computer Networks (LCN) Conferences for the years 1994, 1995, and 1996. He likes to daydream about renouncing computer science research and becoming a professional racquetball player.

John F. Buford

John F. Buford is an Associate Professor of Computer Science and Director of the Distributed Multimedia Systems Laboratory at the University of Massachusetts Lowell. His research interests are in distributed hypermedia and multimedia systems.

Dick C.A. Bulterman

Dick Bulterman completed his PhD at Brown University in 1977 having graduated in 1973 from Hope College with a degree in economics. He is currently a senior researcher and research group head of the multimedia group at CWI. His interests include multimedia networking, authoring and play-back of adaptable multimedia presentations, and dynamic scheduling of synchronized remote data. He is currently involved with a number of Europe-funded research projects, including the technical management of a substantial multimedia authoring system project.

S.K. Chang

Shi-Kuo Chang received the B.S. degree from National Taiwan University in 1965. He received his M.S. and PhD degrees from the University of California, Berkeley, in 1967 and 1969, respectively. He was a research scientist at the IBM Watson Research Center from 1969 to 1975. From 1975 to 1982, he was Associate Professor and Professor at the Department of Information Engineering, University of Illinois at Chicago. From 1982 to 1986, he was Professor and Chairman of the Department of Electrical and Computer Engineering, Illinois Institute of Technology. From 1986 to 1991, he was Professor and Chairman of the Department of Computer Science, University of Pittsburgh. He is currently Professor and Director of the Center for Parallel, Distributed, and Intelligent Systems, University of Pittsburgh.

Dr. Chang is a Fellow of the IEEE. He has been a consultant for IBM, Bell Laboratories, Standard Oil, Honeywell, the Naval Research Laboratory, and Siemens. His research interests include distributed systems, image information systems, visual languages, and multimedia communications. Dr. Chang has published over two hundred papers and written or edited eleven books. His books, *Principles of Pictorial Information Systems Design* (Prentice-Hall, 1989), *Principles of Visual Programming Systems* (Prentice-Hall, 1990), and *Symbolic Projection for Image Information Retrieval and Spatial Reasoning* (Academic Press) are pioneering advanced textbooks in these research areas.

Dr. Chang is Editor-in-Chief of the *Journal of Visual Languages and Computing*, published by Academic Press, and of the *International Journal of Software Engineering & Knowledge Engineering*, published by World Scientific Press.

M.F. Costabile

Maria F. Costabile received her doctoral degree in mathematics at the Universitá della Calabria, Italy, where she worked first as a postdoctoral fellow and later as assistant professor. She has been a visiting scientist in several overseas universities. Her research activity was initially in image analysis and computer vision and currently includes theory of visual languages, visual interfaces, visual languages for querying databases, human-computer interaction, usability of interactive systems, and user models. She has published more than 50 papers on these topics and edited three books. She has been on the organizing and program committees of several international conferences and workshops and has served as program co-chairperson of the International Workshops on Advanced Visual Interfaces AVI'96.

Dr. Costabile is a member of the ACM, IEEE, the Italian Association for Computing, and the Italian Chapter of IAPR. She is chairperson of the Italian Chapter of ACM SIGCHI.

Nevenka Dimitrova

Nevenka Dimitrova is a Senior Member of Research Staff at Philips Research. She obtained her PhD (1995) and M.S. (1991) in computer science from Arizona State University and her B.S. (1984) in mathematics and computer science from the University of Kiril and Metodij, Skopje, Macedonia. Her main research interests are in the areas of content-based video analysis and retrieval, compression-based retrieval, and their applications in advanced multimedia systems.

Arif Ghafoor

Arif Ghafoor received his B.S. degree in electrical engineering from the University of Engineering and Technology, Lahore, Pakistan, in 1976, and his M.S., MPhil, and PhD from Columbia University in 1977, 1980, and 1985, respectively. In the spring of 1991, he joined the faculty of the School of Electrical and Computer Engineering, Purdue University, where he is an Associate Professor and coordinator for the Distributed Multimedia Systems Laboratory. Prior to joining Purdue University, he was on the faculty of Syracuse University since 1984. His research interests include parallel and distributed systems and multimedia information systems. He has published over 100 technical papers in these areas, in leading journals and conferences. His research has been funded by the DARPA, the NSF, NYNEX, AT&T, Fuji Electric Co., Intel, IBM, and General Electric Co.

Dr. Ghafoor has served on the program committees of various IEEE conferences. He has been invited to give tutorials and seminars in the area of multimedia systems at many leading national and international conferences. Currently, he is serving on the editorial boards of *Multimedia Systems* (ACM/Springer-Verlag, publishers), the *Journal on Multimedia Tools and Applications*, and the *Journal of Parallel and Distributed Databases*. He is also a guest editor and co-guest editor of special issues of various journals including *Multimedia Systems* (Nov 1995), the *Journal of Parallel and Distributed Computing* (Dec 1995), the *IEEE Journal of Selected Areas in Communications* (1996) and the *Journal on Multimedia Tools and Applications* (1996). These special issues are on various aspects of multimedia information systems. He is a Senior Member of the IEEE and a member of Eta Kappa Nu.

Simon Gibbs

Simon Gibbs is a senior scientist at GMD—the German National Research Center for Information Technology—and is responsible f r the GMD Digital Media Lab. His activities include coordinating research in the Digital Media Lab and developing the Virtual Studio and Teleport systems. His current interests are in programming environments for multimedia applications and media processing systems.

Carole Goble

Carole Goble is a Senior Lecturer at the Department of Computer Science, University of Manchester, UK. She graduated from Manchester in 1982 with a BSc Hons. in Computer and Information Systems, and has been a faculty member since 1985. She has a wide range of interests centered around information modeling, including hypermedia and multimedia information systems, terminological systems, medical informatics, multidatabase mediation, and user interfaces to databases, with current funding in all of these areas. She has published over 35 papers in these areas.

Forouzan Golshani

Forouzan Golshani is a Professor in the Department of Computer Science and Engineering at Arizona State University. He received his B.S. (1976) from the Ayra Mehy University of Technology, Iran, and his M.S. (1979) and PhD (1982) in computer science from the University of Warwick, England. His research interests include multimedia systems, virtual reality, databases and artificial intelligence, mathematical foundations of software systems, logic, and functional programming and non-conventional architectures.

William I. Grosky

William I. Grosky is currently professor and chair of the Computer Science Department at Wayne State University in Detroit, Michigan. Before joining Wayne State in 1976, he was an assistant professor of Information and Computer Science at the Georgia Institute of Technology in Atlanta. His current research interests are in multimedia information systems, hypermedia, image databases, web technology, object-oriented databases, and database interfaces. He is a founding member of Intelligent Media LLC, a Michigan-based company working on the integration of new media into information technologies.

William received his B.S. in mathematics from MIT in 1965, his M.S. in Applied Mathematics from Brown University in 1968, and his PhD from Yale University in 1971. He has given many short courses in the area of database management for local industries and has been invited to lecture on multimedia information systems worldwide. Serving also on many database and multimedia conference program committees, he is currently on the editorial boards of *IEEE Multimedia*, the *Journal of Database Management*, and *Pattern Recognition*.

R. Hamakawa

Rei Hamakawa was born in Japan in 1957. He received his B.S. degree in mathematical engineering from the University of Tokyo in 1981. He joined NEC Corporation in 1981 and is an engineering manager of its Personal C&C Group Planning Division. From 1988 to 1989, he was a visiting research associate at the Center for Artificial Intelligence of George Mason University, Virginia, where he worked with autonomous intelligent robots. His present interests lie primarily in multimedia communications and intelligent user interfaces.

Lynda Hardman

Lynda Hardman graduated in Mathematics and Physics from Glasgow University in 1982. She is currently a researcher in the multimedia group at CWI (the Dutch research center for mathematics and computer science). Her interests include hypermedia reference models, description languages for hypermedia documents (e.g., MHEG, HyTime), multimedia authoring systems, and the application of multimedia information retrieval to automated authoring of multimedia presentations.

H.V. Jagadish

H.V. Jagadish received his PhD from Stanford University in 1985, and since then has been with AT&T, where he currently heads the Database Research Department. His research interests include the management of multimedia information and the use of database technology for communications networks.

Ramesh Jain

Ramesh Jain is currently a Professor of Electrical and Computer Engineering, and Computer Science and Engineering at the University of California at San Diego. Before joining UCSD, he was a Professor of Electrical Engineering and Computer Science, and the Founding Director of the Artificial Intelligence Laboratory at the University of Michigan, Ann Arbor. His current research interests are in multimedia information systems, interactive video, image databases, machine vision, and intelligent systems. He was the founder and the Chairman of Imageware Inc., an Ann Arbor-based company dedicated to revolutionizing software interfaces for emerging sensor technologies. He is the founding chairman of Virage, a San Mateo-based company developing systems for Visual Information Retrieval.

Ramesh is a Fellow of the IEEE, AAAI, and the Society of Photo-Optical Instrumentation Engineers. He is also a member of ACM, the Pattern Recognition Society, the Cognitive Science Society, the Optical Society of America, and the Society of Manufacturing Engineers. He has been involved in the organization of several professional conferences and workshops, and has served on the editorial boards of many journals. Currently, he is Editor-in-Chief of *IEEE Multimedia*, and is on the editorial boards of *Machine Vision and Applications*, *Pattern Recognition*, and *Image and Vision Computing*. He received his PhD from IIT, Kharagpur in 1975 and his B.E. from Nagpur University in 1969.

M. Farrukh Khan

Muhammad Farrukh Khan is a PhD candidate in the Department of Computer Sciences at Purdue University. He obtained his B.S. degree from the California Institute of Technology. His research interests include multimedia systems, physical limits of computation, human factors in computing, and the social impact of globalization of computers.

Wei Li

Wei Li was born in Shaanxi, China, on April 6, 1964. He received the B.Eng. degree in 1986 from Xidian University, Xian, China, and the M.S. and PhD degrees from the Swiss Federal Institute of Technology in 1989 and 1994, respectively. He was research associate at MIT from December 1994 through August 1995, working on medical imaging. From September 1995 through February 1996, he worked at FutureTel, Inc., California, as Staff Engineer, developing next-generation video solutions. In March 1996, he joined Logitech, Inc., California, as Senior Software Engineer, developing video peripheral products for PCs.

His major research interests include filter bank theory and design, image and video compression, very low bit rate video compression, stochastic optimization algorithms, mathematical morphology, medical imaging technology and standards, and fast implementation of image and video compression standards.

Rajiv Mehrotra

Dr. Rajiv Mehrotra is currently with the Imaging Science Division of Eastman Kodak Company, where he is responsible for the Digital Library-related R&D activities. Previously he held faculty positions with the University of Missouri–St. Louis, the University of Kentucky, Lexington, and the University of South Florida, Tampa. His current research interests include multimedia information management systems and digital image/video library management.

Rajiv received a B.Tech degree in electrical engineering from H.B. Technology Institute, Kanpur, India, an M.Tech degree in electrical engineering from the Indian Institute of Technology, Kanpur, and M.A. and PhD degrees from Wayne State University, Detroit. He was a co-guest editor of a special section of the *IEEE Transactions on Knowledge and Data Engineering* on Multimedia Information Systems (Aug 1993) and of a special issue of *IEEE Computer* on Image Database Management (Dec 1989).

Eitetsu Oomoto

Eitetsu Oomoto received the B.E. degree in 1988, M.E. degree in instrumentation engineering, and the PhD degree in 1994 in computer science from Kobe University, Japan. In 1993, he joined the Department of Information & Communication Sciences, Faculty of Engineering, Kyoto Sanyo University, where he is now a lecturer. His interests include database systems, multimedia systems, and user interfaces. Dr. Oomoto is a member of the ACM and the Information Processing Society of Japan.

Guru M. Parulkar

Dr. Guru M. Parulkar is an Associate Professor of Computer Science at Washington University in St. Louis and Director of the Applied Research Laboratory. He received a PhD in computer science from the University of Delaware (1987). His research emphasis has been on the design, implementation, and evaluation of high-speed network protocols and the host communication subsystem to support network computing applications involving visualization, multimedia, and collaborative work. He is a PI or CO-PI for several projects at Washington University that are aimed at the demonstration of high-performance distributed imaging and multimedia applications on gigabit ATM networks.

His group's past work in this area includes: (1) design and exploration of the "network virtual store" and the "network pipeline" as paradigms for two classes of network computing applications; (2) development of the Axon host communication architecture for gigabit network I/O; and (3) development of a novel internet service abstraction called "congram," which incorporates strengths of both connection and datagram approaches, and thus can effectively support traditional network applications as well as multimedia applications.

Dr. Parulkar is the Publications Editor and a Technical Editor of the *ACM / IEEE Transactions on Networking*, is an editor of *IEEE Network*, served as a guest editor for its special issue on Local Area ATM Networks, and served as a co-guest editor for the *IEEE Journal on Selected Areas of Communication* special issue on Gigabit Network Protocols. He has also served on National Science Foundation review panels and a number of IEEE and ACM conference program committees. He has taught several conference tutorials in the general area of protocols, operating systems, and host-network interfacing support for distributed applications over gigabit networks.

Nilesh V. Patel

Nilesh Patel is currently working at Mandala Sciences, Inc., Detroit, as Research Scientist. He earned his bachelors in control engineering from Gujarat University, Ahmedabad, India, and his masters in computer science from Wayne State University, Detroit. He is also a PhD student at the Department of Computer Science of Wayne State University. Mr. Patel is interested in the application of pattern recognition, image processing, and neural networks in visual information management systems. His recent work includes video indexing using audio-visual information for video database systems. He is also working on behavioral studies of ocular motor reflexes using video analysis at the Neuro-ophthamology Laboratory of the Kresegy Eye Institute, Detroit.

P. Venkat Rangan

Dr. Venkat Rangan directs the Multimedia Laboratory at the University of California, San Diego, where he is a Professor of Computer Science and Engineering. The UCSD Multimedia Lab is one of the leading centers of research and he is well known for his pioneering contributions in the areas of multimedia on-demand servers, media synchronization, multimedia communications, and collaboration. He has over 70 publications and holds two patents in the area of optimal video-on-demand delivery over metropolitan area networks.

Dr. Rangan serves as the Editor-in-Chief of the ACM/Springer-Verlag international journal *Multimedia Systems* and was the program chairman of ACM Multimedia 93 (First International Conference on Multimedia). He was also a member of the multimedia expert panel of the US National Academy of Sciences and the Republic of China Scientific Committee in 1993. He serves on numerous program committees and editorial boards and was a visiting scientist at the Xerox Palo Alto Research Center, California.

Dr. Rangan serves as the Multimedia Technology advisor to the Secretary, Department of Electronics (DOE), Government of India, New Delhi. He has also been a visiting professor at the Supercomputer Education and Research Center (SERC), Indian Institute of Science, Bangalore, and leads multimedia research and development at Tata Consultancy Services, Bombay. He is the Program Chairman of the 1997 Indo-US Bilateral Conference on Multimedia.

Dr. Rangan received his B.Tech degree in electrical engineering at the Indian Institute of Technology, Madras, where he was awarded the "President of India Gold Medal" in 1984. He earned his PhD in computer science from the

University of California at Berkeley in 1988. In 1993, he received the USA's National Young Investigator Award.

Lloyd Rutledge

Lloyd Rutledge currently holds a research position at CWI in Amsterdam in the Interoperable Multimedia Systems Project. Prior to that he was a research associate at the Distributed Multimedia Systems Laboratory at the University of Massachusetts Lowell. He received the Sc.D. and M.S. degrees in computer science from the University of Massachusetts Lowell and the B.S. from the University of Massachusetts at Amherst.

Srihari Sampath-Kumar

Srihari Sampath-Kumar is currently working on the design of hypervideo servers and hypermedia authoring and editing tools at Washington University, St. Louis, where he is pursuing his graduate studies. Previously, he was a visiting researcher at Philips Research, Palo Alto, where he worked on the utilization of distributed multimedia systems in medical imaging. He was also briefly a consultant at the Media Futures Group at SRI International.

Mr. Sampath-Kumar was the key architect of the business plan of Vivid Media, a multimedia software start-up company. As a visiting researcher in the Multimedia Laboratory at the University of California, San Diego, he worked on techniques for the optimal delivery of video on demand over broadband networks. He received his bachelors degree in engineering from the Indian Institute of Technology, Madras, in 1995.

Ishwar K. Sethi

Ishwar Sethi received the B.Tech (Hons.), M.Tech, and PhD degrees in electronics and electrical communication engineering from the Indian Institute of Technology, Kharagpur, India, in 1969, 1971, and 1977, respectively. He is currently a professor of computer science at Wayne State University, Detroit. Prior to joining Wayne State in 1982, he was on the faculty at the Indian Institute of Technology.

Dr. Sethi's current research interests are in the areas of artificial neural networks, computer vision, pattern recognition, and multimedia systems. He is co-editor of the book *Artificial Neural Networks and Statistical Pattern Recognition* (North-Holland, 1991). He currently serves on the editorial boards of *Pattern Recognition*, *Pattern Recognition Letters*, and *Machine Vision and Applications*. Dr. Sethi is the co-chair of the IS&T/SPIE Conference on Storage and Retrieval for Image and Video Databases.

Katsumi Tanaka

Katsumi Tanaka received the B.S., M.S., and PhD degrees in information science from Kyoto University in 1974, 1976, and 1981, respectively. Since 1986, he has been a professor in the Graduate School of Science and Technology, Kobe University, Japan. His interests include object-oriented databases, historical database models, and hypermedia systems. Dr. Tanaka is a member of the ACM and the Information Processing Society of Japan.

Yoshinobu Tonomura

Yoshinobu Tonomura is a senior research engineer, supervisor, and Research Group Leader in the Advanced Video Processing Laboratory, NTT Human Interface Laboratories. He has been engaged in research and development of media conversion techniques for visual communication systems. He was a visiting researcher at the Media Laboratory, MIT, during 1987–1988. He is currently working on structured video handling techniques. He is a member of the IEEE and ACM.

Dennis Tsichritzis

Dennis Tsichritzis is the chairman of the management board and chief scientist of GMD and a professor of computer science at the University of Geneva. He has published extensively in the areas of databases, information systems, and object-oriented programming. His research interests include advanced communications and media systems.

Bhaskaran Vasudev

Bhaskaran Vasudev is a member, technical staff at Hewlett-Packard Laboratories, Palo Alto, California. His research interests include audio/image/video compression techniques, image and video processing, and multimedia information transmission. He is co-author of the book, *Image and Video Compression Standards: Algorithms and Architectures* (Kluwer Academic Publishers, 1995).

Dr. Vasudev received his B.Tech degree from the Indian Institute of Technology, Madras, and did his M.S. and PhD work at Wichita State University, Kansas, and Rennselaer Polytechnic Institute, Troy, NY.

Index

A

Access rights, 461
Active Media Object Stores (AMOS), 399
Admission control, 319–24
    for disk–system based storage servers,
        319–22
    in large–scale storage servers, 322–24
Adobe Premiere, 19
AHM, *See* Amsterdam Hypermedia Model
    (AHM)
Algebraic video model, 20, 228–31
    operation categories, 229
    operation examples, 229–31
Algorithms, 85–90
    deletion, 90
    extending/contracting, 90
    insertion, 86–88
    search, 85–86
    splitting, 88–90
AMOS (Active Media Object Stores), 399
Amsterdam Hypermedia Model (AHM), 58–
    64

spatial layout information, 63
structural information, 59–62
    anchors, 59–61
    atomic components, 59
    components, 59
    composition, 59
    links, 61–62
temporal layout information, 62–63
Anchors, 47–48
    Amsterdam Hypermedia Model (AHM),
        59–61
Annotation data, 369–71
APIC–based interconnect, 296–303
Application level striping, 305
Approximate matching, 75–80
    shape similarity example, 78–80
        dimension mismatch, 79–80
        multiple representations, 77–79
Artifacts, 21
ART MUSEUM, 391–93
    content–based similarity retrieval, 392–93
    data model, 391–92
    query by subjective descriptions (QBD),
        393

D

loop, 226
mark, 226
object hierarchy, 224
overlay, 226
position, 226
relative location, 224–25
temporal glue, 223
time–section, 226
OVID (Oomoto et al.), 231–34
composition operations for video–objects, 232
interval projection, 232–33
merge opertion, 233
operation examples in, 234
overlap operation, 233
video–objects, 231–32
playback, 214
spatial composition, 213
temporal composition, 213–14
absolute positioning of objects, 213–14
relative positioning of objects, 213
Compression, 142–45
intraframe encoding, 144
MPEG video compression standard, 142–43
P and B frame encoding, 144–45
structural hierarchy of MPEG, 143–44
Confidentiality, 461
Constant data streams, 23
Constant frequency streams, 23
Constrained–Latency Storage Acess (CLSA), 412–13
Content, image retrieval by, 372
Content–based indexing and retrieval, 69–93, 147–48, 203–4, 366, 372–75
approximate matching, 75–80
shape similarity example, 78–80
exact feature match, 372
index structures, 80–90
algorithms, 85–90
node structure, 83–85
shape of bounding region, 83
telescoping function, 81–83
tree structure, 85
inexact feature match, 372–73
obtaining the mapping, 90–91

query formulation/presentation, 373–74
query optimization, 374
structural match, 373
transactions, 375
two–phase search, 70–75
shape matching example, 72–75
Content–based search, 139
Content Overviewer, PaperVideo, 205
Content Providers, 289, 325
Continuous streams, 22–23
Control time, 348
CORE, 400

D

Data layouts, 307–19
on disks, 307–16
determining buffer sizes, 314–15
determining read–ahead, 313–14
layout of media blocks, 312–13
merging more than two strands, 315–16
merging storage of two strands, 310–12
storage pattern of a media strand, 309–10
performance metrics, 318–19
in scalable MOD servers, 316–18
Data modeling, 13–68
hypermedia modeling, 39–68
time–based media, 13–38
Data type, image retrieval by, 372
Deadline misses, 337–38
Dedicated Viewing (DV), 287
Derivations, 16–17, 217, 1927–33
changing content, 28
changing media type, 28–29
changing timing, 28
definition of, 27–28
examples of, 29–33
audio normalization, 31
color separation, 29–30
MIDI synthesis, 33
video editing, 31
video keying, 31
video transition, 33
Digital compression, 142–45

The Handbook of Multimedia Information Management **489**

T

U

V

W

X, Y, Z